Studies in Regional and Interregional Co-operation
Series
Volume 2

African and Arab Co-operation for Development

STUDIES IN REGIONAL AND INTERREGIONAL CO-OPERATION SERIES
Edited by Ervin Laszlo

Vol 1: Co-operation in the 1980s: Principles and Prospects

Vol 2: African and Arab Co-operation for Development

Vol 3: Co-operation for Development in Asia

Vol 4: Latin American and Caribbean Co-operation for Development

Vol 5: World Leadership and International Development

Vol 6: Regional and Interregional Co-operation in the 1980s: Policies and Strategies

African and Arab Co-operation for Development

Edited by
ERVIN LASZLO

Published for
UNITED NATIONS INSTITUTE FOR TRAINING AND RESEARCH
by
TYCOOLY INTERNATIONAL PUBLISHING LIMITED, DUBLIN

Published by
Tycooly International Publishing Ltd.
6, Crofton Terrace, Dun Laoghaire, Co. Dublin, Ireland

First edition 1984
© 1984 United Nations Institute for Training and Research
UNITAR/RS/11

ISBN 0 907567 74 6 Hardback
ISBN 0 907567 75 4 Softcover
ISBN 0 86346 048 8 Hardback Set

Typeset by Cahill Printers Limited, Dublin
Printed in Ireland by Iona Print Limited, Dublin

All rights reserved. No part of this publication may be reproduced, stored in a retrieval system or transmitted, in any form or by any means: electronic, electrostatic, magnetic tape, mechanical photocopying, recording or otherwise, without permission in writing from the publisher.

British Library Cataloguing in Publication Data
African and Arab co-operation for development
(Studies in regional and interregional
co-operation, V.2)
1. Africa—Economic integration 2. Arab
countries—Economic integration
I. Laszlo, Ervin II. Series
337.1'6 HC800

Contents

Preface, *Michel Doo Kingué* — vii

Introduction, *Ervin Laszlo* — ix

List of Abbreviations — xv

1. Regional Co-operation in an African Context, *Henri Hogbe-Nlend* — 1
2. The Economic Integration of Africa: Problems and Obstacles, *Makhtar Diouf* — 9
3. Regional Co-operation in Human Resources Development in Africa, *Benedict S. Mongula* — 34
4. The Feasibility of Establishing Jointly-owned Regional Minerals Enterprises (JRMEs) in Sub-Saharan Africa: a Case Study of Institution Building for Collective Self-reliance, *A. R. M. Ritter* — 52
5. Afro-Arab Partnership for Development, *Karl Lavrenčič* — 89
6. Economic Co-operation Between European CMEA Countries and Africa, *Judit Kiss* — 102
7. Regional Co-ordination of Arab National Development Plans, *Mohammed M. El-Imam* — 123
8. Patterns of Regional Co-operation Among Arab Countries, *Mohammed Imady* — 159
9. Towards a Strategy for Arab Food Security, *Khalid Tahsin Ali* — 175
10. Regional Co-operation in Human Resource Development in the Arab Countries, *Abdulla M. Ali and Mohammed Galaleldin* — 183
11. Arab Development Aid Institutions: The Role of the Kuwait Fund, *The Kuwait Fund for Arab Economic Development* — 224
12. Co-operation Between the Arab World and European CMEA Countries, *Mihály Simai* — 240

Annex I. Statements Made on the Occasion of the Meeting
of the UNITAR Panel of Eminent Persons,
Kuwait, January 1983   251

Annex II. Summary of the Issues Raised by the Panel of
Eminent Persons at its Meeting in Kuwait   267

Index   273

Preface

THE VOLUMES THAT APPEAR in the first four of the UNITAR series of studies in regional and interregional co-operation bring the research reports of the UNITAR programme on regional and interregional co-operation in the 1980s to the attention of the international community. The reports are the result of the work carried out by the research network created for that UNITAR programme in various parts of the world. The researchers observed a jointly agreed division of labour, worked out in a series of workshops during 1981 and 1982. Their work was designed to demonstrate the possibilities and objectives, as well as the obstacles and difficulties, of co-operation among and with developing countries, at the subregional, regional and interregional levels. It is hoped that their findings will be of interest to both developing and developed countries, particularly to the members of the Group of 77.

The research reports have taken into account the provisions of the Development Strategy for the Third United Nations Development Decade, the Charter of Economic Rights and Duties of States, and the milestone resolutions on the New International Economic Order of the Sixth and Seventh Special Sessions of the General Assembly, which have served as basic points of departure for the research.

The conduct of research has been co-ordinated by the Programme Director, Dr. Ervin Laszlo, who has benefited from the advice of his panel of eminent persons and was assisted in his work by a drafting commission of distinguished personalities. I wish to express my appreciation and gratitude to all these persons for their kind and invaluable co-operation. UNITAR is particularly grateful to the Government of Italy for its generous contribution, thanks to which a research co-ordination office for the programme was established in Rome and functioned at no cost to UNITAR from December 1981 to January 1984. It is also thanks to contributions from the Government of Italy as well as from other donors, particularly the Governments of Canada, India, Japan, Kuwait, the Netherlands and Spain, that the activities of the programme were carried out. I wish to thank these Governments wholeheartedly for their most valuable support.

As Executive Director of UNITAR, I am authorizing the publication of the reports as edited by the director of the programme in the light of the mandate of the Institute to investigate problems of concern to the international community. The views and conclusions in this study are solely the responsibility of the authors and do not necessarily reflect the opinions of the Board of Trustees, the officials of UNITAR or the governments that so generously supported the project financially.

Michel Doo Kingué
Executive Director
UNITAR
United Nations
New York

Introduction

Ervin Laszlo

Director, Programme on Regional and Interregional Co-operation in the 1980s

AFRICAN AND ARAB Co-operation for Development is the second in the UNITAR series of studies exploring the strategy of co-operation among developing countries on the subregional, regional and interregional levels. Following the first volume, which outlines the principles and prospects of such co-operation and examines the role of developed countries in promoting and facilitating it, the present volume deals with the problems and possibilities of co-operation in two great regions of the Third World: Africa South of the Sahara, and the Arab Nation. Although the studies concerning these regions are published under a single cover, they deal with each region individually: first with Sub-Saharan Africa, and then with the Arab countries. The inclusion of the studies in a single volume is not merely incidental: the two regions overlap in many respects, and have strong mutual ties and interests. Geographically, Arab countries in the regions North of the Sahara belong to Africa. Institutionally, all African countries are member of joint organizations, first and foremost the Organization of African Unity. The United Nations Economic Commission for Africa likewise includes all African countries. At the same time there are numerous reasons for considering the development problems and relations of Sub-Saharan and African countries in their concrete individuality, in view of the many historical ties which bind the Arab countries into a single Arab Nation, and the countries of Sub-Saharan Africa into a brotherhood of Black African developing states.

It would be arbitrary as well as unnecessary to draw a sharp boundary between the two regions. It is sufficient to recognize the specificity of each, and to examine the problems as well as the opportunities of co-operation in the appropriate frameworks and dimensions. This is what the studies published in this volume set out to do. The first four chapters concern themselves with regional and subregional co-operation in Sub-Saharan Africa. Chapter 5 examines the recent patterns of Arab-African co-operation with special attention to financial flows. Chapters 7 through 11 focus on co-operation among all Arab countries, including also those that belong geographically, and in regard to some institutions (such as the U.N.

The opinions expressed in this Introduction, and in the Chapters that follow, are those of their respective authors and do not necessarily reflect the views of UNITAR or of the institutions with which the authors are affiliated.

Regional Commissions), to Western Asia. Chapters 7 and 11 shed light on the relations of African and Arab countries with the Eastern European socialist countries. Facets of interregional co-operation with developed market economy countries, having been treated in detail in Volume 1 of the present series, are not repeated here.)

The problematique of development in Sub-Saharan Africa (henceforth referred to as the region of Africa) is perhaps the most serious of any region of the Third World. The African region is endowed with immense natural resources, yet most of the least developed countries of the world are concentrated in it. The deterioration of food self-sufficiency threatens the very survival of some African nations and populations. African economies depend heavily on the international economic system, and find themselves in a situation resembling economic, although no longer political, colonialism. Some thirty years after achieving independence, the majority of African countries have inadequate economic structures, inherited from the colonial era. If they are to shift from a condition of outside domination to one of collective self-reliance, African states must rely first of all on each other. This makes the implementation of regional and subregional co-operation on this vast continent more important and urgent than anywhere else in the world.

African leaders have recognized the challenge and have taken steps to meet it. Pan-Africanism is a long-standing ideal which has sparked remarkable statements of unity and brotherhood. These culminated, in July of 1979, with the adoption by the OAU Heads of State or Government, of the Monrovia Declaration of "Commitment on the Guidelines and Measures for National and Collective Self-Reliance in Economic and Social Development for the Establishment of a New International Economic Order". Concrete measures for the implementation of the Declaration were outlined by the Heads of State or Government at their meeting in Lagos, in April of 1980. They reaffirmed their commitment to implement a strategy for the economic development of Africa during the 1980s and 1990s, and to establish an African Economic Community by the year 2000. The Lagos Plan of Action, with the Final Act of Lagos, spell out the operational modalities of the strategy, setting objectives for all major economic sectors. The African Economic community, to be created on the basis of a treaty, is to promote the accelerated, self-reliant and self-sustaining development of African states, co-operation among them, and their integration in the economic, social and cultural fields.

Experience has shown, however, that numerous obstacles impede the implementation of the Plan. The document itself identifies the lack of effective follow-up of the agreed decisions as the main impediment to African co-operation. Many member governments, having approved the legal instruments designed to strengthen regional and subregional institutions, failed to give them the necessary support to carry out their mandates. External factors, such as protectionism in the developed world, deteriorating terms of trade for exports vital to African economies, and continued dependence on external actors and market forces exacerbate the difficulties. It is important, therefore, as the Lagos Plan recommends, to assess the existing African intergovernmental organizations with a view to enhancing their relevance and effectiveness. The studies assembled in the first part of this volume contribute to such assessment, placing it in the relevant context of economic and social realities.

Hogbe-Nlend, himself an advisor to the OAU in drawing up the Plan of Action of Lagos, analyses the "wealth/poverty" paradox of the region and finds that its explanation lies in part in the colonial past and in part in the adoption of development strategies based on "micronationalism" and an orientation towards the outside world instead of each other. He suggests that the new strategy of development for Africa must break with the past, revitalize and re-examine traditional African values, open Africa to the outside on the basis of the principle of "assimilation, without being assimilated", adopt a future-oriented long-term vision and, above all, promote systematic regional co-operation among African states. For the latter, careful attention to the political context, a clear definition of expected roles and results, flexible institutional mechanisms, stable budgets, and in-depth training and research are necessary.

The grave problem of making regional co-operation work in Africa is intimately connected with the institutions of co-operation. Diouf shows that there is a proliferation of subregional organizations, especially in Western Africa, causing financial hardship for their members (some belong to as many as eighteen or twenty intergovernmental bodies), a drain on their human resources, and frequent overlap in project design and execution. Lack of harmonized national development planning creates duplication of projects and misses opportunities for exploiting existing and potential complementarities in trade and production. The great variety of national currencies, coupled with over-reliance on the U.S. dollar and French franc, make for conditions of outside dependence and impede intra-African economic ties. Transport and communication infrastructures further exacerbate these problems. Diouf, as does Hogbe-Nlend, concludes that African leaders must be aware that real, endogenous economic development is not possible on the level of individual micro-states: economic integration is a *sine qua non* of development in Africa.

One of the greatest and hitherto largely unexploited resources of the region are its people. Human resource development is at least as important as the development of any natural resource on the continent. Mongula shows that serious efforts are underway in this regard, but much more needs to be done. The potentials of a regional approach to human resource development is fruitful on all levels, since, due to the similarity of the socio-economic structures and problems of African countries, education and training obtained in one country fits well with local conditions in others. A pooling of educational resources in subregional and regional centres of excellence would be cost-effective, would have a multiplier effect, and is far superior to the past strategy of educating African leadership cadres abroad. According to Ritter, a similarly self-reliant approach applies to African mineral resource development. There are feasible alternatives to the foreign-based multinational corporation for the proper utilization of the mineral wealth of the continent. Jointly-owned regional enterprises could assist in the revival of the mineral sector in the region, facilitate the achievement of African control, encourage the development of indigenous personnel, and achieve major economies of scale and management, financing, marketing and risk sharing. Such enterprises could be viable and sustainable if carefully designed with respect to financial autonomy, internal incentive structures and commercial orientation. Financial and personnel constraints make the establishment of such enterprises complex and difficult, but by no means impossible.

There are significant financial flows from the Arab world to Sub-Saharan Africa. Between 1973 and 1982 over $8 billion has been committed by Arab governments and agencies in development aid to non-Arab African nations. The assessment of how the money was used is now under way and is likely to be critical on numerous points. But Arab aid to Africa will continue, as Lavrenčič of BADEA, the main conduit of the flows, affirms.

The Arab world is very likely the Third World region whose member countries are joined with the strongest historical and cultural ties. The countries of the region were practically united under the Ottoman Empire, and large-scale population movements have taken place over the last fourteen centuries. Some of the oldest civilizations were born in this region, which in its long history has also been a crossroad between East and West.

In the contemporary epoch Arab co-operation took institutional form with the signing of the Alexandria Protocol in July of 1944. A year later the Charter of the League of Arab States was adopted, and the League adopted the Treaty for Mutual Defence and Economic Co-operation in April of 1950. Article Seven called for co-operation among member countries in developing their economies, investing their natural resources and facilitating their agricultural and industrial trade. A long series of measures evolved the institutional framework of Arab regional co-operation. Among its milestones, the creation of the Council of Arab Economic Unity in 1957 assumes a prominent place. It gave rise to the Arab Economic Unity Agreement in 1964, as well as to the establishment of the Arab Common Market in the same year.The Council defined at the end of 1973 a Strategy for Arab Economic Action aiming at closer economic integration using a number of different approaches. In 1978 a pan-Arab conference in Baghdad adopted a Joint Strategy which, after a series of further consultations, was adopted at a summit meeting in Amman in November 1981.

Despite such remarkable plans and institutional frameworks, co-operation in the region has not progressed to the entire satisfaction of member states. Numerous obstacles impede progress, including enormous disparities in wealth and income, in territorial and population size, and in natural resources. Countries like Somalia, Mauritania and Sudan are among the poorest in the world; others such as Saudi Arabia, the United Arab Emirates and Kuwait are among the richest. Economic development is at relatively low levels everywhere, despite the great influx of wealth in the oil-producing Gulf states.

A major concern remains that optimum utilization of the existing financial, natural and human resources, in order to create a self-reliant Arab Nation by the end of the century, by which time the oil reserves are likely to become a relatively minor source of wealth accumulation.

For the present, the Arab region lives off its natural riches. Over the last five years exports of manufactured goods came to no more than 2 per cent of total exports, and one per cent was in the form of foodstuffs. The remaining 97 per cent consisted of fuels, minerals and other raw materials. At the same time the region became dependent on imports in all vital areas, including basic foodstuffs. To overcome these pernicious conditions, close co-operation would be required among all Arab countries, exploiting the natural and mineral riches of some states consistently with the agricultural and human potentials of others. Whereas individually, each Arab country is forced into a greater and greater degree of dependence on outside imports and technology, collectively the Arab Nation could be self-reliant and even self-sufficient in many economic sectors. For the present, however, the actual implementation of co-operation is impeded by political factionalism, a certain level of mutual mistrust, and an inward-looking concentration on maximizing each country's own economic potentials. Significant exceptions are provided by the major Arab Development Funds and institutions, which disburse considerable sums for Arab as well as general Third World development, and by the Gulf Co-operation Council which unites the six Gulf oil-producing states in the systematic and legally binding framework of joint action and mutual assistance. In other subregions, such as the Maghreb, actual co-operation is still in early stages despite much discussion and long preparations.

El-Imam, who has been in charge of attempts to co-ordinate the development planning of Arab countries for the past several years, gives a comprehensive overview of the problems and possibilities of the region, and provides a concise but insightful history of such attempts since the beginning. El-Imadi, President of the Arab Fund, likewise reviews the problems and the possibilities, and distinguishes three historically tried approaches to co-operation: trade liberalization and payments facilitation (which produced generally unsatisfactory results due in part to the dearth of products to be put into intra-regional trade); substantive co-operation embracing large numbers of regional bodies, banks and companies in the implementation of joint ventures and projects; and joint financing. The last-named form of co-operation could go well beyond the pooling of financial resources in joint projects; it could achieve horizontal and vertical integration, involving a pooling of activities of enterprises in similar fields in the first instance, and a division of labour with clear-cut specialization among different countries and companies in the second. The new approach to Arab development which, according to El-Imadi, could overcome the shortcomings of the previous approaches, is one that recognizes that development has a regional focus, in addition to national foci.

Food security is a basic aspect of overall economic security in any region; in the Arab world it consitutes a critical issue. Food self-sufficiency has declined precipitously during the past 8 years, with losses of up to 40 per cent in certain commodities. The Arab region is constrained to import 75 per cent of its requirements of sugar, 66 per cent of wheat and edible oil, 50 per cent of all grains and dairy products, and 33 per cent of meats. Today, twenty of the twenty-one Arab countries have a negative agricultural trade balance, whereas six of them enjoyed a positive balance at the beginning of the last decade.

As Tahsin Ali shows, the major problem underlying the low level of Arab food self-sufficiency is the unequal distribution of agricultural potential in the region. To put it simply, the rich countries have poor food potentials while the poor countries often have high potentials; wealth and the ability to produce food do not mesh. The mesh could be brought about through joint efforts, investing some of the wealth of the rich countries in the agricultural base of the poor ones. Such co-operation would have to overcome political divisions and embrace a number of concrete measures including legal and institutional frameworks, long and short-term perspective studies, the standardization of agricultural planning methodology, and the effective co-ordination and strengthening of ongoing and planned joint efforts.

As in Africa, so in the Arab region as a whole, the development of human resources is a basic precondition of self-reliant development. The study by Ali and Galaleldin reviews this complex problem and advances noteworthy recommendations. The fact is that the educational and skill training system of Arab countries has not been able to meet the requirements for certain skills and for highly trained manpower. In higher education especially, the emphasis continues to be on the humanities which, while important, shortchanges the requirement for meeting the demand for people qualified in practical and in managerial skills. The situation is aggravated by the continued "brain-drain" of highly qualified people from the region, while in occupations demanding lesser skills large migrations of labour have developed. On the one hand the Arab region is losing workers to other regions, expecially to Europe, while on the other it is importing non-Arab labour, mainly from Asia, to fill the gap. A rationalization of the labour market on a regional level should thus be a high priority. A Common Arab Labour Market would help to achieve this end; in addition the existing regional training and educational centres should be strengthened and made more accessible to nationals of all Arab countries. Financial assistance could come from the oil-exporting countries, which themselves are in great need of qualified manpower.

In the area of human resource development, as well as in all other sectors of the economy and dimensions of society, the Arab Development Funds and financing institutions, such as the Kuwait Fund, play a key and highly beneficial role. The philosophy as well as the operations of these institutions are concisely and accurately highlighted in the paper presented by the Kuwait fund itself.

Complementing the analyses of the problems and possibilities of regional co-operation in Africa and in the Arab world, two studies focus on the prospects and preconditions of enhanced interregional co-operation of the European socialist countries with each of these Third World regions. Kiss in regard to Africa, and Simai for the Arab region, outline the present, relatively modest levels of co-operation, emphasizing their diversity and pointing to future potentials. Deliberate structural adjustments are required on both sides to realize the East-South interregional potential, with stronger, more concerted regional co-operation promoted by the public sector in the regions of Africa and the Arab world, and closer co-ordination of the national development plans of the European socialist countries within the framework of their own CMEA (Council for Mutual Economic Assistance).

The reader will find the statements made on the occasion of the meeting of the UNITAR Programme's Panel of Eminent Persons in Kuwait annexed to the volume. These, too, provide important insights and merit careful study and earnest consideration.

March, 1984

List of Abbreviations

ACARTSOD	African Centre for Applied Research and Training in Social Development
ACM	Arab Common Market
ACP	Organization of Africa-Caribbean-Pacific Countries
ACSAD	Arab Centre for Studies of Arid Lands and Dry Areas
ADB	African Development Bank
ADFAED	Abu Dhabi Fund for Arab Economic Development
AEUC	Arab Economic Unity Council
AFESD	Arab Fund for Economic and Social Development
ALECSO	Arab League Educational, Cultural and Scientific Organization
ALO	Arab Labour Organization
AMF	Arab Monetary Fund
AOAD	Arab Organization for Agricultural Development
ASEAN	Association of South East Asian Nations
ATF	Arab Thought Forum
BADEA	Arab Bank for Economic Development in Africa
CAEU	Council of Arab Economic Unity
CEAO	West African Economic Community
CEPGL	Economic Community of the Great Lakes Countries
CFA	Communauté financière Africaine
CILSS	Permanent Interstate Committee for Drought Control in the Sahel
CIRDAFRICA	African Centre for Rural Development
CMEA	Council for Mutual Economic Assistance
CODESRIA	Council for the Development of Economic and Social Research in Africa
DAC	Development Assistance Committee
EAEC	East African Economic Community
ECA	Economic Commission for Africa
ECDC	Economic Co-operation among Developing Countries
ECOWAS	Economic Community of West African States
ECWA	Economic Commission for Western Asia
FIR	Flight Information Region
GCC	Gulf Co-operation Council
IBRD	International Bank for Reconstruction and Development (World Bank)
IDA	International Development Association
IDCAS	Industrial Development Centre for Arab States

IFAD	International Fund for Agricultural Development
IFED	Iraqi Fund for External Development
IGO	Inter-Governmental Organization
ILO	International Labour Office
IMF	International Monetary Fund
INPC	Institute for National Planning, Cairo
IsDB	Islamic Development Bank
JAEA	Joint Arab Economic Action
KFAED	Kuwait Fund for Arab Economic Development
LAFB	Libyan Arab Foreign Bank
LAS	League of Arab States
LDC	Less Developed (Developing) Country
LE	Egyptian Pounds
MSA	Most Seriously Affected (Countries)
MULPOC	Multinational Programming Operating Centre
NEIDA	Network of Education Innovation for Development in Africa
NIC	Newly Industrialized Country
NIEO	New International Economic Order
OAPEC	Organization of Arab Petroleum Exporting Countries
OAS	Organization of American States
OAU	Organization of African Unity
OCAM	Common Afro-Mauritian Organization
ODA	Official Development Assistance
OECD	Organization for Economic Co-operation and Development
OFID	OPEC Fund for International Development
OICMA	Organisation Internationale contre le Criquet Migrateur Africain
OMVS	Organisation Mise en Valeur fleuve Senegal
OPEC	Organization of Petroleum Exporting Countries
PAHO	Pan American Health Organization
PANAFTEL	Pan-African Telecomunications Network
PQLI	Physical Quality of Life Index
PTA	Preferential Trade Area
RCDC	Regional Co-operation among Developing Countries
RED	Recent Economic Development
SAAFA	Special Arab Fund for Africa
SADCC	Southern African Development Co-ordination Conference
SAUC	Southern African Universities Conference
SFD	Saudi Fund for Development
TCDC	Technical Co-operation among Developing Countries
UCAO	West African Unit of Account
UDAO	Customs Union of West Africa
UDE	Equatorial Customs Union

UDEAC	Central African Customs and Economic Union
UDEAO	Customs Union of the West African States
UMOA	West African Monetary Union
UNCTAD	UN Conference on Trade and Development
UNDP	United Nations Development Programme
UNIDO	United Nations Industrial Development Organization
UNITAR	United Nations Institute for Training and Research
UNU	United Nations University
WHO	World Health Organization

CHAPTER 1

Regional Co-operation in an African Context

Henri Hogbe-Nlend

University of Bordeaux I

IN RECENT YEARS, and especially since 1979, Africa has undertaken a profound analysis of itself – an analysis which is based on a clear and responsible evaluation of the twenty years which have passed since independence and which aims at perfecting a new development strategy by the year 2000. This evaluation and the elaboration of the strategy have been undertaken at two important meetings, namely the Colloquium of African Experts on "African Development Perspectives at the Horizon of the Year 2000" held in Monrovia, Liberia, in February 1979, and the First Economic Summit of Heads of State and Government of the Organization of African Unity (OAU) held in Lagos, Nigeria, in April, 1980.

The OAU Summit adopted the Lagos Plan of Action and the Final Act of Lagos. These two fundamental documents, which were approved by the continent's highest political authorities, define the new African development strategy – a strategy which is based on regional co-operation.

Having had the opportunity to participate at both the Monrovia Colloquium and the Lagos Summit, in this study I shall set forth and analyze the basic principles and the fundamental orientations of the new strategy.

THE FAILURE OF THE FORMER DEVELOPMENT STRATEGY

The first paragraph of the Preamble to the Lagos Plan of Action summarized the two last Development Decades in Africa as follows:

> The effect of unfulfilled promises of global development strategies has been more sharply felt in Africa than in other continents of the world. Indeed, rather than result in an improvement in the economic situation of the continent, successive strategies have made it stagnate and become more susceptible than other regions to the economic and social

crises suffered by the industrialized countries. Thus, Africa is unable to point to any significant growth rate, or satisfactory index of general well-being, in the past twenty years.

In the sixth paragraph of the Preamble, the Lagos Plan of Action recognizes that, despite all of the efforts which have been made by its leaders, Africa still remains the least advanced continent. Two-thirds of the world's "least developed countries" are in Africa. The continent is also exposed to the disastrous consequences of natural disasters as well as the cruelest endemic diseases. Africa is a victim of exploitation, colonial and neo-colonial domination, of racism and apartheid.

However, African underdevelopment should not be considered as a matter of fate. It is, on the contrary, a paradox when one contrasts levels of underdevelopment with the continent's immense human and natural resources. In fact, the fifth paragraph of the Preamble to the Lagos Plan of Action stipulates:

> In addition to its reservoir of human resources, our continent has 97 per cent of world reserves of chrome, 85 per cent of world reserves of platinum, 64 per cent of world reserves of manganese, 25 per cent of world reserves of uranium and 13 per cent of world reserves of copper, without mentioning bauxite, nickel and lead; 20 per cent of world hydro-electrical potential, 20 per cent of traded oil in the world (if we exclude the United States and the USSR); 70 per cent of world cocoa production; one-third of world coffee production, 50 per cent of palm produce, to mention just a few.

Africa is thus far from being poor. Indeed, it is one of the richest continents in the world. Yet the vast majority of its inhabitants do not live in the most modern sense of the term; they merely survive. They strive for life, they vegetate at the negative end of existence. It is this strange paradox which characterizes Africa in the 1980s.

How can this paradox be explained? It is certainly not the result of divine will, nor of idleness or lack of intelligence, initiative or creativity. In the final analysis, the explanation for the "wealth/poverty" paradox of Africa lies in part in its colonial past, which was characterized by a systematic plundering of the continent. Another explanation stems from the development strategy which has been adopted since independence – a strategy which has been based on policies of "micronationalism" and orientations toward the exterior, or "global extroversion".

While "nationalism" has helped African peoples to struggle for national political independence, it has also led to the creation of very small states which have felt that their only means of survival is through harnessing themselves to the former colonial powers. Hence has derived the global extroversion of politically independent Africa – an extroversion by which African national economies are totally dependent on the international raw materials and mineral markets and thus extremely vulnerable to the influences of international speculation on the part of the industrialized countries and the negative effects on the best interests of the continent. Moreover, there is extroversion by which scientific and technical research is not oriented to meet the priority needs of African societies, and indeed an extroversion of dominant social and cultural values which, through imitation, have come to be abject copies of Western models.

THE FIVE BASIC PRINCIPLES OF THE NEW DEVELOPMENT STRATEGY FOR AFRICA

The New Development Strategy for Africa, as defined in the Lagos Plan of Action, aims at promoting a type of development which is endogenous, Africa-oriented and integrated – in short, development by the people and for the people. This strategy has been founded on the following basic principles:
1. Breaking away from the former development strategy which was based on imitating both the Western and Eastern "developed" countries; "breaking away" from Western and Eastern models should also imply *going beyond* them.
2. Emphasizing the African cultural and civil values; some, and not all, of these values must be reviewed, modernized and revalorized from a critical point of view.
3. Opening Africa to the rest of the world on the basis of the Senghorian principle of "assimilation without being assimilated", or borrowing from others without losing one's own identity.
4. Promoting a *prospective vision* in the elaboration and implementation of development plans; the urgency to resolve certain problems must not result in a systematic "fireman policy" for development and thus prevent the laying of solid foundations for the future.
5. Promoting a strategy of *systematic regional co-operation* based on the collective participation of African countries – countries which are "too small" to achieve development solely as a result of individual efforts. Regional co-operation has come to be called "the new pedagogy of African unity".

I shall now attempt to develop these five basic principles in more detail.

The Principle of Breaking Away

Africa must now break away from certain values, practices and concepts which have proven to be harmful and misguided. I refer to those values based on complacent admiration and senseless imitation of the West and on an egotistical obsession with personal financial and material gains, the most evident of "glories". "Development" must not be confused with "growth".

Among these misguided concepts, special mention should be made of the notion of the "transfer of technology". African experts such as myself have vigorously denounced this concept since the Monrovia Colloquium in 1979, for the transfer of technology, in the direction in which it generally takes place today, is totally unacceptable as a fundamental strategy for the scientific and technological development of the continent. Such development must be based instead on Africa's own creativity. In the final analysis, being "developed" signifies being creative. This is true for individuals, for nations, for peoples and continents. The example of Japan (which is perhaps too often cited, rightly or wrongly) confirms this fact. This country has bestowed commanding importance on both creativity and intelligence.

The concept of "technology transfer" is absurd and illusory: technology cannot be transferred; it is either created or mastered. This erroneous concept (a veritable "dealing of dupes" as it was recently termed by an African Head of State) must be eradicated from the new international vocabulary. Obviously, this is in no way to question the necessity of scientific and technological co-operation and exchange, which has always existed between peoples.

Emphasizing African Values

The second principle of the new development strategy for Africa is that of emphasizing African values, for the roots of African development must lie in values which are truly African. Due to its rich heritage, Africa has not come empty-handed into the twentieth century. Presently recognized as the cradle of humanity, our continent has offered historic contributions of primary importance in the fields of science, technology, philosophy, mathematics and several other sectors of human thought, not to mention the arts. And when I speak of this wise, knowledgeable and creative Africa, I refer to both Black Africa and Arab Africa – two "Africas" which are distinct, but linked to form a presently indivisible unity.

Moreover, one must not overlook the scientific conclusions of the great contemporary Egyptologists who have irrefutably established, on the basis of archaeological evidence, the Black character of ancient Egyptian civilization – "the ancestor of Western science and culture". Just as modern science and technology evolved in Europe, universal knowledge in ancient times flowed from the Nile towards the rest of the world, especially to Greece which would serve as an "intermediary link". This has been very well illustrated by the great African Egyptologist Chiekh Anta Diop in his latest work "Civilisation ou Barbarie" (Présence Africaine, Paris). I heartily recommend an open-minded reading of this book, free of racial prejudices.

The Principle of Openness and of Dialogue

The third principle of the new development strategy for Africa is that of openness and dialogue. Aimé Cesaire has said, "Africa is open to all currents and is full of confluents". Africa would like to "enter the age of dialogue and be reborn through this dialogue", assimilate that which other peoples of the world have created without, in the words of Senghor, "being assimilated".

The dialogue between Africa and its global partners must be developed in "concentric circles" and in four main directions:
1. First, the fundamental dialogue between African countries themselves;
2. Then, the dialogue between Africa and its immediate neighbours who share identical development problems (these are Arab countries and, in fact, the majority of the Arab population is at the same time African);
3. Third, the dialogue between Africa and its partners in the developing world in the framework of the principles and objectives of the United Nations Conference

on Technical Co-operation between Developing Countries held in Buenos Aires in 1978;
4. Last, but not least, the dialogue between Africa and its partners in the industrialized countries, East and West.

In the context of these general orientations, we can maintain horizontal, vertical or "diagonal" forms of international dialogue. But, above all, this dialogue must be between peoples, not only between governments.

As Léopold Sédar Senghor has said, the dialogue between the peoples must first of all be a dialogue of cultures, because culture is the essence of life and the spirit of civilization. We refer, of course, not only to manifestations of folklore, but to culture in its widest connotations, which therefore includes science.

It is culture which allows us to distinguish one people from another. The dialogue between cultures includes economics, as every economic transaction is a human act and therefore a cultural act. The dialogue between cultures includes politics – not the politics of politicians, but Politics in its Aristotelian sense, the prospective management of the "city" and of public affairs. In fact, Senghor has stated that if there exists a primary for culture, then there exists priority for politics. Hence, striving for a "New World Cultural Order" is at the root of achieving a "New World Order" and, in particular, a New International Economic Order.

The Principle of Prospective

The fourth fundamental principle of the new development strategy for Africa is the principle of prospective. In a developing country in a state of general poverty, the pressure to resolve urgent situations is such that the process of "governing" is often reduced to extinguishing a series of brushfires – those of hunger, epidemics, floods, drought, etc. This is what has come to be called the "fireman policy". International aid, in the form of, for example, emergency food and medical supplies or of teachers, is also subject to the same pressures.

Clearly, these methods will not serve to resolve the problems of underdevelopment in any lasting way. These problems will continue to reappear unless they are attacked at the root. Although emergency measures are necessary and useful, they are far from being satisfactory and can even be, at times, counter-productive.

In order to proceed towards fundamental development objectives (the foremost of which for Africans is food self-sufficiency), it is necessary to opt for a prospective vision in the elaboration and implementation of development plans. Aware of this necessity, other African experts along with myself, present in Monrovia in 1979, proposed the creation of an African association for prospective studies, which could be set up in connection with the UNITAR Programme on the Future of Africa.

The Principle of Regional Co-operation

The fifth major principle of the new development strategy for Africa is that of regional co-operation. African countries, taken individually, are "too small" either from the economic, cultural, demographic, scientific or technological point of view, or in terms of room for development. For these micro-states, no lasting solutions can be found for development problems because they lack the necessary "critical mass". Even if major problems occur on the national level, their solutions must be sought beyond the national framework on the regional, inter-state level. The results of such co-operation, in turn, will be felt at the national level.

In this regard, we wholeheartedly support the Final Act of Lagos in which our Heads of State and Government reaffirm their dedication to "create an African Community by the year 2000, on the basis of a treaty to be ratified, in order to ensure the economic, cultural and social integration of our continent".

THE DIFFICULTIES OF INTER-AFRICAN REGIONAL CO-OPERATION

Despite the pressing reasons for intensifying inter-African regional co-operation, experience has shown that the path to such co-operation is lined with difficulties. Some of these difficulties are "universal" and inherent to all actions jointly undertaken by several countries, whether they be African or not; other difficulties are more typically "African".

The universal difficulties inherent to multinational projects involve the lack of harmonization of disparate bureaucratic systems and lengthy delays which occur in the obtaining of common decisions among different political and legal systems, not to mention the complexity of the decision-making process itself, and the differences in the conceptions held by the partners.

Those difficulties which are more typical of Africa have been cited by the Heads of African States in Chapter VIII of the Lagos Plan of Action. They can be summarized in a nutshell: the incapacity of several African states to put into practice certain important signed accords upon which they have agreed. These are mainly financial accords.

The above-mentioned difficulties are not insurmountable. The best example which can attest to this assertion is the success of several inter-African co-operation projects and, in particular, the very existence of the OAU (despite its crises!) in twenty years of overall positive action in furthering first the political, and now the economic liberation of the continent. The existence of the specialized institutions of the OAU, of the African Development Bank (ADB) and of several other regional and subregional projects must also be mentioned as prime examples in overcoming inherent difficulties.

The most important lesson to be drawn from international experience in the domain of regional co-operation is the necessity of maintaining a pragmatic approach: there exists no magic remedy which can be applied universally. Every instance for regional co-operation is a special case in itself for which specific solutions must be found through innovation. We must therefore not allow the trees of difficulties to prevent us from perceiving the forest of existing or prospective successes.

CONDITIONS ALLOWING FOR SUCCESSFUL REGIONAL CO-OPERATION IN AFRICA

Experience in Africa has shown that the eventual success of a common project undertaken by several states will depend on several factors:
1. *Political context.* This entails initiating a project through a clear vision which takes into account the interests of all the partners concerned. In particular, transnational projects must not compete with national projects. They should, instead, complement national projects and be placed "at their disposal". In such a way, transnational projects can supply national projects the means by which they can fulfil their objectives.
2. *Clear definition of roles and expected results.* In order to avoid deceptions and disappointments, it is necessary from the start to clearly define the role and the contribution of each partner and the results that each partner and the group of partners as a whole may expect in the long run.
3. *Flexibility of institutional structures.* Experience reveals that the most flexible structures are often the most effective. In consequence, we should tend to favour the creation of a new international institution and those mechanisms capable of achieving the same results and furthering direct co-operation among the competent national institutions.
4. *Budgetary stability.* Regional projects must be assured financial stability essentially based on approved, pluri-annual budgets, in spite of the fact that such agreements have become increasingly difficult for partner states to sign and respect.
5. *Training and research.* All regional co-operation projects should at the same time serve as a training ground for high-level national specialists. It is necessary to further train these specialists through their own research and by means of advanced courses and seminars, etc.

A NETWORK OF REGIONAL CENTRES OF EXCELLENCE FOR TRAINING AND RESEARCH

The Lagos Plan of Action highly recommends that training and research be considered as integral parts of all inter-African co-operation projects. In order to promote regional co-operation in the fields of training and research, two forms of organization and concerted action must be undertaken: direct action through *centres of excellence* and indirect action through *networks*.

A "centre of excellence" is a high-level, autonomous, inter-state research institution possessing an international juridic statute; an international scientific, administrative and technical staff; international financing; common scientific programmes jointly carried out by the partner states and results which can be obtained and shared among these states.

An "international network" is an international association comprised of several national training or research institutions (public or private) with a centre for co-ordination and activities. The programme of the network is established jointly, but the execution of projects is decentralized. These projects are entirely financed by the member institutions and carried out under their responsibility. The Network Centre assures the co-ordination of this work as well as the exchange of knowledge and experiences. The Network presupposes the existence, on the national level, of member institutions which are capable of carrying out the execution of the common programme and of maximizing its results, which is not always the case in Africa. This formula, however, may offer certain financial advantages.

These two forms of organization and concerted action must be employed simultaneously in Africa. Preference for one form or the other can only be accorded in function of the specific cases involved. The two forms, however, can prove to be mutually enriching, and, according to the circumstances, it would be possible to pass our attention gradually from one form to the other.

A POSSIBLE ROLE FOR THE UNITAR PROGRAMME ON REGIONAL AND INTERREGIONAL CO-OPERATION

In view of the foregoing considerations, and in accordance with the statutes of UNITAR, the Programme on Regional and Interregional Co-operation should essentially aim at helping African countries to make rapid progress in the implementation of the Plan of Action and the Final Act of Lagos. The following activities could be carried out in this connection:
1. Research and training concerning the new strategy of African development;
2. Research and training in regard to the concepts of "African Economic Community" and "African integration", in all relevant fields (economic, social, cultural, technological, etc.);
3. Assessment of the positive and negative experiences of subregional groupings of African States;
4. Helping in the elaboration of a draft Treaty to create an African Economic Community, as stipulated in the Final Act of Lagos;
5. Presentation of the results of the studies to African Heads of State and Government, the African intellectual community, and the public at large.

CHAPTER 2

The Economic Integration of Africa: Problems and Obstacles

Makhtar Diouf

Université de Dakar

As a result of the disappointments which have emerged from the North-South dialogue, development hopes have been re-oriented in a new direction, that of South-South co-operation between underdeveloped countries. This theme, which has attracted a great deal of attention today, presents nothing new; the first attempt at economic integration in Africa, as well as in Latin America, actually predate the recent discussions on the New International Economic Order and the North-South dialogue.

The newly-found interest of the international authorities and the governments of the developing countries can serve to give increased impetus to economic integration schemes which, up to now, have hardly been functioning at full capacity. However, it is first of all necessary to identify those problems which obstruct the potential success of the economic integration of developing countries. The aim of this study is to outline these problems in Sub-Saharan Africa.*

---

*Experiences in African economic integration include:
1. In *Central Africa:*
   - CEPGL: Economic Community of the Great Lakes Countries (1976): Zaire, Ruanda, Burundi.
   - UDEAC: Central African Customs and Economic Union (1966), the forefather of the UDE: Equatorial Customs Union (1969): Cameroon, Congo, Gabon, Central African Republic.

   UDEAC and CEPGL will now be dissolved due to the most recent creation of the Central African Economic Community, which will also include as members Equatorial Guinea, Chad and Sao Tomé and Príncipe.
2. In *Southern Africa:*
   - the Union of the Republic of South Africa (1910): Lesotho, Botswana, Swaziland.
3. In *East Africa:*
   - EAEC: East African Economic Community (1917): Kenya, Uganda, Tanzania.

   The EAEC was dissolved in 1977.

   Two recent integration structures, which are not yet fully operational, should also be mentioned:
1. The PTA (Eastern and Southern Africa Preferential Trade Area), the treaty for which was signed in December, 1981, in Lusaka between Comoros, Djibouti, Ethiopia, Kenya, Malawi, Mauritius,

The process of economic integration in Africa is hindered by a certain number of problems and obstacles, including the following:
1. political problems;
2. problems of compatibility and high costs relating to the proliferation of regional and subregional organizations;
3. problems stemming from the lack of transportational infrastructure;
4. problems relating to industrial complementarity;
5. problems which pertain to payment modalities;
6. problems relating to the unequal sharing of benefits deriving from integration schemes;
7. absence of solidarity.

POLITICAL PROBLEMS

In no region of Africa can an integration project be conceived without implicit or explicit reference to Pan-Africanism. Pan-Africanism is the political and economic process by which Africans have sought not only their liberation from the bonds of colonialism, but also their unification (or reunification) after their dispersion to the four corners of the Earth as a result of the slave trade.

The movement was born at the beginning of the century in Anglo-Saxon surroundings, and its first African proponents were, in fact, Anglophones, such as the Ghanian Nkwame Nkrumah. From the platform of Pan-Africanism, Nkrumah later advocated the creation of the "United States of Africa", an ambitious project of political and economic integration under a single supranational authority.

Uganda, Somalia, Tanzania and Zambia.
2. The SADCC (Southern African Development Co-ordination Conference) between Angola, Mozambique, Botswana, Lesotho, Swaziland, Zambia and Malawi, the declared objective of which is to challenge the Republic of South Africa on the economic front, with the financial assistance of the EEC and OECD for the priority development of transportation systems.

There are three economic communities in West Africa:
1. The CEAO: West African Economic Community (1973), which replaced the UDEAO (Customs Union of the West African States, 1966), which in turn had replaced the UDAO (Customs Union of West Africa, 1959). The numbers of the CEAO are: Senegal, Ivory Coast, Mauritania, Upper Volta, Niger and Mali.
2. The ECOWAS: Economic Community of West African States (1975), whose members, other than the six states members of the CEAO, comprise Guinea, Benin and Togo (French-speaking); Nigeria, Ghana, Sierra Leone, Liberia and Gambia (English-speaking); and Cape Verde and Guinea-Bissau (Portutuese-speaking).
3. The Mano River Union (1974) between Sierra Leone and Liberia, which has included Guinea since 1980.

In West Africa, there are also a great number of intergovernmental organizations of more limited scope. Although each of these operates in a specific domain, it is evident that, through interconnected actions, they may serve as instruments of economic integration.
1. Economic co-operation on a political basis:
   - The Council of Entente (1959): Ivory Coast, Upper Volta, Niger, Benin and Togo.
2. Utilization of natural resources:
   - Organization for the Development of the Senegal River (1972): Senegal, Mauritania and Mali.
   - Gambia River Development Organization (1976): Senegal, Gambia, Guinea (1980), and Guinea-Bissau (1983).

Pan-Africanism, throughout its history, has served to crystallize the major political difficulties which hinder African integration. This has occurred for two reasons:
1. Pan-Africanism is, by nature, a progressive project; as a result, a veritable crusade of hostility was launched against the idea (and against Nkrumah) by the "moderate" African Heads of State, especially at the Addis Ababa Conference in May, 1983, birthplace of the Organization of African Unity.
2. From the start, it has been an Anglophone project. This fact has brought about a certain reticence on the part of the Francophone Heads of State and has thereby served to reinforce the artificial cleavage between the English- and French-speaking Africa of colonial times.

The political difficulties which obstruct African integration may therefore be situated on two levels: political cleavage and colonial burdens.

Political Cleavage

Any successful attempt at economic integration must certainly be based on the necessity of having identical political viewpoints among its partners. No one would consider having a non-communist country as a member of COMECON, or an Eastern European country as a member of the EEC.

In Africa, certain economic groupings, such as the CEAO, are composed of

- River Niger Basin Authority (1980) which replaced the River Niger Commission (1965): Benin, Ivory Coast, Guinea, Upper Volta, Mali, Niger, Nigeria and Cameroon.
- Lake Chad Basin Commission (1964): Niger, Nigeria, in association with Chad and Cameroon.
- Authority for the Integrated Development of the Liptako-Gourma Region (1971): Mali, Niger and Upper Volta.
3. Co-operation in the field of agriculture:
   - Inter-African Committee for Hydraulic Studies (1960): the former members of French West Africa (excluding Guinea) and French Equatorial Africa (excluding the Central African Republic).
   - West African Rice Development Association (1970), the members of which are the same as those of ECOWAS.
   - Permanent Inter-State Committee on Drought Control in the Sahel (1973): Senegal, Mali, Upper Volta, Mauritania, Gambia, Niger, Chad, Cape Verde.
   - *Organisation Commune de Lutte Anti-Acridienne et Anti-aviaire* (1965): the former members of French West Africa (excluding Guinea) in association with Cameroon, Chad and Gambia.
   - International Organization against the African Migrating Cricket (1962): former French, British and Portuguese colonies.
   - African Groundnut Council (1962): Senegal, Mali, Niger, Nigeria, Gambia and Sudan.
4. Co-operation in the field of civil aviation:
   - All West African countries are members of the African Civil Aviation Commission (1969), created within the framework of the Organization of African Unity (OAU).
   - Concerning the management of air space, certain countries (such as Nigeria, Ghana, etc.) have their own F.I.R. (Flight Information Region), while others are grouped into various regional F.I.R. organizations:
     (a) Agency for Flight Safety (1959): former members of French West Africa (excluding Guinea) and French Equatorial Africa, and Madagascar.
     (b) Roberst F.I.R.: Liberia, Sierra Leone, Guinea.
   - For air transportation, Senegal, Ivory Coast, Niger, Upper Volta, Benin and Togo are partners in "Air Afrique", a multinational company for West Africa.

countries with identical political structures. However, other groupings include countries whose political orientations are different from those of the other partners; such is the case of Guinea and Benin in ECOWAS, of the Congo in UDEAC, and of Tanzania in the now defunct East African Community. Moreover, the revolutionary regimes which have recently been set up in Ghana and in Upper Volta have never questioned their membership in such subregional organizations.

It would therefore seem that African leaders do not stipulate similarity of political and economic structure as a precondition to integration. However, this will not suffice to dodge the political problem. After all, the East African Community finally disintegrated some ten years after the radicalization of the Tanzanian regime. In West Africa, Guinea and Benin have refused to join the CEAO which they suspected to be an instrument of French economic domination. At the same time, ECOWAS seemed to offer them more guarantees, taking into account the presence of its English-speaking members.

Since the loss of Nkrumah, Africa has been without a Head of State to defend the principle of a supranational government of the United States of Africa. Jealous of their sovereignty, at least on the intra-African level, African leaders are committed to the functionalist approach to integration, which limits itself to economic co-operation and is to be differentiated from Nkrumah's federalist, political approach.

Even in the context of this conception of integration, a cleavage exists between "moderates" and "progressives". The moderates, by political philosophy, cannot conceive of economic integration beyond the stage of integrating markets. They are perhaps not always cognizant of this tendency. Progressives, on the other hand, call for integration of production. Political will to achieve what is called African Unity does not seem sufficient in itself in order to transcend these forms of opposition.

The Burden of the Colonial Heritage

Other than compensating for political differences, Africa must also support the weight of a heavy colonial heritage.

The experiences of economic integration in Africa which have taken place up to the present have only served to renew, under different forms, the former colonial order. In this manner, the Federation of French West Africa gave rise to the West African Customs Union (UDAO) and, in turn, the CEAO (which excludes Guinea and Benin); the Federation of French West Africa was dissolved in March, 1959, and the UDAO was created three months later. In Central Africa, UDEAC is no less than an extension of the former Federation of French Equatorial Africa; the treaty which founded the Equatorial Customs Union (created just before UDEAC) was actually signed in Paris. The Economic Community of the Great Lakes Countries is a continuation of the Economic Union which was created by Belgium in 1925 between the Congo and Ruanda-Burundi. In East Africa, the East African Economic Community was a British creation dating back to 1917.

On the other hand, there have been no attempts at economic integration which reflect geographic, or simply human logic, as for example between the Congo (a former French colony) and Zaire (a former Belgian colony).

In other words, African leaders have remained at the status quo stage of colonial Balkanization, thus incapable of conceiving an integration of their economies beyond the arbitrary limits established by the colonial powers.

ECOWAS is unique in that it has broken colonial bonds and brought together for the first time French-speaking, English-speaking and Portuguese-speaking African countries. But it must not be forgotten that the initiative which led to the creation of ECOWAS came from the United Nations Economic Commission for Africa, which was backed by the determination of those states in the subregion which were the most independent with regard to France (Togo, and especially Nigeria). This is the same process which recently led Guinea to join the Mano River Union, which is otherwise composed of two Anglophone countries (Liberia and Sierra Leone), after having refused to join the French- speaking CEAO.

THE PROLIFERATION OF INTER-GOVERNMENTAL ORGANIZATIONS (IGOs): PROBLEMS OF COMPATIBILITY AND HIGH COSTS

In West Africa, there are more structures for economic integration than in any other part of the globe: Three economic communities and no fewer than 25 IGO consortia for co-operation.

The existence of three different economic communities derives more from political considerations than from economic logic. Such is the case with ECOWAS, which was created in rather slapdash and hasty fashion in order to counter the CEAO. Hence, in its founding treaty, ECOWAS is presented, in terms of its objectives and functioning, as completely incompatible with the CEAO. ECOWAS was conceived as an integral free trade zone, which the CEAO remained simply a customs preference zone (or an organized trade zone). In the first case, products are exchanged freely and are immune to any form of tariff protections; in the second instance, a reduced customs tax is imposed (in these circumstances, a regional co-operation tax on certain manufactured goods).

A simple example will illustrate the sort of problem which can crop up: if Senegal imports canned pineapple juice from Guinea, an ECOWAS partner, it is totally duty-free in conformity with the regulations of the free trade zone. If, on the other hand, Senegal imports the same product from the Ivory Coast, a reduced import tax may be imposed in accordance with the regulations of the CEAO. The Ivory Coast is thus penalized, unless its membership in ECOWAS becomes the outweighing factor.

In this case, why should the CEAO be maintained? It is not possible that drafters of the ECOWAS treaty had this very idea in mind. Even if this be the case, however, it has served no end; the CEAO has continued to receive solid support from its defenders. This led to the transformation of ECOWAS during the summit of Heads of State into a zone of progressive customs "disarmament", structured in function of the needs of its members. This is, in fact, just a variant of a customs preference zone; the process of customs disarmament will be quicker for the more industrialized countries (Senegal, Ivory Coast, Ghana, Nigeria).

Under the present set of circumstances, the countries of the subregion are confronted with a dilemma: pure logic (not to mention geography) presupposes a 16-member community, such as ECOWAS, which brings together all West African countries. However, concern for efficiency would indicate economic groupings of smaller dimensions (the CEAO, Mano River Union) which have better chances of becoming truly operational. Moreover, the CEAO and the Mano River Union have in fact implemented several projects, while ECOWAS, 8 years after its creation, continues to exist only on paper.

Another peculiarity of West African economic integration is the total number of member countries which make up ECOWAS. In no other continent can one find an economic community comprised of 16 members. This can be used as a persuasive argument by those, like L. S. Senghor, who favours "integration in concentric circles."

The proliferation of IGOs also poses the problem of high costs, as each member state is obliged to contribute to the budgets of several organizations at the same time. The francophone states hold the record for IGO participation – Niger, Upper Volta, Mali and Senegal are members of 20 IGOs, and the Ivory Coast contributes to 18. Nigeria, Sierra Leone, Ghana, Liberia and Guinea belong to no less than 10 such organizations. Cape Verde, on the other hand, is a member of only two IGOs – ECOWAS and CILSS.

Naturally, participation in so many IGOs means very high costs, especially for the Sahelian states. These costs are in fact of two types: human and financial.

The problem of human costs does not generally command adequate attention, yet it is important primarily for two reasons. Firstly, in the process of evaluating costs and benefits, all aspects of cost must be taken into consideration, human costs included. Secondly, in a context of underdevelopment, human costs assume special dimensions.

In the IGOs, the distribution of high-level jobs is implemented according to geographical quotas, as each state has the right to a certain number of top posts. As a result, some states feel the necessity to send their best qualified personnel to the IGOs. At the same time, the developing economies are experiencing a dearth not only of natural and financial, but also of human resources. These countries must try to meet their national economic development needs through foreign technical assistance, which is not always well-adapted to local conditions. The distribution of top-level posts in the IGOs is carried out according to geographical quotas; it therefore automatically excludes competition between various candidates, or scrutiny of their levels of competence. Furthermore, it is not rare to see states fill their quotas with individuals chosen by purely political criteria, without any regard for their particular competence. In such cases, a certain degree of inefficiency is actually inflicted on the IGOs. Indeed, cases of incompetence are present at all levels of responsibility in these organizations.

The financial aspect of the high costs of the IGOs is even more perceptible, owing to their direct effects on national budgets. Membership in various IGOs constitutes a significant financial burden to the participating states. Indeed, for the period 1977-1981 alone, the 16 West African States contributed a total of US $85 million or CFA 20 billion, to these organizations.

The total budget of the CEAO for 1982 amounted to $30 million (CFA 9 billion), of which $3,300,000 (CFA 1 billion) covered the expenses of the General Secretariat. In less than 10 years of existence, the CEAO has received contributions from its members amounting to $133 million (CFA 40 billion).

The 1982 budget for ECOWAS (Lagos Headquarters) came to $7,700,000 (CFA 2.5 billion). This was merely to cover operating costs. In 1980, the ECOWAS Fund for Co-operation, Compensation and Development (in Lomé) operated on a budget of $133 million (CFA 40 billion).

In 1979-80, the Mano River Union cost its two member countries (Liberia and Sierra Leone) a total of $3,721,328 (CFA 1 billion); Guinea had not yet joined the organization at that date. When an external subvention of $1,860,664 (CFA 350 million) is added, the total budget came to $4,864,098 (nearly 1.5 billion CFA francs), of which the expenses of the Secretariat (Headquarters in Freetown and Office in Monrovia) amounted to $1,367,846 (CFA 410 million).

The IGOs clearly cost too much. It is sufficient to note that a good number of states in the subregion grant the advantages contained in the Investment Code to foreign enterprises which accept to set up operations for a local investment of at least $330,000 (CFA 100 million). Herein lies a substantial capacity for external investment which should be attracted in order to create jobs in the short term and to promote economic development in the long term. At the same time, however, we continue to pump money into the budgets of the IGOs which spend 10 times more for their operations without being accountable for their expenses. This is clearly in contradiction with the most elementary principles of economic arithmetic.

Moreover, the proliferation of IGOs has posed a quantitative problem to member states, in that these organisations require increasing contributions from their participants, as well as a qualitative problem, inasmuch as it is necessary to question the way in which the funds received are actually spent.

When an IGO is being created, each member country normally desires either to be chosen as the site of the organization's headquarters or to have one of its citizens named as director. In so doing, the country hopes to obtain a certain economic advantage, i.e., the multiplier effect of the salaries of the organization's headquarters officials on national revenues. In Europe, it has been recently established that a country such as Italy which hosts the headquarters of the FAO in Rome gains a financial advantage much higher than its actual contribution to the Organization. However, the same does not necessarily hold true for an African developing country. No African country can profit, like Italy, from such an economic advantage inasmuch as its economy, oriented towards the exterior, must bear the heavy weight of imports.

The presence of a large number of IGOs in Ouagadougou (CEAO, CILSS, CIEH, Liptako-Gourma, etc.) has no marked effect on the economy of Upper

Volta; local consumption by IGO officials goes largely into imported products. Missions abroad provide opportunities for shopping and, as a consequence, there are "invisible imports". As a result, the multiplier effect on national revenues is nil. As regards that portion of IGO salaries which could be placed as savings in national banks, one should not forget that these funds can be placed in banks outside the host country as well, where interests rates are higher. Does not the ECOWAS Fund provide an example of such a practice?*

One should also draw attention to the manner in which the IGOs are managed and to frivolous expenses for luxury and prestige. The building which houses the CEAO in Ouagadougou cost its six member states nearly $23 million (CFA 7 billion). In 1980 this same organization spent $83,000 (CFA 25 million) for publicity in a Parisian magazine.

Enthusiasm for the IGOs has been maintained in function of relatively satisfactory export profits. The STABEX system, which was developed by the first Lomé Convention (1975-80), helped to nourish hopes for the stabilization of export profits at a fairly high level. Most of the West African IGOs were created in the decade 1970-1980.

The first Lomé Convention ended in 1980, and an initial evaluation of STABEX could then be made. Its resources proved far too limited to cover the enormous losses in profits due to drought (groundnuts) and diminishing market prices for exported raw materials (cacao, coffee, etc.). The repercussions of the financial crisis which has struck the states of the subregion have been felt by the IGOs in the form of overdue contributions from their members:

- At ECOWAS (Lagos Headquarters), up to 1980, only five of the 16 member countries were behind in their contributions. In 1981, only two countries had met their contributions, and on 20 June, 1982, not a single country had yet contributed.
- The ECOWAS Fund (Headquarters in Lomé) has not received a single contribution since 1980. Headquarters operating costs are presently met by interest accrued on the Fund's initial capital deposited in European banks.
- The budget of OCLALAV, which amounted to $1.3 million (CFA 325 million) when it launched its activities in 1965, has dropped to $993,000 (CFA 298 million) despite inflation, although its membership has grown from nine to ten countries.
- The Report of Activities of the Secretary-General of the CEAO for 1979-80 emphasized "a wearing down of the States, which explains a persistently poor economic situation which will cause contributions to become increasingly heavy burdens" (p. 129).

Provisions of the European Development Fund to the CEAO have also posed problems.

From the standpoint of the participating states, there is serious concern over the

---

*There do not even exist any fiscal advantages which may be drawn from the employees of IGOs, as those employees who are not citizens of the host country are exempt from taxes. It also seems that they are not subject to taxation in their countries of origin.

financial repercussions of community contributions which in some cases amount to one per cent of the national budget. This concern has pushed some states to consider abandoning certain IGOs – in particular, those whose basic efficiency has come into doubt. It is curious to note that not all the IGOs are faced with the problem of overdue contributions. Certain of these organizations continue to receive the regular support of their member states because their activities are perceived to be profitable, either in immediate terms, or in the not so distant future.

Discrimination in levels of financial support reveals that some states in the subregion had already implicitly undertaken the process of evaluating the IGOs before the Council of Ministers of MULPOC* explicitly brought up the question in 1981, during a meeting held in Banjul. In this light, the current crisis will have brought about at least one positive outcome, especially if vigorous actions are undertaken by the member states as a result of the request for an evaluation of the IGOs.

Economic cost/benefit considerations regulate all private investment projects. In the public sector, these considerations have traditionally been applied to investment projects for the construction of dams and transportation infrastructure. Investment has been expanded to include such fields as education and health, for which evaluation remains a difficult task. This serves to illustrate that every economic operation which involves the mobilization of a certain volume of financial resources must be subject to evaluation. Such evaluation may be carried out from the beginning in order to sustain or reject a project according to its proven profitability. For sectorial projects (transportation, dams) evaluation may be carried out at a determined point of the project's operations in order to judge if it is worthwhile to continue the project.

The IGOs must be subject to the same type of economic considerations. The high costs of the IGOs is well-known – it is represented in their budgets – and they are expected to pay off through their contribution to the economic development of the member countries. The only means of fulfilling this objective is to ensure that the difference between profit and cost be maximized. At the very least, they must extricate themselves from a perpetual situation of costs without profits if IGOs are to be something other than an impediment to development. Africa cannot continue to permit such luxuries in its underdeveloped economies where the contradiction between the insufficiency of resources and the abundance of needs is most sharply felt.

This applies to all the countries of the region. The limited available financial and human resources could be directed towards different, alternative uses, considering the many needs of the population which must be satisfied simultaneously.

One U.S. dollar, if allocated to Sector A, is lost for Sector B, although it could have provided more effective results there. For example, the sum of $30,000 (a fraction less than CFA 11 million) may seem a modest figure when it is allocated as a contribution to a state or even to the most efficient IGO. However, the same sum,

---

*Multinational Programming Operating Centre. MULPOC is the executing organ of the Economic Commission of the United Nations for Africa (ECA) for each of the fivre subregions of the continent.

injected into a rural community, can finance concrete achievements: the construction of rural child care centres, dispensaries, classrooms, medicines, the drilling of wells, etc. It can satisfy in a direct and immediate manner the fundamental needs of the rural population ("grassroots development").

Sizeable sums of money have been spent on numerous African IGOs in the last 20 years. In consequence, one cannot avoid posing the following questions: would the economic conditions of the region have been affected negatively if the IGOs had not existed? Would they have been altered in a positive direction if these sums had been utilized for different purposes?

No IGO has been created without a precise, *medium-term* economic objective, even if the emphasis of their actual mandates lies more in the context of the promotion of African unity, which is a wider and longer-term objective. When an economist, on the basis of the founding charter of an IGO, requests a summary of its achievements only to be informed that the organization is neither a grocer's shop nor a commercial enterprise, it is proof of the failure of the IGO, and a justification for continuing its chronically deficient operations against the best interests of its region or subregion. It is a sign that the IGO in question has become a brake on the process of economic development.

In conclusion, the financing provided to cover the "operating expenses" of member states should be considered an investment and should therefore be subject to at least a minimum concern for economic profitability.

THE PROBLEM OF TRANSPORTATION

In Africa, the existing transportation network continues to be an important factor underlying the orientation of the continent's economy towards external markets.

West African seaports (Dakar, Conakry, Abidjan, Lagos, Accra) are linked among themselves only by the Atlantic Ocean; the maritime traffic out of reach of these ports is directed towards Europe and America, owing to the fact that the shipping firms belong to foreign interests which find that shipping freight over these long-distance routes is more profitable.

It is the railway network that could be used to best advantage to strengthen inter-African trade, as it is generally the most convenient and economical means of transporting merchandise. However, there exist only 79,185 kilometres of track in Africa, 22,464 of which are located in the Republic of South Africa. This means that in Africa there is a ratio of one kilometre of track per 392 square kilometres of surface area, while in Belgium, for example, the ratio is on the order of one kilometre of track per 7 square kilometres of surface area. Furthermore, throughout Africa, the configuration of the rail network forms the same funnel shape. In each country, interior zones (reservoirs of raw agricultural products and minerals) are linked to ports of export. Such is the case for the Kumasi-Accra line in Ghana; Kano-Lagos and Jos-Lagos in Nigeria; Kankan-Conakry in Guinea; and Parakou-

Cotonou in Benin. The Abidjan-Niger Railway (which links Ouagadougou and Abidjan) and the Dakar-Niger line (which links Bamako and Dakar) were built for the same reason by the colonial authorities of French West Africa. The East African Railways Corporation, which disappeared with the East African Economic Community, had also been set up during the colonial period.

Another inherent difficulty of the African railway network is that the guage differs between many Anglophone and Francophone track systems; in many English-speaking countries, the distance separating the rails is 1.067 metres, while a separation of one metre is common in the former French colonies. An African union of railways was created in 1972 with a view to interconnecting the continent's railway network.

For the moment, a certain number of plans exist to link the railway systems of different African countries: Abadla (Algeria) – Segou (Mali); Tripoli (Lybia) – Gabes (Tunisia) – Nyala (Sudan) – Ndjamena (Chad); Maiduguri (Nigeria) – Yaoundé (Cameroon) – Bangui (Central African Republic). These have been inspired to some extent by the TANZAN (Tanzania-Zambia) system which extends over 1,800 kilometres.

Even more ambitious plans exist for the road network: the African Unity Road (Mombasa-Lagos); the Trans-Sahelian Roads (Dakar – Ndjamena and Nouakchott – Lagos). These seem to enjoy the favour of the African leaders, and of others, who can lend financial support.

But the above are just plans. For the time being, air transportation is the only domain in which there is a certain level of co-operation between African countries, despite the existence of many national carriers.

A similar situation exists in telecommunications. Direct telephone links are not common between one African city and another. The idea of a Pan-African Telecommunication Network (PANAFTEL) came to light during a conference on telecommunications held under the auspices of the CEA and the OAU in 1966. Studies for the project were completed in 1972, but financing problems have so far stalled its implementation.

THE ABSENCE OF INDUSTRIAL COMPLEMENTARITY: THE PROBLEM OF INTEGRATING PRODUCTION

In terms of natural endowments, the countries of some subregions, such as West Africa, are extremely complementary – more so, in fact, than the countries of the European Economic Community. The West African subregion extends over diverse ecological zones, and therefore, in terms of agricultural production, the crops of the Sahelian countries (groundnuts, cotton) can be very clearly distinguished from those of the forested states (wood, coffee, cacao). Livestock production is well developed in the Sahel and in Guinea, which is not the case in the forest zones because of the tsetse fly. Mineral resources are also well distributed.

There is oil in Nigeria, uranium in Niger, phosphates in Senegal and Togo, iron in Mauritania and Liberia, and bauxite in Guinea. It is clear in this case that natural complementarity is no less effective than that between the EEC countries.

Industry, as the transformation of raw materials of animal, vegetable or mineral origin, possesses a natural basis for complementarity among West African countries, both in the agro-food and in the heavy industrial sectors. If, as is often said, African industries are not complementary, the reason is not to be found in nature. Indeed, the lack of complementarity was created and maintained by nationalistic development policies for light, import-substitution industries. Throughout the West African subregion, for example, the industrial landscape is made up of more or less identical configurations, and the result is a low level of intra-community exchanges. Manufactured products are similar and intended for the internal market; agricultural and mineral raw materials are exported to Northern countries. The absence of horizontal forms of integration among African countries only serves to reinforce and perpetuate vertical integration with the developed countries.

Horizontal integration of industrial production can be achieved through intersectorial specialization (for example through the equitable distribution among community partners of the production of air conditioners, refrigerators, electric fans, water heaters, electric motors and other electric appliances). These "footloose" industries may be implanted without regard to local endowments of natural resources; heavy industry, however, must be located with access to the essential raw materials. In either case, an industry must aim at the community itself as a potential market (ECOWAS encompasses more than 130 million inhabitants).

The integration of production may, at the same time, be extended to joint ventures. The co-production system is especially justifiable when individual countries do not have sufficient financial resources for investments of a fairly broad scope.

A system of co-production was attempted several years ago for an oil refinery in Port-Gentil, Gabon. This country, along with its partners in UDEAC, held one-fourth of the shares, the rest of which were held by private French interest. In 1973, the government of Gabon become the sole African shareholder in the company, although it held no more than one-fourth of its shares.

Objective possibilities still exist for co-production schemes in Africa, especially when one takes into account the diversity of its natural resources and the difficulties faced by nations on an individual basis to amass sufficient financial resources. Nevertheless, one must also acknowlege that, in some cases, joint industries have been set up which are not only incompatible with the spirit of the community but also in defiance of pure economic logic. In such cases, the partner is no longer another African state, but a private foreign concern; raw materials are no longer available locally, but imported. Two examples (for cement and sugar production) can be cited in this regard.

Cement can be made directly on the site of limestone and clay deposits, or it may be produced through the grinding of clinker, a semi-finished product. Clinker may be purchased. In French-speaking West Africa, Senegal, Togo and Mali have large deposits of limestone, and cement plants exist in all three countries. On the other hand, the Ivory Coast, which has no such deposits, has nevertheless set up three plants for grinding clinker imported from France and Spain.

Would it not have been more rational to supply the entire ECOWAS market with cement produced directly at the site of these deposits on a co-production basis for financing?

Two models of this type already exist. The former, ONIGBOLO, was created in 1975 by the governments of Benin and Niger, which hold respectively 55 and 40 per cent of the shares. Their partner is a Danish firm which carried out the initial feasibility studies.

The second model is the West African Cement Company, CIMAO, which operates in Togo. The majority of its capital is held by Togo, the Ivory Coast and Ghana (30.7 per cent each). However, CIMAO produces only clinker, which directly interests the Ivory Coast and Ghana in that they hope to supply their own clinker grinding facilities at a lower cost. Since the creation of CIMAO, however, these hopes have not been fully realized. But it seems out of the question that these countries foresake their own "artificial" cement production in favour of their partners who are better endowed with the necessary resources. The argument that clinker is easier to transport than imported cement is hardly convincing. All African countries import products from Europe which are a good deal more unwieldy than cement.

The Ivory Coast has no monopoly on "industrial chauvinism". Practically every state in the subregion has its own cement plant or project. Except for Senegal's installation, which was set up in 1949, these plants were all created either over the period 1965-1971, or after 1978 when both the UDEAO and the CEAO were in existence. Of the 15 plants which operate in nine French-speaking West African countries, more than half are facilities for grinding clinker. Among West African countries, only Upper Volta and Mauritania do not yet have their own cement producing facilities; both of these countries, however, plan to set up at least one such operation in the years ahead. As regards Central Africa, the Central African Republic is in a situation similar to that of Mauritania and Upper Volta, which leaves Chad as the only francophone African country with no plans to set up cement production facilities.

In the sugar industry similar irrational policies exist. In 1971, the government of the Ivory Coast created the state-owned company SODESUCRE which originally was to set up a complex of 15 refineries in order to produce 600,000 tonnes of sugar annually. The internal market of the Ivory Coast could absorb only about one-tenth of this quantity. The raw material for the refineries is in the form of sugar cane grown under irrigation in the North of the Ivory Coast, which does not pose great difficulties as the country suffers no dearth of rainfall. The Ivory Coast is capable of covering the entire sugar demand of the CEAO and is the biggest sugar producer in Africa.

In fact, however, the original SODESUCRE project has been reduced to more modest proportions. Only six refineries have been installed so far for an initial production of 180,000 tonnes in 1980-81, half of which was destined for export.

Production should be gradually brought up to 280,000 tonnes by 1985, at which time national sugar consumption is estimated to reach 100,000 tonnes.

In light of the above, clear possibilities exist for increasing production in order to cover the needs of the CEAO market at least. This would include the financial participation of the other states in the subregion to augment the capital base of SODESUCRE. (The high cost of the project – CFA 300 billion – was especially due to fraudulent billing practices which have been quite rightly denounced by President Houphouet-Boigny).

At the same time, however, all the other states of the subregion have also launched sugar production projects – even the countries of the Sahel, regularly plagued by drought, have envisioned the cultivation of sugar cane, which necessitates a good supply of water. The government of the Ivory Coast holds 16.29 per cent of the shares of the Upper Volta Sugar Company, an agro-industrial complex.

Starting in 1972, lands which had previously been used for rice crops for local consumption in the river region and in the north of Senegal were converted to sugar cane production. The cane supplies a specially created refinery, but the local crops alone will not suffice for the plant's needs. As a result, unrefined sugar is imported from Europe as a semi-finished product. The unrefined sugar which arrives in Dakar, where it will be consumed, must first be transported to and from the refinery – a distance of 740 kilometres, round-trip. Naturally, these transportation costs are reflected in the consumer price of the product. Furthermore, at times when the refinery cannot meet local demand, the only recourse lies in importing refined sugar from Europe.

The Ivory Coast, on the other hand, is faced with the problem of surplus sugar production. The European authorities in Brussels have failed to guarantee purchases of Ivory Coast sugar at a higher market price than going world rates, as stipulated by the Lomé Convention. It should be added that the Ivory Coast launched its sugar project at the moment when world sugar prices went from CFA 50 to 300 per kilo. Thus the project, right at the start, was part of a process of vertical integration with the world market.

In Central Africa as well, each member country is equipped with its own sugar refineries. As is the case for cement, sugar is not part of trade within UDEAC.

These examples of cement and sugar production demonstrate that African states formulate their development plans without consulting one another, quite as if the economic communities did not exist. One is therefore led to question the purpose of these organizations, especially if they cannot even fulfil their role as technical advisers or co-ordinators for the governments of their member countries.

The multiplication and hence the dispersion of efforts is common also to the field of higher education and advanced training. In French-speaking Africa, the 1970s witnessed the creation of several national universities, always with a certain regard for the countries' prestige. But these institutions were characteristically ineffectual, due to the limited availability not only of material means (libraries, laboratories) but also of human resources (educators, trainers). Hence there developed a massive need for French technical assistance, which served to reinforce vertical dependence. From the integrationist's point of view, there has been a clear regression since the colonial period, at which time all higher level personnel in French West Africa were trained in Senegal. Of course, it is no longer admissible that one single country be allowed a monopoly of all training facilities; it is possible, on the other hand, to rationalize efforts and bring together the means necessary to establish subregional university-level centres of excellence distributed between partners. An example of such co-operation has been provided by the Common Afro-Mauritian Organization (OCAM) with the creation of the Inter-State School of Veterinary Sciences and Medicine in Dakar, the African Data-Processing Institute in Libreville, and the Advanced Training Centre for Administrative Personnel in Abidjan. Similar institutions were established by the East African Economic Community, and some of these have outlived that organization.

On the whole, the irrational aspects of national industrial strategies can be explained quite simply by the fact that individual governments are anxious to see their countries included in the mainstream of the industrialization process which they consider, with good reason, to be the basis of economic development. The most industrialized African countries wish to consolidate their advantages, the others do not wish to play forever the role of agrarian "appendages".

If this is indeed the case, it is because there does not exist a community strategy for the integration of production. Such a strategy would present considerable advantages:
- Based on industrial complementarities, it would almost automatically serve to develop trade between member states.
- It is the only path to industrialization of the different subregions of the continent which can allow countries to develop their own industrial branches (metallurgy, siderurgy, mechanics, petrochemistry, etc.) with the assurance of some level of independence from external competition.
- It would regulate the problem of unequal development. The equitable distribution of major industries among member countries would be determined by the economic community itself, and not only by market criteria and the search for immediate profits.

The existence of community-run operations in heavy industry would in no way jeopardize the existence of light industries in each member country, since the latter serve basically the needs of local markets.

In legal terms a community enterprise may be either an inter-state company, a mixed capital company or it may be privately owned. In any event, it must be run according to the rigorous norms of management in the private sector, as is the case with the multinational firm Air Afrique. Development finance institutions such as the ADB (African Development Bank) can bring effective support to schemes of production integration. The charter of the ADB gives special importance to multinational projects, which, however, received only three per cent of all funds allocated over the period 1967-1981; a total of 12 million units of account was allocated to the CEAO and the OMVS dam projects (Diama and Manantali). Otherwise, the ADB has financed a certain number of studies for identifying multinational projects in the fields of transportation, telecommunications, tourism, energy, etc. However, these studies have not resulted in the implementation of concrete projects due to the absence of a strategy for the integration of production.

Certain African states have realized the need for the integration of production, and the shortcomings of the existing economic communities have prompted them to take initiatives on their own. In this regard we can cite the example of Senegal's industrial chemical company (ICS) which is being set up to produce fertilizer. The government of Senegal has invested 23.3 per cent of the company's capital; the governments of the Ivory Coast, Nigeria and Cameroon have each invested 9.4 per cent of the capital, and the Indian government is also associated with the project.

Under Nkrumah, in the early 1960s, the government of Ghana built the Akossombo dam which was designed to furnish electric power not only to Ghana itself, but also to neighbouring Togo and Benin. To date, the latter countries still receive their electricity from Ghana, at a kilowatt per hour rate which is by far the lowest in the region. Presently, a project has been set up to link the electric power distribution networks of Ghana and the Ivory Coast. The advantage of the project is that it will allow for the surplus electric power of one country to be consumed by the other.

The above-mentioned initiatives were taken either before the creation of ECOWAS, or, in some cases, outside the framework of this subregional organization. This is also true for the multinational cement companies CIMAO and ONIGBOLO.

THE PROBLEM OF THE MEANS OF PAYMENT

Within ECOWAS, there is a veritable mosaic of currencies made up of the Nigerian naira, the Ghanian cedi, the leone of Sierra Leone, the Liberian dollar, the Gambian dalasi, the Mauritanian ouguiya, the Malian franc, Guinea-Bissau's escudo, the Guinean sily and the CFA franc of the six member countries of the West African Monetary Union.* Apart from the Liberian dollar (which is the same as the American dollar) and the CFA version of the French franc, the above currencies are limited to domestic transactions and cannot be utilized for international payments. Nor can these currencies be converted to those of another country of the subregion, which obviously does not serve to foster trade in the area.

For many years, the states of the subregion relied on bilateral accords (such as between Niger and Nigeria, and Senegal and Gambia), or were obliged to pass through financial centres in Paris or London to regulate payments with neighbouring states. Neither of these solutions served to stimulate commercial flows within the subregion itself.

For this reason, the West African Clearing House was established in 1975, with its Headquarters in Freetown, Sierra Leone.† Members (participating states of

---

*Senegal, Ivory Coast, Upper Volta, Niger, Benin and Togo./
†Guinea, Guinea-Bissau and Mauritania joined the Clearing House in 1976. Cape Verde is not yet a member.

ECOWAS) are represented by their respective central banks, with the exception of the West African Monetary Union states which are represented collectively.

Because there were no links between the different currencies of the subregion, the UCAO (West African Unit of Account) was established as an equivalent to SDRs. All ECOWAS currencies are convertible to West African Units of Account (UA); the rate of exchange of each currency is calculated every 15 days, from the 1st to the 15th and from the 16th to the 30th of every month.

The UCAO now constitutes the previously missing link between the different currencies of ECOWAS. Individual states may no longer arbitrarily establish rates of exchange for their own currencies, often over-evaluating their real value.

A clearing house for subregional payments has also been established in Central Africa between the member states of UDEAC with the addition of Zaire. Headquartered in Kinshassa, the clearing house has been operational since February, 1982.

The West African Clearing House, on the other hand, became operational in July, 1976. From August 1976 to September 1978, the volume of transactions was UA 50.713 million; in August 1980, the volume had risen to UA 108.340 million. This represents an increase of 69.64 per cent from 1977-78 to 1978-79, and of 54.73 per cent from 1978-79 to 1979-80 – or a progression of 45 per cent annually.*

However, the increase in the volume of transactions within the West African Clearing House does not – for diverse reasons – reflect a corresponding increase in the volume of intra-community trade within ECOWAS. In the first place, the fact that the central banks of three countries (Guinea, Guinea-Bissau and Mauritania) adhered to the Clearing House inflated the volume of transactions. Further, transactions in CFA francs (which account for three-quarters of intra-community trade within ECOWAS) are not directed through the Clearing House.

The totality of transactions within the Clearing House is not limited to commercial transactions. In 1979-80, commercial transactions amounted to UA 58.961 million, financial transactions came to an additional UA 47.345 million, while "non-classified" transactions (such as sums transferred by governments to their embassies) represented UA 2 million.

Generally speaking, the West African Clearing House has yet to gain its "cruising speed", as its normal operations have run up against several difficulties:
- Trade btween border areas (which is considerable in the subregion) does not pass through the channels of the Clearing House;
- The communications situation of the subregion for telegrammes, telexes, etc. is disastrous; often important messages are not received, or arrive after long delays.
- It is not clear that all potential users of the Clearing House (importers, exporters) are even aware of its existence.
- Even those who are aware of the Clearing House have failed to use it for one simple reason: local African currencies are not desirable forms of exchange in the subregion.

*West African Clearing House, *Annual Report 1979-80*.

One does not have to subscribe to the body of diagnoses and recommendations contained in the 1981 World Bank Report to recognize that these currencies are overvalued. It is for this reason that a black market is active in the subregion – outside the CFA franc zone and, of course, Liberia. On the black market, rates of exchange are from two to fifteen times lower than official rates, according to the currencies transacted. On might even wonder if the black market rates do not correspond to the real worth of these currencies, given the lack of official exchange in the market-economy countries. A shunning attitude has thus developed in regard to "autonomous" African currencies. (Recent devaluations of the currencies of Ghana and Zaire under the aegis of the IMF were followed by reductions in their worth on the black market as well.)

The markets of Liberia (for dollars) and the UMOA countries (for CFA francs) are much sought after by the subregion's exporters. This has led some states to adopt safeguard measures such as exchange controls which have slowed intra-community trade, particularly that involving Liberia.

At the same time, the substantial import needs of other countries have not been satisfied. Ghana, for example, respresents a considerable potential market for livestock from Upper Volta. But a livestock merchant of Upper Volta has no desire to be paid in cedis in accordance with the procedures of the Clearing House. By the same token, a grower in Ghana would prefer to sell his crop in the Ivory Coast for CFA francs, rather than selling it to the Ghana Marketing Board for cedis.

It should be added that states do not always play by the rules of the game which they themselves have set up. Nigeria does not channel payments for its oil sales to ECOWAS partners through the West African Clearing House; Lagos would not consider accepting nairas in payment for oil, even from a community partner. The result is that partners who lack foreign exchange can have serious problems in acquiring their oil supply. At the same time Nigeria utilizes the Clearing House more often than other countries for its imports from the ECOWAS group, and it pays for these imports in nairas. Furthermore, the Central Bank of Nigeria has always been in a debtor position at the Clearing House. Its negative balance amounted to UA 43.260 million in 1979-80; over the same period, Nigerian transaction represented 60 per cent of total transaction in the Clearing House.*

If West Africa is to overcome the drawbacks of the CFA franc zone (or of adopting the US dollar), and if it is to avoid having separate currencies for each country, the only solution is to establish a joint Bank issuing a common currency. The CFA franc zone entails a monetary dependence on France, as much for periodic devaluations as for credit operations which clearly favour the short-term. This monetary dependence serves as vehicle for other forms of dependence (commercial, financial, political). The situation in which each state issues its own currency is merely a *pro forma* kind of independence: overvaluing a national currency causes serious balance of payments problems and results in an indirect devaluation by the IMF. Neither of these situations permits a currency to become an instrument of economic development.

*West African Clearing House, *Annual Report 1979-80*.

Thus serious monetary problems exist in West Africa. Monetary authorities (such as the Association of West African Central Banks, whose secretariat is presently in the West African Clearing House) are well aware of this fact. In this regard, certain initiatives have been taken to stimulate intra-community trade, among which there is a project for the establishment of support funds for balance of payment deficits; the setting up of a system of travellers' cheques; an ECOWAS study on the convertibility of currencies; a study by the Centre Africain d'Etudes Monétaires on exchange regulations in the subregion, etc. These initiatives should be encouraged, but we must not forget that they are only steps towards the all-important goal – that of setting up a joint Bank and a Monetary Union to cover the subregion as a whole. This is the equivalent of establishing an enlarged UMOA with 16 members instead of six, and without foreign trusteeship. Similar attempts should be made in the other four subregions of the continent, with the future goal of establishing a joint bank and currency for all of Africa.

THE PROBLEM OF THE EQUAL DISTRIBUTION OF THE BENEFITS OF INTEGRATION

In strategies for economic integration, benefits are perceived in the medium-term for industrial development, i.e. in terms of the exportation of manufactured products to the markets of partner countries. Frustrations and conflicts arise when a country perceives that its markets have been flooded by its partners' products when it cannot make reciprocal gains on its own. Such fears are fully justified, for no country wishes to be a mere agricultural appendage to its more developed neighbours. This would only prolong on the subregional level the vertical division of labour present in international relations – the major complaint of the developing countries.

This problem was to a large degree responsible for the dissolution of the East African Economic Community in 1977, while it had also caused Chad to withdraw from UDEAC in 1968.

In West Africa, the fear of unequal distribution of the benefits of integration explains why the member states of UDAO-UDEAO did not relax customs practices despite their agreed accords. In fact, this IGO, an ancestor of the CEAO, never existed except on paper.

The CEAO learned from this lesson and instituted an apparatus for financial compensation: the Regional Co-operation Tax (RCT) and the Community Development Fund (FCD). By this system, industrial products generally continue to be subject to duties and taxes. But preferential treatment is accorded to certain industrial products and regulated by the system of RCT. This applies to products entirely composed of local raw materials. When imported raw materials make up a proportion of more than 40 per cent of a product, the value added by the local processing of the product must represent at leat 35 per cent of the wholesale price of the product in a first period and 40 per cent thereafter.

To date, RCT products have included:
- in the food industry: roasted coffee, ground coffee, crude groundnut oil, refined cane sugar, pasta, biscuits, canned vegetables, beer, vinegar, etc.
- in the chemical industry: bleach, pharmaceutical products, soap, perfume, disinfectants, plastic products, paper, etc.;
- in the textile industry: fabric, clothes, knitted goods, etc.;
- tobacco, cigarettes and matches.

When, for example, Niger imports such a product from Senegal, it imposes a level of RCT which is effectively lower than previous customs duties and taxes for the same product. Two-thirds of the difference between the RCT and previously prevalent levels of taxation will be reimbursed to Niger by the Community Development Fund of the CEAO; the remaining one-third represents Niger's contribution towards the financing of "community development actions". The FCD is financed by member states in proportion to the relative importance of their exports within the CEAO. For the time being, the Ivory Coast and Senegal are by far the Fund's major contributors.

The CEAO is unique among experiences of economic integration in Africa in that it has set up the RCT and the FCD in advance, as mechanisms to correct unequal development.

Signs of unequal industrial development are already clearly perceptible in the distribution of officially recognized enterprises for the RCT. In 1980, 66.42 per cent of the industrial products which qualify for RCT were from the Ivory Coast, and 27.40 per cent from Senegal, for a combined total of 93.82 per cent.

Difficulties have arisen from contrasting short-term financial concerns. On the one hand, the governments of the landlocked, importer countries (Upper Volta, Niger and Mali) are anxious to keep their budgets afloat through expected refunds from the FCD. On the other hand, the governments of the coastal, exporting countries (Ivory Coast, Senegal) have become increasingly reticent to supply funds to the FCD in order to subsidize the exports of private sector producers who have set up operations within their territories.

It is certain that the landlocked partners will one day (quite legitimately) pose the

Table 2.1. Distribution of Officially Recognized Enterprises for the RCT in the CEAO

Country	1975	1976-77	1978	1979	1980
Ivory Coast	46	81	94	113	119
Senegal	30	52	58	61	66
Upper Volta	4	6	10	12	18
Mali	8	10	12	12	13
Niger	3	5	5	5	5
Mauritania	0	0	0	1	1

Source: *Intégration Economique,* special edition, September 1981.

issue of their own industrial development, should the CEAO continue to operate through these mechanisms.

As regards ECOWAS, the government of Nigeria provides one-third of the financial resources of the Co-operation, Compensation and Development Fund.* However, this has not served to dissipate some partners' fears of the "Nigerian giant". Fears of seeing their markets flooded by Nigerian products have forestalled the participation of many ECOWAS partners.

Nonetheless, the Summit of Heads of State held in Lomé in January, 1980, clearly defined a schedule for the liberalization of customs duties, drawn up in the spirit of the Lagos treaty and calculated in function of the different products of the countries. In the range of products distinctions were made between products of Community enterprises, priority industrial products and other goods. Although the term "Community enterpise" is still being defined and the list of priority products is still in development, it is clear that only the products of Community enterprises will be entitled to full free-trade conditions.

A distinction has been made between two groups of countries. The first is made up of the more advanced countries (Nigeria, Ghana, the Ivory Coast and Senegal), and the second by the other 12 less developed partners.

The schedule for customs liberalization for *priority industrial products* is as follows:

First Group of Countries (Nigeria, Ghana, Ivory Coast, Senegal)

– 25 per cent to 28 May 1981
– 50 per cent to 28 May 1982
– 75 per cent to 28 May 1983
– 100 per cent to 28 May 1984

Second Group of Countries (the remaining 12 partners)

– 15 per cent to 28 May 1981
– 30 per cent to 28 May 1982
– 50 per cent to 28 May 1983
– 70 per cent to 28 May 1984
– 90 per cent to 28 May 1985
– 100 per cent to 28 May 1986

Liberalization is to take place over a four-year period for the first group and over a six-year period for the second group.

For *all other products,* the schedule is as follows:

First group of Countries:

– 15 per cent to 28 May 1981

---

*The balance is provided by the Ivory Coast (13 per cent), Ghana (12.9 per cent), Liberia (6.7 per cent), Senegal (5.4 per cent), Cape Verde (1 per cent).

- 30 per cent to 28 May 1982
- 50 per cent to 28 May 1983
- 75 per cent to 28 May 1984
- 90 per cent to 28 May 1985
- 100 per cent to 28 May 1986

Second Group of Countries:

- 10 per cent to 28 May 1981
- 20 per cent to 28 May 1982
- 30 per cent to 28 May 1983
- 45 per cent to 28 May 1984
- 60 per cent to 28 May 1985
- 75 per cent to 28 May 1986
- 90 per cent to 28 May 1987
- 100 per cent to 28 May 1988

Liberalization here is scheduled over a period of six years for the more developed countries and over a period of eight years for the less developed group.

The intended objective is to place the less developed group of countries in a more favourable situation for tariffs for a period of time. Thus (with the exception of the products of Community enterprises which are immediately exempt from customs duties and taxes) the exports of, for example, Benin to Nigeria will not be subject to customs duties for a period of two years. For the same period Benin will be able to impose customs duties on the same types of products imported from Nigeria.

The Summit of Heads of State of ECOWAS held in Conakry in May, 1983, established a third group of "intermediate-level" countries: Liberia, Sierra Leone, Guinea, Togo and Benin. (A strategy which differentiates between countries according to levels of development for purposes of customs liberalization is already operative in the Andean Pact for the benefit of Bolivia and Ecuador. The ECOWAS strategy may have been borrowed from this model.)

Experience has already shown that such financial operations will not suffice in themselves to eliminate the problem. The East African Economic Community had initiated a duty system which allowed Tanzania and Uganda to protect themselves from Kenya's production capacities and to increase their own customs revenues. This action did not prevent the Community from breaking up. In fact, no short-term financial compensation can made up for the terrible losses incurred in industrial "non-development". Only an equitable distribution of profits through industrial specialization (integration of production) can resolve the problem of sharing the benefits of integration.

THE PROBLEM OF REVENUES

African economic communities are almost always modelled after the EEC and share the objective of establishing a common market. But Africa is not Europe, and none of the African common markets have evolved beyond the stage of free trade zones. In African countries, as in all developing nations, duties on imports and exports make up an important percentage of national revenues. When these countries are grouped together in a free trade zone or a customs union, the more developed partners are able to export manufactured products on the community market duty-free. These same products, if they come from a country outside the community, are subject to duty. Thus, in the short-term, the community is faced with substantial customs losses. The country concerned can only console itself with the vague perspective of long-term economic development, resulting from economic integration. But such a perspective is hardly a certainty, and in the meantime a solution must be found for the problem of public finances. The necessary compromise between these short-term financial imperatives and the goals of integration has been reached in a formula which allows each member state to impose moderate customs duties on its intra-community imports of industrial products. Throughout Africa, this mechanism has been essentially the same, whether it was the transfer tax in the East African Economic Community, UDEAC's single tax or the Regional Co-operation Tax in the CEAO.

In the CEAO, raw materials are exchanged freely, but an organized trade zone has been established for industrial products on which tariffs are imposed. Certain of these products are subject to the RCT, others are subject to the regulations of each member state. For the latter, economic distortions could arise in the Community's operations as long as the customs legislations of the individual states are not harmonized.

When, after 12 years of operations, the CEAO succeeds in establishing a common external tariff, certain problems will still persist. In effect, when for a given country the common external tariff is lower than the tariff previously applied to imports from other countries, the country will face a loss of revenues. This will be the case until compensation measures are established, which is not yet the case.

A nearly identical mechanism exists within UDEAC in the form of the single tax and the complementary tax imposed on intra-community industrial imports.

INSUFFICIENT SOLIDARITY

Experience has revealed that solidarity between African governments is insufficient. Countries have entered community schemes of integration and co-operation with an "everyone for himself" attitude, as if they were participating in a struggle for their own existence. Strategies of economic integration are perceived as zero-sum games in which the gains of one partner are the losses of the others.

Nigeria has systematically refused to sell oil to its partners dealing through the West African Clearing House. Instead of being paid in its own, non-convertible currency, the naira, Nigeria prefers hard currency settlements in U.S. dollars. In so doing, Lagos has lost the opportunity of dispelling its partners' suspicions of Nigerian economic hegemony in the subregion, based on its demographic weight and industrial infrastructure. (The USSR sells oil to its COMECON partners through the intermediary services of the International Bank for Economic Co-operation which deals in a single unit of account – the convertible rouble. Indeed, the price of Soviet oil within COMECON is much lower than oil prices on the world market, just as Cuban sugar is purchased at a figure higher than world market prices.)

Why must the current government of Ghana rely on Libyan oil to meet its balance of payments difficulties when Nigeria is so nearby?

The lack of a spirit of solidarity was particularly evident when OCLALAV and OICMA were to be united. OCLALAV was created to combat both millet-eating "quelea-quelea" birds and small grasshoppers, while the scope of OICMA is limited to actions against desert locusts. Basic economic logic would call for the fusion of these organizations, but certain states in the Sudano-Guinean zone did not feel concerned by the fight against the quelea-quelea which is only found in the millet-growing countries of the Sahel. They therefore decided not to finance a joint organization, a part of whose activities would not benefit them directly.

The livestock and meat market is another area in which there is a lack of solidarity. A few examples illustrate this point:
- Modern slaughterhouses have been constructed in Northern Ghana for livestock from Upper Volta. This livestock is not always delivered.
- In 1982, Mali and Mauritania chose to export their flocks of sheep to Algeria and Libya, in so doing depriving many Senegalese families of their ritual mutton sacrifice during the Islamic "Aid el Kebir" feast.
- The Ivory Coast has increasingly tended to buy meat from Argentina, rather than from Upper Volta, the former being less expensive despite air transport costs.

Many other anomalies could be cited, despite the resounding calls for African unity.

CONCLUSION

Africa's political leaders must be aware that real economic development, which is to say endogenous development, is not possible on the limited level of micro-states. Historically, major achievements have taken place in large contexts, either in the form of national territories of continental dimensions (the U.S.A., the U.S.S.R.) or through colonial holdings (France, Great Britain).

Economic integration is a *sine qua non* for the economic development of Africa. The greatest significance of the Lagos Plan of Action is its awareness of this necessity and the resulting call for an African Economic Community by the year 2000. However, in order to achieve economic integration, obstacles must be not only identified, but overcome. From this point of view, the passwords to success are solidarity, and political will for endogenous development.

CHAPTER 3

Regional Co-operation in Human Resources Development in Africa

*Benedict S. Mongula**

*Institute of Development Studies
University of Dar Es Salaam*

DEFINITION OF THE HUMAN RESOURCES PROBLEM

HUMAN RESOURCES DEVELOPMENT has been a subject of central concern in Africa over the last two decades of independence of most countries on the continent. This is also one area in which Africa can rightfully claim to have made exceptionally great efforts for modest achievements.

The term resources often refers to the economically active part of the human population, those employed or seeking to be employed. That is the labour force. But human resources could be extended to include children and the youth, the labour force of the future.

Concern with human resources arises basically from the human being's capacity to produce and is therefore an important factor for development. Since the ability to produce is related to the physical and mental well-being of the human population, talk about developing human resources would therefore address itself to the promotion of such characteristics. This is possible through providing the population with access to knowledge and skills, along with the satisfaction of basic needs.

Nowhere else in the world has the problem of development of human resources been a greater challenge than in Africa. Here, the home of most of the 700 million people of the world's poor and an area long neglected in the fields of education and training, development of human resources is a number one priority. Poverty must be eliminated by expanded health and basic education programmes and appropriate income distribution. Investment in human capital through education and training must be undertaken to promote general knowledge and specialized skills. In

---

*Prepared with the assistance of R. Mkenda.

addition, efforts must be undertaken to further the utilization of the underemployed labour, to eliminate brain drain, to avoid misallocation of manpower and to promote equal opportunities for employment for both sexes.

CO-OPERATION BETWEEN AFRICAN COUNTRIES

Co-operation in Africa has a long history. It first started during the colonial period when the colonizing powers used it chiefly to consolidate their colonial powers. The British, for example, had started a federation in central Africa, consisting of what was then Nyasaland, Northern Rhodesia and Southern Rhodesia. For East Africa, they had worked out the Eastern African Common Services Organization in which what was then Tanganyika, Kenya, Uganda and Zanzibar shared common rail, air and postal and other kinds of services.

After independence, the African countries sought even greater co-operation between themselves. Before independence, Tanganyika, Kenya and Uganda had already contemplated the formation of a Federation once they became independent. Nkrumah of Ghana, one of the founders of the OAU, spoke strongly of African unity and indeed, by 1963, the OAU itself had been established. Tanganyika and Zanzibar formed a Union in 1964. In 1965 Thirteen Francophone states signed a treaty to create the African Malagasy Community (OCAM). In East Africa, efforts were being made to correct problems in EACSO, culminating with the formation of the East African Community in 1970.

The spirit of co-operation has continued until today. In West Africa there exists the well-known ECOWAS, first conceived in 1970, and in Southern Africa SADCC, conceived in late 1970s, both of which are important sub-regional organizations aimed at the economic liberation of Africa. Co-operation has also evolved on a bilateral basis between the African countries.

One of the greatest setbacks to the growing spirit of co-operation was nationalism. After independence, African countries started to undertake measures to build national identity and sovereignty and to choose for themselves the appropriate development approaches to follow. At the same time, a number of these countries got entangled in territorial claims and border clashes. All these, plus instability in the different post-independence African regimes, undermined the desire and attempts to strengthen co-operation. This was the basic cause, for example, of the collapse of the East African Community which had a long (nearly 30 years) history (since the days of EACSO).

More recently, following the intensification of discussions on the New International Economic Order in the mid-1970s, there has been a growing interest in co-operation between African countries. This led, in effect, to regional Summits of the Heads of the OAU Member States in 1979 and 1980. The result was a Plan of Action for the African countries individually and collectively to overcome the problems they were facing. African countries feel more of a need now than ever before to chart common strategies and to practice collective self-reliance in order to overcome their common problems.

AFRICA'S CONCERN OVER THE HUMAN RESOURCE PROBLEM

Two-thirds of the 36 low-income countries in the world are in Africa. Most of the world's 700 million poor people live there. The majority of Africa's population lives in conditions of destitution, illiteracy and squalor and are unable to afford the barest essentials of anything near a decent life.

The causes of this poverty and misery are the subject of great dispute. However, at this stage of development of the debate on the New International Economic Order, it is generally agreed that colonialism had a strong hand in it. Now that colonialism is no more, save for Namibia, the stage for eliminating this problem has been set. African countries should now be able, or potentially able, to overcome this problem through their own collective efforts. For this they may also enlist international support from outside the continent, especially the advanced countries, who are obliged to compensate for the role they played in the past, of enriching themselves at the expense of African underdevelopment.

Fighting poverty has for a long time been taken as a welfare problem *per se*. It was sometimes even considered to be inversely related to economic growth. It is not until recently that fighting poverty was seen not as a welfare problem alone, but also as an important factor for economic growth and development. A more literate and healthier society is capable of greater production. This view today is shared by many people, even conservatives, and was heeded by the World Bank in its 1980 report. The World Bank, in view of the relevance of satisfying basic needs to economic development, has undertaken a number of programmes in support of the poor in the developing countries.

THE ANSWER TO THE BASIC NEEDS PROBLEM

Basic Education

Africa is one place in the world that has given prominence to the fate of the poor. Many of the African countries have given it such high regard that some of them have even shaped their definitions of national development around it. For example, Tanzania's Ujamaa, Zambia's Humanism are man-centred philosophies and essentially basic-needs approaches to development.

One of the areas which has received a great deal of attention in this respect is basic education. Many of the African countries launched massive campaigns aimed at universal primary education and adult education. Countries such as Nigeria, Ethiopia, Somalia and Tanzania have even made primary education compulsory to all children in the relevant age group. Literacy campaigns to provide both basic and functional education are common in Africa. In general, basic education is a top priority throughout Africa, though in a few cases (Ghana and Swaziland) efforts are more modest.

While it may not be easy to get precise estimates of expenditure on basic education *per se,* a safe guess is that it is a significant proportion of the total budget in countries such as Ethiopia, Kenya, Tanzania and Sierra Leone where basic education policy is very important. It would not have been otherwise possible to raise the African literacy rate to where it is today, about 40 per cent. The remarkable successes in Tanzania (65 per cent), Somalia (60 per cent), Lesotho (55 per cent), etc. are the results of efforts and resources directed towards literacy. Education expenditures run at between 13 and 20 per cent of total government budgets in most countries, or on average 4.5 per cent of Gross Domestic Product. In 1975, Zambia spent US $23.00 per capita (about 16 per cent of her budget), Tanzania US $7.00 per capita or 13 per cent and Malawi $4.00 or 11 per cent.

African countries have also realized that education and social reforms present special problems. Education may cause social alienation of the educated and increase rural migration. As a result, some of the African countries have started to structure their education systems to be able to offer education which is as complete as possible and which promotes self-reliance on the part of those who complete school. A good example of such a policy of education for self-reliance exists in Tanzania.

Co-operation Towards Solving the Basic Education Problem

African countries demonstrated clearly their common concern with the basic needs problem in the Extraordinary Heads of State Summit, held in Lagos in 1980. The Lagos Plan of Action, produced by this historic meeting, proclaimed: "A primary socio-economic development is the improvement of life for the entire population of a nation. The attainment of this objective requires full participation of all segments of the population in gainful employment and provision of essential services for enrichment of the life of the community. . . . "

In an earlier meeting of African leaders, such common concern also featured prominently. In a conference of African Ministers of Education in 1976, it was noted: that "a literate population promotes national economic development and that harmonious overall development needs to enlist all the productive forces of the nation". The conference called on African countries to commit themselves resolutely to the eradication of illiteracy among the masses of the people so as to make it easier for them to receive training in their national languages in order that they may be able to participate more effectively in development and in raising their own standards of living.

Apart from this kind of co-operation, which brings together policy-makers such as ministers and heads of state, co-operation is carried out through meetings of educational experts. In April 1977, for example, following a 1976 UNESCO General Conference in Nairobi, an important seminar of experts from 20 African UNESCO member states was called to deliberate on post-literacy programmes. Towards the end of the 1970s, UNESCO's Africa region established a technical arm, referred to as the Network of Education Innovation for Development in Africa (NEIDA). This institution brings together national and regional educational innovation institutions to share experiences, promote group reflection and stimulate co-operative action. By December 1981, 25 African countries had already officially become members of NEIDA, and about 105 projects were associated with it. NEIDA undertakes inter-project visits, seminars, workshops and other programmes aimed at improving education.

A number of other units of regional co-operation have been created to bring together educational experts. For example, in an effort to develop methods of assessing adult literacy, African countries created a Regional Council for Adult Education and Literacy in Africa. The council devoted two training sessions to the subject of evaluation in Lomé (Togo) in 1977 and 1979. Some non-governmental organizations such as the African Adult Education Association, the Afrolit-Association based in Nairobi, National Adult Education Associations, and a few others, have also been established.

Of course, success in providing basic education in Africa calls for co-operation not only between the African countries themselves, but also with the rest of the world. It is already clear that Africa has the will to implement as quickly as possible basic education for all its population but is facing a problem with resources. Assistance in technical, financial and material form would be highly valuable in this direction. In recognition of this fact, the 1976 Lagos Conference of Ministers of Education of UNESCO Member States urged UNESCO and other competent organizations to assist the African countries in implementing their basic education programmes and organizing sub-regional and regional workshops.

ACCESS TO BASIC NEEDS

Health Services

Like education, health facilities are very poor in Africa. Data show that Africans have the poorest health in and the highest death rate in the world. For example, the crude death rate in Mali is 30 per 1,000, life expectancy 37 and infant mortality 100 per 1,000 live births.

The greatest health hazard is malaria followed by alimentary diseases. The incidence of disease, especially intestinal cases, could be greatly minimized through access to clean water supplies, proper sanitation and decent feeding. Undernourishment also plays a substantive part in the health prospects of Africans, especially in rural populations, since it reduces their resistance to disease.

Many countries are seriously concerned about the health situation. On paper, they have made firm commitments to provide more health services, especially primary health care. Nonetheless, lack of resources has meant low government expenditures on health (about 5.5 per cent of total budget, or less than US$10.00 per capita, as compared with Europe and America where expenditures run to over $1,000 per capita). Furthermore, it has become clear that Africa must change inherited attitudes towards health which exphasize curative services and underplay preventive health care. Africa also must aim at primary health care, and reach the bulk of the rural population who are especially prone to disease. Some countries such as Mali, Kenya, Tanzania and (Northern) Nigeria have established village-based rural health services which can be considered quite successful.

As in other fields, there is a lot of room for regional co-operation in health. In the days of the East African community for example, co-operation in research was common and concentrated on malaria, schistosomiasis and tuberculosis, some of the most prevalent diseases in the region. Research stations were located in Tanzania, Kenya and Uganda, under community administration.

The World Health Organization provides opportunities for the African countries to co-operate in the field of health. Member-States often come together and make group decisions on different aspects of the health problem which are of interest to their countries. For example, WHO Member States of the African region have agreed to ensure primary health care to their citizens so as to assure them a socially and economically productive life by the year 2000. The Member States signed a charter for the health development of the African Region whose provisions include: "Improvements in primary health care, manpower development and training, provision of safe water and sanitation, promotion of maternal and child health and control of communicable diseases. The charter affirms the commitment of Member States in areas they jointly consider important for health development."

The OAU provides another forum for co-operation. In the Lagos Summit of 1980, a number of recommendations were made regarding health strategies of African countries. These included involving villages in health education, strengthening centres for training health personnel, improving the organization of primary health care, strengthening maternal and child health centres, etc. The summit encouraged the exchange of country experiences through analytical case studies.

Co-operation in the field of health takes place also at professional and technical levels. Doctors in Africa, both as a region and in its constituent sub-regions, come together under professional associations to deal with different health problems. Under the Commonwealth African Region for example, surgeons, pediatricians, obstetricians and gynaecologists and public health experts meet to exchange research findings in their respective fields.

DEVELOPMENT OF HIGH LEVEL MANPOWER

It was earlier pointed out that because of the neglect of education and training, Africa had only a tiny pool of educated and skilled people to rely on to run newly independent countries. In Zambia there were only 1,200 Africans with secondary education and 100 university graduates at the time of independence in 1964. In a number of other countries the situation was still worse.

During colonial times, not only were overall expenditures on education too small to allow for opening many schools and colleges, but there were open discriminatory policies restricting education and training for Africans. In Mozambique, only about 5 per cent of university places went to Africans at the time of independence. Discrimination was also common in British East Africa. A government bulletin produced by the Ministry of Manpower Planning Development in Zimbabwe put it as follows: "Prior to independence vocational training in this country was a privilege, only accessible to the white community and an insignificant number of blacks. Furthermore, even where there were openings for blacks, it was invariably in the lower skills such as bricklaying and carpentry. . . The subsequent emigration of some of these artisans following independence left the country under threat of serious skills shortages." On placement of apprentices, the bulletin notes: "In the past there has been radical discrimination with regard to the distribution of apprenticeship within all industries."

Skill shortage in independent Africa is more critical if consideration is made of specific skill categories. The few educated people at the time of independence had been oriented towards the humanities. For some years this continued to be the case especially because the first challenge of the independent African governments was to ensure a smooth running of governments. Thus training lawyers and public administraters was a first priority. In Tanzania for example, the earliest higher educational institutions established after independence were a law school, a civil service training school and a public administration school.

COUNTRY INITIATIVES TOWARDS HIGHER EDUCATION AND TRAINING

The critical shortages of skills in all categories in the African countries at the time of independence called for immediate action by the countries themselves. Not only were there too few Africans who could fill the existing vacancies, but also, in the wake of departing whites the shortage was becoming even more critical.

Many countries therefore adopted manpower development as a leading policy objective. Enrolment in schools and colleges was expanded rapidly. In Zambia enrolment in secondary schools rose sharply between 1960 and 1970, from 2,600 to 52,500. In Malawi, there was a rise from 1,500 to 9,300 and in Tanzania from 9,500 to 31,200. In a number of countries the expansion was so high that today they are already experiencing a problem of unemployed secondary school leavers. In Ghana, Gabon and some other countries the problem of unemployment among graduates is beyond control.

In most countries, secondary education is aimed at laying down a broad foundation for further training. Recently, considerable attention has been devoted to science education in an attempt to orient education and training to meet expanding technological requirements. Some countries such as Tanzania have come up with major structural changes in the education system, creating definite biases in favour of the secondary school level and training in the fields of commerce, agriculture and engineering. For Tanzania, this fits in well with the education for self-reliance policy of 1968.

As with general education, vocational and technical training was not developed until after independence. Even where it existed, as in the countries with mining and some industrial activities like Zimbabwe and Zambia, it concentrated on simple carpentry and brickwork skills, and open discrimination was practised against the black population. In 1964, at the time of independence, Zambia had 805 vocational trainees, but 75 per cent of them belonged to these two trades.

After independence, however, the shortage of artisans and technicians was not critical. Most countries had no substantial industrial base, the basis for a large part of demand for such skills. Given the nature of the socio-economic situation then, even carpentry and brickwork did not suffer a critical shortage. But with the rapid industrialization that characterized most of Africa, and the changes in structure of societies and economies, it did not take long before shortages of skills started to appear in most countries. By the end of the decade, the demand for machine operators, mechanics, electricians, draughtsmen, tailors and shoe-makers had increased and surpassed supply.

This phenomenon was even more true in regard to professional qualifications in architecture, engineering, surveying, geology, etc. Critical shortages were registered in these fields, and supply had to be greatly supplemented with the recruitment of professionals from abroad.

As shown in Table 3.1, expatriate employment in Africa in the 1960s comprised a significant proportion of total trained manpower.

It is the high percentage of expatriates which made African governments regard higher education and training a number one priority during the early years of their independence. Most countries worked out fairly elaborate education and training plans and schemes to cope with the problem. Tanzania's education and training plan for example was the most elaborate of the different sectoral plans of its 1964-1969 Five Year Development Plan.

In a matter of a few years, Africa had turned out a large number of skilled personnel. A number of countries in Africa are already over 80 per cent self-sufficient in high level manpower and almost self-sufficient in the lower skill categories.

As compared to an enrolment in higher education of 142,000 in 1960, Africa had

Table 3.1 Expatriate Employment as a Percentage of Total Employment of Trained Manpower:

Country	Year	Expatriates as % of Trained Manpower
Botswana	1967	42%
Ivory Coast	1962	45%
Kenya	1964	48%
Malawi	1966	18%
Nigeria	1964	13%
Somalia	1970	2%
Sudan	1967-68	3%
Swaziland	1970	35%
Tanzania	1975	31%
Uganda	1967	21%
Zambia	1965	62%

Source: Richard Jolly and Christopher Colclough, African Manpower Plans: An Evaluation, International Labour Review, 106 Aug./Sept., 1972.

attained an enrolment of 1,169,000 in 1980. The number of universities had also increased from 32 located in 23 countries to 68 located in 35 countries.

In 1982, 700,000 university enrolments were registered in 27 African countries (excluding notably Nigeria and Ghana). Out of these, about 91,000 (or 12.9 per cent) were in law and 90,000 (or 12.8 per cent) in the humanities. Education and teacher education had about 10.9 per cent of the total and by this time health and medicine, engineering and agronomy had also been significantly developed and had respectively 82,000 (11.6 per cent), 70,000 (10.0 per cent) and 57,000 (8.1 per cent).

CO-OPERATION IN HIGHER EDUCATION AND TRAINING

The fields of higher education and training offer greater potential for regional/sub-regional co-operation than any other sphere of human resource development. It is also the area with longest history of co-operation, dating back to the colonial period.

For many years, co-operation in higher education and training involved mainly the industrialized countries. They received students from Africa for long and short-term education and training and sent their people to teach in African countries. This form of co-operation proved highly valuable for Africa during the crisis of manpower in the early years of independence. But it was not without problems. Because of the great differences in the socio-economic and cultural environments between these countries and those of Africa, the skills obtained were often not totally relevant to African conditions. A doctor trained in Western Europe, for example, would take long to be able to acquaint himself with tropical diseases. An engineer trained in the USA similarly had to adjust greatly to the local environment with less technological sophistication. People coming from overseas transferred alien values, attitudes and tastes to the local environment.

Some of those problems could be overcome by regional and subregional co-operation. Because African countries have similar socio-economic and cultural structures, education obtained in one country fits well with the local conditions of another.

There are several other reasons for co-operation at the regional and sub-regional levels between neighbouring countries. For the more specialized skills for which demand is low, the price of having a national training centre in each country is too high. Regional and subregional training co-operation would greatly minimize training costs. Co-operation between training centres offering the same programmes is also mutually beneficial and would stimulate levels of innovation and efficacy in these centres. With such co-operation, countries are able to avoid inward-looking education and training systems.

Co-operation in higher education and training has a long tradition in the African continent. The colonizing powers, in an attempt to minimize training costs, established training centres which were shared by a number of their colonies. In East Africa, there was the University of Makerere, catering for Kenya, Uganda and Tanganyika and in Southern Africa, the University of Botswana, Lesotho and Swaziland at Roma, Lesotho. This was also true with the French colonies. Such centres supplemented overseas training which was more dominant. This arrangement had many advantages and would have been most economical if pursued after independence.

However, independence meant national sovereignty for each African state; national identity and paramount national interests. Prestigious projects identified as symbols of development, such as national universities, were established irrespective of costs. That kind of nationalism plus growing national differences caused the collapse of early co-operative programmes and the proliferation of training centres over the continent. In the new system, training centres were oriented to cater exclusively for national interests and requirements.

In the light of increasing economic hardships and growing awareness of the world economy in Africa, the African governments discovered that collective self-reliance was the best way out of their present predicament. This was part of a world-wide feeling that replacement of the current North-South Co-operation with South-South Co-operation would create greater potential for the advancement of the developing countries.

This led to a renewed interest in co-operation in training. A 1976 Conference of Ministers of Education noted the potential of such co-operation and stressed the role of the association of African Universities as an instrument of co-operation. It urged the OAU and UNESCO to support this association.

The Conference of Ministers and other meetings of officials to exchange experiences and deliberate on common policies is a good foundation for co-operation relating to education and training. Two important ministerial conferences were held in the mid-1970s to deliberate on education, training and related fields. They laid a strong foundation for the development of specific programmes of co-operation. The historic Monrovia and Lagos Summits of the Heads of State of the OAU Member Countries, which dealt with a wide selection of issues including education and training, were perhaps the greatest political foundations for future co-operation.

In order to increase co-operation between African Universities, a number of associations have been established at regional and sub-regional level. These include among others: The Council for the Development of Economic and Social Research in Africa (CODESRIA) based in Senegal, the Association of African Political Scientists, the Southern African Universities Conference (SAUC) and the Association of African Women for Research and Development. These associations are important fora for exchange of research findings by experts and therefore promoting professional efficiency. Other co-operative arrangements include the Network of Education Innovation for Development of Africa (NEIDA) based in Dakar, Senegal; the Science Education Programme in Accra, Ghana, the Pan African Institute of Development in Cameroon, and others.

Another type of co-operation entails the sharing of joint education and training centres. A number of such centres have been established under U.N. and OAU auspices to offer training to nationals of different OAU member countries. These include the East and Southern African Management Institute based at Arusha, Tanzania; the African Institute for Economic Development and Planning in Dakar, Senegal; the Institute of Population Studies in Ghana, the Institute of Development Management in Gaborone, Botswana, and the African Women Training and Research Centre in Addis Ababa, Ethiopia. Closely related are the U.N.-OAU centres to co-ordinate research and offer short-term training such as the African Centre for Technology based in Dakar, Senegal; the African Centre for Rural Development (CIRDAFRICA) based in Arusha, Tanzania; and the African Centre for Applied Research and Training in Social Development (ACARTSOD) based in Tripoli, Libya.

Finally, there are bilateral co-operative arrangements involving different national universities. Under such arrangements student and staff exchange programmes are carried out, and it is possible to send students to centres outside their countries for the more specialized skills whose training facilities are not available at home. These arrangements are fairly common in Africa, especially between neighbouring countries.

HUMAN RESOURCES DEVELOPMENT: MANPOWER PLANNING

Manpower planning is a necessity in order to alleviate the acute scarcity of skills experienced in different African countries. Of course, the form and content of such plans are not the same in all the countries concerned.

The institutional framework for planning, management and administration of manpower varies from country to country. Two different types of institutional setups can be distinguished, namely a system involving a fully fledged Ministry of Manpower Development, and one in which such processes go through non-exclusive and less powerful institutions. Zimbabwe and Tanzania both have a Ministry of Manpower Development while Nigeria has instituted a Manpower Board and a Manpower Secretariat of the Ministry of National Planning. Lesotho employs a National Manpower Development Secretariat, and Zambia has established a Department of Manpower Planning.

It is difficult to judge *a priori* which kind of institutional set-up would be best suited to handle the manpower development task. While creation of a full ministry appears to raise the status of such task, it risks a break in co-ordination between manpower development and other socio-economic policies and plans. In Tanzania, where manpower planning was conducted for a number of years in the Minister of Economic Affairs and Development Planning and later in a new Ministry of Manpower Development, planning officials of the new Ministry share the view that manpower planning processes have been swallowed-up by manpower management and administration processes and that returning manpower planning to the Ministry of Economic Affairs and Planning would strengthen the results.

Zambians feel differently. Manpower planning officials believe that a high-powered and exclusive body like a government ministry would remove defects being experienced in planning. "It is therefore the realization of defects in the First and Second National Manpower Development Plans of the country that in the third National Plan, a high-powered manpower formulation body will be set up. . . It is felt now in government circles that a Ministry of Manpower Planning should have been created at the time of independence in 1964."

Lesotho has been moving in this direction by taking the manpower planning function away from the Central Planning and Development Office and creating instead a National Manpower Development Secretariat.

Another but more important difference in manpower planning lies with the approaches used. Some countries simply collect statistical data about the manpower market for use by the government to determine their training programmes, including the establishment and expansion of training centres and scholarship awards.

In other countries, however, the function of planning extends beyond statistical data collection. It includes the allocation of manpower across the different sectors and occupations, including graduates of training institutions. Indeed, in some cases, wage and salary structures, work incentive systems, etc., are arranged on a centralized basis.

Nigeria, through the Manpower Board, determines manpower needs and formulates policies regarding expansion and training, scholarships and fellowships and co-ordinates Federal and State manpower activities. Tanzania, however, through its Ministry of Manpower Development goes the whole length to include allocation of its trained manpower to different workplaces and centrally organizes remuneration systems for workers.

In planning the development of education and training, various institutions have been created in African countries. Such institutions shape the content and methodology of the education and training process to suit and meet specific national requirements. Nigeria, for example, has a National Universities Commission, a National Board of Technical Education, etc. Tanzania has a National Technical Advisory and Co-ordinating Council, a National Board of Accountancy and Auditors, etc.

CO-OPERATION IN MANPOWER PLANNING

What kind of interrelationship could be developed between African countries in the area of manpower planning is not easily identifiable, for this is one area in which potential for co-operation is less obvious.

However, through the OAU and the ECA, African countries have worked out a training and fellowship programme involving 8,000 Africans to be trained in five years in the fields most required. Such training is to be carried out in Africa.

Certainly greater room for co-operation exists in several spheres. For example, some countries experience excesses in particular skills where others have shortages. Under such a situation co-operation in manpower development and mobility of labour across countries would help to put into economic use manpower resources presently wasted in some countries of Africa and alleviate shortages in others.

At the Lagos Summit in 1980, the African Heads of the OAU States emphasized co-operation and collective self-reliance in the continent through (1) the use of manpower studies to determine national training needs, (2) "support for an information and placement service facilitating the identification and employment of African experts and consultancy organizations" as is currently operated by ECA (3) "adoption of employment policies that permit free movement of labour within subregions, thus facilitating employment of surplus trained manpower of one country in other members lacking in that requisite skill." In general, this co-operation, whose potential and prospects seem great, will rely heavily on, and will be guided by, concrete and complete manpower studies.

The Summit also called for the Member States to actively support not only a clearing house for African experts and consultancy organizations but also to jointly establish research and training centres.

SADCC envisages co-operation in education and training in areas requiring a small number of highly specialized personnel. It has identified as important co-operation arrangements the exchange of education and training, exchange of information on education and training systems, evolving common strategies of education and training, exchange of regionally produced documentation and publications, establishment of regional training insitutions, exchange of teaching staff and other qualified personnel, and utilization of regional potential in designing and producing school materials and equipment.

However, the present economic crisis in Africa poses, though temporarily, a serious threat of this kind of co-operation. With the impending decisions to cut down government expenditures across the board, the jointly established research and training centres (which depend substantially on subventions of Member States) are directly threatened. Thus international support in this area would be even more necessary than before. This also affects labour mobility across the African nations. Recently Nigeria expelled hundreds of thousands of Ghanians and other non-nationals to create jobs for citizens. Kenya has done the same. And the trend is likely to be followed by other countries.

Nonetheless, setbacks in co-operation are likely to be both temporary and isolated. Prospects for increased co-operation can be found in Southern Africa where in recent years Losotho, Botswana, and Zimbabwe have been absorbing increasing numbers of Africans from other countries in the subregion and the African region as a whole. Zimbabwe recently accepted hundreds of Mauritians into their education system as teachers. Tanzanians, Malawians, Kenyans, Ugandans etc., are starting to migrate southward.

Unemployment and Misallocation of Manpower

Unemployment should be made antithetical to human resource development policies. Differently stated, resource development policies should be designed to avoid the unemployment, underemployment or compulsory employment of the labour force, or part of it, irrespective of profession, religion, sex or age. But for human development institutions to define exactly the requirements of the various sectors of the economy is one thing, to allocate manpower to these sectors is another. No matter how much effort is devoted to develop the human resources for optimal social application, there are just not enough physical, intellectual and financial resources to meet required investments for each sector. Rapid expansion of the economy would create enormous demand for skills and know-how, the magnitudes of which cannot be met by either local or foreign institutions. At this juncture, policy-makers in Africa should increase co-operative efforts to combat unemployment and avoid the misallocation of manpower. They should work together for optimal use of training facilities as well as provide adequate and rational utilization of the manpower so created.

Unemployment in Africa means an under-utilization of human resources. No one would expect unemployment to occur as a result of the factors which characterize this phenomenon in the advanced industrialized countries.

Yet, by empirical observation, unemployment in African urban centres could be even more rampant than it is in the cities of the advanced countries. In addition to unemployment in the urban settlements, widespread underemployment prevails in the rural sections of the population. The social and economic interplay between rural and urban employment has several causes:

1. Economic reasons:
   (a) Where the marginal returns are too little, as occurs in agricultural activities

in those places which border on deserts (Sahelian States). In this case able-bodied people leave their homes in search of jobs in urban centres.
   (b) Where low productivity prevails in the rural area; in this case output from agricultural employment is small due to the application of rudimentary technologies. This has two effects (i) the nominal incomes of the peasants (in monetary terms) is due to low output, and (ii) little is available for industrial processing and manufacturing. This phenomenon accounts for rampant underemployment in agriculture and shortage of employment opportunity in the advanced urban centres of the towns.
   (c) Variations in technologies: Policies by governments to effect industrial development are often prone to technological dislocation; people who migrate from the countryside require substantial training before they are able to achieve the required skills in industry.

2. Behavioural factors:
   (a) Barter terms of trade: corollary to section (b) of (1) above: nominal incomes derive dually from low productivity and low prices paid to farmers. With regard to low prices, the farmer is discouraged to engage in agricultural employment and therefore decides to seek alternative, more rewarding, employment in cities. With regard to real earnings, the trade-off between agricultural products and industrial manufactures further discourages the farmer. Whereas greater controls are exercised on producer prices with little consideration to the well-being of the workers, factors like inflation, turmoils in the international scene and inefficiencies in production regularly force the prices of manufacturers higher and higher. In this case the barter terms of trade between agricultural products and industrial manufactures are heavily weighted against agriculture.

The flight of people from rural to urban milieus is dynamic. The squalor prevailing among the urban unemployed is maintained or rather aggravated over time. Governments sometimes engage in ambitious industrial programmes to absorb these masses but as soon as the situation improves, fresh replenishments leave the rural areas in search of city jobs.

It is important to observe the variations in the supply of development services, especially comparing urban establishments to the rural countryside. The urban centres are necessarily provided with better housing, road communication, water supply, sanitary services, medical services and, in some countries, even educational services and business convenience. These are material incentives which indirectly explain the size of unemployment in towns, despite ample opportunities in agriculture.

CHARACTERISTICS OF UNEMPLOYMENT IN AFRICA

In measuring unemployment, one has to consider the magnitude of the masses seeking jobs. One has to examine the composition of the unemployed in terms of sex, skills, profession, religion, geographical position, ethnic origin, and age. With regard to skills, unemployment occurs because of discrepancies between the demand for specific skills and their supply. In most of Africa this is due to the absence of planning for such skills. In effect training institutions produce unnecessarily large numbers of available manpower for certain skills, while other skills receive too little attention.

It has to be noted however, that unemployment in Africa does not refer to skilled categories of labour. In Africa, only a very small fraction of the unemployed comes from the skilled group; the bulk of unemployed labour comes from the unskilled work force.

Unemployment of skilled workers does not arise in countries which engage in planning. In this case, skilled people are trained to man places as specified in various economic investment programmes. In most newly independent countries, rapid economic progress creates new jobs. Usually such jobs are more numerous than the ability of training institutions to turn out the necessary skills.

Another variable that merits consideration is planning of economic development. Countries which engage in planning (like Tanzania), do not face as big an unemployment problem of skilled and professional groups as those countries which rely on the labour market. This remark is made with careful reservations because most countries in Africa do not depend entirely on the labour market, and only few plan their manpower resource development as part of their overall national economic plans.

Countries which do not plan their manpower development often rely on initiatives by employers or private establishments for training their cadres. As a result of unco-ordinated training, there are usually shortfalls in demand or supply. For a demand shortfall, there will be a shortage of jobs and a pool of unemployed people in the market. If the shortfall is on the supply side, then there will be a skilled labour reserve. Neither of these situations can be perpetuated for political, social or economic reasons.

For both planned and non-planned manpower development, there is one common problem; immobility of labour. Individual countries, as has been cited earlier, cannot satisfy all their manpower needs. And as long as labour mobility is restricted within their borders, no substantial improvement can be expected in allocating and employment.

AREAS OF CO-OPERATION IN AFRICA IN SOLVING UNEMPLOYMENT AND MISALLOCATION

Having identified the nature of the problem related to unemployment in Africa, it is now possible to show that policy measures need to be taken co-operatively by African countries. Policies should be designed to strike a balance of physical, social and economic development between rural and urban sectors of the economies of African Countries. This is crucial because it is the imbalanced development between the two sides which accounts for African unemployment even in countries with ample rural opportunities. The manpower element can be satisfied indirectly from agricultural and industrial development programmes. A balance of rural/urban incentivre structures can be satisfied at national levels but co-operation among countries can enable the production of required physical inputs in the co-operating region in urban and rural sectors equally. A choice of techniques in agriculture might be a determinant of success.

Another area of co-operation involves the development of incentive structures in such areas as water supply, health services, educational facilities, communication networks, roads and transport facilities. Although it will not be possible for the rural countryside to equal the supply of services in urban areas, the price structure of farm products should balance income distribution between urban and rural societies.

Technological improvements and balanced growth will, if pursued vigorously, ameliorate the extent of rural emigration, unemployment in towns and underemployment in agriculture. This applies mainly to unskilled labour.

For skilled labour, demand-supply imbalances can be eliminated only by:
1. The careful planning of training by the responsible authorities, implementing the development programmes on schedule, identifying their manpower needs and initiating training programmes.
2. Common development projects allowing for greater mobility of labour from state to state.
3. Harmonization of the social and economic benefits of employment to eliminate the "brain drain".
4. The creation of adequate training facilities through regional co-operation, colleges, institutes, universities, including the sharing of training equipment, intellectual resources and training materials.

SUMMARY

Development of human resources is a subject that is given great attention in Africa. African countries place a high priority on both human capital and raising the human production capacity in a broad way by solving the basic poverty problems. With this outlook it is both possible to build a capacity to produce and also, and more importantly, to raise the welfare of the society, which indeed is the ultimate end of all processes of development. Africa has been able to raise in a significant way her potential in the field of human resources.

For many years African countries have been co-operating in different fields, including in areas of education and training. Such co-operation, however, was interrupted by deep nationalist sentiments, differences between states, etc.

Among the specific areas of human resource development are access of the African poor to basic needs, skill promotion through education and training, manpower planning and management, solving the problems of unemployment and misallocation of manpower and eliminating the brain drain.

In all these areas African countries have established various kinds of co-operation arrangements, some of which are fairly old while others count less than a decade. Formation of such arrangements illustrates the increasing realization in Africa that the African peoples' development will ultimately depend on their collective self-reliance. Under such arrangements the African countries do not only share their experiences in their attempt to seek best policies for their rapid social, economic and cultural development, but also share their resources in such areas as education and training.

Over the last decade the desire among African Countries to co-operate between themselves in order to solve their problems has been increasing. This healthy development cuts across co-operation in the areas of trade, transport, energy, industry, agriculture, education and training, etc. It is even more promising the way Africa has grasped her problems in a broad way and therefore has worked out global co-operation arrangements. In the field of human resources development, Africa has shown a lot of concern as revealed in the Lagos Plan of Action of 1980 and other Statements and Commitments of African Heads of State, and Ministers in various regional, subregional or bilateral meetings.

At this stage, however, in order to facilitate greater and more effective co-operation it is important to identify and assess clearly different specific fields of co-operation. This applies to all areas of human resources development. Africa must raise even further not only her technical capabilities through promoting the skills of her people and their physical abilities, but also their welfare, which is what ultimately development is all about.

CHAPTER 4

The Feasibility of Establishing Jointly-owned Regional Minerals Enterprises (JRMEs) in Sub-Saharan Africa: a Case Study of Institution Building for Collective Self-reliance*

A. R. M. Ritter

School of International Affairs, Carleton University, Ottawa

INTRODUCTION

AN IMPORTANT but still neglected aspect of deepening the co-operation among developing countries, that is, of furthering their collective self-reliance in order to achieve basic developmental objectives is the creation and gradual expansion of Third World multinational enterprises. In this essay, the desirability and feasibility of establishing such enterprises as alternatives to foreign-owned multinational enterprises are examined in the context of the mineral sector of Sub-Saharan Africa. The central objectives of the essay are to review the case for the establishment of Jointly Owned Regional Minerals Enterprises or JRMEs as they will be labelled here, to discuss how such enterprises could be designed in order to be commercially and politically viable, and to suggest ways in which such enterprises could be established and developed to maturity.

In the longer term, there is little doubt about the desirability of establishing African owned and controlled enterprises, public or private or mixed, and in a

---

*I would like to thank the following individuals for their assistance, support and encouragement: John O'Manique of the School of International Affairs, Carleton University, Ottawa; Willie Sweta of the Ministry of Mines, Lusaka, and N. Peter Mwanza, Director, Natural Resources Division, U.N. Economic Commission for Africa, Addis Ababa. The individuals who provided interviews and other assistance, and who are listed in Appendix A also have my gratitude. None of the above-mentioned individuals or interviewees are implicated in the argumentation and conclusions of this study, the responsibility resting solely with the author.

variety of sectors. The advantages which such enterprises would generate vis-à-vis foreign multinationals include reduced profit exportation from the region, improved potentials for managerial and technical learning and the genuine adoption and diffusion of technology, and improved harnessing of production linkages, interindustrial and intersectoral. In many sectors, African multinationals could share many of the advantages which foreign multinationals display vis-à-vis smaller nationally-oriented public or private firms. Among these advantages would be (i) economies of scale in production, marketing, management, and in the use of expertise; (ii) the ability to pool personnel and financial resources and to spread risk over a variety of activities; and (iii) better access to markets and to sources of investible resources.

Public, or mixed public/private African multinational enterprises would, at least "in theory" share the possible advantages listed above for private multinationals. Public African multinationals also are more politically acceptable to many African countries; and they could build on or spin-off from existing public-sector enterprises. On the other hand, the difficulties of establishing African publicly-owned multinationals must not be underestimated. The financial, technical and personnel constraints are severe. Ensuring that such enterprises, once established, would be commercially viable and sustainable as well as self-activating and dynamic would be difficult. The rather dismal record of many state-owned enterprises throughout the world is not encouraging. The problems of state-owned multinationals would be compounded further by the complexities of inter-governmental relationships.

There are a number of interesting and positive African precedents for the establishment of Jointly Owned Regional Enterprises. One of the most interesting state-owned multinationals in Africa is Air Afrique, founded in 1961 with twelve contracting states, and often viewed as one of the best airlines in Africa. Another enterprise, the Central African Power Corporation is jointly owned by Zambia and Zimbabwe and has survived and thrived despite the political problems of the transition to Independence for Zimbabwe. Unfortunately, there are also examples of regional state-owned enterprises established before Independence which have been unsuccessful, the best-known examples consisting of the railway, airline and communications system of the East African Common Services Organization.

It is also of relevance to note that some developing countries, usually "newly industrializing countries" such as Hong Kong, Singapore and Brazil, but also including India and Malaysia have become the home countries to dynamic multinational enterprises. Most of these are private sector firms but some like Petrobras, the state petroleum company of Brazil are in the public sector (Economist, July 23, 1983). It is also of interest that in developing countries, state-owned enterprises have frequently been adopted as the chosen institutional form, especially in the mineral sector of African countries (see Table 4.4 for an idea of the African countries relying on state ownership in mining). In some countries, the minerals parastatals have developed or are developing broad ranges of technical, managerial, financial and commercial expertise covering the various phases of mineral activities from production to marketing. Examples of state sector mining houses which seem to be evolving well would include Codelco in Chile, and Zambia Consolidated Copper Mines.

The need to strengthen economic and technical cooperation through institution building has been stressed by a variety of organizations including UNITAR, the OAU and ECA. The UNITAR project on Regional Development among Developing Countries, or "RCDC" (Lazlo, 1981) the Lagos Plan of Action for the Implementation of the Monrovia Strategy for the Economic Development of Africa (OAU, 1980) and the mineral resource development document produced by the U.N. Economic Commission for Africa (UNECA, 1981) all emphasized the importance of institution building. Among the numerous types of institutional innovation necessary for deepening cooperation among countries, jointly-owned regional enterprises were mentioned specifically in the UNITAR "RCDC" statement (Lazlo, 1981, 28).

In the Preamble of the Lagos Plan of Action (OAU, 1980, 45), a number of objectives of special relevance to the formation of regional joint enterprises in the mineral sector were listed:

–More specifically, we commit ourselves, individually and collectively on behalf of our governments and peoples to:
–realize the subregional and regional internally located industrial development;
–co-operate in the field of natural resources control, exploration, extraction and use for the development of our economies for the benefit of our peoples and to set up the appropriate institutions to achieve these purposes;
–develop indigenous entrepreneurial, technical manpower and technological abilities to enable our peoples to assume greater responsibility for the achievement of our individual and collective development goals.

Jointly-owned regional mineral enterprises could be important vehicles for the achievement of these objectives (as will be argued later). In discussing co-operative institutional development in the mineral sector, the Lagos Plan of Action (LPA) emphasized regional co-ordination in a number of areas: (i) geological surveys and mineral resource inventories, (ii) training of specialized personnel and (iii) the exchange of scientific technical and economic information pertinent to activities in the mining sector. It was also stated in the document that objectives for the mineral sector were to be achieved through "the active participation of Member States in the operation of African multinational mineral resources development institutions through political and material support" (OAU, 1980, 36). This statement includes the possibility of regional enterprises, but subsequent discussion in the LPA did not pursue this option.

The potentials and problems involved in intensifying co-operation in the mineral sector have been explored in some detail by the Economic Commission for Africa in documents prepared for the 1981 Arusha Conference on the development and utilization of mineral resources in Africa (UNECA, 1981). A variety of areas for improved and intensified co-operation in the mineral sector were discussed in the Conference Proceedings. Of special relevance here is the recommendation that "ECA should undertake feasibility studies . . . of institutions at the regional or sub-regional level for the mobilization of finance and for investment in mineral exploration and mineral development prospects in the region" (UNECA, 1981, 307). These institutions might be of a financial, insurance, advisory or operational character, and "would, *inter alia*, advise on appropriate investment incentives for mineral projects in Africa, assist Governments in financing feasibility studies of high priority projects, . . . raise funds from member countries and other sources including international institutions to finance mineral projects . . . . and prepare standard forms of agreement for possible use by member states in mineral projects in Africa." The Economic Commission for Africa was apparently thinking about the possibility of regional minerals enterprises when it stated that: "ECA should also promote study tours to national and multinational companies established in selected Third World countries to finance mineral exploration and mining development, with a view to gaining experience on their organization, management and operations. Thus the proposal being explored in this paper, namely the establishment of jointly-owned regional multinational enterprises, is an idea that is not new in general terms. Moreover, it has been specifically considered for the mineral sector of Africa by the U.N. Economic Commission for Africa.

This examination of the feasibility of the creation of jointly-owned regional enterprises in minerals proceeds with a background section which argues for the necessity and desirability of this type of institutional innovation. In this section, the past and prospective marginalization of the mineral sector in Sub-Saharan Africa in the world mineral economy is outlined and explained, the contribution of the mineral sector to national development is emphasized, and the positive case for a new form of minerals multinational enterprise, namely the jointly-owned regional mineral enterprise (JRME) is outlined. Following the background discussion are a number of sections which outline some of the organizational prerequisites for viability, some major institutional alternatives for a JRME, financial arrangements and personnel considerations. A further section outlines some of the structural and operational features of a JRME. Finally, the strands of the argument are drawn together in a Summary and Conclusion section.

THE CASE FOR JOINTLY-OWNED REGIONAL MINERALS ENTERPRISES (JRMEs)

The Marginalization of Sub-Saharan Africa in the World Minerals System

Since their achievement of Independence, the nations of Sub-Saharan Africa (excluding South Africa) have been increasingly marginalized from the development of the world mineral system. The region's share of total world production and exports has decreased steadily. Moreover, mineral exploration has largely neglected the region, and major mineral multinational corporations (MMNCs) generally but with some exceptions, have refrained from investing there. In consequence, new investment in minerals slated to come "on stream" in Sub-Saharan Africa in the 1980s is limited. It is probable that in the absence of major policy initiatives and/or institutional innovations, most countries of Sub-Saharan Africa will be largely left out of the development of the mineral system for the remainder of the decade of the 1980s and perhaps into the 1990s.

The mineral production and export shares of the Sub-Saharan African countries as a proportion of global production and exports have been declining in aggregate terms for much of the post-war era. As can be seen in Table 4.1, the share of "Developing Africa" (excluding the Union of South Africa but including the countries of North Africa) in total world exports has fallen steadily, from 13.2 per cent in 1955 to 6.0 per cent in 1979. The declining export shares are particularly notable for non-ferrous minerals, falling from 15.6 per cent to 5.4 per cent of total world exports from 1955 to 1979. The decline in export market shares of crude fertilizers, mineral ores and scrap was less pronounced in this time period, but nonetheless significant. Even the value in real terms of non-fuel mineral exports seems to have declined from 1965-1970 to 1979, as indicated in the lower portion of Table 4.1.

Table 4.1 African Mineral Export Shares and Values, 1955 to 1979

	1955	1960	1965	1970	1975	1979
Export Market Shares, % of World Exports	Percentage					
Crude Fertilizers, Minerals, Ores and Scrap	10.7	8.6	9.6	6.0	10.7	6.7
Non-Ferrous Metals	15.6	13.6	12.4	13.5	7.8	5.4
Combined	13.2	11.0	11.1	10.1	9.3	6.0
Value of Mineral Exports	billion $, constant 1979					
Crude Fertilizers, Minerals, Ores and Scrap	1.39	1.62	2.19	2.03	3.31	2.20
Non-Ferrous Metals	2.14	2.34	2.99	5.29	2.18	2.00
Total	3.53	3.96	5.18	7.32	5.49	4.20

Source: UNCTAD (1976) and UNCTAD (1981).
Note: Crude Fertilizers, Minerals, Ores and Scrap include SITC 27 and 28. Non-Ferrous Metals excludes iron and steel, and includes SITC 68. The constant dollar values for mineral exports were calculated by deflating the nominal value by an index of inflation for the imports of the developing countries. (UNCTAD, 1981, 47).

The production of most non-fuel minerals also declined in the post-war era as illustrated in Table 4.2. Of the more important non-fuel minerals, only for uranium and bauxite did Africa's production shares increase from 1958 to 1978. From 1970 to 1980 export volumes declined for a number of major minerals including iron ore, copper, lead, zinc, and tin although for uranium and bauxite they undoubtedly increased. The declining export shares for African minerals are also illustrated in Appendix Tables A and B which show the overall changes in the global pattern of exports for non-ferrous metals, and for crude minerals, fertilizers, ores and scrap.

Sub-Saharan African participation in the world mining system will likely continue to decline substantially in the remainder of the 1980s. The information on global

Table 4.2 Africa's Major Minerals, Production Shares and Export Growth Rates

	Production Shares; Percentage of World Production				Share of Total African Exports	Average Annual Growth Rate of Export Volumes	
	1984	1958	1968	1978	1978-1980 (Per cent)	1960-1970 (Per cent)	1970-1980 (Per cent)
Cobalt	66.6	64.1	70.8	50.8	0.9	25.6	-3.9
Chromium	19.9	21.5	8.8	9.9	0.3	14.1	0.2
Iron Ore	2.6	3.0	7.7	4.3		2.3	-0.3
Manganese Ore	19.3	13.7	15.3	15.6	2.7		
Copper	18.0	22.6	20.0	15.0	0.2	-0.3	-6.4
Lead	6.8	11.4	6.4	4.9	0.1	-0.3	0.2
Zinc	5.1	10.1	4.8	3.9	0.1	5.0	-11.4
Tin	15.0	13.4	8.4	5.3	0.2	12.5	25.0
Bauxite	1.7	3.0	5.7	15.5			
Uranium	0	0	8.4	10.4			
Phosphates	35.6	34.0	24.2	22.7	1.1	20.2	6.7
Gold	7.7	6.4	2.9	3.1			
Petroleum	0.5	0.5	12.9	10.3	56.0	-2.2	18.2

Source: UNECA (1981, 27-28); World Bank (1983, 24); World Bank (1981, 157).

Table 4.3 World Investment Projects in the Mineral Sector by Geographic Area for the 1980s: Number of Projects under "a"; Estimated Investment Value under "b"

	Developing Countries									Developed Market Economies											
	Africa				Latin America and Caribbean				Developing Asia		Canada		USA		Australia		S. Africa		Europe	
	Sub-Saharan		North		Total		Brazil														
	(a)	(b)	(a)	(b)	(a)	(b)	(a)	(b)	(a)	(b)	(a)	(b)	(a)	(b)	(a)	(b)	(a)	(b)	(a)	(b)
Major Metals																				
Bauxite/Aluminum	3	4,000*	1	800	16	10,717	8	6,146	8	4,855*	7	6,167*	2	900	9	6,430			9	1,159*
Copper	2	242	3	122	15	9,601	1	n.a.	17	3,995*	5	1,320	8	1,781*	6	1,997	1	69	5	596*
Iron	4	2,100*	2	1,010	8	3,663	3	2,455			2	388	1	11			1	30	4	300*
Lead/Zinc			4	109	5	92*		—	10	333*	4	652	3	327	1	324			8	644
Nickel			1	n.a.	1	570					3	70*	1	300*					1	n.a.
Uranium	4	545*		—	1	150			1	n.a.	6	660*	9	80*	6	1,996			1	65
Lesser Metals																				
Chromium	1	n.a.							4	241									2	n.a.
Cobalt	1	130							1	n.a.										
Manganese	1	200	1	100	2	500	2	500					2	400						
Molybdenum																				
Silicon					1	96	1	96					4	1,784	1	76				
Tungsten					1	25			1	n.a.	1	150					1	25	1	100
Light Metals					2	341	1	280			1	n.a.	3	n.a.	1	200			2	245
Others					1	n.a.			4	262	2	170			2	179			3	92*
Precious Metals																				
Gold	3	359			7	337*	3	283*	5	376	20	1,064*	21	1,797*	14	355	24	5,243*	1	35
Others	1	12			6	26.5*					1	24	10	189*		*			1	n.a.
Industrial Minerals																				
Phosphates			6	733*	4	1,150	2	300	3	830	1	n.a.	7	1,588*					1	n.a.
Potash					2	760	2	760	1	90	6	4,102	1	n.a.						
Others	4	329*							2	4*	2	15	3	465	1	475			3	88
Oil Shale and Sands			2	500	1	110	1	110			4	717	9	5,925*						
Total	24	7,717*	20	3,374*	73	28,138.5*	24	10,930*	57	10,986*	65	15,499*	82	15,547*	41	12,032*	27	5,367*	42	3,324*

Source: Calculations based upon *Engineering and Mining Journal* (Jan. 1984).
Note: See the text for a discussion of the limitations of this Table.

investment plans in the mineral sector, presented in Table 4.3, indicates that relatively few new or expansion projects are likely to come on-stream in the 1980s in that region. This Table, constructed from information in Engineering and Mining Journal, emphasizes the shift of new mineral investment to some of the developed market economies (DMEs), especially to Australia and South Africa, together with the maintenance of the roles of Canada and the United States as leading mineral producers. The emergence of Brazil as a major participant in the world mining economy is also illustrated in the Table. Further disaggregation of the data would show that a number of non-African developing countries are maintaining or expanding their production shares, notably Peru, Mexico, Chile, the Philippines and Indonesia, all in copper. (EMJ, January, 1984) A list of the specific mineral projects is presented in Table 4.4. Of the 24 projects, eight are under construction, five are "on the shelf", awaiting improved market conditions or the arrangement of financing, and ten are in the initial proposal stage.

There are a number of limitations to the information presented in Tables 4.3 and 4.4, however. First, the detail of the coverage for different regions varies, some countries are excluded, and Eastern Europe is omitted entirely (with the exception of Yugoslavia). Second, estimates for the value of investment projects are incomplete. Third, the investment projects are in various stages of implementation, ranging from projects already under construction to projects at the proposal or feasibility study stage. Fourth, the project number and value figures are for gross investment, not net or new investment. In the light of these limitations, the information in Tables 4.3 and 4.4 must be treated as indicative only, and not completely accurate.

It is discouraging to note that, according to these figures, the number of new projects in Sub-Saharan Africa is similar to that of South Africa alone. Brazil, the United States and Australia, each taken individually have shares of planned new investments which are larger than the share of all of the Sub-Saharan African region.

There are two main factors relevant for explaining why mineral development in the region has slowed down. The first factor is the increasing avoidance of mineral exploration in the region by the major DME-based MMNCs in the 1960s and 1970s–despite the relatively high quality of ore bodies in the region. The reduction in investment in exploration is illustrated in Figure 4.1. The MMNCs have generally avoided Sub-Saharan Africa in favour of Australia, South Africa, and Brazil due to a general perception of high "political risk". Although seldom clearly articulated, high "political risk" referred to the possibility of expropriation, to the chances that contracts between governments and MMNCs could be redrawn after physical investment was in place so that profits could not be repatriated, and to political instability in some countries. Other relevant factors explaining the aversion of MMNCs to investing in the region include lack of profit mobility, relatively high taxes in some cases, the absence of credible mining law in some countries, and lack of information on basic geology of major areas.

Second, some established state-owned mineral enterprises in countries have been employed by those countries as "milk cows", generating foreign exchange and

Table 4.4. Prospective Mineral Projects in Sub-Saharan Africa

Commodity	Country	Company	Capacity (thousand mt/yr)	Class*	Estimated Value (Millions U.S.$)
Bauxite/ Aluminium	Ghana	Government	800 alumina	A	n.a.
	Guinea	Government	1,200 alumina	C	3,000
	Zaire	Consortium	210 alumina	C	1,000
Copper	Zambia	Government (ZCCM)		A	242
	Zambia	Government (ZCCM)	120	A	n.a.
Iron Ore	Angola	Ferrangol	1,100	B	n.a.
	Guinea	Government (partial)	15,000	B	1,100
	Nigeria	Associated Ore	3,000	C	n.a.
	Senegal	Government (28.5%)	12,000	BC	1,000
Chrominum	Malagasy Rep.	Government		C	n.a.
Cobalt	Zambia	Zambia Eng. Serv.		n.a.	130
Manganese	Upper Volta	Gov't (majority)	500	B	200
Gold	Ghana	Government		B	14
	Upper Volta	Gov't (60%)		A	100
	Nigeria	Government (partial)		A	45
Tin	Zaire	Government (20%)		A	12
Uranium	Central African Rep.	Government (partial)		C	500
	Namibia	General Mining		C	n.a.
	Gabon	Government		C	45
	Niger	Government (33%)		C	n.a.
Asbestos	Sudan	Gulf/Johns Manville	100	C	115
Diamonds	Bophutheswna	Rio Tinto		C	n.a.
	Guinea	Aredor		A	96
	Sierra Leone	Government		A	118
Total	24 projects				7,717

Source: Engineering and Mining Journal (January 1984).
*Note: Class Symbols: A: projects now under construction.
B: construction not yet begun; awaiting financing or appropriate market conditions.
C: projects in the initial proposal stage.

See the text for a discussion of the limitations of this Table.

public revenues for general developmental and/or governmental purposes. In view of the foreign exchange crises faced by these and other oil-importing countries since the OPEC price increase of 1973, and especially since the oil price increase of

(a)
European mining companies' capital spending on mining projects (US$×10⁶ in real terms. European companies' share).

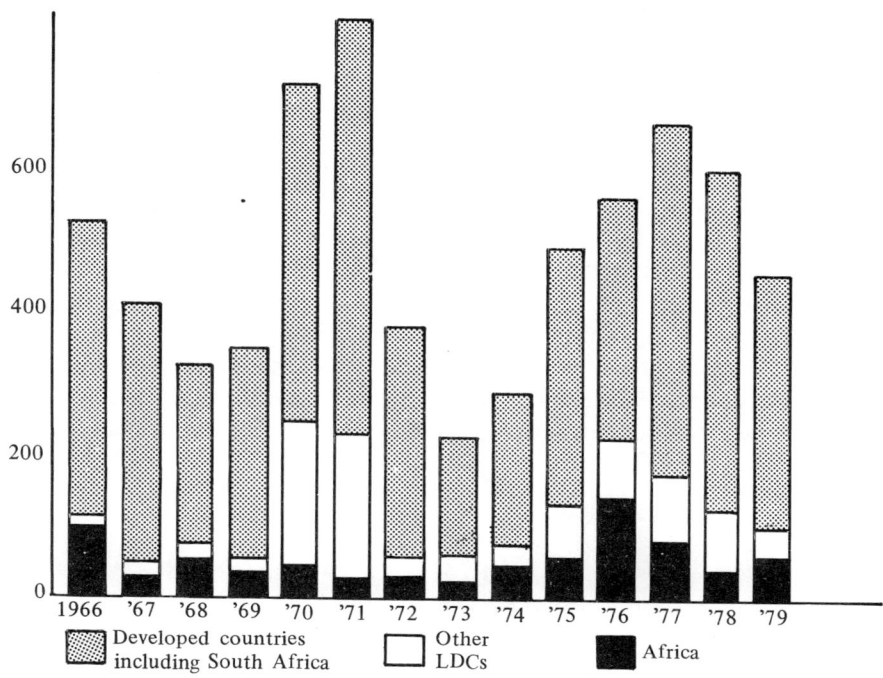

(b)
European mining companies' exploration expenditure (US$×10⁶ in real terms. European companies' share).

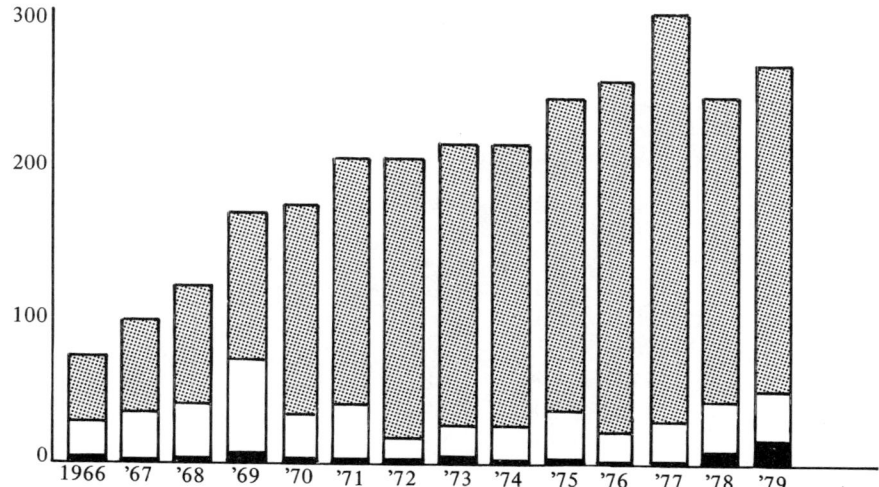

Source: MacLeod-Smith, A. (1981, 28).

Figure 4.1.

1979-80 and the following world recession, it is not surprising that relatively little funding has been available for further mineral exploration and development.

In summary, Africa's share of global mineral production and exports has been declining. This is likely to continue at least for the decade of the 1980s in view of the prospective number and size of new mineral development projects and the global pattern of mineral exploration, both of which are largely bypassing Sub-Saharan Africa.

Intra-African trade in non-fuel minerals does not seem to have been expanding rapidly. Although Intra-African mineral trade as a proportion of total exports has risen slightly, it is still low, amounting to 4.5 per cent of total for non-ferrous metals and 1.9 per cent for crude fertilizers, ores and scrap in 1979. Intra-African non-fuel mineral imports seems to have been more variable with no clear tendency to increase or to decrease. Information on Intra-African mineral trade is presented in Table 4.5. There are a variety of factors underlying this low volume of Intra-African non-fuel mineral trade, which will not be discussed here. But the low current trade volume also creates an interesting opportunity for expanded interregional exchange. (See UNECA, 1981, 52-57).

Table 4.5 Intra-African Trade in Non-fuel Minerals

	Year	Total Exports $ millions	Intra-African Exports $ millions	Intra-African Exports as Percentage of Total	Total Imports to Africa $ millions	Intra-Africa Imports as Percentage of Total
Non-Ferrous Metals (SITC 68)	1955	560	5	0.9	34	14.7
	1960	620	3	0.5	45	6.7
	1965	830	9	1.1	79	11.4
	1970	1,670	14	0.8	130	10.7
	1975	1,451	303	20.9	568	53.3
	1979	1,977	88	4.5	537	16.4
Crude Fertilizers Ores and Scrap (SITC 27 & 28)	1955	365	2	0.5	16	12.5
	1960	430	3	0.7	19	15.7
	1965	610	9	1.5	33	27.3
	1970	648	8	1.2	50	16.0
	1975	2,206	30	1.4	141	21.3
	1979	2,204	41	1.9	317	12.9

Source: UNCTAD (1976) and UNCTAD (1981).
Note: The figure for Intra African Exports of Non-ferrous Metals for 1979 reproduces the UNCTAD figure, but is likely erroneous or extraordinary.

Does Sub-Saharan Africa Need the Mineral Sector?

Squeezing the potential benefits from the mining sector is difficult for developing countries in the best of circumstances. Indeed, excessive reliance on a productive mineral sector can create problems for a small country, problems similar in nature although quantitatively less significant than those faced by some major petroleum exporters (the "petroleum economy syndrome"). But neglecting the development of the minerals sector means that substantial foreign exchange earnings and public revenues, some job creation and infrastructural cost-sharing are also foregone. This is an especially serious loss for those oil-importing African countries which have been confronting excruciating balance of payments deficits which in turn are suffocating both growth and the ability to meet basic human needs.

The greatest benefit from the existence of a productive mineral extraction and processing sector is the earning of foreign exchange which can then be used for various developmental activities, including industrial and agricultural diversification, infrastructural projects, or to meet the import costs of basic needs-oriented activities. The revenues generated by governments through royalties, taxes or profit shares can also be employed for pro-developmental activities of all sorts. Mineral development may facilitate the opening up of new regions of a country, and may help pay for infrastructure–transportation and power systems, for example–which can be used by individuals and enterprises. Some employment is also generated in the sector, although due to its capital intensive nature job-creation in mining is limited.

In the future, it is likely that as African consumption of minerals will grow more rapidly than consumption in the developed market economies (DMEs) due to the high minerals-intensity of prospective African growth patterns and greater market saturation in the DMEs (Energy Mines and Resources Canada, 1982, 144). This factor, together with the drive towards greater collective self-reliance within Africa should create growing opportunities for Intra-African trade in minerals. Non-fuel minerals are, of course, a basic building block for industrial and agricultural development and for infrastructure and construction generally. One may expect, therefore, that in time there will be important intersectoral as well as interregional linkages emanating from the development of the non-fuel minerals sector.

But other potential benefits from mineral development are difficult to harness, and indeed there are some specific problems arising from the presence of a wealthy mineral or petroleum extractive sector. First, while there are strong backward and forward linkages from mineral extraction, few countries–DCs or DMEs–are equipped to harness a large proportion of these linkages. The fabrication of much of the machinery and equipment used for mineral extraction/concentration/smelting/refining is often complex, large-scale, and highly specialized so that it has to be imported, mainly from a few countries which have specialized minerals machinery industries (notably the United States, Japan and Western Europe). Because most minerals (with the exception of crude fertilizers) are used mainly as inputs in the capital equipment and consumer durables, the markets for refined metals are largely in the DMEs, and to an increasing extent in the middle income "Newly Industrializing Countries" or "NICs" rather than in Sub-Saharan Africa. In other words, resource-based industrialization is difficult.

The so-called "consumption linkage" or "final demand" linkage–that is the stimulus to consumer goods activities to supply the labour force in the mineral sector–is also weak. This is because the relative size of the labour force in capital-intensive mining activities is small, and the level of incomes is relatively high so that the consumption pattern of the labour force tends to become import-intensive. In summary, mineral extraction/processing activities in small and undiversified countries have tended to become an "enclave" activity, unintegrated with the rest of the economic structure.

Moreover, if the foreign exchange earnings from mineral – or petroleum – exports are very high, there can be adverse ramifications of a macro-economic nature which can deform the development of other sectors of the economy. For example, if high mineral exports push up the exchange rate, imports of foodstuffs may become relatively inexpensive, and traditional agricultural exports may become "expensive" and may lose their markets. Similar impacts on industrial imports and exports may occur through the exchange rate, and industrial development may thus be impaired. If a "high-rent" mineral sector permits relatively high wage levels in that sector, there may be a tendency for wages and salaries in other "formal sector" activities to be pushed upwards. This then tends to reduce the competitiveness of local industry, thereby making manufactured exports expensive and imports cheap – with consequent impacts on the potential for industrial diversification. The exchange rate and wage/salary structure impacts of resource wealth may therefore worsen the employment-generating potential of industrial development. Diversification of exports into non-traditional manufactures and agricultural products also tends to be stifled. This type of development pattern is especially typical of oil-exporting countries (including Trinidad, Nigeria, Gabon, Iran, and Venezuela), but is in lesser degree present in the experience of mineral-based economies such as Zambia.

There are a variety of other problems of mineral development. For example, the infrastructure constructed to service a mineral sector – typically of a mine-to-port character – may not be useful as a means of integrating the economy and may not be of much benefit to other individuals or enterprises. The prices of some major minerals are notoriously volatile so that reliance on one or a few may contribute to unstable foreign exchange earnings with consequent macroeconomic destabilization, and vulnerability to the international business cycle.

Finally, some analysts have argued that mineral development in DCs merely ties them more tightly into the innately unjust international capitalist system whereas they should instead be attempting to disengage themselves.

A careful weighing of the advantages and disadvantages of mineral development cannot be undertaken here in the space and time available. My conclusion on this, however, is that the limitations of mineral development are severe, but that the imperative to expand foreign exchange earnings for virtually all of the oil-importing Sub-Saharan African countries is more severe. To regain greater internal freedom of action, to finance developmental activities of all sorts, to diversify economic structures, to pay for petroleum imports and to finance the development of domestic petroleum supplies or of substitutes and to continue to improve the fulfilment of basic human needs requires foreign exchange earnings. In sum, to reduce the severe dependence engendered by the current balance of payments crises in most Sub-Saharan African countries requires increased foreign exchange earnings. Minerals provide one important potential contributory source of foreign exchange earnings.

Diversified mineral development in the region should also provide some of the basic building blocks for diversified and hopefully integrated industrial development in the region.

Some of the harmful effects of great resource wealth discussed above are a long way off for most Sub-Saharan African countries. Expansion of the mineral export sector from very small bases in most countries would not generate the macroeconomic problems present recently in some of the oil exporting countries.

Wise public policy is vital in harnessing the benefits and reducing the negative consequences of mineral development. The central task of mineral policy is then to squeeze the maximum net benefits out of the sector in terms of foreign exchange earnings, public revenues, industrial linkages, infrastructural externalities, and the building of indigenous capabilities to manage and expand the sector autonomously.

Reviving the Minerals Sector in Sub-Saharan Africa

Sub-Saharan Africa has been regarded for many decades as "one of the great storehouses of mineral wealth" (World Bank, 1981, p. 97) even in the absence of detailed exploration for much of the post-war period. Despite the promise of such mineral wealth, the mineral sector has declined in relative and even absolute terms since the early 1960s. This is unsatisfactory in view of the urgent need of most countries in the region for foreign exchange earnings and in view of the other developmental benefits which may be generated by the sector, as discussed in the previous section.

What can be done to revive the sector and to "turn it around" so that its share of global production and exports is maintained and increased rather than diminished? The successful establishment of Jointly-Owned Regional Mineral Enterprises would contribute to a revival and expansion of mineral sector activity. But the contribution would be minor, and many other types of policy change would also be necessary. It should be stated emphatically that the JRME proposal is no panacea for the problems of the mineral sector. Instead it is viewed here as just one of the many types of initiative which are necessary.

The conference on the Development and Utilization of Mineral Resources in Africa, held under the auspices of the U.N. Economic Commission for Africa has perhaps done most to analyse the functioning of the sector, and to make an integrated set of proposals for reviving it (UNECA, 1981, pp. 1-7; 106-110; and 299-307). At this Conference recommendations were put forward on building the geological and technical knowledge base; development of national and multinational capabilities for extraction, processing and marketing; developing intra-African minerals markets; manpower development; developing the capital goods industries providing machinery and equipment for the sector; the creation of financing, investment and insurance institutions; and environmental protection. The specific recommendations will not be outlined here, however, except to state that under each of the above-mentioned headings there were proposals for action at the national as well as the regional levels. All of the types of recommendations are relevant and appropriate.

It has often been thought that countries face a strategic choice in the minerals sector between "going it alone", utilizing parastatal enterprises rather than multinationals, on the one hand, and "coming to terms" with the western multinational minerals corporations.

It may be more appropriate to follow both options simultaneously. The particular blend of state-ownership and foreign participation probably should be custom-designed to fit the degree to technological complexity required for different types of minerals, and the degree of maturity of established parastatals and/or private firms in the sector. Relatively straightforward and technologically simple open pit extraction of a mineral can often be handled by relatively new parastatals without long mining traditions, but able to fill any gaps in expertise through hiring expatriates or technical contracts with foreign companies. On the other hand, technically complex underground extraction with difficult processing may require closer contact with established multinationals through joint ventures or turnkey arrangements plus management contracts. In any case, there is no reason why individual countries should not utilize both domestic parastatals and foreign firms, the particular blend being determined by a pragmatic weighing of relative costs and benefits of each.

For countries which wish to follow an institutionally pluralistic approach to mineral sector development, including not only national parastatals but also Jointly-Owned Regional Minerals Enterprises, domestic private firms and major western mining houses (as joint venture partners or with foreign majority ownership), a number of policy changes or modifications may be appropriate. One of these, for some countries at least, is the codification of a more clear-cut "mining law". A second is the elaboration of tax legislation and profit remittance law which would not be too lenient but also would not be uncompetitively punitive. (Standardization continent-wide or within certain subregions would be of obvious benefit, but is politically complex.)

A third type of policy initiative which would be appropriate for the institutionally pluralistic countries would relate to small scale domestically-owned mining enterprises – "junior" mines as they are labelled in the Canadian context. The almost complete absence of such small-scale independent firms in the minerals sectors of most countries in the region is a serious gap. Such enterprises – often consisting of a few self-employed prospectors, or a good deal larger – can perform crucial exploration activities at a detailed grass-roots level, in a manner not currently performed adequately by parastatal exploration, by UNDP funded prospecting, or by the large scale mining houses. The most frequent *raison d'etre* of such "junior" enterprises is to discover mineable ore bodies, and then to sell out the mineral rights to a major private or public company which undertakes to delineate the ore body more precisely, to arrange financing and to establish extraction and processing operations. In a few cases, the "juniors" themselves may be able to bring a discovery into production and become "majors", but this is rarer. The near-absence of such enterprises in many African countries means that relatively little exploration is performed by nationals, aside from the parastatal sector. In view of the contribution which such enterprises can make to exploration and the development of the sector, various types of policy changes may be in order in some countries. Mining legislation, clearcut and especially favourable tax arrangements, access to basic geological information and technical training for prospectors may all be appropriate depending on the specifics of the case.

Fourthly, improvements in the capability of mines ministries or other ministries to bargain effectively with multinational corporations may also be relevant in some countries in order to ensure that optimum national benefits are obtained from joint ventures, management contracts, or the design of contracts for foreign majority owned operations.

To summarize, the JRME proposal on its own may be a useful innovation for reviving the mineral sector in some African countries, but it is no panacea. A variety of other policy changes, legal and taxation provisions, and institutional innovations at the level of governments and the region are also necessary. Indeed for some countries, it is not likely that a JRME would establish operations without clearer taxation and profit remittance provisions and mining law more generally, and some assurance concerning the stability of the "rules of the game".

African Jointly-Owned Regional Enterprises and Western Multinationals

Western-based minerals multinationals possess important strengths and advantages which have permitted them to survive and expand into the global arena. Western multinationals have also generated a variety of benefits for the host countries in which they operate. But the minerals multinational also is disadvantageous to host countries in a number of respects which go beyond the inherent limitations of mining as a propellant of growth and development as discussed in the previous section. Perceptions of these disadvantages have led many developing countires to nationalize established foreign-owned mineral enterprises either fully or partially, to enter into joint venture or management contract relationships with the foreign firms, or to place limits on their operations through the design of contracts or through foreign investment policy. This is not the place to undertake an evaluation of the role of the minerals multinational in developing countries, nor to weigh the relative advantages of the minerals multinational vis-à-vis state-owned minerals enterprises or joint ventures between state-owned and multinational firms.

The essence of the argument in this section is that Africa needs its own multinational – or supranational – minerals enterprises. Such enterprises would in time develop the same types of strengths currently possessed by western multinationals, without some of the drawbacks of the latter. They would, it is hoped, contribute towards the resuscitation of the mineral sector in African countries, with all of the national benefits this would entail, and facilitate the development of African expertise in all facets and stages of mineral production, processing and marketing. African jointly-owned regional minerals enterprises might also overcome some of the disadvantages of smaller-scale nationally-oriented state-owned mining companies as a result of their larger multinational orientation. (The avoidance of some of the problems and inefficiencies which have plagued national state-owned firms by the jointly-owned regional enterprises is a major challenge, and is discussed subsequently).

What are the advantages of the western-based minerals multinational enterprises which have permitted them to develop into multi-stage, multinational mining houses which have sustained themselves for long periods of time? A few of their basic strengths are listed below: (Mikesell, 1979; Cunningham, 1981; Shirley, 1983).

Financial autonomy and responsibility: Their long-term viability and expansion has been forced upon them in a sense, in that they have been responsible for their own financial solvency as autonomous enterprises. This is an obvious source of their strength which is useful to recall in the context of a discussion of jointly-owned regional minerals enterprises. Managers of mining houses are also likely to be relatively independent of political pressures, so that their decision-making will reinforce enterprise viability.

Development of Organically-Integrated Sets of Expertise: Over substantial periods of time they have developed complex constellations of skills in exploration, extraction, processing and marketing and of a technical managerial and commercial character at a range of levels.

Economies of Scale in Management and Technology: Western mining houses are able to pool expertise through their operations in a variety of minerals and in a number of countries and regions throughout the world. Pooling of expertise on a global basis facilitates problem-solving in mine development and operation.

Pooling of Financial Resources and Spreading of Risk: Pooling of financial resources from many operations in many regions provides retained earnings for exploration and project development in new areas where prospects for success may be high. Global operations also permit the spreading of risk. Through their access to profits from other regions or other minerals, mining houses are able to buffer themselves partially from losses due to unsuccessful exploration, project failures, production dislocations arising from political instability and price volatility for specific minerals.

Access to Markets: Vertically integrated minerals enterprises for some minerals such as bauxite/alumina/aluminium have significant control over access to end markets for cruder mineral ores.

Access to Financial Resources: The presence of an established minerals multinational may facilitate access to financial resources from commercial banks or even international financial institutions anxious to be assured of the commercial viability and credit-worthiness of a specific project.

These advantages of western-based minerals multinationals are not usually available to nationally-oriented state-owned enterprises, except for the larger developing country mineral producers, such as Chile, Zambia or Brazil. For some of the smaller producers of Sub-Saharan Africa, however, regional multinational mining enterprises perhaps can be developed which could possess some of the above advantages. The rest of this paper is an exploration of the technical, economic and commercial feasibility of the establishment of African regional jointly-owned minerals enterprises.

BASIC DIMENSIONS FOR VIABLE JOINTLY OWNED REGIONAL MINERAL ENTERPRISES

The establishment and development of any enterprise is a difficult and complex process. For the type of enterprise under consideration here, the process is much more difficult. In addition to the requirements for an integrated constellation of skilled personnel and for financial resources, is the question of institutional design, for which there are no close precedents. However, there are a number of organizational prerequisites which must be fulfilled if any type of jointly-owned regional mineral enterprise is to be successful and sustainable. These are considered in the next section. Some alternative institutional forms are then analysed and assessed, including (i) an inter-governmental joint enterprise, or the "air Afrique" model; (ii) a "parastatal spin-off" model; (iii) joint ventures of governments and international or regional institutions; and (iv) mixed public-private enterprises. The possible sources of financial resources for the JRMEs are then considered, along with personnel constraints.

Prerequisites for Viability

Objectives: The ultimate goals of establishing any type of African JRME are to stimulate the development of the mineral sector directly, and to generate a broad range of indigenous capabilities in exploration through to processing and marketing. In the long run, the JRMEs would become integrated mining houses not too dissimilar from established multinationals such as Anglo-American, Amax, Alcan or Rio Tinto, but African owned and operated.

To achieve these long-term goals, the immediate, medium-term and long-term objective of the enterprises must be commercial in character. JRMEs must become financially responsible and autonomous as soon as possible; after a transition period of perhaps five to eight years, they should generate revenues exceeding costs. Profits are of the utmost importance for financing new investment and in order to compensate the owners, which would be mainly governments. Sustainability for the JRPE depends upon earning profits. If the enterprises were not self-financing but had to rely on continuous allocations of funds from governments, their survival would be improbable if not impossible. In a word, the enterprises must be "profit maximizing" if they are to survive in the long run.

This does not mean that JRMEs cannot be expected to orient their activities towards the achievement of other "social" objectives aside from commercial profits. But if they are expected to aim directly at providing non-commercial social benefits such as regional or frontier development, or provision of general-purpose infrastructure, the "social benefit" elements of minerals investment should be covered by governments. On the other hand, social costs which might be imposed by the enterprises on the rest of society, pollution, or waste and tailings disposal – should be covered by the companies themselves through preventative measures.

To reiterate, a JRME must be commercially-oriented and profitable if it is to generate over time sustainable flows of direct and indirect social benefits, including foreign exchange earnings, tax revenues, employment and some contribution to the provision of social and economic infrastructure.

Autonomy with Accountability: A most vexing issue with respect to state-owned enterprises everywhere is how to maintain ultimate public control and managerial accountability while providing the enterprise with a high degree of autonomy in its operations. This is a continuing dilemma which has not been completely resolved anywhere, and for which there is no single universal resolution.

Maintenance of operational independence of the JRMEs from governments is of the utmost importance. Such enterprises must be able to hire on the basis of merit, not national quotas. They must be free to develop the best projects within the relevant region without political influence, or, again, without national quotas on project location. (This creates problems of equity among the participating countries. This perhaps can be handled by ensuring profit distribution from any projects wherever located to all of the equity-owning governments, as discussed subsequently.) The JRMEs must be able to procure inputs and process and market outputs on the basis of commercial criteria. If the enterprises did not have autonomy in investment allocation as well as in their operations, their commercial failure would be virtually assured. Survival of the enterprises, and the sustaining of benefits from their operation requires such independence from political interference.

How then could ultimate social control of the activities of JRMEs be assured? Three general mechanisms should serve to establish a significant and suitable degree of control. The first is competition through markets. Large proportions of the output of JRMEs undoubtedly would be sold in international mineral markets in which there are relatively large numbers of suppliers and buyers so that price determination is highly competitive, approaching the purely competitive market model for the major minerals. This means that monopoly or oligopoly power, common for the output markets of nationally-oriented state-owned enterprises, would be insignificant for JRMEs. International market forces would thus provide a powerful discipline and a degree of social control over the enterprises. These market forces would provide powerful stimuli towards efficient operation and careful project selection. They would also make abusive practices, such as excessive managerial salaries and benefits counter-productive, if the viability of the enterprise was thereby threatened.

A second mechanism for public control would be the Board of Directors of the JRMEs (also discussed below) which would represent the equity-owning participating governments and perhaps bodies such as regional development banks. The Board of Directors would monitor the operations of the JRMEs but not interfere in their operations, leaving this to management. The Board would oversee the general functioning of the enterprise, under an enterprise charter which was clearly commercial in orientation. A danger, of course, is that the Board of Directors might become heavily politicized, serving as a medium for the transmission of political pressures from governments. This perhaps could be avoided if regional bodies such as development banks had major representation on the Boards.

Thirdly, in their operations within specific countries, JRMEs would be oriented and constrained by national legislation. Presumably they would operate within normal company law within the country concerned, and, for example, would be dependent on national banks for foreign exchange allotments for the purchase of imported inputs. But the JRMEs probably should not be subject to national legislation designed to define the terms and conditions of employment in the domestic parastatal sector as is done by Tanzania's Standing Committee on Parastatal Organizations (SCOPO). Greater operational autonomy within more competitive international markets would be more appropriate.

Incentive Structures: A most important prerequisite for success of the JRME is the design of the incentive structure for harmonizing the efforts and eliciting the full and focussed energies of the personnel, including managers, technicians and workers. There probably would be powerful forces at work pushing the enterprise into the mold of a standard international civil service. Likely there would be pressures towards international United Nations salary scales, benefits and emoluments, and "terms and conditions of employment" at the managerial and technical level. The problem with this is that the JRME might be converted into an international bureaucracy rather than an enterprise. Management personnel, recruited partly for their energy and enterpreneurial talents, may in time become more concerned with the emoluments of the position rather than with the strenuous tasks of developing projects.

This real danger can be avoided in a number of ways. First, a "sunset" provision in the charter of the enterprise could serve to concentrate the energies of management and technical personnel. Under this type of provision, the JRME would have to be financially autonomous after the five to eight year transition period or it would face automatic dissolution. This would provide a strong stimulus for the enterprise to become self-activating and self-financing quickly. Secondly, optimum efforts might be elicited from personnel if there were a strong incentive element in their income, probably a profit-sharing arrangement. Indeed, some type of generalized profit-sharing arrangement would likely be appropriate as a means of mobilizing additional exertion, not only at managerial and technical levels, but also for workers at production sites. Such an incentive would need to be designed carefully and adapted to the structure of the JRME as it evolved.

Alternative Institutional Forms

A wide variety of possible organizational structures are conceivable for the JRME. Only a few general possible types are examined here.

(i) Intergovernmental Joint Enterprises: the "Air Afrique" Model: This variant would consist of two or more countries or particular groupings of countries such as the Southern African Development Coordinating Committee (SADCC) or the Economic Community of West African States (ECOWAS). The governments of the participating countries would contribute equity capital through the purchase of shares. The voting powers would then be allocated on the basis of share ownership (or common share ownership), and would be reflected to some extent in the Board of Directors of the enterprise.

Which entities within the governments would actually fund the JRMEs? This could be done through a variety of institutions, including National Development Banks, major parastatal mineral enterprises, or through budgetary allocations and national treasuries or departments of finance. It is not possible to determine which of these types of source might be most desirable and feasible. Presumably different countries could utilize different funding instruments as they saw fit. For major minerals producers with well-established parastatals, perhaps the ZCCM would constitute the relevant source of or channel for funds as well as locus of domestic monitoring. For countries with smaller minerals sectors or little public ownership, the National Development Banks might be more appropriate.

Other sources of funds could be tapped for the JRME. International or regional development banks such as the World Bank, the African Development Bank or the East African Development Bank, and publicly owned or private commercial banks could lend to the enterprise. Such debt financing would *not* involve equity ownership. In the case of regional development banks, however, such equity participation may not be undesirable. Private shareholding by individuals or companies might also be encouraged.

The intergovernmental enterprise, as outlined here, has a precedent in Air Afrique, established in 1961. Air Afrique is one of the most successful jointly-owned regional enterprises in the developing countries and perhaps the world. Twelve countries were initial signatories to a Treaty establishing Air Afrique (ICAO, 1970). Each had an equal share in the Corporation's capital, although it is not clear whether all countries have since subscribed to increases in authorized capital. Each contracting state was guaranteed a minimum of two members on the Board of Directors, but could obtain greater representation proportional to subsequent financial subscriptions. (The Treaty also went beyond the establishment of Air Afrique to include standardization of laws and regulations in matters of civil and commercial aviation, and harmonization of taxation arrangements and the treatment of financial transfers.) Unfortunately, to the knowledge of the author, there has been no analysis of how and why Air Afrique has been able to survive and prosper while other jointly owned regional enterprises have failed.

(ii) The "Parastatal Spin Off" Model: A second possible institutional form could involve the creation of an internationally-oriented spin-off from the major minerals parastatals of one or a number of countries in the region, buttressed by equity participation form the Development Banks of countries with smaller mineral sectors, by regional development banks, and by loans and for grants from international bodies. In this variant, for example, Tanzania's State Mining corporation (Staminco) and the Zambia Consolidated Copper Mines (ZCCM) might take a lead role in establishing an international affiliate with participation from the Development Banks of other contracting states. Participation by major private mines in the relevant region might also be considered. The resulting type of JRME might not be dissimilar from variant (i), but a stronger initiating role would have been taken by major national minerals enterprises. This JRME variant might be of particular relevance for the SADCC region in view of Zambia's improving mineral sector management capabilities and its official role as coordinator for minerals in that region.

The principal advantage of this JRME variant would be close contact between the international company and major national enterprises, which could facilitate the transfer of managerial and technical personnel, of technology, and perhaps of equipment. The advantage to countries with smaller mineral sectors and lacking a depth of experience in mineral exploration, extraction, processing and marketing is that they could get access to the know-how of the neighbouring countries with accumulated managerial and technical expertise.

There are no direct precedents for this particular JRME variant. Perhaps the closest is Petro-Canada International, which is a subsidiary of Petro-Canada. This, however, is an "aid" oriented non-profit energy assistance organization funded by CIDA, the Canadian International Development Agency (Petro-Canada International, 1982). Its mission is to assist in the financing of energy exploration activities in oil importing developing countries using Canadian equipment and specialized personnel wherever possible. It currently has projects on land or offshore in cooperation with Jamaica, Barbados, Senegal, The Gambia, Tanzania, Thailand and the Philippines. Petro-Canada International is obviously different from the type of enterprise proposed here. The JRME would be commercially-oriented, would be owned by a group of African countries, and would be involved in production activities on its own or in joint venture with public or private minerals companies in its participating countries. But the Petro-Canada International example does illustrate that innovational institutional arrangements are possible. Perhaps ZCCM, for example, might think of establishing an affiliate of this sort in the future when its national operations have more fully matured.

(iii) Joint Ventures of Governments and International or Regional Institutions: A third organizational variant would consist of two or more governments together with certain international or regional institutions such as the World Bank, or the

African Development Bank, or one of the oil producers international development funds. Equity participation by non-African banks would dilute African control, but on the other hand might facilitate the generation of initial financing.

(iv) Mixed Public/Private Consortia: A final organizational possibility might be an international enterprise jointly owned by some established parastatals and nationally oriented private minerals enterprises (most likely foreign owned) with issue of share capital to private citizens in the relevant region. This JRME variant may be advantageous in that the expertise of the MMNEs could be tapped with greater ease than with some of the other variants. But the disadvantages may be a dilution, or a pre-empting of control and a truncation of the managerial learning process on the part of indigeneous personnel.

Relative Attractiveness of JRME Variants

It is probably impossible to judge unequivocally which of the above JRME variants is most viable and most desirable in all situations. Instead, different variants are likely most applicable for different groupings of countries. In the SADCC region, for example, perhaps variants (ii) the "Parastatal Spin Off" model and (iv) the Mixed Public/Private model may be the most applicable, in view of the size and relative maturity of ZCCM, and the presence of some major minerals multinationals in a few of the countries (Rio Tinto in Zimbabwe and De Beers in Botswana). But variant (iv) would not likely be politically appealing to some of the members of SADCC. In East Africa, or among the French-speaking West African countries, the first variant, the "Air Afrique" model may be most appropriate and politically acceptable. In any case, a careful canvassing of national viewpoints and interests, and analyses of existing mineral sector structures would be necessary to arrive at any conclusion on the relative attractiveness and appropriateness of different JRME variants.

Financial Arrangements

A crucial question in considering the feasibility of any type of JRME is, "Where is the money to come from?". This question should be broken into two parts, however, a first part referring to the initial and temporary funding of the organizational centre, and the second part referring to the financing of specific mineral projects. The potential sources of funds are different for each of these components.

The financing of the initial organizational structure would likely be small relative to the financing of specific projects. It would nonetheless be onerous if undertaken by governments at the present time. In view of the current foreign exchange crisis facing most African countries as a result of the 1980-1984 global recession coming on the heels of the 1979-1980 increase in oil prices, raising the financial resources for a relatively high-risk JRME would be difficult. There are also other urgent developmental uses towards which public revenues and foreign exchange earnings need to be applied. Any decision by national governments to allocate funds to a JRME would be hard, at this time and in view of other needs.

Most variants of the JRME require equity participation by contracting governments. How much would be required on an annual basis for the transitional phase is impossible to determine in general terms. Only a specific proposed organization could be "costed" with any accuracy. But in any case, the sums involved would be large relative to the other urgent uses. The equity subscriptions would also likely have to consist of proportions of convertible currencies as well as national currencies.

In the longer term when the JRME is standing on its own, further equity subscriptions would not be necessary. Instead, the enterprise should at some point begin to return shares of its profits to the governments which own it. Indeed, as emphasized earlier, the JRMEs should be seen as "money-makers" for the governments initially subscribing share capital. But the question of how contracting governments are to raise the equity capital for the initial and transitional phase remains.

There are a number of possibilities: (a) foreign exchange earnings and tax revenues could be used for equity subscription. The difficulties with this do not need repetition. (b) The dedication of bilateral aid for this specific purpose. A promising JRME proposal might elicit aid funds which would have to be substantially untied from OPEC or certain OECD donors. This source would obviously be worth exploring. It is conceivable that access to such funding would be instrumental in determining whether a JRME could be tried, at least for some groups of countries. (c) The profits – in the form of hard currency as well as local currency – of national parastatals could be used for front-end financing. (d) The UNDP might be a potential source.

Financing mineral projects, either extraction or processing, can be large scale and extremely expensive, as indicated in Table 4.4 above. This is especially true for the extraction of ferrous and non-ferrous metals and for processing. Mineral extraction projects for national construction purposes may be small-scale and relatively cheaper. There are a number of foreign sources of financing for projects, especially if hard currency will be earned from exported minerals. These sources include the World Bank Group (including the International Development Agency), foreign commercial banks, the African Development Bank, Regional Development Banks, and perhaps the Development Funds or Aid programmes of some donor countries, most likely the Arab OPEC countries. The EEC "Sysmin" might be a potential source for project funding, as well.

Likely there would not be great difficulty in obtaining the financing for specific projects if their expected commercial rates of return were high enough. The major problem would be to finance the basic organizational structure of the JRME until such projects could be brought on stream and started to earn profits, so that the enterprise could become self-financing.

Personnel

A serious constraint on the development of the mineral sector in Sub-Saharan

Africa is the insufficiency of skilled personnel, especially mining engineers and metallurgists, geologists and chemists. Even Zambia, which has a long mining tradition, an emphasis on indigenization of personnel, and a strong program for manpower development and University level training, is still reliant upon a significant number of expatriate employees – 2,572 out of a total labour force of 58,795 in ZCCM at the 1982 year end (ZCCM, 1983). This dependence on expatriate employees has been diminishing steadily in Zambia, however. The reasons for the critical shortage of skilled personnel include the past and present hiring, training and promotion practices of multinationals, the difficulty of establishing training facilities, and the novelty of the types of skills required in mining for some of the countries with smaller minerals sectors. The causes and character of personnel contraints will not be explored here, however.

This shortage of appropriate manpower obviously constitutes a problem for the establishment of JRMEs as well as for some existing parastatal, or private sector minerals enterprises. Would there be sufficient personnel to staff a JRME or a set of JRMEs? Would the creation of JRMEs simply drain skilled managers and entrepreneurs away from national parastatals, private sector enterprise, or ministries where they are also urgently needed?

These are difficult questions which could be answered definitely only with a more detailed examination of a concrete JRME proposal in the context of a specific sub-region. Some groupings of countries such as SADCC have larger pools of skilled mineral sector personnel from which to draw. (This is especially true for SADCC if Euro-Zimbabweans are included.) Generalist manager-entrepreneurs would likely be forthcoming in SADCC and elsewhere without seriously impairing existing minerals enterprises. Finding the more technical personnel from indigenous sources would be more difficult. Probably some expatriate personnel would have to be hired, especially for the tasks of bringing operating mineral projects on stream. This is because specific projects, both of a rehabilitation and "greenfields" character, require technical skills which are often rather rare, depending on the nature of the project concerned.

In summary, personnel constraints are serious but not incapacitating if gaps in expertise can be filled initially from expatriate sources.

STRUCTURE AND OPERATIONAL FEATURES

The Long-Term Vision

The JRMEs envisaged in this study would in the long run evolve into large scale multinational, multi-project, multi-metallic and multi-stage enterprises, African owned and controlled. They would constitute integrated "mining houses" not unlike some of the major western mining houses, with exploration, extraction, processing and marketing capabilities. They would enter into a variety of arrangements with parastatals, private companies, western multinationals and international and national financial institutions for the development of specific projects.

Ultimately, the JRMEs would build capabilities from exploration through to marketing. They would develop exploration affiliates or sections which would locate minable ore bodies. A good deal of exploration could be farmed out or subcontracted to independent exploration enterprises. Even in the long run, however, it would be beneficial if a wide array of "junior" mining companies as well as governmental entities engaged independently in exploration, with the JRMEs being willing to move in and buy out the rights to particular mineral properties explored by the "juniors" but beyond the capability of the "juniors" to develop into producing mines. (The important role which can be played by the "juniors", and the absence of such enterprises in Africa was discussed briefly in the section entitled "Reviving the Minerals Sector in Sub-Saharan Africa" p. 65). One would also expect the JRMEs to develop a variety of types of extraction, concentrating and smelting refining activities in different countries and in a variety of mineral products. Different JRMEs would likely develop different types of expertise and capabilities in different sets of minerals, with enterprises emphasizing ferrous, or non-ferrous metals, industrial minerals, or precious minerals perhaps.

After a transition period, the JRMEs would be expected to be self-financing. Retained earnings from established operations should finance major proportions of new projects. But additional equity capital could also be raised, and debt financing (on various hard to soft terms) would also be appropriate for some projects.

The JRMEs could establish a range of types of relationships with parastatals and foreign companies in specific projects. These could include joint ventures with foreign companies, joint ventures with national parastatals, management contracts with foreign companies, management contracts with African parastatals where the JRME was providing the managerial and technical services, "turnkey" contracts where a foreign enterprise constructed a complete facility to be handed over and managed by the JRME, technical service contracts with foreign companies, or simply hiring non-African technical experts. All of these may be appropriate on their own or in various combinations depending upon the circumstances. The JRME would ultimately have a considerable number of affiliates related to the parent in a variety of ways.

In their mature state, the JRMEs would have established a set of concentrating, smelting, and refining activities appropriate to the minerals being produced. They would also be involved in the development of the basic transport, electrical energy, water supplies, town site and other types of infrastructure. The JRMEs might undertake these directly in some frontier regions, but more likely governments would play a major role in infrastructural development in consultation with the enterprises, and recouping a proportion of their costs through user fees.

In the long term, the JRME would play an important role in stimulating the minerals machinery and equipment industry among the signatory countries. The major instrument for this purpose would be the practices relating to procurement of inputs by the enterprises. It would be most unwise in terms of the international competitive position of a JRME to incorporate a high level of discrimination in procurement practices in favour of suppliers in the participating countries, as this would force higher priced or lower quality inputs on the enterprise. But while forcing the pace of local procurement would be counter-productive, there is reason to believe that non-discriminatory procurement by a JRME would be directed towards local suppliers more so than is the case with foreign companies which have a procurement bias towards foreign suppliers. Foreign mining houses often have traditional suppliers based in their home countries; in some cases they are also producers of mine machinery and equipment; and they have a natural tendency to standardize their machinery and equipment on a world-wide basis (making spare parts and repair personnel interchangeable globally). A JRME, on the other hand, would usually look to regional suppliers – and seek them out – for the high bulk and lower value equipment which can be produced by established capital goods and heavy engineering firms, and which are afforded a "natural" type of protection due to transport costs. Thus by maturity, one would expect that the JRMEs would foster important inter-industry or inter-sectoral linkages with this portion of the capital goods industry.

Getting There from Here: Start Up and Transition

How is a potential JRME to be established and to expand and evolve into an integrated African mining house? A number of scenarios may be envisaged, but only the most probable type of sequence is outlined here. The discussion below assumes that the first JRME considered in the previous section – the Intergovernmental Joint Enterprise along the lines of Air Afrique – is the type of enterprise to be established.

The first step in the creation of a Jointly Owned Regional Minerals Enterprise would be for a particular group of countries to reach an Agreement or perhaps a Treaty establishing the legal status of the enterprise; defining the governing bodies, and presenting the "articles of incorporation". The latter would include the purpose of the enterprise, a specification of its head office, the allocation of equity share capital and provisions for increasing capital contributions and for controlling share transfers. The basic administrative structure of the enterprise in terms of the composition, chairmanship, and powers of the Board of Directors would be defined. The constitution of the enterprise would be established. Other elements such as the distribution of profits and payment of dividends, the initial design of the management system could be included in the Agreement. The Agreement should also specify a standardized arrangement concerning the fiscal and financial provisions granted to the enterprise by the signatory states. This last item would be important in clarifying the legal and tax situation of the enterprise in individual countries in which it operates. The Treaty on Air Transport in Africa, establishing Air Afrique would provide a useful model or inspiration for a Treaty establishing a JRME. (ICAO, 1971)

Following the creation of the legal corporation and perhaps defining the legal framework in which it was to operate, the contracting states would have to provide their share of the initial subscription of equity capital, and select representatives for the Board of Directors. The Board then would select a General Manager, providing instructions for his subsequent actions. The General Manager, presumably, would then hire appropriate managerial and technical personnel and commence operations.

The immediate task of the enterprise would then be to establish projects as expeditiously as possible. This would be vital if the enterprise were to become self-financing quickly. New "greenfields" projects, or projects which must start "from scratch" working new ore bodies usually require a long gestation period, from five years minimum to 10 years more often. This may be too long to wait initially. Such projects could be evaluated and perhaps begun quickly, recognizing that a long time would likely elapse before they began to earn significant profits for the enterprise.

There are many potential rehabilitation projects in Africa, however, which could be brought on stream relatively quickly in periods ranging from two to five years (World Bank, 1981, 98). These would be especially appropriate for the JRME, which needs to generate its own cash flow quickly. Mine rehabilitation would be not only profitable for the JRME, but also most beneficial to the specific countries. Potential mine rehabilitation projects are numerous, because there have been many mines and/or processing facilities which shut down prematurely in the post-independence period as a result of administrative problems in some parastatals, disagreements between foreign companies and governments and consequent decapitalization or truncated reinvestment, problems of political instability or civil turbulence, and inadequate foreign exchange allotments for the purchase of imported inputs. There are probably inventories of such projects maintained by national governments, some major foreign mining companies, and perhaps the U.N. Economic Commission for Africa.

Financial resources for rehabilitation projects could be obtained from the range of sources mentioned previously in the Section entitled "Does Sub-Saharan Africa Need the Mineral Sector" p. 63, and include the Lome II "Sysmin", Arab OPEC Investment Banks or Funds, the World Bank, the African Investment Bank, African sub-regional investment banks, the European Investment Bank, or the European Development Fund. For goods projects which gave promise of earning reasonable rates of return and foreign exchange, there is little reason why western commercial banks would not lend. Or foreign minerals processing companies or mining houses might also invest. There is probably no serious lack of investible funds if the projects are good enough. But obviously with mineral process at 1981-1984 levels, there are fewer projects with high rates of return vis-à-vis a time period when mineral prices were higher.

A second way in which cash flow for a JRME could be generated quickly would be through the acquisition of certain existing minerals operations. This might be considered where better general management or pieces of crucial missing expertise could be inserted to "turn a company around" and make it commercially attractive. The problem with this alternative, however, is that it would require a lot of capital which might be difficult to raise internationally for the purpose of acquisitions.

Another type of activity with which a JRME could become involved quickly is exploration. A JRME could become a major conduit for the exploration monies provided by the UNDP for example. A JRME could consider assembling its own exploration arm or affiliate, or it could establish sub-contractual links with other exploration enterprises, or it could do both. Its exploration endeavours would most profitably be directed to specific potential mine sites rather than to the more general aerial mapping activities. Exploration would not generate cash flow except insofar as overheads were extracted from the exploration expenditures of foreign bodies administered by a JRME or utilized by its exploration arm.

In view of the wide varieties of ways in which a JRME might evolve as it approaches maturity, it would have to be designed so as to be flexible, adaptive and responsive to different opportunities.

Relationships with Governments

A serious stumbling block to the survival and flourishing of economic integration schemes among developing countries has been the uneven incidence of costs and benefits arising from the establishment of common external tariffs. (Typically the more industrially advanced countries in such schemes receive the benefits from increased demands for their industrial output, while the less advanced countries incur the costs of having their imports diverted to higher cost suppliers within the scheme.) The problem of uneven incidence of benefits could stifle the expansion of a JRME or lead to its dissolution.

The need for some sort of mechanism to ensure distributional equity among participating states is apparent in the JRME proposals. Once created, a JRME would search for viable projects in the member countries. It would start specific projects according to their commercial merit rather than on a national quota basis. This means that some participating countries would not have projects initially, and indeed for some time. Why would such countries, losing out initially in project development and the foreign exchange earnings, tax revenues and employment generated, remain as participants in a JRME? The major reason would be that such countries would still benefit from their share of the profits which they earned through their equity ownership in the JRME. Moreover, the JRME would hold some promise of future project development in such countries, and presumably attempt to fulfill this promise through the allocation of exploration expenditures in the countries initially losing out. These two mechanisms, profit earnings and investment in exploration to contracting states participating in the JRME but not having specific mine projects immediately should be useful devices for ensuring an equitable allocation of benefits from the functioning of the JRME, and should maintain the interest or enthusiasm of participating states.

A second important dimension of the relationship of a JRME to the member governments concerns the treatment of the JRME by national laws and provisions concerning taxation and profit remittance. The best of all possible arrangements would be for the contracting states to agree through a treaty to standardize tax treatment, profit remittance provisions and other relevant aspects of company or mining legislation. This again follows the precedent of the treaty establishing Air Afrique (ICAO, 1970). Such an agreement would undoubtedly be difficult to achieve. Among some groups of countries, mining legislation and taxation/profit remittance legislation may be harmonious enough already to be attractive to a JRME and to permit it to function well. On the other hand, among other groups of countries fiscal and legislative harmonization to some degree may be imperative for the functioning of a JRME. In such cases harmony would have to be established with the formation of a JRME.

SUMMARY AND CONCLUSION

This essay has examined the desirability and feasibility of establishing Jointly-Owned Regional Multinational Enterprises (JRMEs) – that is, state-owned or mixed public/private multinationals – in the mineral sector of the countries of Sub-Saharan Africa. The endeavour to establish such enterprises is of course relevant to a variety of other sectors, not only minerals. In the long term, the establishment of African-owned multinational enterprises, privately-owned as well as of the JRME variety, will be an important aspect of institutional development for improved indigenous control of economic activity, for greater regional integration and "collective self-reliance", for enhanced learning-by-doing and technological diffusion, and for stimulation of more efficient economic organization of economic activity.

There is little debate as to the innate desirability of establishing JRMEs as they are envisaged here. The mineral sector in many of the countries of the region has been languishing since Independence and probably will continue to do so for the decade of the 1980s, in view of levels and patterns of mineral exploration and project development. The sector could make a much more significant contribution to the development of many countries in the region in terms of foreign exchange earnings, tax revenues, inter-industry and inter-sectoral linkages, technological transfer, and infrastructural cost bearing. JRMEs could assist in the revival of the mineral sector. If successfully established as multi-stage, multinational mining houses, JRMEs may also develop many of the strengths demonstrated by private mineral multinationals, including economies of scale in management and technology, the pooling of financial resources and the spreading of risk, the development of organically-integrated sets of expertise, improved access to markets, and improved access to financial resources.

But how feasible is the JRME proposal? The basic conclusion of this study is that the establishment of viable and sustainable JRMEs is difficult and complex but possible. The essential requirements for such an enterprise include certain organizational characteristics to ensure viability, commitment and agreement among the governments of a group of countries, appropriate personnel, and adequate funding.

With respect to the required organizational features, a JRME must be commercially oriented. It must be operationally independent and financially autonomous yet ultimately accountable to the governments which own it (wholly or partially). It must also have an internal incentive structure which elicits the full energies and entrepreneurship of its personnel. An organizational structure can be designed to incorporate these necessary features.

Financing the initial organizational core of a new JRME constitutes a major hurdle for most Sub-Saharan African countries, especially in the international recessionary environment of the early 1980s. Raising equity subscriptions from contracting governments would be particularly difficult, as such subscriptions would have to be mainly in a convertible currency. One possibility, however, is that aid funds might be utilized in part for the subscription of the initial equity of the enterprises. Specific mineral development projects would likely be somewhat easier to finance. For good projects, there are a variety of international financial institutions, commercial banks, development funds, and aid donors which could be tapped for the hard currency cost components. External funding sources such as the UNDP might also be utilized for exploration activities.

The availability for a JRME is also a constraint, as qualified mining engineers, geologists, accountants, etc. are limited in most Sub-Saharan African countries. Some such personnel would likely have to be acquired initially from expatriate sources, for a period of time. Generalist managers for a JRME could likely be obtained more readily from the region. It must be emphasized, however, that an important facet of the functioning of such an enterprise, and also an important consequence of its operation is "learning by doing", that is, developing skilled managerial personnel on the job (a potentiality that is sometimes impaired through private multinational enterprises.)

The mature JRMEs, as envisaged in this study, would be similar to large western mining houses in that they would be multinational, multi-stage from exploration to marketing, multi-metallic or multi-mineral and multi-project. But they would be African owned and controlled. How is such an enterprise to be established and to expand and evolve into an integrated African mining house? The essential scenario would involve an intergovernmental agreement such as the Treaty which founded Air Afrique, to establish a JRME legally, to define the legal framework within which it is to operate, and to establish a Board of Directors which would select the General Manager. Second, governments would have to raise and pay their initial subscriptions of the equity capital. The General Manager, in accordance with instructions from the Board of Directors, would hire the appropriate personnel. Third, with the organizational nucleus in operation, the overriding imperative would be to bring on stream as soon as possible high quality mineral projects which would generate cash flow and profits, in order to achieve self-financing and autonomy very quickly. The types of projects most appropriate would be mine rehabilitation projects rather than "greenfields" projects due to the very long gestation period of the latter compared to the former. The foreign exchange costs of these likely could be financed externally. Once well established and earning profits, a JRME could consider "greenfields" projects. Externally funded exploration could be commenced quickly, through sub-contracting with exploration enterprises.

One most important issue has not been addressed in this study, nor could it have been. This is the question of the relative value for the countries of Sub-Saharan Africa of investing funds, allocating personnel, and devoting political attention and energy for the establishment of JRMEs in comparison with all of the other projects and institutions which would be of worth. In other words, what priority should the establishment of JRMEs have in view of the other urgent demands on the governments and on investible resources of the region? This is a question which cannot be answered adequately in general terms and from a distance. The benefits and costs, broadly conceived, of establishing JRMEs *vis-à-vis* other endeavours can only be weighed by the governments of a particular African sub-region. Such an evaluation of relative worth can only be made by those governments likely to be involved. All that has been suggested in this study is that the JRME proposal specifically, and jointly-owned regional enterprises more generally, are potentially of significant value as development-generating institutions in the Sub-Saharan African region.

This study of JRME feasibility has also been conducted in rather general terms. There has been no attempt to put forward a specific organizational design or plan of action for the creation and development of a JRME which would be suitable for a specific group of countries. Nor has there been any attempt to quantify the financial requirements or to determine a precise idea of the personnel which would be required for a concrete JRME proposal. Clearly, this would be premature in a study such as this. What has been attempted is to establish that the JRME proposal is worthy of consideration by the countries of Sub-Saharan Africa. The next stop in the exploration of the feasibility of establishing JRMEs would involve consultation by a body such as the United National Economic Commission for Africa with governments in a particular sub-region in Africa to ascertain their interest in the proposal. If there is sufficient interest on the part of governments, a further detailed elaboration and examination of a concrete JRME propals would be appropriate.

Appendix Table A. Non-Fuel Minerals and Metals*: Export Shares, 1955 to 1979

	1955	1965	1973	1979
	%	%	%	%
Developing Countries	21.0	18.8	15.9	15.6
Developing America	9.2	8.4	6.1	6.7
Developing Africa	8.1	6.4	5.0	3.0
West Asia	0.3	0.3	0.4	0.4
South & S.E. Asia	3.5	3.7	3.5	4.7
Oceania	—	—	—	—
Developed Market Economies	67.7	68.3	73.2	74.8
Canada	9.9	9.2	7.6	5.8
United States	11.5	8.1	6.4	6.5
Australia/New Zealand	1.2	1.5	3.2	2.6
Japan	2.9	6.3	9.4	10.9
South Africa	2.0	1.9	1.7	—
Centrally Planned Economies	11.2	13.0	11.1	8.8
USSR	5.1	8.0	6.4	4.9
Other Eastern Europe	4.0	4.0	3.9	3.2
Asia	2.1	1.0	0.8	.7
World	100.0	100.0	100.0	
	$11.4b	$34.3b	$60.1b	$140.7

*Note: "Non-Fuel Minerals and Metals" include SITC 27 28 67 68, that is, crude minerals, crude fertilizers, ores, scrap, ferrous and non-ferrous metals.
Source: UNCTAD, *Handbook of International Trade and Development Statistics, 1976*, and *Supplement 1980*, New York: United Nations, 1976 and 1980.

Appendix Table B. Crude Minerals, Fertilizers, Metallferrous Ores and Scrap: Export Shares, 1955-1979

	1955	1965	1973	1979
	%	%	%	%
Developing Countries	33.0	33.9	30.2	28.7
Developing America	14.5	16.7	14.0	13.4
Developing Africa	10.7	9.6	7.1	6.7
West Asia	0.9	0.8	1.0	1.1
South & S.E. Asia	7.2	6.8	5.9	5.9
Oceania	—	—	—	—
Developed Market Economies	52.6	54.7	58.2	59.5
Canada	13.7	15.9	16.3	12.6
United States	11.8	10.6	10.0	13.3
Australia/New Zealand	1.5	2.0	7.6	5.3
South Africa	5.0	4.3	2.8	
Centrally Planned Economies	14.4	12.1	11.6	11.7
USSR	4.4	7.1	8.0	7.5
Other Eastern Europe	6.0	3.3	2.4	2.7
Asia	4.0	1.0	1.2	1.4
World	100.0	100.0	100.0	100.0
	$3.4b	$6.3b	$14.8b	$33.06b

Appendix Table C. Non-Ferrous Metals: Export Shares 1955 to 1979

	1955	1965	1973	1979
Developing Countries	33.9	28.6	24.4	22.4
Developing America	14.4	11.1	7.5	10.0
Developing Africa	15.6	12.4	11.3	5.3
West Asia	0.0	0.2	0.2	—
South & S.E. Asia	4.2	5.0	4.7	6.3
Oceania	—	—	—	—
Developing Market Economies	59.2	63.1	66.3	69.9
Canada	16.1	13.0	9.8	6.9
United States	6.3	8.2	6.3	6.7
Australia/New Zealand	2.1	2.4	3.3	3.2
South Africa	1.4	1.5	2.4	—
Centrally Planned Economies	5.9	8.4	9.9	7.7
USSR	3.5	6.1	7.0	4.3
Other Eastern Europe	0.7	1.7	2.1	2.6
Asia	1.7	0.6	0.8	.8
World	100.0	100.0	100.0	100.0
	$3.6b	$6.7b	$16.9b	$37.0b

Source: UNCTAD, *Handbook of International Trade and Development Statistics, 1976*, and *Supplement, 1980*, New York: United Nations, 1976 and 1980.

List of Interviews

United Nations, Economic Commission for Africa

Dr. N. Peter Mwanza, Director, National Resources Division
Dr. Moshe, Chief, Minerals Sector, National Resources Division

Kenya

Mr. Andango, Chief Mining Engineer, Mines and Geological Survey
Mr. R. Geddes, Geologist, Mines and Geological Survey
Mr. John Lang, Management Enterprise Ltd.
Mr. Colin J. Richards, Managing Director, Magadi Sodu Company, PLC

Tanzania

Prof. M. Bagachwa, Economic Research Bureau, University of Dar es Salaam
Mr. P. Bowani, Minister, Ministry of Minerals
Mr. A. N. Kassum, Minister, Ministry of Energy
Mr. Lwakatare, Deputy Minister, Ministry of Minerals
Prof. B. Mongula, Institute of Development Studies, University of Dar es Salaam

Zambia

Dr. E. M. Kolsko, Deputy Director, Corporate Planning, Zambia Consolidated Copper Mines Ltd.
Mr. L. M. Likulunga, Assistant Manager, Development Bank of Zambia
Mr. James Mtomgo, Director of Economic and Technical Cooperation, National Commission of Development Planning
Prof. G. B. Misra, School of Mines, University of Zambia
Dr. Mwanang'onze, Permanent Secretary, Ministry of Mines
Mr. Willie Sweta, Director, Mines Development Department, Ministry of Mines
Dr. Ernest H. Tere, Dean, School of Mines, University of Zambia
Mr. P. K. Verma, Senior Mining Engineer, Mines Development Department, Ministry of Mines
Dr. F. D. Yamba, Dean, School of Engineering, University of Zambia

Zimbabwe

Mr. F. C. Bohmka, Managing Director Rio Projects Ltd., Rio Tinto Zimbabwe Ltd.
Mr. J. M. Clutten, Chief Geologist, Anglo American Corporation Services Ltd.
Mr. M. J. Harris, Director, MTD Management Services Ltd., MTD Group
Mr. D. Robinson, Ministry of Mines
Mr. Fairbairn, Ministry of Finance, Economic Development and Planning

Bibliography

Baldwin, W. L. (1983) *The World Tin Market: Political Pricing and Economic Competion,* (Durham, N.C., U.S.A.: Duke University Press).

Bosson, R. and Varon, B., (1977). *The Mining Industry and the Developing Countries,* (New York: Oxford University Press).

Choksi, A. M., (1979). *State Intervention in the Industrialization of Developing Countries: Selected Issues,* World Bank Staff Working Paper, No. 341, (Washington, D.C., World Bank).

Cobbe, J. H. (1979). *Governments and Mining Companies in Developing Countries* (Boulder Colorado: Westview Press).

Cronje, S., Ling Mu, and Cronje G., (1976). *Lonrho: Portrait of a Multinational* (London: Penguin).

Cunningham, S., (1981). *The Copper Industry in Zambia: Foreign Mining Companies in a Developing Country.* (New York: Praeger).

Economist, (July 23, 1983) "Here Come the Third World Multinationals".

Energy, Mines and Resources Canada (1983) Mineral Policy: A Discussion Paper, (Ottawa: EMR).

Engineering and Mining Journal (January, 1984) "Mining Investment, 1984, (New York).

Faber, M. and Brown, R. (1981) "Reply", *Overseas Development Institute Review,* 1: 1981.

Hance, W. A. (May, 1971). "Africa's Minerals: Myths and Realities", *Africa Report*, 16:5.

International Civil Aviation Organization (1970), *Treaty on Air Transport in Africa: Establishment of Air Afrique* (Montreal: ICAO).

Lanning, G. and Mueller, M., (1979), *Africa Undermined: Mining Companies and the Underdevelopment of Africa*, (London: Penguin Books).

Macleod-Smith, A. (1981), "Is the International Mining Industry Necessary to Africa?", *ODI Review*, 1: 1981.

Mikesell, R. F. (1979 a), *New Patterns of World Mineral Development* (New York: British-North America Committee).

Mikesell, R. F. (1979b) *The World Copper Industry: Structure and Economic Analysis*, (Baltimore, Johns Hopkins University Press).

Mikesell, R. F. (1983) *Foreign Investment in Mining Projects*, (Cambridge, Mass: Oelgeschlager, Gunn and Hain).

Mining Journal (1981) *Annual Review, 1981*, (London: Mining Journal).

Nankani, G., (1979) *Development Problems of Mineral Exporting Countries*, World Bank Staff Working Paper No. 354 (Washington, D.C.: World Bank).

Ochala, S. (1975) *Minerals in African Underdevelopment*, (London: Bogle-L'Ouverture).

Petro-Canada International Assistance Corporation (1983) *1982 Annual Report*, (Ottawa: Petro-Can International).

Radetski, M. (1982) "Has Political Risk Scared Mineral Investment away from the Deposits in Developing Countries?", *World Development* 10:1.

Ritter, A. R. M., (1984), "Policy Making in the Mineral Sector: Global, Continental and Regional Dimensions" in Pammett, J. and Tomlin B. (editors), *The Integration Question: Political Economy and Public Policy in Canada and North America* (Toronto: Addison-Wesley).

Sideri, S., and John, S. (1980), *Mining for Development in the Third World: State Enterprises and International Economy* (New York: Pergamon Press).

Shirley, Mary M. (1983), *Managing State-Owned Enterprises* World Bank Staff Working Paper No. 577 (Washington, D. C., World Bank).

Smith, D. N., and Wells, L. T. (1975) *Negotiating Third World Mineral Agreements*, (Cambridge Massachusetts: Ballinger Publishing Publishing Co.).

Thoburn, J. (1981), *Multinationals, Mining and Development: A Study of the Tin Industry*, (Westmead U.K.: Gower).

United Nations, Centre on Transnational Corporations (1983), *Transnational Corporations in World Development, Third Review*, (United Nations, New York).

United Nations, Conference on Trade and Development, (May, 1983) *The Promotion of Multinational Marketing Enterprises of Developing Countries, Production and marketing of copper by developing countries*, TD/B/C.7/56 (Geneva: UNCTAD).

United Nations, Economic Commission for Africa (1981) *Proceedings of the First Regional Conference on the Development and Utilization of Mineral Resources in Africa* (UNECA, Addis Ababa).

World Bank, (1981) *Accelerated Development in Sub-Saharan Africa: An Agenda for Action* (World Bank, Washington, D.C.).

World Bank, (1983) *World Development Report 1983,* (World Bank, Washington, D.C.).

Zambia Consolidated Copper Mines Ltd. (1983) *1982 Annual Report* (Lusaka: ZCCM).

CHAPTER 5

Afro-Arab Partnership for Development

Karl Lavrenčič

BADEA

As the Arabs and Africans look back on the past ten years of their mutual co-operation they can scarcely avoid a certain feeling of disappointment. The high hopes initially placed in that co-operation or partnership have not been fulfilled, or have only in part. Yet after these years the co-operation continues and some valuable experience has in the meantime been accumulated. The Arab Governments and their Funds have asserted their presence in the Sub-Saharan region where they had little connection before.

If today many of these Arab Governments and their institutions are household names in Black Africa this is in no small measure due to the work and influence of one agency, which the Arab countries had created especially to help the non-Arab region of the Continent and promote friendship and solidarity with it. The Arab Bank for Economic Development in Africa, usually referred to as BADEA, has all these years been very much more than a financial institution for supplying concessional loans, although this was important. In sum, what BADEA has been is what its Tunisian President and Managing Director, Dr. Chedly Ayari, had said in 1975 that it was going to be, "we are acting as spokesmen for the Africans in the Arab world and spokesmen for the Arabs in Africa." The dialogues have continued, enriching mutual knowlege and experience.

From 1973 to 1982 the Arab Governments and their agencies had committed a total of over US$8 billion in development aid to the non-Arab African nations. This was a vast sum of money by any standards and now when the coffers of several formerly rich Arab States are all but empty as their commitments have far outpaced the rapidly shrinking revenues, questions are bound to be asked whether it was wise to spend so much money for aid to others and whether the assistance could not have been used more effectively. Such questions are legitimate and they have indeed been put. It was announced in April 1983 that Arab donor agencies would take a long, hard look at their activities, and a report is due to be published on the results of the reappraisal early in 1984.

But it is unlikely that the report will be negative. The President of BADEA has repeatedly made clear that Arab commitment to help Africa stands. However critical one can be of the way Arab aid was used, there is little doubt that the ten years of financial co-operation for development, marked by a steady flow of Arab funds to the African region, resulted in many important projects being executed – roads, ports, airports and other transport infrastructure, agricultural and rural development, hydroelectric stations, manufacturing plants and others. These developtment schemes are of lasting value and they could almost certainly not have been realized without Arab financial help.

If not all the hopes entertained in the heady days of Arab-African rapprochement have been fulfilled, it is nonetheless plain today that the need for the partnership is still there and that it has, in fact, never been greater. When the Third World is more and more compelled to turn to itself and draw strength from its own resources and solidarity, Afro-Arab co-operation fits in this wider pattern of self-reliance of developing and non-aligned nations.

Politically, there is little cause for jubilation on the part of either the Arab or the Black African communities, as these go through their respective agonies and tribulations which one day may well appear as so many teething troubles of recently emerging nations.

The two "catalyst" adversaries, Zionism and South Africa, although themselves by no means the actual source of Arab-African co-operation, have nevertheless done more than anything else to bring the two communities closer together. Yet they have not been eliminated or overcome – quite the contrary. Having partly drawn force and encouragement from the weaknesses and dissensions of their victims, each of the two has grown in power and influence, representing a much more serious menace now than they did even ten years ago.

In the economic field, too, things have changed for the worse. The celebrated Arab "oil weapon" has been blunted through the vagaries of world demand for oil and declining revenues which mean that the Arab petroleum exporting countries put together now register a large deficit on their current account compared with sizeable surpluses in the seventies.[1*] Africa, for its part, has been passing through an economic and financial crisis of unparalleled and unprecedented gravity. At the end of 1983, 20 out of the 41 African developing countries were facing serious food shortfalls, and some 150 million people were actually on the brink of starvation.[2]

For a variety of reasons more and more African countries are unable to pay their way and are forced to seek external assistance. The ultimate result can only be even greater dependence on the industrialized world, especially on the former colonial powers, and a serious erosion of economic as well as political independence and sovereignty. A continuation on this road would almost unavoidably result in a return to colonial slavery, as the world dominated by greed and lust for power will have no mercy for the weak and helpless.

There are, it is true, perfectly sound theories about a fundamental convergence of interests between the developed and developing countries, the North and the South. Many influential and far-sighted men in the industrialized countries have

*See Notes section at end of Chapter.

been exposing the folly of a policy based on the impoverishment of the developing world, of the oil-exporting as well as the oil-importing countries. It stands to reason that all mankind would benefit from greater and more evenly distributed purchasing power and trade among nations, not least the industrialized countries themselves.

But by 1983 we could see in a considerable number of international conferences and meetings, including UNCTAD VI in Belgrade, that such theories cannot as yet prevail over sectional interests. What is surely needed is to create a shift in the balance of economic power and in the current pattern of exchanges. The developing countries have no choice but to do more themselves and help each other more in order that the New International Economic Order may be brought about. In this respect closer co-operation between the Arab and African regions with their huge development potential assumes extraordinary and timely significance.

IMPORTANCE OF THE POLITICAL FACTOR

Two events occurred by November 1973 which made the Arab Governments decide, at their summit conference in Algiers, to start a new era of their relations with Black Africa. The new era, as they saw it, was to extend mutual support and sympathy, lent consistently to the United Nations and other international fora, to an institutional reality. The Arab Heads of State and Government decided to create three institutions designed to assist non-Arab developing Africa following *first* a large increase in revenues of the petroleum exporting countries in that year, this being the "enabling" factor, and *second*, the impressive show of solidarity on the part of Black African countries when nearly all of them had broken their diplomatic relations with Israel.

The Arab Governments were to set up and finance a development agency, a fund to help in balance of payments emergencies, particularly when resulting from higher prices of petroleum, and a small fund for technical assistance to be used particularly for teaching the Arabic language.

The development agency, BADEA, opened for business in Khartoum in March 1975. The Special Arab Aid Fund for Africa (SAAFA) began work a year earlier but was wound up in 1977 after having disbursed a total of US $214.244 million and its capital of $350 million was added to that of the Bank which had already been administering the Fund for some time.

In another important development, Arab Funds were to be made available to non-Arab countries as well, particularly those in Africa while these agencies, including the Saudi Fund for Development (SFD), Kuwait Fund for Arab Economic Development (KFAED) and the Abu Dhabi Fund for Arab Economic Development (ADFAED) also had their respective capital bases substantially increased.

These gestures were not to be regarded as a "quid pro quo", a kind of reward to

African countries for having broken their diplomatic ties with Israel. Neither did the Africans see it as such; for them, or most of them, this was a decision of principle, taken in order to demonstrate solidarity in an area of special concern to the Arab world – the problem of Palestine.[3]

The matter was to come up for comment and discussion many times over the following ten years. But queries were answered very much in the same vein, even after the international situation changed somewhat, especially when one important Arab country itself made peace with Israel in 1979.

Would these changes, including the fact that Israel withdrew from the Sinai peninsula, allow a resumption of diplomatic relations on the part of African countries which wished to do so but were at the same time reluctant to lose Arab support? The Arabs made perfectly plain that resumption of diplomatic relations with Israel was regarded by them as a hostile act. An African country committing such an act was to be seen as opting out of the concept of Afro-Arab friendship and solidarity. Dr. Ayari, the President of BADEA, explained this Arab thinking to a gathering of British businessmen in London in September 1983 when he said:

> The African countries renewing diplomatic ties with Israel offend against the Afro-Arab Charter of Cooperation signed in Cairo by 60 Arab and African leaders. These 60 States said in their Charter that as long as an inch of either Arab or African land was not free, "we shall consider ourselves totally mobilized in order to make such territory free". I am talking about total Arab and total African land, not Egyptian land, or Namibia. And this statement in the Charter is linking us, the Arabs and Africans in our political struggle. In 1983 there was still some Arab and some African land which was not free. So, there can be no change in our solidarity. When a country, be it Arab or African, chooses to violate the Charter by renewing diplomatic ties with a country that is responsible for the occupation of that land we shall regard such country – which of course has sovereign right to do what it has done – as having opted out of our Charter of Afro-Arab Co-operation and stipulations of that Charter, including economic and financial co-operation, as no longer applying to the country concerned. For this reason we have done in the cases of Zaire and Liberia exactly what the Charter tells us to do: no more co-operation. If tomorrow an Arab State would resume diplomatic relations with South Africa, I think, this Arab State would also be expelled from the Afro-Arab co-operation and its Charter.

It was significant that the decision to stop all aid to Zaire was made in 1982 by all the Arab Governments and institutions, on the initiative of BADEA, the only Arab institution specifically designed to foster Afro-Arab friendship and solidarity. This showed that these factors were equally important to agencies whose terms of reference do not expressly refer to political relations, such as for example the KFAED. At the time of writing no such decision was formally announced by the Arab agencies in respect to Liberia, but there is no doubt that it would be, in due course, although it is understood that BADEA and other Arab Funds would continue to honour the commitments already undertaken in favour of that country.

Political consensus between the Arabs and Africans, as represented by their respective regional organizations, the League of Arab States and the Organization of African Unity, found its high point at the above-mentioned Cairo summit conference in March 1977. The occasion was used to agree on a detailed programme of political, economic, financial, social and cultural co-operation with the tasks of implementation entrusted to a number of institutions, to consolidate the first permanent machinery of Afro-Arab co-operation.

The Summit itself was to be the supreme organ of the alliance, meeting at least every three years. Plenary meetings at a ministerial level were to be held every 18 months. A Standing Commission of Afro-Arab Co-operation, consisting of two delegations of 12 Foreign Ministers each, appointed by the respective organizations, the Arab League and OAU, was to become the policy-drafting and chief executive organ of the new partnership, to be convened every six months. In addition, there was to be a Co-ordinating Committee, including the two Secretaries-General and the heads of the delegations to the Standing Commission, to monitor and help the implementation of joint decisions. Various technical committees for specific areas of co-operation were also appointed.[4]

Yet this elaborate machinery could not be said to have worked properly, from the start. The first major stumbling block arose in 1979 when Egypt, a member of the African delegation of 12 to the Standing Commission, was expelled from the Arab League and was ostracised by the Arab world after concluding the peace treaty with Israel. The Standing Commission could no longer meet and it was not until July 1981 that the OAU appointed a new delegation of 12 which did not include Egypt. The Commission then resumed its meetings, but no important decisions or new initiatives were recorded as it was generally felt that the long overdue summit conference of African and Arab countries was needed to bring the co-operation forward.

It should be pointed out that the large and somewhat unwieldy institutions for Afro-Arab co-operation created in Cairo in 1977 could not be expected to function smoothly at a time when both the Arab League and the OAU were facing serious problems, arising from external aggression as well as internal dissension. Afro-Arab co-operation could not be regarded as a priority by preoccupied national leaders, yet they alone were in a position to reform the institutions and machinery and bring out new ideas.

Having said that, however, one ought to add that the institutions and programmes agreed by the first Afro-Arab Summit have never been officially disowned. On the contrary, both the Arab League and the Organization of African Unity have repeatedly reaffirmed their commitment to the blueprint of co-operation agreed in 1977, stressing the urgent need for the partnership to continue and expand and more particularly to see an integration of the respective development plans, the Arab Amman Economic Strategy and the Lagos Plan of Action of the OAU.

THE FLOW OF ARAB AID

From 1975 to the end of 1982 Arab oil-exporting countries committed a total of US$7,373.6 million for the benefit of the 41 Sub-Saharan African developing countries, of which $6,135.2 million was supplied as Official Development Assistance, i.e. on concessional terms with a grant element of at least 25 per cent. Forty-six per cent of this aid was destined for 19 Least Developed Countries, and in this case the grant element averaged 92.7 per cent.[5]

Arab aid commitment in favour of Africa rose in 1980 to $1,327.1 million from $552.8 million in the previous year, to decline in 1981 to $1,160.6 million and to 1,066 million in 1982. It is nevertheless remarkable that the commitment held up so well in the latter year when the revenues of the oil-exporting countries went down quite sharply. No figures are available for 1983, but it is expected that there is a further decline in commitment, since only four Arab countries, Saudi Arabia, Kuwait, The United Arab Emirates and Qatar, still offered financial assistance to other Third World countries.

Geographically, there was a certain bias in favour of West Africa, partly explained by the larger number of countries and greater population than in the eastern half of the Continent. The Sahel region's seven non-Arab countries benefited from nearly a third of the total aid effort. One can notice a stress on aid for Islamic countries and those with large Muslim communities on the part of some Arab donors. The Islamic Development Bank, which is an important instrument of Arab economic aid, is, of course, reserved for Muslim countries only. But it should be pointed out that African Muslim countries, for instance those in the Sahel belt, are also among the poorest of the Continent.

In 1974-81 Mali and Guinea, both Muslim, received $411.3 million and $647 million of Arab aid respectively, but the non-Muslim countries of Africa also shared substantially in the total, for instance Zaire with $411.4 million, Kenya with $340.2 million and Zambia with $323.6 million.[6] Zimbabwe received more than almost any other country in the short period of time since independence because of its special reconstruction problems and its exposed position in regard to South African aggression and subversion. For similar reasons countries like Mozambique, Angola, Lesotho and Botswana received substantial support. For example, the latter two countries were enabled to construct international airports in order to lessen their dependence on South Africa. On similar grounds Lesotho is being assisted in a large farm development programme.

There has never been any partnership on account of the nature of a country's political regime. Countries with systems based on Marxism-Leninism, such as Benin and Guinea-Bissau, received no less favourable treatment than countries with free-market economies, such as Kenya.

While all Arab aid comes from a depletable source, namely petroleum, it has the additional merit of not being tied for procurement in any particular country, as is much of the aid supplied by industrialized countries. This has been an additional reason for the heavy emphasis in Arab aid on the Most Seriously Affected (MSA) Countries, while some industrialized countries prefer to direct their aid to medium-rich developing countries in the hope of gaining better and quicker commercial advantages. Arab spokesmen have consistently supported proposals at international fora for all development aid to be free of all ties. No supplies or services have, however, been permitted for Arab-assisted projects from companies and agencies figuring in the black lists of boycott of Israel and South Africa.

In their technical criteria for project aid, Arab agencies have generally adhered to the principles applied by other international institutions, such as the World Bank, stressing in particular the need for all assistance schemes to be well-researched, and economically and financially viable. But over the years the Arabs have been developing a distinct philosophy and approach to reflect the principles of solidarity with the Third World, political as well as economic and social. The long-term economic and social significance of a road construction programme may thus outweigh its strictly commercial value and traffic density considerations as in case of a highway to open up an isolated region of high agricultural potential.

Most of the Arab aid commitment (nearly 64 per cent of the total) has been for specific economic development projects; just over 36 per cent has been allocated to non-project assistance. Transport infrastructure, including roads, railways, airports and ports, and agricultural and rural development each recieved about one-fifth of the total in 1975-82, followed by energy schemes and manufacturing ventures. Much of the non-project aid was for balance of payments support, and less than 5 per cent of the overall commitment was for social services, which covered help for Muslim religious communities and the construction of mosques.

Although the major part of the Arab aid to the Third World in general and to Africa in particular has been dispensed directly by the Governments, with Saudi Arabia well in the lead, an increasing portion is channelled through special institutions created by the Arab Governments, mostly after the first oil boom in 1973-74. These institutions, which have preserved close working ties with the Arab donor Governments, include the Arab "Co-ordination Committee", meeting as a rule twice a year at the level of operational department heads and once a year at the level of chief executives.[7] ADFAED, KFAED, SFD, the Iraqi Fund for External Development (IFED), the Libyan Arab Foreign Bank (LAFB) and the State of Qatar as bilateral agencies, the two Arab multilaterals, BADEA and the Arab Fund for Economic and Social Development (AFESD – dispersing aid only for members of the Arab League) and the two mostly Arab-financed institutions, the OPEC Fund for International Development (OFID) and the Islamic Development Bank (IsDB) are members of the Committee which serves to co-ordinate Arab aid policies and to standardize their practices. A major subject of discussion is usually the question of co-financing, as the Arab agencies have been increasingly endeavouring to pool their resources in order to finance jointly much or part of a development project. This enables the Arab interests to exercise a certain control over the section of the scheme which they fund, but co-financing among Arab Funds as well as between these and a large number of non-Arab international agencies, including the World Bank and its affiliates, and bilateral governmental institutions, is more and more seen as a necessity given the high cost of many projects and the ceiling set by the respective institutions for their commitments. Normally, Arab co-financing agencies appoint one agency as co-ordinator or leader, to direct and supervise joint operations in a given project.

The Arab institutions or Funds (which now command a combined capital of nearly $24 billion) are all independent agencies, each with its own juridical personality and statute. Their terms of reference often differ. For instance, the IsDB is allowed to participate in a project with equity, while the KFAED may only dispense loans and grants.

What may at first seem a bewildering variety of Arab sources of aid is much more coherent and simple in practice. Often the same people are involved in a number of institutions, especially the Ministers of Finance of the leading donor countries. At all events, the Arab governors and chief executives are a relatively small group of experts who know each other well and usually arrive at joint decisions with the required speed and efficiency. The variety of institutions makes for greater flexibility and choice, for the benefit of the donors as well as the recipients.

CONCLUDING REMARKS

If Afro-Arab co-operation appears at this moment in some difficulties, the same can be said of many other projects, movements and organizations in this time of crisis, especially in the Third World. Indeed, the Afro-Arab partnership can only be as effective and successful as the two parent organizations – the Arab League and the Organization of African Unity – allow it to be or are capable of making it. This in turn depends on the Governments and States which make up the two communities and their mutual relations.

Good intentions are not enough. If they were, many of the proposals and plans regarding closer Afro-Arab co-operation would long have been put into effect.[8] The need for further progress has been confirmed and reaffirmed by the Heads of State and Government of both sides on many occasions, as recently as 1983.

A proposal for a closer working relationship between the Arab League and the OAU has in principle been agreed. This provides for consultation between the two organizations at international meetings and co-operation in matters of common concern. The two Secretaries-General are to maintain a close and permanent contact through special representatives attached to the respective headquarters.

Both sides agree that there should be more trade between African and Arab countries, as this so far has been negligible and in some respects shrinking in relative terms. Exports to and imports from Africa represent considerably less than 1 per cent of the Arab region's total. Studies on the subject have been made, including one by the Economic Commission for Africa on the initiative of BADEA. Private investment, particularly Arab investment in Africa, ought to be encouraged, according to other proposals and an investment guarantee fund set up to protect against non-commercial risks, such as nationalization. In cultural affairs the establishment of a Centre of African and Arab Studies has been proposed. For all these suggestions to materialize effective Government intervention is needed. Governments alone can introduce trade prferences, enact investment inducements, and undertake other measures. For this purpose new initiatives, and above all another Afro-Arab summit would be necessary.

There is little doubt that the Afro-Arab movement needs a fresh boost in order to enable it reach new horizons.[9] It cannot indefinitely remain a largely one-sided affair, confined to flows of concessional capital from one region to the other.

ANNEX

BADEA: "PRIMUS INTER PARES"

BADEA is the first specialized development agency set up by one Third World region for the benefit of another. With its current capital at $988.25 million, the Bank had by the end of 1983 committed a total of $597.889 million in project aid, to which the SAAFA supplied non-project aid of $214.244 million which should be added to arrive at the overall commitment of the Bank so far.[10] All the 41 qualifying countries, except two, Nigeria and Malawi, have been assisted to some degree.

BADEA has clearly endeavoured to cover as many of the eligible countries as soon as possible because the Bank's presence makes it easier for the country concerned to attract other Arab and to some extent even non-Arab finance. BADEA has been taking its role as a catalyst of capital flows to the region very seriously; this is reflected in the large amount of co-financing done with BADEA.*

By the end of 1982 BADEA participated with other Arab agencies in co-financing 35 projects costing $3.318 billion with the combined Arab contribution amounting to $930.56 million.[11] The ratio between Arab participation and total investment cost has been increasing in recent years; in 14 out of the 35 projects Arab money was responsible for more than half the total finance. There has been a noticeable tendency on the part of Arab agencies to make their impact felt on the project they co-financed. BADEA's statutes now permit an investment of up to $15 million in a single project and a maximum coverage of 80 per cent of the project cost.

In Arab financing of development projects in non-Arab Africa, the role of BADEA is as a rule that of the "primus inter pares". This makes the role played by BADEA in financing African development and generally in Afro-Arab co-operation much greater than the actual money committed and disbursed by the Bank, which has been only about one-tenth of the Arab total for the region.

*One should point out, however, that there have been cases when other Arab Funds rather than the Khartoum-based Bank had taken the lead and given the initiative for funding a development scheme in non-Arab Africa, in which BADEA later joined.

BADEA, which is funded by 18 Arab countries (with Saudi Arabia supplying the largest single share) and whose Ministers of Finance are the Bank's Governors, has the status of an inter-governmental agency and its representatives are regularly invited to the relevant international and regional conferences, including those sponsored by the U.N., the OAU and the Arab League. On all such occasions the Bank has been prominent in influencing moves to deepen and expand Afro-Arab co-operation in all its various features. The Bank has furthermore concluded many formal agreements of co-operation with such institutions as the World Bank and the United Nations Development Programme as well as the individual governments involved in African development. The Bank has also financed studies of particular African development issues, one notable example being a study on the Sahel, made at the request of Arab Funds.

The Bank, which only lends for economic development (and does not finance social services, provide balance of payments or budgetary support or participate in equity) had earmarked 48.1 per cent of its commitment of $513.96 million in 1975-82 for various infrastructure projects, particularly transport facilities. Several of these projects have recently been implemented, as has for example the Ndola-Kitwe road project in Zambia for which the Bank had supplied a loan of $10 million with 4 per cent interest repayable over 25 years, including a grace period of 5 years. Another important project operational in the transport sector is the extension of the Cotonou port in Benin for which the Bank has disbursed two loans totalling $7.3 million. The port now plays an important regional role apart from serving Benin itself.

Agriculture, fisheries, forestry and general rural development come second in the list of commitments by sector in the period referred to, accounting for 21.6 per cent of the total. Most of the projects under this heading are now already serving the respective economies – in Kenya, Tanzania, Senagal, Mali, Guinea, Upper Volta, and elsewhere.

Industry came third with 18 per cent of the commitment, as well as building materials, which figure prominently as vital supplies for local construction industries. A clinker factory in Guinea and a cement plant in Benin are just two examples of such ventures, which are now successfully integrated in the economic life of the recipient countries and regions.

In the energy sector, which received 12.3 per cent of the total during the first eight years of the Bank's operations, the Sélingué Dam, Mali's major development scheme, was officially commissioned in December 1982. Over $60 million was supplied by various Arab interests for this project, $15 million by BADEA itself on terms which included interest at 2 per cent, maturity of 25 years and a grace period of 10 years. The Andekaleka (Madagascar) and Kpong (Ghana) hydroelectric stations co-financed by BADEA were also commissioned in 1982.

BADEA lending terms have stiffened somewhat in recent years, with the grant element averaging 19.24 per cent in 1982, compared with 21.74 per cent in the previous year and 47.42 per cent in 1976. The reduction accorded with general world trends, but concessionality of BADEA loans has remained well above the average lending terms available to Sub-Saharan Africa.

At their annual meeting in April 1983, the BADEA Governors approved a five-year plan prepared by the management, according to which the Bank would be lending at an average annual rate of about $80 million, an amount that was exceeded in the first year of the programme when nearly $84 million was committed for 12 development projects and 5 technical assistance operations.

Table 5.1. BADEA Commitments in 1983 ($ thousands)

Recipient	Project	Amount	Interest (%)	Maturity (years)	Grace Period (years)
Association of Faculties of Agriculture in Africa	Technical assistance	20	(grant)		
Benin	Tech. ass. for study of rural development	463	(grant)		
Burundi	Road project	8,000	6	10	5
Central African Republic	Rural development	1,450	6.5	10	4
Chad	Tech. ass. for study of land reclamation	50	(grant)		
Equatorial Guinea	Airport	4,700	5.5	8	4
Guinea	Road programme	9,000	6	12	4
Lesotho Agr. Dev. Bank	Line of credit	3,000	8	12	3
Mozambique	Telecommunications	10,000	7	15	4
Niger	Road project	8,000	6	16	4
Sao Tome and Principe	Tech. ass. for study of fruit canning complex	150	(grant)		
Senegal	Water supply installations	5,000	6.5	15	5
Sierra Leone	Road project	8,000	5	10	4
Togo and Benin	Hydroelectric station	10,000	6.5	11	4
Uganda	Tech. ass. for study of poultry and fishery development	100	(grant)		
	Sugar scheme	8,000	8	16	4
Zimbabwe	Telecommunications	8,000	7	10	4
Total:		83,933			

Source: BADEA.

The latter are likely to be further favoured in subsequent years, as the Bank's management feels such assistance to be particularly important at a time when scarcer resources available to African countries should be used with optimal effect. A new form of technical assistance for BADEA will also be given greater importance in the future. The development of local skills and human resources, of which the first item in the above table of commitments in 1983, is an example of such assistance.

In 1983 there was a stress on infrastructure as financial facilities for such type of development are particularly difficult to obtain for African countries at the present juncture, and as concessional aid is needed to finance schemes involving long-term gestation rather than rapid financial returns.

Zimbabwe now received its third $10 million facility in succession, which showed BADEA's concern for that country, a concern also applying to other members of SADCC, including Mazambique and Lesotho.

The credit line granted to Lesotho reaffirms a trend that BADEA is likely to pursue with greater emphasis in the future: lending to local banking organizations so that they in their turn can help the industries and activities which the country concerned regards as a priority. This form of assistance approaches programme aid, which many developing countries would like to see expanded because such finance affords them greater freedom of action than money allocated for a specific development project.

The Bank has generally had little preference for any particular region, although the urgency of need has always been an important consideration. BADEA's assistance, like that of the rest of the Arab world, is heavily weighted in favour of the most underprivileged countries. The President of the Bank indicated that there may be a certain shift now from aid to West Africa to the Eastern half of the Continent, and there may also be proportionally more money going to the Anglophone countries of Africa than has been the case in the past.

Notes

(1) IMF Annual Report 1983, pp. 18 and 77.

(2) Food Emergencies in Africa, FAO, Rome, October 1983, pp. 2-6.

(3) See "Africa's International Relations", by Ali Mazrui, Heinemann, London, p. 144.

(4) See "Afro-Arab Relations in the New World Order", by E. C. Chibwe, Julian Friedmann, London, 1977, pp. 137-146.

(5) Survey of the Arab Programme of Co-operation with Africa, BADEA, Khartoum, March 1983, pp. 8-12.

(6) BADEA Annual Report 1982, p. 73.

(7) See Co-operation for Development, BADEA Bulletin for April 1982 and April 1983.

(8) For details see, Cinquième réunion du comité de coördination pour la coöpération Arabo-Africaine, BADEA, Khartoum, March 1981, pp. 51-77.

(9) "The Concept of the South and the South-South Co-operation Project", lecture delivered by Dr. Chedly Ayari in Kuwait, May 1983, pp. 15-16.

(10) BADEA Press Release No. 19/83, December 1983.

(11) BADEA Annual Report 1983, p. 26.

CHAPTER 6

Economic Co-operation Between European CMEA Countries and Africa*

Judit Kiss

Institute for World Economy, Hungarian Academy of Sciences

THE SIGNIFICANCE OF CMEA-AFRICA RELATIONS IN LIGHT OF THE COMMODITY TURNOVER

IN EVALUATING and analyzing economic relations between the socialist and the African countries, it is necessary to point out the mutual significance of the relations. A usual method is the presentation of the role played by foreign trade, by bilateral commodity turnover in the external economic relations of the two groups of countries, so much the more as today foreign trade is still the most important form of co-operation. On the other hand it must be taken into consideration that the role played in each other's foreign trade may only partly reflect the significance of economic relations, since beyond mutual commodity deliveries economic relations also cover other forms of economic co-operation, often having implications of greater significance than foreign trade.

SOCIALIST EXPORTS AND THE AFRICAN MARKET

Examining the socialist countries' exports to developing countries, and within them those to Africa, it can be shown that while between 1960 and 1981 the socialist countries' total exports – in terms of value and calculated at current prices – increased by 10.4 times, exports to the developing countries grew by 22.2 times.

---

*This study is limited to the European CMEA countries (the Soviet Union, Bulgaria, Czechoslovakia, the GDR, Hungary, Poland and Romania) since the extra-European CMEA countries (Vietnam, Mongolia and Cuba) have slight or no relations with Africa.

Consequently the developing countries' weight within the socialist countries' total exports rose from 6.5 per cent in 1960 to 13.8 per cent in 1981. An even more dynamic growth than that of socialist exports to the developing countries as a group was registered by exports to Africa (27.2 times increase in terms of value between 1960 and 1981), as a result of which a considerable growth occurred in Africa's share both within socialist exports to the developing countries and within the overall exports of the socialist countries. While in 1960, 29 per cent of socialist exports to the developing countries went to Africa, in 1981 the corresponding share was already close to 36 per cent, i.e. in 1981 5.0 per cent of all socialist exports were to Africa, as against 1.9 per cent in 1960.

The African countries, consequently, represent a very dynamic developing market, but a fairly modest outlet, for the commodities of the socialist countries. This is to be attributed partly to a later attainment of political independence by the African countries, to stronger ties with the ex-colonial countries, and capitalist economic and financial organizations (monopolies and multinational companies), to an instability of economic and political systems, to the small size and narrow internal market of the majority of African countries, to transport difficulties, to a lack of information on markets by the socialist countries, to an insufficient adjustment to special climatic conditions; and partly to competition becoming keener on the markets of African countries and an unsatisfactory level of competitiveness in the socialist countries' own commodities.

What do the socialist countries' supplies mean for the African countries? As shown by the tables later in this chapter, the socialist countries – despite a dynamic growth of the volume and value of their exports to Africa – satisfy a very slight share of the import needs of the African developing countries: while in the early '70s the socialist countries satisfied some 6-8 per cent of all African imports, by the end of the '70s this share declined to around 5.0 per cent, that is to say, in the last decade the African countries increased their procurements more dynamically from other countries, primarily from the developed capitalist countries who account for 80-85 per cent of their trade relations. An increasing role is played in African purchases also by other developing countries. Consequently, the socialist countries continue to occupy a modest place within the African countries' imports. It is difficult for them to counterbalance the dominance of the developed capitalist countries.

Despite the fact that the greater part of socialist exports (35-40 per cent) is accounted for by machinery and transport equipment (agricultural machinery, mining and construction equipment, tractors, aeroplanes, machine-tools, etc.) and by manufactured goods (20-25 per cent), even in the case of these products the socialist countries meet a modest and declining share (4-5 per cent) of African import demands. It may be anticipated that also in the future the greater part of socialist deliveries will consist of capital goods, machinery, complete equipment of fundamental significance for the economic development of the African developing countries, besides certain foodstuffs and food industry products. On the other hand it is expected that the export of manufactured consumer goods will decline in both dynamism and share, as a result of the African countries' endeavours at import substituting industrialization.

SOCIALIST IMPORTS AND AFRICAN SUPPLIES

Examining the dynamism of the CMEA countries' imports from developing countries, and those from Africa, it becomes clear that while between 1960-1981 the socialist countries' total imports increased by 10.1 times, their imports from the developing countries grew by 14.9 times. Consequently the devreloping countries' weight within the total imports of the socialist countries rose from 7.4 per cent in 1960 to 10.8 per cent in 1981. Since 13.8 per cent of total CMEA exports goes to the developing world, a 4 billion rouble surplus obtains in the trade balance in favour of the socialist countries.

Socialist imports from Africa grew less dynamically between 1960 and 1981 than the total imports of the CMEA countries from developing countires. Consequently the weight of Africa – which has not been of particular significance before – continued to decline in the course of the '60s and '70s. Currently the CMEA countries cover just 2.0 per cent of their imports from Africa, although of their exports 5.0 per cent goes to that region. The socialist countries' trade balance with Africa showed a surplus of 3.7 billion roubles in 1981. The ratio of imports to exports amounted to some 250 per cent. It is probable that in the future there will be a considerable decline in the surplus, as the East-European socialist countries will increase their fuel and raw material purchases from African countries, and the industrial division of labour will deepen between them.

As Tables 6.4 and 6.5 show (at end of chapter), the most important commodity groups of the socialist countries' imports from Africa are tropical agricultural produce, food, fruits and beverages (about 40 per cent of imports), crude materials and mineral fuels (20-30 per cent of imports). The African countries' exports to the socialist countries – similar to the commodity structure of all African exports – are characterized by an 80 per cent crude products dominance; on the other hand a considerable increase occurred in the socialist countries' imports of manufactured and consumer goods. Among the manufactured goods worthy of mention are various items, leather, shoe and clothing industry manufactures, and products of iron and non-ferrous metallurgy.

The significance of the procurement of tropical agricultural produce and of crude and basic materials is shown by the fact that while just 2.0 per cent of all socialist imports comes from the African countries, some 6 per cent of CMEA imports of tropical agricultural produce, about 10 per cent of crude and basic materials, and 4 per cent of mineral fuels are of African origin, i.e. in respect of these items Africa represents a relatively important source of procurement for socialist countries.

The above products are not only significant from the viewpoint of the socialist countries' procurements; also the CMEA countries represent an outlet of greater significance than the average for African exports, in comparison to total exports. For example, while in 1979 some 3.0 per cent of all African exports went to the socialist countries, the latter accounted for 7.4 per cent of the exports of agricultural produce and mineral raw materials, and for 7.9 per cent of food and beverages.

In view of the fact that in certain crude materials Africa is a leader in global production and world reserves;* that the socialist countries participate in the development of the extractive industry of the African developing countries; and that in view of their wish to ensure part of their crude material needs from external (including African) sources, it is probable that within the socialist countries' imports from Africa, crude products and their processed variants will continue to play a leading role. Africa's weight in respect of the imports of these products may even exceed their current, relatively high share. In the future, the African crude material base may be an area of mutual economic interest forming a basis for the economic co-operation of the two groups of countries. In order to take advantage of this, greater activity, flexibility and an increase in the competitiveness of the socialist countries will be required. On the other hand, the African countries – besides wanting to ensure solid markets for their crude products – will search for expanding outlets (which are readily available in the socialist countries) where they can sell the products of their industries.

A one-sided picture would be given of the economic relations of the socialist and the African countries if economic co-operation were evaluated only on the basis of foreign trade figures, and no account were taken of the distinctive features of co-operation with the socialist countries' economic relations. In the co-operation of the two groups of countries other forms of co-operation are at least of the same significance as commodity trade.

OTHER FORMS OF ECONOMIC CO-OPERATION

Economic co-operation between the socialist and the developing countries differs in the basic principles of the establishment of economic relations, in the indirect and direct impacts of co-operation and, to a certain extent, in the forms of co-operation, relative to those with the capitalist countries. It is often these distinctive features that permit a strengthening of the impact of co-operation, and a quantitative expansion of relations.

The basic principles of co-operation between the two groups of countries are observance of sovereignty, equality, mutual advantage, freedom from exploitation

*Africa accounts for 96 per cent of the world's diamond reserves, 90 per cent of the chromium reserve, 50 per cent of the cobalt reserve, 50 per cent of the phosphate reserve, 55 per cent of the manganese reserve, 40 per cent of the bauxite reserve, 30 per cent of the thorium and uranium reserves, and 20 per cent of the copper reserve, and this continent accounts for 72 per cent of the world's cobalt production, 67 per cent of the gold production, 36 per cent of the manganese production, 35 per cent of the chromium production, 28 per cent of the phosphate production, 22 per cent of the copper production, 10 per cent of the iron production, and 7 per cent of the bauxite production.

and dependence, full equality of rights, and non-intervention in each other's internal affairs.

Long-term Agreements

Among the fundamental forms of co-operation is commodity turnover which – despite its slight volume and weight – is of particular significance for the partners, because it is generally handled within the framework of long-term trade agreements and related agreements on payments and economic co-operation and thus introduces stability, safety and continuity. With a view to both market assurance and an assurance of the sources of procurement it is in the interest of both parties. It counterbalances political uncertainty and brings to expression mutual economic interests. Currently the socialist countries have long-term agreements and arrangements with 34 African countries.

In co-operation concerning raw materials, an even more frequent phenomenon is the conclusion of long-term supply contracts for 10, 20 or 30 years, where the relation between the partners may range from usual selling and buying, through barter-type mutual commodity deliveries, to co-operation covering credit and technical co-operation.*

Delivery of Complete Equipment and Facilities

A distinctive trait of the socialist countries' commodity turnover with African countries is the delivery of turnkey plants and complete equipment,† and participation in the construction of various facilities of significance for the national economy. Though this form of co-operation depends to a greater extent on the shaping of political relations than simple commodity deliveries, and often it also serves demonstrative purposes, considering its effect exercized on the developing countries' economy it is superior to the direct and indirect impact on commodity deliveries. Complex deliveries, the setting up of facilities of national economic significance, permit in the first place the establishment and development of complete vertical lines of production of individual industries, of a research and development base, of agriculture and of infrastructure in the developing countries. They increase

---

*In 1978 Poland concluded an agreement with the Moroccan firm Office Cherifien des Phosphates, in accordance with which Poland receives from Morocco an annual 500,000 tons of phosphate in exchange for sulphuric acid factory equipment. In accordance with a Polish-Tunisian phosphate contract Poland receives an annual 300,000 tons of phosphate between 1977 and 1985 in exchange for complete factory equipment. In 1978 Poland concluded a long-term oil supply contract with Libya, within the framework of which Libya supplies a definite amount of oil for the Polish party's building industry, services and power plant construction. Oil supply contracts were also concluded with Libya by Hungary and Czechoslovakia, while the Soviet Union drew up a bauxite supply contract with Guinea and a 30-year phosphate supply contract with Morocco.
†In 1978 some 53 per cent of the Soviet Union's machinery and equipment exports to the developing countries was made up of complete equipment.

productive capacity and the possibility of accumulation, promote indirectly a modernization of the production pattern, a decrease in one-sidedness, possibly the establishment of export capacities, an easing of the employment problem, and (if deliveries are complete with a transfer of know-how and technology) to the lessening of technological dependence and easing of concern about the shortage of specialists.

The greatest significance of this form of co-operation lies in its comprehensive character, that is to say in that:
- it includes the design, erection and placing into service of machinery and equipment, occasionally the sending of specialists, the transfer of technology, technical and scientific assistance, the training of local workforce, possibly the granting of credit, and the buyback of part of the goods produced;
- it contributes to reducing the unilateral dependence on the developed capitalist countries' machinery and equipment supplies, technology transfer, and credit granting;
- it promotes the development of the given country's national economy and means of production, a realization of its economic integration, an increase in export capacities, in many cases a reduction of its dependence on imports, an active and mutually advantageous involvement in the international division of labour and the development of interregional relations; and
- it contributes to a long-term development of systematic, mutually advantageous economic relations, creating mutual economic interests.

Until the beginning of 1981 the socialist countries participated in the establishment of 4,918 facilities* in the developing countries, of which 3,300 are already in service,† with total annual production capacities of 30 million tons of steel, 67 million tons of oil, 50 million tons of oil products, and 23 million kw of electrical power. Some 90 per cent of the facilities established by the socialist countries are in key branches of the productive sphere; 70 per cent in the field of processing and extractive industry, energy production and agriculture, and 30 per cent in the domain of infrastructure, education, health and culture.‡

Of the facilities the CMEA countries helped create in developing countries, 1,964 are on the continent of Africa (with 1,507 already in service); four fifths of them are in the possession of African countries with a socialist orientation. The distribution by branch on the African continent is characteristic of the whole of the developing countries: the greater part (three-quarters) of the facilities are in the productive sector – primarily in heavy and in extractive industry, in energy production and in agriculture – but in view of the considerable underdevelopment of the continent's infrastructure and the backwardness of the transport and communication sectors, the socialist countries laid great stress in Africa on the establishment of infrastruc-

---

*Of which 2,752 are in Asia, 1,964 in Africa and 202 in Latin America.
†1,947 in Asia, 1,507 in Africa, and 140 in Latin America.
‡The CMEA countries assisted in the construction in developing countries of 193 machine factories and metal-working plants, 161 chemical industry plants, 103 oil producing and processing plants, 1,969 energy supply facilities, 229 mine and extractive industry plants, 96 iron and nonferrous metal smelting works, 663 food industry plants, 239 light industry facilities, 172 building industry factories, 335 transport, traffic and telecommunication networks, 344 agricultural farms, and 641 facilities in the field of public health and education.

tural facilities. The majority of the facilities contribute to a strengthening of the public sector of African countries.*

The Soviet Union established some 500 facilities of national economic significance in Africa (168 in industry, 57 in agriculture, 11 in transport and telecommunication, and 108 in public health and education). Of these, 150 are in Sub-Saharan Africa; 45 in industry and energy, 11 in transport and telecommunications, 15 in the extractive industry, 19 in agriculture, and 45 in the field of education and public health.

The facilities in the field of industry are designed to contribute to the foundation of a domestic national industry, establishing an energy base, developing the forces of production, increasing employment, and raising the level of work force qualifications. They also contribute to an improvement of the developing countries' external economic balance, through import substitution and the increase of exports.

Besides concentrating on heavy industry, the socialist countries also participate in the setting up of light industry (textile, clothing and shoe) and food industry to satisfy the needs of the population and possibly increase the country's export potential.†

Co-operation in the extractive industry is based on the one hand on the African countries' wealth in raw materials (oil, phosphate, iron ore, manganese, nonferrous and rare metals, copper, tin, lead, etc.), and on the other on the comprehensive character of the co-operation of the socialist countries, covering practically all phases of extractive industry activity (sending of geologists, surveying, development of natural resources, delivery of extractive industry equipment, mining machines, production, concentration, treatment, pipeline construction, training of geologists, etc.).‡

The most important areas of co-operation in the field of agriculture are supply of agricultural means of production, comprehensive facilities, turnkey plants and entire production systems; mechanization of agricultural production; establishment of state farms, agro-industrial complexes, agricultural machine stations, stock-raising farms and systems; improvement of veterinary hygiene and plant protection; subjecting new land to cultivation, complex utilization of stocks of land and waters,

---

*Of the facilities established on the African continent, 107 are in Egypt, 100 in Algeria, 36 in Somalia, 21 in Ethiopia, 30 in Guinea, 15 in Sudan, 14 in Mali, and 5 in Morocco. Other facilities constructed with the help of the socialist countries are in Angola, Benin, Ghana, Congo, Libya, Mozambique, Nigeria, Zambia, Tanzania and Tunisia.

†Hungary, for example, brought into existence mills, bread factories, slaughter-houses and meat processing plants in Algeria; slaughter-houses and meat complexes were established by the Soviets in Guinea, Somalia, Ethiopia and Sudan; dairy plants in Ethiopia, Somalia and Sudan; the Soviet Union set up in Guinea four fish canning plants, and established fish processing plants in Somalia and Angola; the GDR set up a textile complex in Mozambique.

‡The CMEA countries' co-operation covers above all the following African countries: Algeria (iron ore, oil, nonferrous metals, mercury); Libya (oil, gas); Morocco and Tunisia (phosphate); Egypt (raw phosphate and bauxite); Ethiopia and Guinea (bauxite); Ghana (manganese, iron ore, gold, bauxite); Sudan (bauxite, copper, magnesite, asbestos); Congo (zinc, lead, gold); Benin (copper, tin, zinc, molybdenum, cobalt, nickel, chromium); Mali (cement basic material, iron, gold); Mozambique (coal); Nigeria (iron, coal, metallurgical basic material); Senegal (titanium, gold); Tanzania (gold, zinc, rare metals), the Ivory Coast (iron ore, manganese ore); Angola (oil, raw phosphate); Zaïre (nonferrous metals, copper, lead); and Zambia (copper).

soil amelioration, soil protection, irrigation; processing of agricultural produce; design, establishment and equipment of pilot farms and laboratories; education and training of agricultural specialists, sending agricultural experts and consultancy.

Another significant domain of co-operation is the development of infrastructure (construction of railways, bridges, roads, airports, telecommunication systems), public health (establishment of hospitals, maternity homes, training of physicians), and education.

Technical and Scientific Co-operation

From the viewpoint of the developing countries' economic development, an important role is played by CMEA technical and scientific co-operation, sending and training specialists, and technology transfer. This form of co-operation is important because it alleviates the shortage of specialists, a reduction of technological and technical dependence, and helps to counterbalance the ideological and political influence of the developed countries. It contributes to an expansion of the scientific and technical potential of African countries.

The socialist countries' scientific and technical assistance is realized either within the framework of, or in relation to, other forms of co-operation (e.g. supply of complete equipment, turnkey plants, usually complete with technology, licence, know-how transfer and training of specialists), or is conducted independently, under autonomous technical and scientific co-operation contracts and agreements. The socialist countries concluded technical and scientific agreements with some three dozen African countries.

The most important areas of technical and scientific co-operation are the following:
1. Transfer of licences, know-how, technology, experience in production, management and work organization; co-operation in the development of appropriate technology; joint research; joint solution of scientific and technical problems; exchange of information; consulting-engineering activities; technology transfer in designing and technical services; and the elaboration of economic and social development plans.
2. Assignment of specialists and instructors for technical assistance in the construction and operation of various facilities or as consultants in local educational institutions. In the late 1970s some 90,000 specialists worked in the developing countries from the Soviet Union, the East-European socialist countries and Cuba. About half of the experts on assignment are active in Africa.*

---

*The socialist countries' specialists work in various economic fields: Soviet experts (geologists, engineers, physicians, agronomists) are active mainly in Algeria, Libya, Nigeria, Ghana, Guinea, Mali and Ethiopia in the field of extractive industry and in the development of heavy industry, agriculture and food industry; Bulgarian stock-breeders, agronomists, engineers, technicians, economists work in Tunisia, Mali, Sudan, Algeria, Nigeria, Tanzania, Kenya, Ethiopia; Rumanians carry out geological development work in Mauritania, Guinea, Nigeria, Kenya; Hungarian specialists are in Libya, Algeria, Nigeria, Tanzania, Ghana, Zambia, Ethiopia, Mali, Sudan and Guinea.

3. The training of specialists by the socialist countries includes the education of Africans at socialist country universities and colleges and the secondary-level training of technicians and postgraduates. These services extend to educational and research institutions within African countries. The socialist countries helped establish 56 African higher and secondary educational institutions, and 158 centres for special technical-professional education.

Co-operation in Production Joint Ventures

More stable and lasting co-operation than the above is assured by forms of co-operation that cover production based on common economic interests. In production co-operation with African countries, the motivation of the socialist countries is not to make profits, but to create an alternative for investments, to create new markets, and assure supplies.

In principle, production co-operation may be realized in various forms. Traditional forms are sectoral or infra-sectoral co-operation between autonomous producing units, production specialization, mutual use and development of licences and technologies, joint ventures in the field of marketing, services and research, joint ventures relying mainly on the developing countries' own raw materials and labour, "tripartite co-operation", which includes enterprises from socialist, developing and advanced capitalist countries, and horizontal and/or vertical comprehensive co-operation combining various forms of the above.

In Africa, the socialist countries have availed themselves in only slight measure of the above-enumerated possibilities of production co-operation. Just 100 joint ventures serve the sales of the socialist countries' commodities; the overwhelming majority of joint ventures are in the African countries' extractive industries. In raw material ventures the CMEA countries generally hold 10 to 49 per cent of the shares. The greater part of socialist shares is made up of machinery and equipment supplies and various technical and scientific services, whereas the smaller part is represented by convertible currency contributions.

It is probable that in the future there will be an increase in the number of African joint ventures with socialist countries, mainly in the extractive industries, and possibly in light and food industries. The activity of the enterprises is expected to cover the exploitation and processing of the raw materials in Africa, and the export of processed raw materials and finished products to the socialist countries. By these activities African countries will obtain capital goods, modern technologies and reliable sales outlets, while the socialist countries will have assured continuous deliveries of the products.

Financial and Credit Relations

It is perhaps not accidental that among the forms of co-operation the last to be mentioned is financial co-operation – credit assistance. The socialist countries do not wish to put credit and financial assistance first. They do not want to promote the "assistance" of developing countries by a transfer of financial means, but through the forms of co-operation outlined above, enforcing to the full the basic principles. Naturally the socialist countries also grant credit and render assistance, considering it as a means that furthers, accelerates and strengthens co-operation between the two groups of countries.

In the interest of achieving this goal, the socialist countries conclude financial agreements with African countries. Instead of the previous clearing account procedures, a changeover is being made toward accounting in convertible currencies with greater dynamism and flexibility. There is a definite tendency toward making accounts multilateral and making use of transferable roubles for financing plants in developing countries and for amortizing debts, settling them on a multilateral basis. A new possibility is offered by the one billion rouble Special Fund of the International Investments Bank of the CMEA, which may be used for the establishment or reconstruction of energy generating, metallurgical, chemical, textile and other industrial plants.

Within the framework of financial agreements, the socialist countries grant state or government credit and commercial firm credit to African countries. The credits are on favourable terms: their government credits are for 8 to 12 years, with a 2-3 per cent interest. Repayment is in convertible currency, or by deliveries of the developing country's traditional export products, or (most often) by deliveries of the products financed by the credits. Since the greater part of government credits are loans for the construction of specific facilities, the distribution of credits by use and sector fully coincides with the sectoral structure of the establishments constructed by the socialist countries. In 1979 three-quarters of the credits granted by the Soviet Union and the socialist countries went to industry, whereas in the same year 19 per cent of Official Development Assistance by the advanced free-market countries went to the developing countries' productive sector, 6.1 per cent going to industry. In the case of the Soviet Union 71.5 per cent of credits went to industry and energy, 9.7 per cent to agriculture, 1.6 per cent to transport and communication, 9 per cent to the extractive industry, 7 per cent to education and public health, and 0.7 per cent to housing.

While between 1965 and 1972 Africa received half of the loans provided by the socialist countries, by the mid-70s the share of the African continent fell to below 30 per cent, due to the diversification of the socialist countries' credit allocations. The most important donor in the CMEA is the Soviet Union, which accounts for 50-60 per cent of all loans. This is of particular significance for African countries since 80 per cent of Soviet loans are from the State, granted on more favourable terms than commercial loans. (While state loans are granted with a 2.5-3 per cent interest rate, for 10-15 years, with a grace period of 1-3 years, in the case of commercial loans the rate of interest is 3-3.5 per cent and the period of repayment is 5 years.)

While in the 1960s and early '70s socialist loans went mainly to certain Arab countries (Egypt in the first place), from the mid-'70s onward the countries of Sub-Saharan African gained in significance. Within the African region the most important recipients are Sudan, Ghana, Guinea, Ethiopia, Mali and Zambia, and from the late '70s Angola and Mozambique.

GEOGRAPHICAL DISTRIBUTION OF RELATIONS AND PARTNER SELECTION

Economic co-operation between the two groups of countries may be stable and advantageous for both sides if the partners' economic and political-strategic interests coincide in the long run. Where partner selection is made in the interest of one party only, the other's interests lead to a disorganization of relations. From this viewpoint political and economic interests are not equivalent. Where partner selection is based on political motivation alone, with a deterioration in political relations economic ties regress, stagnate, or decline to a minimum level (e.g. in the evolution of economic relations with Somalia in 1978). If political change is in favour of the socialist countries, they may develop rapidly (as in the case of large-scale deliveries to Angola and Ethiopia). On the other hand, relations based on mutual economic interests alone remain stable or may develop even if the political situation is unstable (e.g. relations with Nigeria and Sudan).

While in the 1960s economic relations with African countries were concentrated on just a few countries, from the mid-'70s – simultaneously with the increase of Africa's international political weight – we can witness an establishment of relations on grounds of political motivation with Angola, Mozambique and Ethiopia. A further development of relations will probably depend on the mutuality of economic interests as well.

In the future the most important partners of the socialist countries will be the potential raw material and fuel exporters, countries having considerable markets, and the socialist-oriented countries (Angola, Mozambique, Ethiopia, Tanzania).

On the part of the socialist countries the most important supplier to Africa is the Soviet Union followed by Romania, Bulgaria, Poland, Czechoslovakia and Hungary. Among the CMEA countries the USSR is also the most significant importer (with half of all CMEA imports of African origin); the second place is taken by Romania. Then come Poland, the GDR, Hungary, Bulgaria and Czechoslovakia.

POSSIBILITIES FOR DEVELOPING INTERREGIONAL CO-OPERATION

Taking into account the present, relatively low level of economic co-operation between the two groups of countries, the experience gained by the socialist countries in national economic planning, industrialization, developing and transforming agriculture and creating a national scientific and technical base; and their interest in deepening the international division of labour with developing countries, there are a great number of possibilities for increasing interregional co-operation.

The main criterion and basis for increasing interregional economic co-operaton will be common economic and political interests. On the side of the socialist countries this involves increasing reliance on the raw materials, fuels and tropical agricultural resources of the African region, increasing their purchases not exclusively in crude, but also in processed or semi-processed form. Besides the raw materials sector the socialist countries – and especially the small European socialist countries – are more and more interested in establishing a real industrial division of labour with African countries, first of all in the field of industrial consumer goods (textiles, clothing, footwear, etc.), in certain heavy industry branches (metallurgy, steel industry, petro-chemical industry) and in food processing. For the socialist countries the importance of the African region will increase not only on the import side, but on the export side as well, especially in the field of capital goods, machinery, complete plant, turnkey projects deliveries, and in exporting expertise and skills.

As far as African interest in interregional economic co-operation with the CMEA region is concerned, the main objective will be to liquidate backwardness and promote economic development through an international division of labour on the basis of equality and reciprocity. Deriving from the common economic and political interests of the two regions, the main fields of interregional co-operation can be the following:

1. Industry. For the African countries the main driving force in economic development is industrial development; consequently the main emphasis will have to be laid on industrial co-operation and division of labour. The necessity to deepen industrial co-operation is due to the fact that most of the European CMEA countries, especially the small ones, would like to (or will have to) stop the production of certain manufactured goods – mainly labour-, energy- and raw material-intensive products – transfer production activity to the developing countries.

2. Raw material sector. Taking into consideration that for the majority of the African countries the most important (or in most cases the single) export revenue derives from the export of raw materials (minerals, fuels and agricultural raw materials) and that demand for raw materials will increase in the socialist countries in the coming years, the raw materials sector will remain an important sector of interregional co-operation. Both regions' interest is to increase the stability and security of raw material deliveries and enlarge the share of processed and semi-processed goods. The deepening raw material co-operation will necessitate the co-ordination of the activity of the CMEA, ECE, ECA and UNIDO, and various African regional integrational groupings.

3. Agriculture. In contrast with the past, one of the most rapidly developing fields of interregional co-operation could be the agricultural sector. This is necessitated by the need to increase domestic agricultural and food production in Africa to achieve higher regional self-sufficiency and re-orient the structure of agricultural production towards staple food-stuffs. The fulfilment of the African agricultural plans laid down in the documents of FAO (FAO: *Agriculture Towards 2000*) and ECA (*African Food Plan*) necessitates not only the development of the agricultural production forces, increasing the use of inputs, reclaiming and improving agricultural infrastructure, but also the development of production relations. Co-operation with the socialist countries can promote the elimination of agricultural underdevelopment and contribute – although modestly – to counterbalancing the increasing role of agro-businesses. The socialist countries can deliver agricultural machinery, equipment, inputs, production systems and technology contributing to the development of agricultural production forces, and they can change production relations through providing agricultural expertise and skills, and sharing their experience in the field of agricultural development. Agricultural co-operation between the two regions can be helped not only by the harmonization of the activities of CMEA and competent African organs (the ECA and regional integration groupings) but also by the FAO and UNIDO, especially in the field of food processing industry, agricultural machinery, technology and fertilizers.

4. Technological and scientific co-operation. As in the past, the socialist countries will continue to attach special importance to co-operation in the field of science and technology. This type of co-operation can include technology transfer, sending specialists, and educating and skill training of Africans on location or in the socialist countries. Possibilities in this field could be enhanced with the help of UNESCO and UNITAR. A more active co-operation with CODESRIA could also contribute to the development of scientific co-operation with the African countries.

Apart from advantageous or disadvantageous changes in the world economic and political order, interregional co-operation between the European CMEA countries and African countries will play a modest role in each other's external relations. By the author's own calculations – elaborated within the framework of an international world trade model – in 1990 only 4 per cent of Africa's total exports will go to the socialist countries (but 10-11 per cent of their chemical exports, 12-16 per cent of their consumer goods exports and 12-15 per cent of their agricultural product exports), while in the field of imports 6 per cent of Africa's total imports will be covered by the socialist countries. For the socialist countries Africa will remain a very modest outlet; by 1990 about 6 per cent of the European CMEA countries' exports will go to Africa, while 3-4 per cent of their imports will be covered by African sources.*

SUMMARY

1. The significance of foreign trade shows that for the socialist countries' exports

---

*For more details see the author's forthcoming publication: *What kind of future for Africa*, Studies on Developing Countries, Budapest, Institute for World Economy.

the African countries represent a dynamic but modest market, as at the beginning of the 1980s only 5 per cent of all socialist exports went to Africa, meeting only 5 per cent of Africa's import demands.
2. The greater part of socialist exports (35-40 per cent) is accounted for by machinery and transport equipment, while 20-25 per cent by manufactured goods meeting only 4-5 per cent of Africa's imports.
3. By the beginning of the 1980s the socialist countries covered only 2 per cent of their import demands from Africa, and as 5 per cent of their exports went to Africa the socialist countries' trade balance with Africa showed a surplus of 3.7 billion roubles in 1981.
4. Tropical agricultural produce, foods, fruits and beverages made up 40 per cent of socialist imports from Africa, while raw materials and fuels made up 20-30 per cent, meeting 6 per cent and 10 per cent of the socialist countries' import requirements respectively. For these products the African countries represent a relatively important source of procurement for the socialist countries.
5. Economic co-operation by the socialist countries with African countries differs from the co-operation of capitalist countries mainly in basic principles, its indirect and direct effects, and in its forms.
6. The most important institutional form for economic co-operation between the two groups of countries are long-term trade agreements on payments, and scientific-technical co-operation aiming to assure markets and sources of procurement.
7. A distinctive feature of the socialist countries' economic co-operation is the delivery of turnkey plants, complete equipment, participation in the construction of various facilities, complete vertical lines of production in the field of industry, energy, agriculture, research and development.
8. Within technical and scientific co-operation the socialist countries are sending specialists to African countries, educating Africans at the schools of the socialist countries as well as locally, establishing educational centres in the African countries, and transferring technology.
9. The rare examples of production co-operation vary from sectoral and intersectoral co-operation through production specialization to joint ventures in the field of marketing, services and research, and different varieties of tripartite co-operation.
10. The socialist countries' financial co-operation with African developing countries covers credit and aid as well as various financial clearing agreements and convertible currency accounts.
11. On the side of the socialist countries the most important supplier to, and importer from, Africa is the Soviet Union.
12. The main criterion for increasing and deepening interregional economic co-operation between the European CMEA and African countries is common economic and political interests.
13. The main potential fields of interregional economic co-operation are industry, the raw materials sector, agriculture, and science and technology.
14. The future and possible forms of economic interregional co-operation will vary

with the aims, fields and partners of co-operation. The most common form will remain foreign trade, within which an increasing role will be played by comprehensive, long-term delivery agreements, intergovernmental or interregional trade and economic co-operation agreements, mixed intergovernmental commissions, sub-committees and working groups for concrete areas, sectoral agreements and frame-work agreements, exchange of trade missions, and high level economic delegations. The importance of production co-operation will also grow.

15. As far as the participants of co-operation are concerned, a wide range of possibilities exists, ranging from narrow bilateralism to total multilateralism.
16. The realization of the proposed changes and developments will depend on the one hand on the internal economic, financial and trade policy, institutional and political changes within the two regions' countries, and, on the other, on developments in the world economic and political situation.
17. In all possible and feasible development alternatives, interregional economic co-operation will play a modest role in both regions' external economic relations.

Table 6.1. The Socialist Countries' Exports to Africa by Commodity Groups (million US $, fob)

	1970	1973	1974	1975	1976	1977	1978	1979	1980
Food, beverages and tobacco (SITC* 0+1)	105	105	300	280	275	364	431	491	–
Crude materials (SITC 2+4)	58	110	185	145	125	214	193	209	–
Mineral fuels (SITC 3)	69	87	220	180	175	204	146	210	–
Chemicals (SITC 5)	35	47	99	110	115	165	194	209	–
Machinery, transport equipment (SITC 7)	425	560	590	670	660	884	1,134	1,228	–
Other manufactured goods (SITC 6+8)	195	265	475	450	435	563	536	722	–
Total exports (SITC 0-9)	1,000	1,280	1,910	1,960	1,890	2,508	2,913	3,234	4,098

Source: Calculation based on U.N. Yearbook of International Trade Statistics 1980.
*Standard International Trade Classification.

Table 6.2. Commodity Structure of the Socialist Countries' Exports to Africa (%)

	1970	1973	1974	1975	1976	1977	1978	1979
Food, bev., tob.	10.5	8.2	15.7	14.3	14.6	14.5	14.8	15.2
Crude materials	5.8	8.5	9.6	7.3	6.6	8.5	6.6	6.5
Mineral fuels	6.9	8.7	11.5	9.1	9.2	8.1	5.0	6.5
Chemicals	3.5	3.6	5.1	5.6	6.0	6.5	6.6	6.5
Machinery, transport equipment	42.5	43.7	30.8	34.1	34.9	35.2	38.9	38.0
Other manufactured goods	19.5	20.7	24.8	22.9	23.0	22.4	18.4	22.3
Other	11.3	8.6	2.5	6.7	5.7	4.8	9.7	5.0
Total	100.0	100.0	100.0	100.0	100.0	100.0	100.0	100.0

Source: Calculation based on U.N. Yearbook of International Trade Statistics 1980.

Table 6.3. The Weight of Socialist Countries' Exports within African Imports (%)

	1970	1973	1974	1975	1976	1977	1978	1979	1980
Food, bev., tob.	6.6	3.6	6.1	5.0	5.2	5.6	5.8	5.8	–
Crude materials	11.4	12.6	11.7	9.8	8.4	10.8	9.1	7.7	–
Mineral fuels	9.9	9.4	7.8	5.9	5.4	5.6	3.8	3.7	–
Chemicals	3.6	3.0	3.9	3.8	4.2	4.8	5.0	4.4	–
Machinery, transport equipment	9.4	6.4	5.0	3.9	3.4	3.8	4.5	4.9	–
Other manufactured goods	5.8	5.3	5.9	4.4	4.4	4.5	3.8	4.5	–
Total imports	8.4	6.3	6.0	4.8	4.4	4.8	5.1	5.1	4.8

Source: Calculation on the basis of U.N. Yearbook of International Trade Statistics 1980.

Table 6.4. The Socialist Countries' Imports from Africa by Commodity Groups (million US $, fob)

	1970	1973	1974	1975	1976	1977	1978	1979	1980
Food, bev., tob.	265	385	520	630	650	621	635	710	–
Crude materials	330	350	700	760	400	516	319	438	–
Mineral fuels	31	200	115	230	335	175	155	632	–
Chemicals	21	26	39	66	42	45	47	37	–
Machinery, transport equipment	1	4	3	9	2	0	0	0	–
Other manufactured goods	135	170	255	345	235	251	264	199	–
Total imports	783	1,135	1,632	2,040	1,754	1,608	1,415	2,016	3,114

Source: Calculation on the basis of U.N. Yearbook of International Trade Statistics 1977 and 1980.

Table 6.5. Commodity Structure of Socialist Countries' Imports from Africa (%)

	1970	1973	1974	1975	1976	1977	1978	1979
Food, bev., tob.	33.8	33.9	31.9	30.9	37.1	38.6	44.9	35.2
Crude materials	42.1	30.8	42.9	37.3	22.8	32.1	22.5	21.7
Mineral fuels	4.0	17.6	7.0	11.3	19.1	10.9	11.0	31.3
Chemicals	2.7	2.3	2.4	3.2	2.4	2.8	3.3	1.8
Machinery, transport equipment	0.1	0.4	0.2	0.4	0.1	0.0	0.0	0.0
Other manufactured goods	17.2	15.0	15.6	16.9	13.4	15.6	18.7	9.9
Total imports	100.0	100.0	100.0	100.0	100.0	100.0	100.0	100.0

Source: Calculation on the basis of figures in Table 6.4.

Table 6.6. The Socialist Countries' Credits to Developing Countries (in million US $)

	1954-1972	1973	1974	1975	1976
Bulgaria	334	43	117	17	8
Czechoslovakia	1,341	303	108	168	1,064
GDR	857	–	46	277	105
Hungary	542	148	110	151	20
Poland	719	247	107	54	52
Romania	910	36	752	465	261
Soviet Union	8,147	1,230	1,260	1,642	1,208
CMEA countries, total	12,850	2,007	2,500	2,774	2,718
Credits granted to Africa	6,193	746	761	639	720
Share of Africa (%)	48.2	37.2	30.4	23.0	26.5

Source: *Afrika v 70-80-ye gody, stanovlenie natsionalnoy ekonomiki i strategiya razvitiya*, "Nauka" Publisher, Moscow, 1980, p. 297.

Table 6.7. Geographical Distribution of the Socialist Countries' Exports to Africa (%)

	1970	1975	1977	1978	1979
Algeria	9.8	14.4	18.2	15.1	–
Egypt	60.0	35.4	24.7	19.9	19.0
Libya	5.8	23.1	22.2	26.0	28.2
Morocco	5.8	7.4	5.6	5.8	4.1
Tunisia	1.4	1.9	1.6	1.7	2.4
North African countries	82.8	82.2	72.3	68.5	53.7
Cameroon	0.3	0.3	0.4	0.5	0.5
Ethiopia	0.7	0.6	1.8	3.9	2.9
Ghana	1.7	1.1	1.3	0.8	–
Guinea	1.2	2.0	1.5	1.2	1.4
Ivory Coast	0.1	1.4	0.8	0.8	0.6
Nigeria	3.7	6.9	8.4	9.0	5.4
Somalia	0.3	1.6	0.5	0.0	0.0
Sudan	6.2	2.0	1.4	1.6	1.0
Tanzania	0.2	0.4	0.5	0.8	0.8
Sub-Saharan countries	97.2	98.5	88.9	87.1	66.3
Total for Africa	100.0	100.0	100.0	100.0	100.0

Source: Own calculations based on figures on pages XXX, XXXI, XXVIII, XXIX of Monthly Bulletin of Statistics, July 1981, Vol. XXXV, No. 7.
[1]Without Algeria. [2]Without Algeria and Ghana.

Table 6.8. Geographical Distribution of the Socialist Countries' Imports from Africa (%)

	1970	1975	1977	1978	1979
Algeria	10.2	15.0	6.2	9.0	7.9
Egypt	57.8	45.0	37.1	22.6	19.2
Libya	0.1	4.8	13.3	21.3	31.7
Morocco	6.4	11.5	9.0	9.1	8.9
Tunisia	1.6	2.1	1.7	1.4	0.6
North African countries	76.1	78.4	67.3	63.4	68.3
Cameroon	1.1	2.7	2.1	1.3	0.7
Ethiopia	0.1	0.3	0.3	0.6	1.1
Ghana	6.9	4.9	8.6	8.0	8.3
Guinea	1.1	1.4	3.3	2.6	1.4
Ivory Coast	0.5	1.5	2.8	6.4	4.7
Nigeria	3.5	5.5	1.4	4.6	0.6
Somalia	0.0	0.3	0.0	0.0	0.0
Sudan	8.2	1.4	2.3	2.3	2.7
Tanzania	0.4	0.5	0.3	0.2	0.3
Sub-Saharan countries	97.9	96.9	88.4	89.4	88.1
Total for Africa	100.0	100.0	100.0	100.0	100.0

Source: As for Table 6.7.

Table 6.9. Distribution of the Socialist Countries' Exports to Africa (%)

	1970	1975	1977	1978	1979
Bulgaria	4.9	10.5	13.5	13.8	13.4
Czechoslovakia	11.3	11.4	8.2	9.8	9.0
GDR	6.1	6.4	8.9	10.3	10.6
Hungary	4.9	4.7	6.6	6.9	6.8
Poland	8.4	12.3	12.9	11.5	9.9
Romania	5.8	14.3	14.8	15.0	17.2
Soviet Union	58.6	40.4	35.1	32.7	33.1
Total	100.0	100.0	100.0	100.0	100.0

Source: as for Table 6.7.

Table 6.10. Distribution of the Socialist Countries' Imports from Africa (%)

	1970	1975	1977	1978	1979
Bulgaria	3.5	4.1	4.6	3.1	4.0
Czechoslovakia	7.9	8.0	9.0	4.3	2.2
GDR	6.5	6.0	11.4	9.3	6.0
Hungary	4.6	5.6	6.4	7.5	4.0
Poland	6.4	11.1	7.0	5.4	7.4
Romania	3.6	10.6	9.5	21.2	24.7
Soviet Union	67.5	54.6	52.1	49.2	51.7
Total	100.0	100.0	100.0	100.0	100.0

Source: as for Table 6.7.

Bibliography

Barenkiewicz, B. Africa's role in the international division of labour and the question of co-operation between the socialist countries and the African countries, in.: Economic Relations of Africa with the Socialist Countries, Vol. 3. Budapest, 1978, Institute for World Economy of the Hungarian Academy of Sciences, *Studies on Developing Countires,* No. 93. pp. 17-41.

Afrika v 70-80-ye gody. Stanovlenie natsionalnoy ekonomiki i strategiya razvitiya, "Nauka" Publisher, Moscow, 1980, p. 325.

Andreasyan, R. N. *Sotsialisticheskoe sudruzhestvo i razvivayushchiesya strany: ekonomicheskoe sotrudnichestvo, Narody Azii i Afriki,* 1981, No. 2, pp. 3-13

Bartkowski, T. The conditions of effective economic relations of the socialist countries with the African states, in.: Economic Relations of Africa... op.cit., pp. 41-49.

Berezin, V. A KGST és a fejlödö országok /The CMEA and the developing countries/ = *KGST-együttmüködés,* 1979, No. 1, pp. 4-8.

Blahó András. *A szocialista és a fejlödö országok közötti technológiai transzfer kapcsolatok néhány kérdése* (Some issues of technological transfer relations between the socialist and the developing countries), Manuscript, Budapest, 1979, p. 44.

Bogatiy, N. *A KGST-tagállamok gazdasági együttmüködése a fejlödö országokkal* (Economic co-operation of CMEA countries with the developing countries). *A KGST-tagállamok gazdasági együttmüködése,* 1982, No. 1-2, pp. 53-58.

Cass, A. Moscow aid woos the Third World = *Financial Times,* March 4, 1980, p. 23.

Chekhutov, A. *Razvitie finansovo-ekonomicheskogo sotrudnichestva sotsialisticheskikh i osvobodivshikhsya stran, MEIMO,* 1981, No. 4, pp. 50-63.

Chinese and Soviet Aid to Africa (ed. by W. Weinstein/, New York, 1975. Praeger Publ., p. 200.

A Communist Call to Africa. *The African Communist,* No. 75, 1978. 4.

Dobozi István. *A KGST-országok nyersanyag-együttmüködése a fejlödö országokkal* (Co-operation on raw materials of CMEA countries with the developing countries). *Külgazdaság,* 1982, No. 1, pp. 23-38.

Economic Relations between the European CMEA Countries and the Developing Countries and their role in the Development. Institute for World Economy, Hungarian Academy of Sciences, Research Project directed by Professor József Bognár, Budapest, 1980, p. 355.

Ganev, I. *A KGST és a fejlödö országok együttmüködésének jellege és alapelvei* (Character and basic principles of co-operation of the CMEA and of the developing countries). *KGST Együttnüködés,* 1978, No. 9, pp. 1-3.

Gromyko, A. A. — Lopatov, V. V. *Sotrudnichestvo stran-chlenov SEV s nezavisimoy Afrikoy. Narodi Azii i Afriki,* 1978, No. 3, pp. 3-16.

Gukasjan, L. G. The economic co-operation of the Soviet Union with the developing countries of Africa, in.: Economic Relations... op.cit., Vol. 2, p. 19-29.

Ilyin, Y. *Nauchnoe sotrudnichestvo SSSR s afrikanskimi stranami. Aziya i Afrika segodnya,* 1977, No. 5, pp. 18-20.

Kapranov, Y. *Sotrudnichestvo SSSR s razvivayushchimisya stranami. Aziya i Afrika segodnya,* 1981, No. 9, pp. 2-6.

Kiss Judit. *A szocialista országok gazdasági kapcsolatai Fekete-Afrikával* (Economic relations of the socialist countries with Black Africa), (Manuscript), Budapest, 1979, p. 53.

Kiss, Judit. What kind of future for Africa (Lessons from an econometric world trade model for Africa. Studies on Developing Countries, Budapest, 1982, (forthcoming).

Koshelev, P. Y. *Ekonomicheskoe sotrudnichestvo SSSR s afrikanskami gosudarstvami. Narodi Azii i Afriki,* 1982., No. 2, pp. 3-12.

Lopatov, V. V. *SEV i razvivayushchiesya strani: sotrudnichestvo v oblasti selskogo khozyaystva. Narodi Azii i Afriki,* 1981, No. 3, pp. 87-93.

Lopatov, V. V. Some results and tendencies in the development of economic relations of the European CMEA countries with the African countries, in.: Economic Relations of Africa . . ., op.cit., Vol. 2, pp. 57-62.

Marx, P. *A KGST-tagállamok együttmüködése a Mozambiki Népi Köztársasággal* (Co-operation of the CMEA member countries with the People's Republic of Mozambique) = *A KGST-tagállamok gazdasági együttmüködése,* 1982, No. 1-2, pp. 59-61.

Olshaniy, A. *A KGST-tagállamok együttmüködése a fejlödö országokkal* = *A KGST-tagállamok együttmüködése,* 1982, No. 1-2, pp. 77-79 (Co-operation of the CMEA countries with the developing countries).

Orosz Árpád. *Gazdasági kapcsolataink a fejlödö országokkal* (Our economic relations with the developing countries), Budapest, Kossuth Publisher, 1978, p. 107.

Panchenko, V. I. *Vneshneekonomicheskie svyazy SSSR,* "Nauka", Moscow, 1979, p. 63.

Plan of Action for the Implementation of the Monrovia Strategy for the Economic Development of Africa, UN, Addis Ababa, 1980, p. 200.

Rubinstein, G. I. The situation of the African countries in international economic relations and the Soviet-African countries' economic cooperation, in.: Economic Relations with the Socialist Countries . . ., op.cit., Vol. 2, pp. 85-91.

Shitov, V. *Sotrudnichestvo stran SEV s afrikanskimi gosudarstvami. Aziya i Afrika segodnya, 1978,* No. 11, pp. 7-9.

Surányi Sándor. *Az afrikai országok külgazdasága a 80-as évek küszöbén* (External economy of the African countries on the eve of the 80s). *Külgazdaság,* 1981, No. 4, pp. 55-62.

Survey of Economic and Social Conditions in Africa, 1979-1980, United Nations, Addis Ababa, 1981, p. 140.

Smirnov, G. V. The conditions of expanding the CMEA countries' economic and trade co-operation with the independent states within the next 10-15 years, in.: Economic Relations with Africa . . ., op.cit, Vol. 2, pp. 93-102.

Smirnov, G. *Torgovo-ekonomicheskoe sotrudnichestvo stran SEV s razvivayushchimisya stranami Afriki,* Moscow, 1976, Manuscript.

Soviet economic and political relations with the developing world (Ed. by R. E. Kanet, D. Bahry), New York, 1975, Praeger Publ., p. 242.

The Soviet Empire. Expansion and Détente (Ed. by W. E. Griffith), Toronto, 1976, Lexington Books, p. 417.

Tanulmányok az új világgazdasági rendről (Studies on the new world economic order) (Ed. by Bognár József), Akadémiai Kiadó, Budapest, 1981, p. 287.

U. N. Yearbook of International Trade Statistics, 1977, 1979 and 1980.

UNCTAD Handbook of International Trade and Development Statistics, 1977 and 1980.

USSR and countries of Africa, Progress Publishers, Moscow, 1980, p. 319.

Voloshina, T. *Ekonomicheskoe sotrudnichestvo SSSR s razvivayushchimisya stranami na sovremennom etape* = *Ekonomika Sovyetskoy Ukrainy,* 1981, No. 4, pp. 77-82.

Zevin, L. — Prohorov, G. *Ekonomicheskoe sotrudnichestvo sotsialisticheskikh i razvivayushchimisya stran: novye tendentsii* = MEIMO, 1977, No. 3, pp. 37-48.

CHAPTER 7

Regional Co-ordination of Arab National Development Plans

Mohammed M. El-Imam

Arab Monetary Fund

THE ARAB WORLD is perhaps the region of the Third World whose member countries are the most closely tied together. Apart from the active population movements that have taken place over the last fourteen centuries, the countries of the region were practically unified under the long reign of the Ottoman Empire. In the nineteenth and early twentieth centuries, many of these countries fell under British and French colonialism, and others under that of Italy and Spain. They shared with the Europeans the perils of the two World Wars. A few of them gained their independence during the first half of this century; others had to wait until the early 1970s.

The region is well known for its long history. Several civilizations, among them some of the oldest in the history of mankind, were born there. Three major religions, Judaism, Christianity and Islam found their way to humanity through the centre of the region. Lying in the heart of the Old World, the region acted as a vehicle between East and West. Apart from its role in the diffusion of culture and science, it proved to be vital for the smooth passage of world trade. More recently, its possession of a good deal of crude oil reserves added to its importance for the development of the world economy. And its central position has exposed it to the major disease of Western civilization, consumerism.

In 1944, towards the end of World War II, the few independent Arab countries agreed to form the League of Arab States. In 1950, Ministers of economy and finance met and adopted a number of resolutions raising the level of co-operation among their countries. They also decided to create the Arab Economic Council which became the economic arm of the League. Soon the inter-Arab System grew into a full-fledged network of specialized agencies, centres and organizations. The system was later supplemented by funds for economic development. In 1964, the agreement of the Council of Arab Economic Unity became operative, and a resolution to create the Arab Common Market was adopted. In 1971, the Arab Fund for Economic and Social Development was created, to be followed in 1977 by the Arab Monetary Fund. This completed the sophistication of the regional network, which further gained in weight as a result of the attention given by Arab summit meetings to economic matters, especially in the eleventh meeting held in Amman towards the end of 1980.

Like most of the countries of the Third World, Arab States adopted national planning as a means to hasten economic and social development. Some of them attempted partial planning during the 1950s. The 1960s witnessed overall planning efforts in many countries, while the seventies carried with them attempts at planned co-ordination. The advent of the eighties was marked by the formulation of strategies and plans of regional joint action. Nevertheless, meaningful efforts for co-ordination of national policies and plans are still a long way off. This paper aims at presenting the experiences and indicating the areas of success and failure, and their reasons.

CHARACTERISTICS OF THE REGION

Table 7.1 lists the twenty-two countries which are members of the League of Arab States. It indicates that thirteen of them are situated in Asia, and out of these, six are members of the recently created Gulf Co-operation Council. Egypt links the two continents, while the last five countries are usually classified as North Africa. This geographical classification serves some purpose in analysis; but there are other meaningful classifications, as we shall indicate later.

The overall area of the region is about 13.7 million square kilometers. Countries falling in Asia occupy 27 per cent of that area; the rest belongs to Africa. None of the countries is land-locked. The whole of the Red Sea falls in the region, which also includes the eastern and southern areas of the Mediterranean. The remaining shores belong to the Atlantic and Indian oceans as well as the Gulf. Three major rivers flow into the region: the Euphrates and Tigris in the second subregion (essentially in Iraq) and the Nile in the third (Egypt and Sudan).

Perhaps the most distinctive feature of the Arab region is the wide disparity of per capita income. Countries like Somalia, Mauritania and Sudan are among the poorest in the world. At the other end of the list are some of the small oil-producing states, such as the U.A.E., Qatar and Kuwait. The third subregion is the largest in size and the poorest in income. Comparing the region with a single country, such as Canada, we notice that overall GNP is 146.5 per cent that of Canada, while population is 666.6 per cent greater. It follows that per capita income is only 22 per cent of that of the average Canadian. In fact, the region's GNP hardly matches that of Italy with its 57 million inhabitants.

As we know, per capita income is not necessarily the best indicator of develop-

Table 7.1 The Arab Region; Basic Indicators, 1980

Country and Subregion	Area (,000 Square kms)	Population (,000)	G.N.P. ($ per Capita)	Life Expec. at Birth (years)	Income Expec. at Birth ($,000)	Energy Consum. kgm. per capita
Bahrain	0.6	344	5,560	63	350	6,254
Kuwait	17.8	1,374	19,830	69	1,368	6,573
Oman	212.5	984	4,380	51	223	1,435
Qatar	11.0	243	26,080	63	1,643	8,754
Saudi Arabia	2,149.7	9,229	11,260	53	597	3,461
U.A.E.	83.6	983	30,070	65	1,955	6,067
Subregion I	2,475.2	13,157	13,170	56	764	4,000
Iraq	434.9	13,025	3,020	57	172	1,305
Jordan	97.7	2,092	1,420	66	92	792
Lebanon	10.4	2,452	1,660	68	113	979
Palestine	27.1	—	—	—	—	—
Syria	185.2	8,979	1,340	65	87	867
Yemen, Arab R.	195.0	5,225	430	42	18	116
Yemen, P.D.R.	333.0	1,858	420	45	19	244
Subregion II	1,283.3	33,631	1,825	57.5	108	890
Djibuti	22.0	352	480	44	21	197
Egypt	1,001.4	40,085	580	56	32	362
Somalia	637.7	3,914	350	44	15	90
Sudan	2,505.8	18,371	410	46	19	73
Subregion III	4,166.9	62,722	515	52	27	260
Algeria	2,381.7	18,919	1,870	56	105	575
Libya	1,759.5	2,978	8,640	56	484	1,824
Mauritania	1,030.7	1,634	440	43	19	244
Morocco	446.6	20,182	900	56	50	263
Tunisia	163.6	6,354	1,310	60	79	559
Subregion IV	5,782.1	50,067	1,765	56	99	610
Total Arab Region	13,707.5	159,577	2,225	55	127.6	780

Sources: U.N. Statistical Abstract — The World Bank — OAPEC.
U. N. ECWA: Demographic and related Socio — economic Data Sheets.

ment. This is clear from the fact that some Arab countries, especially in subregion I, are rich, but still they are underdeveloped. Some writers would prefer the expectancy of life at birth. Table 7.1 indicates that while some of the rich states enjoy relatively high life expectancies, the subregional averages are close to the general average of 55. However, the poorest countries exhibit quite low life expectancies, lower than the world average (48) for low-income countries (excluding China and India). The overall and subregional averages are below the general average (57) for all low-income countries.

Table 7.1 gives also what we call "expected income at birth". This is simply the product of per capita GNP and the life expectancy at birth for a given country. The resultant represents the total income expected for the child born under the some social and economic conditions. Such a child is expected to live a given number of years if it experiences the current health conditions throughout its life. At the same time, each of those years it gains the same per capita income realized from the current economic structure. In a sense, such an indicator is a socio-economic indicator, reducing the deficiencies of either of its two factors. It may be noticed that this indicator more realistically reflects the process of development. When growth takes place, per capita income rises. But if development is on its way, life expectancy increases. This generally implies a lower per capita income, as a result of the more rapid increase in population growth, and due to the higher proportion of children accompanying the rising expectation of life. The complete index reflects more accurately the part of welfare which is not measured by per capita income in the case of developing countries due to relatively fast population growth.

Expected income at birth is under $20,000 in the five poorest countries: Somalia, the two Yemens, Sudan and Mauritania. Djibouti follows with $21,000. At the other end is the U.A.E., where an infant born in 1980 expects to earn about $2 million. The ratio of the highest per capita GNP to the lowest (that of Somalia) is 86. The ratio of the highest income at birth to the lowest (that of Oman); expected income at birth shows a wider dispersion, namely, 8.77 times. These comparisons illustrate our remarks regarding the inadequacy of GNP per capita as an indicator of development.

By the same token it would be misleading to consider the so-called "rich oil-producing countries" as enjoying a better level of living than industrial countries. For example, the average GNP per capita for the first sub-region is 27.6 per cent higher than that of the developed market economies. Taking into consideration that life expectation in the latter is 74, the expected income at birth is $764,000, which is the same as the average for the first sub-region. In other words, per capita GNP overstates the measure of welfare of that sub-region by some 27 per cent. For the region as a whole, total expected income at birth is $20,362 billion. This exceeds the total of $17,947 generated as expected income at birth by the 24 million Canadians by only 13.4 per cent.

Modern economic strength is energy dependent. The Arab region is well known as a major oil producer and exporter. The last column of Table 1 gives per capita consumption of energy, which roughly moves with the income indicators. Here again, the dispersion is quite large – a ratio of 120 to 1. However, the sum total of energy consumption for the whole region is 124.5 million tons of coal equivalent. This is less than 40 per cent of the total consumption of a single country, Canada (314.6). Excluding OPEC Countries in subregion I (Algeria, Iraq and Libya), the average per capita consumption is 345.7 which is 84 per cent of the average for all low-income countries. Oil aside, the region is energy poor. If it is going to catch up with world standards, it has to provide for a rather heavy energy bill. So far the non-oil producing countries have been facing difficulties in providing for their modest consumption. More countries are expected to face a similar situation, as their oil reserves are drained away.

The low level of energy consumption is a symptom of a relatively retarded economy. Table 7.2 indicates the structure of GNP by country and subregion. The classification here differs from the geographic one of Table 7.1. The first two subregions comprise the major oil exporters. The first is heavily dependent on oil, with an otherwise limited resource base. The second enjoys a wider resource base, and is more densely populated. As it happens, two countries in that subregion suffer from deficits on the current account. The fourth subregion contains the poorest, or least-developed countries in the region. The third group covers the remainder.

Table 7.2. Arab Region, GDP and its Structure

Country	Sector Shares (%) 1980						GDP at Factor cost ($ m.)
	Agri-culture	Extrac-tive	Other Indus.	Cons-truction	Distribu-tion	Other Services	
Kuwait	0.2	70.0	6.3	2.5	9.4	11.6	27,280
Libya	1.6	64.7	3.0	8.8	9.9	12.0	33,025
Qatar	0.7	63.5	4.9	8.8	15.8	6.3	6,131
Saudi Arabia	1.2	62.7	4.4	11.0	10.4	10.3	116,597
U.A.E.	0.7	63.5	4.9	8.8	15.8	6.3	30,067
Subregion A	1.1	64.0	4.5	9.2	11.1	10.1	213,100
Algeria	6.3	36.1	12.1	12.0	16.7	16.8	38,541
Iraq	7.2	63.3	5.8	3.8	9.5	10.4	35,809
Subregion B	6.7	49.2	9.1	8.1	13.3	13.6	74,350
Bahrain	2.1	28.1	15.0	13.2	24.6	17.0	3,255
Egypt	26.2	14.0	15.9	4.3	19.3	20.3	18,308
Jordan	7.7	4.5	15.2	9.9	38.2	24.5	2,552
Lebanon	8.5	–	18.5	3.4	39.7	29.9	3,985
Morocco	18.5	4.9	20.0	6.8	23.3	26.5	17,642
Oman	2.0	69.2	1.7	5.5	9.5	12.1	5,279
Syria	20.9	–	20.9	6.1	33.6	18.5	12,905
Tunisia	16.4	12.6	14.8	7.7	27.4	21.1	7,394
Subregion C	17.8	12.7	16.7	6.2	25.1	21.5	71,320
Djibuti	3.1	–	9.7	7.3	51.2	28.7	348
Mauritania	23.4	13.7	6.3	7.9	20.4	28.3	640
Somalia	60.6	0.4	7.6	3.0	19.6	8.8	1,424
Sudan	37.6	0.1	8.0	5.5	34.3	14.5	7,190
Yemen, A.R.	33.7	1.5	7.0	9.8	27.7	20.3	2,247
Yemen, P.D.R.	12.1	0.2	12.8	9.8	35.5	29.6	540
Subregion D	36.7	1.1	7.9	6.3	31.3	16.7	12,389
Total Arab Region	6.6	49.1	7.9	8.3	14.9	13.2	371,159

Source: AMF and others: Unified Arab Economic Report, 1982.

The predominance of the primary sectors is quite clear. As the level of income decreases, the share of agriculture rises and that of extractive industries falls down. On the other hand, the share of industry increases except for the fourth subregion. The higher incomes of major oil-producers allow for a more active construction sector. For the whole region, 49 per cent of GDP is derived from the extractive industries. This results in smaller share for other sectors as compared with other developing economies. However, the share of agriculture in the fourth subregion is in line with the average share of 36 per cent exhibited by all low-income countries. Again its share in the third subregion is slightly higher than the average share of 15 per cent for all medium-income countries.

The structure of final demand (Table 7.3) reflects the peculiarities of the different subregions. The first subregion is forced to produce oil according to world demand, with the result of a large surplus in the balance of goods and services, amounting to 38.3 per cent of GDP at market price. In spite of the fact that these countries adopt a free economy system, a great deal of resources are transferred to the consumers through public consumption, which constitutes 31.3 per cent of domestic demand. Further, they allocate 38.1 per cent of domestic expenditure to capital formation. The second group adopts a more vigorous investment policy, allocating 42.5 per cent of domestic demand to investment. In spite of their socialist systems, the ratio of public consumption is the smallest among the four subregions, being 15.7 per cent of domestic demand. The relatively higher domestic demand reduces the ratio of exports and simultaneously raises that of imports.

The third subregion exhibits a ratio of private consumption equivalent to that of medium-income developing countries. But it shows a higher ratio of public consumption, hence a lower savings rate, 17 per cent against 25 per cent. At the same time, the rate of gross domestic investment is 25 per cent, which is similar to that of the low-income countries, hence lower than the 27 per cent observed for medium-income countries. This subregion shows also a stronger degree of dependence on the rest of the world. Exports are 36 per cent of gross expenditure as against 25 per cent. The resource gap is 8 per cent as against 2 per cent, which raises the ratio of imports to 44 per cent, compared with 27 per cent for medium-income countries.

The reliance on the rest of the world is more pronounced for the least-developed subregion. At the same time, the limited productive base allows for the modest 10 per cent export ratio, which is in line with the 9 per cent ratio for low-income countries. However, the resource gap is as high as 27.5 per cent, to finance the 23 per cent rate of investment as well as the 4.5 per cent rate of loss. In fact, the $3.8 billion gap is only partly covered by transfers on the current account amounting to $2.0 billion. The rest was financed through capital inflows. This is in contrast with subregion C which receives current transfers of $11.6 billion which is about double the gap of $6.2 billion. It is interesting to note that transfers over the whole region total only $27 billion. The net recipient countries obtained an amount equivalent to the $24 billion flowing out of the first subregion.

Table 7.3. Arab Region, Structure of Final Demand, 1980 (% of GDE)

Country	Final Consumption		Domestic Saving	Gross Investment	Exports of Goods & Services	Imports of Goods & Services	Gross Expenditure ($ m)
	Private	Public					
Kuwait	23.2	11.6	65.2	11.2	91.0	37.0	27,280
Libya	22.1	22.6	55.3	22.5	70.2	37.4	33,025
Qatar	4.2	10.2	85.6	15.5	93.9	23.8	6,041
Saudi Arabia	18.2	22.8	59.0	25.8	67.9	34.7	116,166
U.A.E.	17.3	10.9	71.8	28.4	77.9	34.5	29,626
Subregion A	18.9	19.3	61.8	23.5	73.4	35.1	212,138
Algeria	45.4	14.2	40.4	41.7	36.5	37.8	40,600
Iraq	26.6	12.6	60.8	31.6	70.9	41.7	39,787
Subregion B	36.1	13.5	50.4	36.6	53.5	39.7	80,387
Bahrain	61.0	15.0	24.0	9.3	132.5	117.8	3,255
Egypt	63.4	14.2	22.4	27.9	33.1	38.6	23,196
Jordan	86.6	30.0	−16.6	41.0	53.2	110.8	2,908
Lebanon	98.1	21.0	−19.1	20.4	34.1	73.6	3,985
Morocco	66.0	22.5	11.5	21.8	19.0	29.3	17,642
Oman	17.4	22.4	60.2	24.1	71.0	34.9	5,279
Syria	66.9	23.5	9.6	25.1	18.3	33.8	12,905
Tunisia	60.8	15.1	24.1	27.4	41.7	45.0	8,570
Subregion C	63.7	19.3	17.0	25.0	36.0	44.0	77,740
Djibuti	68.8	30.4	0.8	8.0	36.7	43.9	404
Mauritania	72.1	28.0	−0.1	32.2	29.2	61.5	691
Somalia	79.3	25.2	−4.5	17.7	13.5	35.7	1,513
Sudan	85.4	11.6	3.0	14.9	7.1	19.0	7,890
Yemen, A.R.	102.0	18.4	−20.4	43.9	6.7	71.0	2,612
Yemen, D.R.	98.0	41.6	−39.6	48.9	11.9	100.4	668
Subregion D	87.3	17.2	−4.5	23.0	10.0	37.5	13,778
Total Arab Region	34.0	18.0	48.0	26.6	59.4	38.0	384,043

Source: See Table 7.2.

The Arab region is essentially an exporter of raw materials. Over the last five years, exports of manufactured goods amounted to 2 per cent of total exports. Another one per cent was in the form of foodstuffs. The remaining 97 per cent were fuel, minerals and other raw materials. On the other hand, there was modest growth in the already limited agricultural products, especially foodstuffs. The share of the region in world imports of agricultural products rose from 5.8 per cent in 1977 to 7.6 per cent in 1980 and 8.5 per cent in 1981. The rise in foodstuff imports was even faster: from about $4.3 billion in 1977 to $12.2 billion in 1980 and $14.5 billion in 1981. As a result, they rose from 6.8 per cent of total Arab imports to over 10 per cent in 1981.

For the first two subregions (the oil exporters), the ratio of imported manufactured goods was around 82 per cent in 1980. The ratio for the third subregion was 60 per cent, and for the fourth 70 per cent. This gave an average of 69 per cent, compared with 75 per cent in 1977 and 67 per cent in 1981. The fall was essentially in favour of imports of raw materials and fuels whose share rose from 11 per cent to 19 per cent during the same period. The disparity between the structures of exports and imports has its implications for inter-Arab trade, as will be shown later.

It should be noticed that recent years have witnessed a rapid fall in the surplus on current account. Table 7.4 indicates that the overall surplus fell from $82 billion in 1980 to half as much in 1981 and to only $7.2 billion in 1982. This was partly due to recent developments in the oil market, and partly due to the Gulf War which seriously affected Iraq's exports. The situation was further affected by the increase in the deficits of the last two subregions. This gives warning of what might be a trend in the near future.

INDICATORS OF ECONOMIC INTEGRATION

One of the earliest agreements adopted by the League of Arab States in 1953 was that relating to promotion of regional trade and regulation of transit trade. The agreement has been amended several times since that time. On the other hand, one of the main objectives of the CAEU (Council of Arab Economic Unity), which was created in 1957 but did not become operative till 1964, is to ensure the free exchange of goods and services. In 1964, the ACM (Arab Common Market) was formed, starting with a free trade area. Only four countries (Egypt, Iraq, Jordan and Syria) joined the ACM.

Table 7.5 indicates the development of regional trade during the 1970s, in terms of averages, for three two-year periods, 1971-1972, 1974-1975 and 1979-1980. The share of regional to total trade (exports + imports) declined from 7.15 per cent in the first period to 6.4 per cent in the second and 6.09 per cent in the third. As a result of the overall regional surplus, essentially due to oil, the ratios of exports are smaller than those of imports. After the 1973 oil price correction, the ratio fell from 5.75 per cent to 4.60 per cent, a drop of 20 per cent. It rose slightly at the end of the decade to 4.68 per cent. The pattern of imports was somewhat different, though total regional imports are the same as total regional exports. The second period indicates a rise of 11 per cent, from 9.45 per cent to 10.51 per cent. But as major surplus countries engaged more actively in large development programmes and oriented their consumption towards more sophisticated products, their demand on goods from other subregions did not grow as fast. As a result the imports ratio fell by some 17 per cent, to 8.7 per cent.

Out of total regional trade, about half took place among countries belonging to the same subregion. These are calculated as the sum of ratios along the main

Table 7.4. The Arab Region, Resource Gap, 1980-82 ($ million)

Subregion	Foreign		Domestic		The Gap
	Exports	Imports	Savings	Investment	
(A)	155,691	74,489	131,043	49,841	81,202
(B)	42,990	31,930	40,543	29,843	11,060
(C)	27,948	34,183	13,251	19,486	6,235
(D)	1,373	5,167	627	3,167	3,794
Total, 1980	228,002	145,769	184,210	101,977	82,233
(A)	153,765	86,549	126,314	59,098	67,216
(B)	24,221	34,657	18,762	29,198	10,436
(C)	30,956	42,029	12,846	23,919	11,073
(D)	1,673	5,814	974	3,167	4,141
Total, 1981	210,615	169,049	156,948	115,382	41,566
(A)	128,855	91,755	105,308	68,208	37,100
(B)	21,180	33,978	22,691	35,489	12,798
(C)	26,305	39,253	9,567	22,515	12,948
(D)	1,567	5,718	712	3,439	4,151
Total, 1982	177,907	170,704	136,854	129,651	7,203

Source: AMF and others: Unified Arab Economic Report, 1982, 1983.

diagonals in Table 7.5. During the first period, this sum was 54.5 per cent; during the second, 47.4 per cent, and during the last, 50.4 per cent. As the distance grows longer, the ratios drop quickly. As a result the bulk of trade has been taking place among countries in the first two subregions in Asia. Their share rose from 68 per cent to 70 per cent, then to 77 per cent. However, countries in Africa exhibited an opposite pattern, their share falling from 14 per cent to 8 per cent and eventually to 2 per cent.

The role of the first (oil-exporting) subregion is quite predominant. Its share of exports rose from 30 per cent to 50 per cent then to 66 per cent. Its share of imports rose from 47 per cent to 55 per cent, but fell back to 50 per cent. As a result, the share of regional to total trade improved slightly on the export side but retreated markedly on the import side, in spite of the increase in the internal share. The third group, which is essentially an agriculture-based one, shows the weakest internal share, and a downward trend in regional trade. This is partly due to difficulties in financing trade, and partly to decisions to boycott Egypt after its signing of the Camp David treaties.

Trade within the ACM was not more fortunate. In fact, its share in overall trade is much less than the share for the whole region. There has been a distinct drop in the second period, and a clear rise in the third, as percentages of regional trade indicate (Table 7.6). However, that rise hardly brought it back to the original ratios of total trade.

Table 7.5. Interregional Trade (% of Total Arab Trade)

Subregion	Ratios of Exports to Region's Total					Ratio to Total Exports of Subregion
	I	II	III	IV	Total	
I	23.52	5.35	0.57	0.80	30.24	3.26
II	18.90	20.17	4.02	2.81	45.90	23.80
III	4.63	4.66	3.65	2.17	15.11	11.75
IV	0.05	0.59	0.94	7.17	8.75	1.79
Total, 1971-72	47.10	30.77	9.18	12.95	100.00	5.75
% of Total Imports	16.76	11.87	6.23	3.50	9.45	(7.15)
I	33.95	8.45	6.14	1.15	49.69	3.47
II	18.77	8.50	3.98	6.42	37.67	13.44
III	2.41	1.68	0.85	1.43	6.37	11.88
IV	0.10	0.38	1.72	4.07	6.27	1.55
Total, 1974-75	55.23	19.01	12.69	13.07	100.00	4.60
% of Total Imports	20.23	8.28	10.94	3.92	10.51	(6.40)
I	37.60	19.26	4.34	4.59	65.79	4.68
II	8.88	11.15	0.38	4.95	25.36	8.24
III	3.36	2.26	0.34	0.32	6.28	18.18
IV	0.33	0.89	0.07	1.28	2.57	0.66
Total, 1979-80	50.17	33.56	5.13	11.14	100.00	4.68
% of Total Imports	9.63	12.46	7.50	3.84	8.71	(6.09)

Regional breakdown same as in Table 7.1. Source as in Table 7.6.

We may conclude that the most decisive factors governing inter-Arab trade were geographical adjacency and oil. As may be seen from Table 7.7, the share of mineral fuels in total exports is quite high, not only for OAPEC countries,* but for others like Tunisia which is a small producer and Yemen P.D.R., whose refinery depends on oil imported from neighbouring Arab countries. Hence, over 95 per cent of the region's total exports are in the form of oil and its by-products. Part of this goes into Arab trade, especially among members of subregion I, and between that subregion and others. The second most important group is essentially raw materials designed

*OAPEC's membership covers subregion I, Iraq and Syria in II, Egypt in III, and Algeria, Libya and Tunisia in IV.

Table 7.6. Relative Importance of ACM Trade

	Ratio of Inter-ACM Trade to the Trade of ACM Countries with			
Period	Arab Countries		The Whole World	
	Exports	Imports	Exports	Imports
1971-1972	36.4	36.0	3.8	3.6
1974-1975	30.5	24.4	1.5	1.8
1979-1980	49.3	42.8	3.4	3.6

Source: AMF: Foreign Trade for Arab States, 1971-1982.

for the world at large. The most important of these are cotton (Syria, Egypt and Sudan), phosphates (Jordan and Morocco) and iron ore (Mauritania). In the case of Mauritania, ore exports are tied to European parties involved in the mining process. In the other two cases, there is strong competition in world markets, affecting both Jordan and Morocco. Finally, most of the food items exported by Arab countries are cereals, or vegetables and fruits (as in the case of Jordan, Lebanon and Syria) or live animals as in the case of Somalia whose major client is Saudi Arabia. Manufactured food products such as Tunisian olive oil are again designed for the rest of the world. These, as well as other agricultural raw materials, fluctuate heavily with changes in climatic conditions, calling in many cases for compensatory loans.

Thus the structure of exports is not conducive towards intra-regional trade. In spite of lack of data, there is evidence that a good deal of Arab trade takes place in oil, especially with respect to subregion I. On the other hand, the close relationships between subregion IV and Europe explain the rather poor ratio of exports to other Arab countries. This had been used as an argument to prove the fallacy of the trade approach towards integration (the Balassa doctrine), which underlined the philosophy of the CAEU and the ACM. A movement appeared calling for integration through measures designed for restructuring the economies. It is in this context that the call for the co-ordination of plans was made.

Another objective of both CAEU and ACM was to ensure freedom of movement of citizens among member countries. This was to be accompanied by the right for engagement in gainful occupation. One of the major characteristics of the region is the heavy population movement which has gained in momentum over the last decade. It still has to be proved that this movement is actually an introduction towards longer term integration. The movement is often described as importation of labour force by some rich and thinly-populated oil-producing countries. In spite of the fact that the majority of migrants are Arab, there is a fast-growing proportion of non-Arab origin, especially Asians.

The phenomenon is quite clear for the Gulf Co-operation Council (GCC) i.e., subregion I. Table 7.8 summarizes the composition of both total and economically active populations. For the whole group 31.7 per cent of the population are non-

Table 7.7. Total Exports by Commodity Groups, 1980

Country	Value of Total Exports	Distribution of Total Exports (%)				Share of Regional Exports
		Food & Beverages	Crude Materials	Mineral Fuels	Other Goods	
Bahrain	3,602	1.1	0.2	88.9	9.8	25.9
Kuwait	20,421	0.5	0.2	92.6	6.7	8.7
Oman	3,295	0.4	—	99.6	—	0.4
Qatar	4,465	—	—	100.0	—	2.5
Saudi Arabia	102,112	—	—	99.9	0.1	3.9
U.A.E.	20,516	1.3	0.2	94.8	3.7	3.6
Subregion I	154,411	0.3	0.1	98.0	4.9	
Iraq	26,346	0.4	0.1	99.2	0.3	4.1
Jordan	574	17.0	29.2	0.2	53.6	49.9
Lebanon	1,129	20.0	4.9	0.3	74.8	58.0
Syria	2,108	4.2	10.3	78.9	6.6	7.0
Yemen, A.R.	23	26.5	6.2	—	67.3	28.5
Yemen, P.D.R.	472	5.3	2.7	91.6	0.4	37.5
Subregion II	30,652	1.8	1.6	92.1	4.5	7.7
Djibouti	n.a.	n.a.	n.a.	n.a.	n.a.	n.a.
Egypt	3,047	6.2	12.6	61.5	19.7	12.0
Somalia	141	84.2	7.2	—	8.6	73.4
Sudan	542	22.2	72.1	—	5.7	34.7
Subregion III	3,730	11.5	21.1	50.2	17.2	17.6
Algeria	13,662	0.9	0.4	98.0	0.7	0.1
Libya	22,574	—	—	100.0	—	0.5
Mauritania	240	17.8	64.2	—	18.0	0.3
Morocco	2,450	26.9	42.6	4.9	25.6	4.6
Tunisia	2,201	3.6	6.0	53.3	37.1	4.0
Subregion IV	41,127	2.2	3.4	90.6	3.8	0.8
Total, $ million	229,920	2,305	2,771	218,681	6,163	10,923
Percentages	100	1.0	1.2	95.1	2.7	4.75

Source: AMF: Trade Among Arab Countries, 1971-1982.

nationals. The ratio rises to over 50 per cent for the smaller sized countries, reaching 76 per cent in the case of the U.A.E. and 73 per cent for Qatar. At the same time, the ratio of non-national labour force for the whole subregion is 57.4 per cent, reaching about 90 per cent for the U.A.E. and Qatar. The smallest ratio is 37.2 per cent in the poorest member, Oman. It is 47.4 per cent in Saudi Arabia, which accommodates 70 per cent of the total population of the subregion, or 79 per cent of nationals. The phenomenon is accompanied by distinctly low participation ratios among nationals, 18.6 per cent, as against 53.9 per cent among non-nationals. The poorest member, Oman, exhibits the largest ratio, but even this is quite low (23.6 per cent) by world standards.

Other countries have been attracting migrants in sizeable numbers. Libya proved to be a big importer from neighbouring countries, especially Egypt. Both Iraq and Jordan represented a somewhat different case. While importing some non-Arabs for specific jobs, they opened their frontiers to Arabs to enter and share their economic rights. This attracted a lot of Egyptians in particular, either to go and stay and become gainfully occupied, while enjoying a mode of life similar to their own, or to consider their trip as a first step in getting them closer to more remunerative opportunities in Gulf States.

Table 7.8. Composition of Total and Economically Active Populations, Subregion I (% of Total Population)

Country	Nationals			Non-nationals		
	Males	Females	Total	Males	Females	Total
A — *Total Population*						
Bahrain	34.9	34.0	68.9	23.3	7.8	31.1
Kuwait	20.4	20.8	41.2	37.0	21.8	58.8
Oman	41.3	40.5	81.8	12.6	5.6	18.2
Qatar	13.5	13.4	26.9	54.3	18.8	73.1
Saudi Arabia	39.4	37.3	76.7	15.6	7.7	23.3
U.A.E.	12.5	11.6	24.1	56.5	19.4	75.9
Total Gulf	34.9	33.4	68.3	21.6	10.1	31.7
B — *Economically Active Population*						
Bahrain	41.8	3.7	45.5	52.0	2.5	54.5
Kuwait	22.4	2.1	24.5	67.1	8.4	75.5
Oman	59.4	3.4	62.8	34.3	2.9	37.2
Qatar	10.3	0.3	10.6	85.0	4.4	89.4
Saudi Arabia	50.0	2.6	52.6	43.5	3.9	47.4
U.A.E.	9.1	0.3	9.4	86.3	4.3	90.6
Total Gulf	40.3	2.3	42.6	53.0	4.4	57.4
C — *Participation Rates*						
Bahrain	41.3	3.8	22.8	77.1	10.9	60.5
Kuwait	36.1	3.3	19.6	59.9	12.8	42.4
Oman	44.3	2.6	23.6	83.9	16.0	62.9
Qatar	40.7	1.3	21.1	83.5	12.3	65.1
Saudi Arabia	32.7	1.8	17.7	71.9	12.8	52.3
U.A.E.	39.8	1.2	21.2	83.5	12.3	65.3
Total Gulf	34.4	2.0	18.6	73.2	12.8	53.9

Source: ECWA: Demographic and Related Socio-Economic Data Sheets, May, 1982.

The major exporting countries are Egypt, Jordan, Yemen A.R., Syria, Sudan and Oman. Egypt is the major exporter, as a result of its population size and relatively low income per capita. Oman represents a case where imports to replenish its needs had been accompanied by exporting to neighbouring rich countries. A similar situation has arisen in Jordan, which is essentially an exporter. The opposite flow for migration is workers' remittances, which proved to be a major source of foreign exchange, to the extent that the foreign exchange systems of exporting countries were altered several times to maintain regularity of the flows.

Data on movements are scanty. The reference study in this respect was commissioned by the ILO in 1978, and appeared as a report by Birks and Sinclair: "International migration and Development in the Arab World". This study gives a detailed analysis of the situation as it was in 1975. It was estimated that the labour force imported by oil producing countries (excluding Iraq whose statistics were affected by the fact that Arabs were not required to obtain work permits) amounted to 1.75 million workers. Out of these, 1.28 million, or 73 per cent, were Arabs, while 0.426 million were Asians. By 1980, the total was estimated to have risen to around 2.68 million, out of which 1.65 million (61.5 per cent) were Arabs. The share of Asians rose to about 0.95 million, or 35.4 per cent. The trend is still persisting.

The bulk of migration is directed towards the construction sectors of recipient countries, as a result of the rapid increase in investment programmes over the last decade. Others went into administration, helping to build up the relatively new national administrations in those States. Most of the rest were assigned to service sectors, especially education, health and personal services. In so far as such services were under government control, exporting countries could regulate the movement allowing for their own needs. They did not suffer from serious shortages, although they had to give up better qualities for exportation, with an adverse effect on performance at home. The matter could be taken into account in national plans, and in many cases ample provisions were made for training.

Perhaps the most serious bottlenecks have arisen with respect to construction. For example, the 1970s witnessed a rapid increase in demand for construction workers in Egypt as a result of the shift from a war to a peace economy. But the large external competition led to a lacuna in many basic professions and a general decline in productivity. This adversely affected the costs of investments. At the same time, agriculture suffered a great deal, not only as a result of the migration of peasants to external agricultural sectors, but mainly as a result of the shift from agriculture to construction at home and abroad. There has arisen a peculiar situation where a heavily populated country suffering from overt and disguised unemployment faced shortages of labour in several professions, a rapid rise in wages, a decline in productivity, hence a shift to more capital intensive techniques and even importation of labour. This adversely affected national plans, which found that the benefits gained through workers' remittances were practically wiped out by the tendency for holders of those remittances to accelerate real estate speculation, and the continuous devaluation encouraged by large foreign exchange deals outside the banking system.

Other types of movements of persons occurred in the form of tourism. The main points of attraction were Egypt, Lebanon and Tunisia. However, political events affected the first two, while the third is showing some progress. There is a growing tendency for tourism to shift outside the region. It is estimated that Egypt comes out with a debit balance on this account. Apart from some joint ventures in the field of tourism, there had been little efforts to introduce the industry within a framework for the co-ordination of plans.

To conclude, the large population movements which took place, although they manifested signs of complementarity, far from satisfied basic conditions for integration. Apart from Iraq and Jordan, importing manpower is subject to the most strict rules of entry and permits for work. Further, there is a growing tendency towards restricting Arab migration, in preference for non-Arabs, especially Asians. Soon importing countries will be shifting to new categories, especially as their manufacturing industries expand. The industrial branches eligible to grow and the technologies to be introduced are hardly likely to induce new waves of migration. Even if they were to do so, they would add more adverse effects, since they are most likely to concentrate on professionals and technicians, already in shortage in the exporting countries.

Another aspect of the transfer of factors of production through regional integration is that of capital. As was mentioned earlier, the distinctive feature of the Arab region is that it includes some of the major donor countries and institutions. The ratio of official aid to GDP of Arab donor countries averaged 3.7 per cent over the period 1974-1981 (Table 7.9). Its ratio to surpluses averaged 14.9 per cent and was as high as 51.5 per cent in 1978 which witnessed a big drop in surpluses. The bulk of assistance (70 per cent) was in the shape of grants. Loans themselves included some 78 per cent grant element, which brings the grant element to about 90 per cent. However, the main source of aid has been bilateral, which averaged about 85 per cent of the total (Table 7.10). It is mainly directed towards balance of payments support, and public budget finance.

Kuwait initiated the concept of a national development fund in 1961, mainly to assist other Arab countries. This was added to in the mid-sixties by the Funds of Saudi Arabia and Libya, and later by Iraq, Qatar and Abu Dhabi. The AFESD started its operations as a regional fund in 1972. Arab countries contribute also to other institutions which act within the Third World at large, such as the Islamic Bank, the OPEC Fund and the Arab Bank for Economic Development in Africa (BADEA). A good deal of aid from Arab countries is channelled through international institutions to which they contribute in substantial amounts.

At the beginning, aid was mainly directed towards Arab countries. After 1973 and the rapid cumulation of reserves, the scope was greatly enlarged to include other developing countries. Thus, up to 1973, the general philosophy of aid was regional. Starting 1974, the issue took new dimensions and became related to overall co-operation among developing countries. This trend was encouraged by calls to assist in situations arising from changes in oil prices at a time when world inflation was already on its way. As a result, the share of non-Arab countries rose rapidly to over 40 per cent and settled eventually at 60 per cent. The share of Arab,

Table 7.9. Flow of Official Aid from Arab Countries

Year	Surpluses $b.	G.D.P. $b.	Official Aid $b.	Aid as % of	
				Surpluses	G.D.P.
1974	53.2	88.3	3.0	5.6	3.4
1975	35.2	105.0	4.9	13.9	4.7
1976	35.7	125.2	4.6	12.9	3.7
1977	33.5	150.4	6.6	19.7	4.4
1978	13.4	167.9	6.9	51.5	4.1
1979	61.3	217.4	7.4	12.1	3.4
1980	87.0	297.6	11.0	12.6	3.7
1981	43.2	323.1	9.4	21.8	2.9
Total	362.5	1,474.9	53.9	14.9	3.7

Source: AMF & Others: Unified Arab Economic Report, 1983.

Table 7.10. Official Aid, Source Type ($ million)

Year	According to Source		According to Type		Total
	Bilateral	Multilateral	Grants	Loans	
1973	1,036	80	1,012	104	1,116
1974	2,639	398	2,322	715	3,037
1975	4,342	514	3,034	1,822	4,856
1976	3,913	692	2,466	2,139	4,605
1977	4,414	2,214	3,561	3,067	6,628
1978	5,576	1,335	4,980	1,931	6,911
1979	6,481	905	5,075	2,311	7,386
1980	10,126	975	7,822	3,279	11,101
1981	8,074	1,344	8,262	1,156	9,418
Total	46,601	8,457	38,534	16,524	55,058

Source: See Table 7.9.

least-developed countries (subregion D) fluctuated around 20 per cent. This meant that the share of non-Arab countries was essentially at the expense of that of subregion C, as shown in Table 7.11. The further drop of that share after 1978 was brought about by suspension of aid to Egypt.

The bulk of aid provided by Arab Funds was directed towards infrastructure (see Table 7.12). Transport and communications, energy (electricity, oil and gas), and water and sewage obtained about 56 per cent of total disbursements up to the end of 1982. Agriculture and livestock received about 15 per cent, while industry and mining shared one per cent. The remaining 12 per cent went to other sectors, such as education, training and tourism. This means that contributions to "productive" sectors were essentially left to movement of other types of capital.

Table 7.11. Flow of Assistance among Arab Countries

Year	Percentage Shares, Arab Subregions					Share of Non-Arab	Total in $ million
	(A)	(B)	(C)	(D)	Total		
(i) Bilateral Assistance							
1974	–	0.3	64.9	7.7	72.9	27.1	2,909
1975	0.2	1.7	69.0	9.4	80.3	19.7	4,712
1976	–	0.0	47.9	16.3	64.2	35.8	4,362
1977	1.0	−0.2	62.9	19.8	83.5	16.5	3,303
1978	–	−0.2	61.5	20.2	81.5	18.5	2,906
1979	–	−0.1	78.6	13.9	92.4	7.6	4,262
1980	–	0.7	64.4	14.9	80.0	20.0	5,743
1974-80	0.2	0.4	64.3	14.4	79.3	20.7	28,197
(ii) National & Regional Development Funds							
1962-69	–	13.8	67.1	19.1	100.0	–	194
1970	–	29.4	41.2	29.4	100.0	–	29
1971	–	63.7	31.5	4.8	100.0	–	17
1972	–	–	87.1	12.9	100.0	–	45
1973	–	–	43.7	56.3	100.0	–	58
1962-73	–	13.4	61.9	24.7	100.0	–	343
1974	–	5.9	66.2	19.3	91.4	8.6	348
1975	–	0.1	47.9	25.2	73.2	26.8	847
1976	–	–	35.9	19.2	55.1	44.9	1,384
1977	–	2.5	35.6	19.0	57.1	42.9	2,148
1978	0.3	2.6	42.2	11.8	56.9	43.1	1,490
1979	0.5	1.8	18.5	37.0	57.8	42.2	2,154
1980	0.5	2.0	19.6	17.1	39.2	60.8	2,363
1981	–	3.1	23.3	13.4	39.8	60.2	2,801
1982	–	3.9	19.9	16.5	40.3	59.7	2,630
Total %	0.2	2.6	29.0	19.5	51.3	48.7	100.0
$ m.	26	435	4,780	3,223	8,464	8,044	16,508

Since 1953, the Arab community has paid much attention to the facilitation of movement of Arab capital within the region. The general argument runs as follows: Financial resources are in ample supply, especially in recent years. The problem lies on the demand side. However, two major issues have been raised. The first is the identification and formulation of viable projects capable of attracting finance. The second is the creation of a favourable environment, providing investors with ample guarantees against economic and non-economic risks. This problem was felt by the Kuwait Fund, and it eventually led to the creation of the Arab Organization for Investment Guarantee. But the issue was treated on a much wider scale through the "Unified Agreement for Investment of Arab Capital in Arab Countries". Again, this Agreement (like that on trade) underwent long deliberations over the last thirty years, until it took its final shape in 1980.

There is very little evidence on the flow of private capital within the region. This has motivated AFESD to undertake a recent field study, the results of which are not yet available. But one interesting feature has emerged during the early stages of the survey. It seems that the stronger movement is from deficit countries towards surplus countries, rather than the other way around. In search of safe and profitable investment opportunities, private capital has moved against the tide. (The exact magnitudes and the net results have to await the conclusion of the survey.)

To conclude, capital movements within the Arab region have been quite substantial. However, there is a tendency for Arab aid to flow more and more outside the region. Movement of private capital is still quite limited, and it seems to be flowing in the wrong direction. The bulk of aid is directed towards infrastructures in recipient countries. This is hoped to ease the pressure on their payments balances, and render productive investments more remunerative, hence capable of attracting more equity capital. The selection is made on the basis of project-by-project approach; and projects are generally identified through national plans. Any plan co-ordination is a side result, emerging as an expression of preferences of donor institutions. As will be shown later, attempts to refer to an overall regional development programme have actually been frustrated. Still, AFESD is trying its best to give more weight to joint ventures, or projects of regional impact.

ATTEMPTS AT PLAN CO-ORDINATION

Over the last thirty years, the Arab World has undertaken several steps towards co-ordinating developmental efforts. Concepts have been changing over time, especially as achievements proved to lag considerably behind expectations. We may classify efforts under several headings:

Table 7.12. Assistance from Development Funds by Sector

Sector	Arab Subregions					Non-Arab	Total in $ million
	(A)	(B)	(C)	(D)	Total		
Transp. & Comm.	42.2	29.5	24.2	27.2	25.7	22.5	3,983
Energy	–	1.7	22.9	21.3	21.2	33.2	4,461
Water & Sewerage	–	–	9.2	5.1	7.1	2.4	800
Agric. & Livestock	–	–	14.4	15.8	14.1	15.9	2,472
Indus. & Mining	38.2	63.2	18.0	14.2	18.9	15.1	2,817
Others	19.6	5.6	11.3	16.4	13.0	10.9	1,975
Total	100.0	100.0	100.0	100.0	100.0	100.0	16,508

Source: See Table 7.9.

1. Classification according to sphere. This includes:
   (a) Co-ordinating institutional frameworks.
   (b) Co-ordinating data bases.
   (c) Co-ordinating policies, at sectoral and overall levels.
   (d) Co-ordinating programmes and plans proper.
2. Classification according to level.
   (a) The sectoral level.
   (b) The overall level, subregional.
   (c) The overall level, national.*
3. Classification according to approach to economic integration:
   (a) The trade expansion approach.
   (b) The structural adjustment approach.
   (c) The joint action approach.

Essentially what is meant by co-ordination of national development plans are the activities related to the co-ordination of development plans, at the overall levels, within the structural adjustment approach. As shall soon be illustrated, this calls for the emphasis to be put on long-range development and hence long-range planning. Another dimension of great importance is to consider the regional and its countries in relation to the rest of the world, rather than in isolation. This has its bearing on the so-called "global modelling" techniques.

The first attempt at co-operation among Arab countries in modern times dates back to the "Alexandria Protocol" signed in July 1944, which defines its objective to be co-operation in economic, cultural, social and other affairs. This was further stressed in the Charter of the League of Arab States (LAS), signed a year later. Due to the importance of security in the region, the Council of the LAS adopted the "Treaty for Mutual Defence and Economic Co-operation" in April 1950. Its seventh article called for co-operation among member countries in developing their economies, investing in their natural resources and facilitation of trade in their products, both agricultural and industrial. For this purpose, a ministerial Economic Council was created to suggest ways and means of promoting such co-operation.

Thus, at that early period, economic co-operation was regarded as a means to strengthen political and economic independence, recently obtained by member countries. Planning in the modern sense was not yet practised although attempts were made to formulate sectoral programmes. Concern was focused on issues of an institutional character. These covered amending legislations and creating bodies which would encourage movement of trade, transit trade, settlement of current payments, participation of capital in the finance of developing projects, and removal of barriers limiting movements of persons and their rights for residing in sister countries and for being gainfully occupied therein. At that early date, the concept of pan-Arab projects was emphasized. Minister of Finance and Economy, meeting in Beirut in 1952 added to the above list a proposal for creating a joint financial institution to assist in development through financing Arab projects.

*In the Arabic usage, "national" is synonymous with "regional", as against "domestic" or "country" level.

The basic institutional framework was constructed through adoption in 1953 of two agreements on trade and on current payments and capital movements. As mentioned before, these two agreements were amended several times, and they took their latest form in February, 1981. The financial institution was decided upon in 1975, and its capital was increased from L.E. 20 million to L.E. 25 million in 1964, when Kuwait decided to participate. The project never saw light, and was later replaced by the Arab Fund for Economic and Social Development, which started operations in 1972.

The most important step was the decision in 1957 to create the CAEU as an agent for economic unity. The concept governing its treaty was the *laissez-faire, laissez-passer* doctrine, ensuring freedom of movements for products, factors of production and equality in economic rights, and the ultimate creation of a customs union. It aimed also at co-ordination of policies relating to agriculture, industry, domestic trade, money and finance, and at unifying legislations in those areas. Article 8 of the treaty spoke of co-ordinating economic development and formulating programmes for the execution of joint development projects. An ultimate objective was monetary union, and the co-ordination of fiscal and labour legislation.

The Economic Unity Agreement was strongly affected by the current literature and by the experiences of Europe and Latin America. The makers of the Agreement failed to recognize that any success realized through this approach has been achieved in cases where regional development, after being launched, started to suffer from arbitrary obstacles leading to imperfect allocation of resources at the regional level. In fact, the idea was to bring about integrational efforts as levers for economic development at both the country and regional levels. It is interesting, however, to notice that the Agreement embraced the major approaches to integration:
- Its backbone was free movement, or what has been described as the trade approach.
- It allowed for various degrees of policy co-ordination, up to complete unity.
- It stressed the concept of joint development projects, which came to take the lead afterwards.
- It insisted on co-ordination of economic development activities.

The ratification of the Agreement took some time. Consequently, Egypt insisted in 1959 on creating a temporary Council as a forerunner of the permanent one which became active in 1964. The early activities concentrated on sectoral co-ordination, again from a basically institutional point of departure. It was decided to create a permanent technical bureau and request countries to provide it with all relevant information, data and legislation needed for co-ordinating industrial activities. The objective was to undertake studies which would reduce excessive competition and produce higher levels of integration, thus helping to bring about economic unity not only in the industrial sector, but also in other sectors as well, and thus to assist in developing individual economies and pave the way for an Arab Common Market. The LAS picked up the issue, and in 1966 it approved a proposal for creating the IDCAS (Industrial Development Centre for Arab States). This Centre was later transformed into a fully-fledged Industrial Development Organization to give it a higher degree of autonomy.

It should not be concluded that other sectors escaped attention. In fact in 1954, the Economic Council invited member countries to create offices concerned with the formulation of agricultural policy, whenever such units were lacking. It encouraged studies on nutrition and rural education, as well as veterinary activities and fisheries. In 1957, it drew attention to development of livestock, co-operatives, and finance of small-scale farmers. In 1963, it created an agricultural Committee whose role was defined in 1966 to be the development of agricultural production via the co-ordination of agricultural plans and programmes. As a result of the failure of member countries to fill in an agricultural questionnaire, the Council paid more attention to the improvement of the statistical base. It further called member countries to give prominence to agricultural planning conducive to optimum utilization of available agricultural resources, and hence increasing the quite low per capita income in the sector, and arresting the rural exodus to urban centres. In 1970 it asked for measures to be taken for the creation of the Arab Organization for Agricultural Development.

The year 1964 represents a landmark in the history of Arab economic integration. In that year, the permanent CAEU came into existence, and one of its early resolutions was the creation of the Arab Common Market. Pursuing its steps towards industrial co-operation, the CEAU asked member countries to supply its secretariat with copies of their economic development plans, with the purpose of formulating an integrated plan. The non-response of member countries led the CAEU to invite them to provide the Secretariat with ten copies of their development plans and programmes and data related to them. It also directed its subcommittees to study each plan according to its field of interest, and supply the permanent economic committee with their recommendations to enable it to carry out an overall study. Again, lack of response forced the Council to affirm its resolution in 1966.

In other words, those early attempts at co-ordination of national plans were of an *a posteriori* nature. They were referred to experts forming technical and economic committees. This approach was frustrated as a result of two factors:

1. The limited membership of CEAU. Only five countries joined at that time, namely Egypt, Iraq, Jordan, Kuwait and Syria. A few years later, membership increased by two – Sudan, and Yemen Arab Republic.*
2. The lack of response on the part of the authorities of those countries, in spite of the fact that they have already adopted socio-economic planning as a means of realizing development.

At this point we may stop to consider a rather unique experience in plan co-ordination. In 1958, both Egypt and Syria entered into an interesting precedent of unity, forming the "United Arab Republic". Since Egypt was actively involved in formulating its first development plan, it sent some of its leading experts to Syria to assist in creating a planning authority. The first preoccupation of those experts was to build up the data base. Both parties of the union went ahead with their five-year plans, 1960-65, with the general common objective of doubling national income

*At present membership also includes: Libya, Mauritania, Palestine, Somalia, U.A.E. and Yemen P.D.R.

over the next ten years. Before adoption of plan proposals, the two parties met for co-ordination. It became apparent that there were wide divergences in technical structures as well as in contents. While Egyptians concentrated on the details for the first five-year plan, lack of information in Syria barred such a detailed formulation. To cover for that, they came up with a plan frame covering the whole ten years. Egyptians then had to rush the formulation of the plan frame for the second five-year period. Eventually co-ordination had to be realized through a series of committee meetings. But they failed to produce tangible effects. In the ensuing annual plans, little was done for co-ordination, apart from participation of top level officials in supreme planning committees of both countries. One of the major problems that faced Syrians was the drought which reduced the output of the main productive sector, agriculture, by more than 50 per cent. As it happened, this state persisted until the breach of the Union in September, 1961. Under such conditions, the main concern was to obtain assistance from Egypt to compensate for export shortage and lack of finance. In 1961, Egypt itself faced hardships with its major crop, cotton. This caused both Egypt and later Syria to be among the early beneficiaries of the new window opened by the IMF to assist its growing membership of developing countries, viz., compensatory financing. After separation, Egypt found it easy to go ahead with its original plan, while Syria discarded hers as a sign of resentment. This put a sad end to an unrepeated experience.

There was a growing feeling of failure of most country development plans to achieve their basic objectives. At the same time, it was realized that integration cannot be actively on its way unless the trade liberalization approach is supplemented by structural adjustments. The delay in co-ordinating plans was considered to be due to the non-direct involvement of planning ministers. Hence Iraq put forward a proposal for convening a meeting for them, and this took place in 1970. The first task undertaken by that meeting was the listing of basic principles for the co-ordination of plans. These related to:
(a) adoption of consistent objectives;
(b) application of criteria for specialization and division of labour at regional level;
(c) giving more weight to projects strengthening regional co-operation and tying together country economies;
(d) emphasizing industrial branches for co-ordination in the light of specific studies undertaken by CAEU (iron and steel, yarn and textiles, fertilizers, petrochemicals, paper pulp and synthetic silk, agricultural tractors and machinery, and medicines) in the hope that planning activities according to regional rather than domestic demand would help promote regional trade and raise the degree of self-sufficiency;
(e) observing both important-replacement and export promotion policies;
(f) increasing degrees of interdependence among individual economies;
(g) reducing dependence on outside markets, through taking into account regional patterns of consumption;
(h) joint financing of some projects which were eligible for efficient joint management; and

(i) creation of joint finance institutions, and appeal for the implementation of AFESD and the Investment Guarantee Organization.

Planning Ministers adopted a plan of operation to implement the above objectives. It called for the creation of a unit for planning, statistics, and follow-up in the CAEU, and the formation of a joint permanent committee from member countries to direct the activities of the said unit, and to forward recommendations to the attention of future meetings of Planning Ministers. Member countries were to supply that unit with all material relating to plan co-ordination, either directly or through missions from the CAEU Secretariat. The Secretariat was asked to collaborate with specialized centres and institutes and experts from member countries, and Planning Ministers were to meet once a year at least to monitor those activities and to develop co-ordination activities.

The CAEU created the proposed unit at the end of the same year, 1970. In 1971, it requested member countries to apply the unified system of national accounts developed by the LAS. The unified dates for plans were to begin with plans starting 1975-1976. The Council decided on 1 January 1972 as a target date for a detailed analysis and comparison of current country plans, showing areas of complementarity. Another study defining principles and priorities for co-ordinating those plans, their programmes, investments, production, conumption, trade and policies conducive to economic integration, was scheduled for mid-1973. The Council urged its sectoral subcommittees to conclude their studies and present their recommendations. It also asked them to present final technical and economic studies of joint projects which would be included in country plans. In 1973, the Council emphasized the need for the co-ordination of plans and the formulation of feasibility studies based on the objectives adopted by each member country, and on the outlook for the co-ordination among their economies. The guiding principles were to help the eventual achievement of economic unity, and to apply the principle of mutual benefit so as to compensate any country for the sacrifice of some joint project, by similar benefits from another, while observing this rule over time.

Joint projects were to be such that they would add to growth of the economies of member countries. In other words, rather than waiting for a complete co-ordination of plans, the CAEU, under the influence of its new Secretary-General, Dr. A. A. Al-Sagban, shifted its emphasis to Arab joint projects. It asked its Secretariat to propose one agricultural joint project and other industrial, to set the wheel moving. As a result it decided in 1974 to create the Arab Company for Development of Livestock (with a nominal capital of K.D. 50 million) and the Arab Mining Company (with a nominal capital of K.D. 100 million). At that point of time, three important developments took place:

1. The emergence of the "long-range Planning for Arab Countries" as a research group in the INPC (Institute of National Planning in Cairo).
2. The assistance provided by UNCTAD to CAEU in the shape of EIATE project (Economic Integration and Trade Expansion among members of CAEU). Among its major objectives was the assistance in plan co-ordination.*

---

*This was assigned, early in 1975, to the present author in his capacity as Planning Expert and Leader of the team.

3. The formulation by UNDP of a technical assistance project for identification and promotion of multi-country projects. This was assumed to help mobilize financial resources, which had begun to be in abundance in the region. The AFESD acted as a co-manager of that project, and some degree of co-operation took place with the CAEU in this respect.

The "Long-range Planning Group" was initiated by Dr. I. H. A. Rahman (former Executive Director of UNIDO). The objective was to promote the application of global modelling and systems analysis techniques to co-operation and planning in the Arab region. The group got in touch with other groups in those fields and attempted to formulate its own approach. Thus in 1975 it managed to do some joint work with Mesarovitch and Guernier from the Club of Rome. The computer programme of the Mesarovitch-Pestel model was set on a computer in Cairo, and experimentation with it brought some interesting results on potentials of co-operation among Arab countries. However, the group felt the need to develop working relations with the Latin American Barilochi group, who tailored their model to conditions in developing countries. In 1977, they got in touch with the AFESD with the purposes of turning into a pan-Arab group and putting their efforts in the service of actual operations agencies. The management of the Fund was ready to commission the services of the group in order to provide its technical departments with an overall view of the Region. This was considered as a means for improving the operations of identifying, formulating and evaluating projects eligible for promotion on the basis of an analysis of potentials of the region and its member countries. However, the AFESD Board of Directors was not ready to allocate some of the Funds' resources to such scientific research projects. Eventually the group was dismantled. Some of its ex-members found an opportunity to invest their expertise in other projects.

It may be worth mentioning that other modelling exercises occurred, but with different emphases. Thus the OAPEC, in collaboration with the Italian ENI group, formulated a model for co-operation between the OAPEC region and Europe. Further, the centre for Arab Unity Studies in Beirut recently paid attention to the study of the future of the Arab World. The original proposal was to carry the work of the "long-range Planning Group" still further. Eventually it was decided to cover some major issues pertinent to the development of the Arab region. In a sense they came closer to the futuristic studies undertaken by Dr. I. S. Abdullah Cairo under the auspices of the U.N. University. These studies concentrate on projection, and have gone beyond co-ordination activities. Another chapter seems to have been closed.

The EIATE project was set up to examine in a more concrete way the concept of the co-ordination of plans, but has so far failed to produce tangible results. A few points of clarification were made. The first is the inherent contradiction in the concept of plan co-ordination. The argument runs as follows. Any plan proposal does not acquire the nature of a plan unless it is approved by relevant authorities. The trouble is that planning technicians formulate their proposals and submit them to those authorities. At that stage they are not normally at liberty to present their findings to the outside world. Thus there is little room for co-ordination *a priori*.

Once proposals are endorsed by authorities, it would be difficult to convince them to amend legislation to fit in with co-ordination requirements. This means again that there is little scope for effective co-ordination *a posteriori*.

Another point relates to the length of term involved. Facts of life indicate that a good deal of a medium-term (e.g. five-year) plan is inherited from previous plans. This in fact leaves limited room for manoeuvring at either the country or the regional level. The issue gains further strength from the fact that integrational activities are by definition of a considerably long-range nature. If a long-range planning activity is undertaken on the regional level, it may be of great help to country authorities, who usually give the bulk of their attention to medium-term planning.

The third point considered is the fallacy of talking about a "regional plan."* For such a thing to exist, there should be a regional legislative power. If its decisions are to be implemented, that power should be in a position to overrule country authorities. This type of organism does not exist in the network of regional institutions. Even decisions by CAEU which possess a more imperative nature than those of the LAS Economic Council (not to mention decisions at the Summit level) are frequently ignored by member countries participating in their formulation, or even proposing them. It is quite indicative that even repeated requests for supplying mere information were not met.

With these considerations in mind, I advised to move first towards "co-ordination among planners" rather than co-ordinating plans. This was motivated by the observation that planners are mainly occupied with matters relating to their own economies, and possess little or no knowledge of conditions or potentials of others. If they were supplied with ample information, their plan proposals would be closer than otherwise. The programme of operations of the CAEU Secretariat should be geared towards this objective.

The programme proposed may be summarized as follows:
1. To undertake country, sectoral and cross-sectional studies for the region, in collaboration with other specialized agencies and research institutions. These would serve as benchmark studies, and may be considered in a matrix form, where columns stand for countries and rows for sectors and cross-sections. However it should be emphasized that these studies do not follow the traditional lines of e.g. IMF RED's. More attention has to be given to chapters on economic integration and co-operation.
2. As a synthesis those studies would lead to a regional study indicating areas of contradiction, gaps and potentials. At that stage, a gathering of Arab planners would provide the Secretariat with important observations.
3. Another stage would be to build up a regional model capable of expressing alternatives for development and integration. A second gathering of planners would bring out elements of a regional preference function in a more concrete shape.

---

*True there are so-called regional and global plans (e.g. FAO World Indicative Plan). But these are in the nature of background studies rather than plans proper.

4. This would then help the Secretariat in building up a long-term plan frame and a series of long-range studies of sectors and major economic variable to fit with them.

It was intentional to speak of "long-term" in one case, and "long-range" in others. In the latter, there is no unified term (e.g., 15 or 20 years) but several terms according to the nature of the subject. Thus population may be considered over a longer term, energy on a still longer one. Education and manpower may be detailed for the next decade or two, and so on. An overall plan would have a given "term", and it would select from long-range studies what is relevant to that term.

It was considered that such a programme would take place during the second half of the seventies. The objective of co-ordination among planners was to be realized by 1980, and hence reflected in the 1981-85 plans. However, the door was not closed to other approaches. In particular, country planners were encouraged to invite fellow planners from other Arab countries to discuss their plans on the eve of their endorsement. It was expected that this would persuade them to emphasize points of co-ordination and integration. Observations from other participants would help reduce contradictions and enhance co-ordination. Benefits may be multiplied if those discussions occurred at close dates, as a result of unified starting dates for all plans.

In June 1975, the CAEU approved the last proposal. It is interesting to note that the approach was later adopted by world organizations, such as UNCTAD and the World Bank. The emphasis there was on ensuring sources of finance, especially for least developed countries. At the same time, the Council invited member countries to construct long-range development planning units, with the assistance of its Secretariat. The latter was to prepare long-range projections taking into consideration findings of those units, and strategies declared at a regional level by specialized pan-Arab organizations. It was also to prepare development alternatives which help to realize country and regional objectives. Finally, it asked the Secretariat to prepare a methodological study to eliminate discrepancies among planning concepts and practices.

Later the same year, the Council approved the detailed programme of work. This included:
- Holding a symposium on long-range planning. This took place in early 1976 in collaboration with the INPC (The long Range Planning Group).
- Undertaking country, sectoral and cross-sectional studies;
- Follow-up of current plans and evaluation of development achieved during the first half of the 1970s;
- Participation in discussing plan projects of member countries;
- Identification and promotion of joint ventures;
- Co-ordination of planning concepts and techniques;
- Engagement in long-range planning;
- Formulation of long-range projections;
- Model-building.

The Council decided to unify plan periods starting from 1981. In 1977, it requested member countries to promote the Secretariat with necessary information. As a result of rapid manpower movements, the Council emphasized the importance of manpower development, and of the optimum allocation of the labour force. Again realizing the increasing shifts of financial resources outside the region, the CAEU asked in June 1978 for the detailing of sources of financing the Arab plan proposal.

It also invited all Arab financial institutions to contribute to the financing of projects in country plans, especially those of a joint nature and those assisting in integration. One year later the Council asked for the presentation of the frame for a joint Arab plan, and definition of sources of finance, means of execution and techniques of follow-up. The plan frame would take care of economic integration while observing the specific conditions of Arab countries. At the end of 1979, the Council invited all Arab countries (and not only members) to provide its secretariat with documents on their 1981-85 plans before actually launching them to enable the Secretariat to prepare its views on areas of co-ordination and complimentarity.

Here again, efforts seem to have been fading away. Both plan co-ordination and joint ventures were giving way to another approach: the *joint action approach*. This approach derives roots from partial attempts to define rules of action in specific areas of joint action by means of so-called "strategies". Thus, the CAEU defined by the end of 1973 what it considered as a strategy for Arab Economic Action. The purpose was to emphasize the need for closer economic integration and the imperativeness of ultimate economic unity. Its resolution listed the various approaches to integration and indicated the possibility of other Arab countries joining the CAEU, selecting one approach or more. In 1974-1975, the Arab Labour Organization presented what it considered to be an Arabic strategy for economic development. Ministers of industry approved in April 1974 the principles of an industrial development strategy. Education ministers adopted a strategy in their own field.

The Economic Council of LAS felt that those strategies were formulated in the absence of an overall strategy, hence liable to be contradictory. Further, as Arabs engaged in various dialogues, they felt the need for a clear vision of their own strategy vs. that of the rest of the world. Hence it decided in early 1975 to undertake a study on the strategy of Arab joint economic action. A committee of experts (sometimes called the Committee of Twenty, according to its size) was formed. In 1978, a pan-Arab conference was arranged in Baghdad in collaboration with the CAEU and the Arab Economists Association. About 150 experts joined, and many presented papers and studies relating to overall strategies and issues of a sectoral nature up to the end of the century. One school believed in the need for an *integrated overall approach,* while the second was content with partial treatments. The first school indicated that mankind has reached a point where the Third World should divorce itself from historical patterns of development, and look for a new framework based on more balanced cultural and political systems for the individual and society. The Arab World, being a part, should define overall and comprehensive objectives beyond economic sectors, to cover its genuine culture, political existence and behavioural patterns. It should select its optimum development paths making use of a unique incident, namely the availability of financial resources. This group gave the term "Strategy" its full meaning: it should be comprehensive, bringing development into its proper context of human life in all its aspects, and it should suggest future paths of action and weigh them against objectives.

The other group of thinkers, belonging to the *partial outlook school*, did not question the importance of global issues, but indicated that this may be time-consuming. By the time agreement is achieved, favourable chances may have evaporated for good. Real development patterns may require actions difficult to implement in the foreseeable future. For example, there is little that can be done immediately to reduce dependency on technologies developed by industrial countries. The main concern should be to introduce new mechanisms which render a better allocation of resources not only feasible, but also politically desirable, through creating vested interests in co-operation for all parties concerned.

The partial outlook school was subdivided into a number of sub-schools. One group was happy to confine research into the peculiar and unrepeatable phenomenon of the temporary abundance of financial resources. Their theme was to suggest actions that would utilize those resources to maximize development of the whole region. Another noted that past experiences in integration lagged considerably behind aspirations. They decided to evaluate them and come up with practical solutions. A third group, though sharing the same opinion, felt that, modest as they were, achievements to date had brought about what may be considered as a small joint sector. They would be happy to suggest ways and means of letting it grow in the future, without any illusions about its size. They shared with the first sub-school the view that achievements have centred around joint finance which may be pushed ahead still further.

One important implication of the partial outlook was the lack of agreement on long-term goals. Once development and transformation of society were subdued, there existed a vacuum. Inherent in the "what-could-be, rather than what-should-be" approach is a pessimistic attitude toward the possibility of securing political will around broad aspirations. It followed that to mobilize political will, there was need to bring in some threats to the mere existence of political entities. Hence the term "security" came to take the lead. Threats to security in various aspects of life were considered as prime motivators to achieve unanimity of opinions on joint action.

The final document came out as a synthesis, paying lip-service to overall objectives and listing what may be considered as priorities for the period 1981-2000. Objectives stated were:
- Liberalization of man and his capabilities to participate in the development process and to enjoy its fruits;
- National security, including cultural, military, food and technological security;
- Confrontation with the imperialistic Zionist entity, which is closely tied to world monopolies, and whose expansionist attitudes threaten Arab existence;
- Accelerating comprehensive development, through collective self-reliance, and the achievement of ample levels for sectors and areas providing for the expanding basic needs;
- Reducing the development gap among and within countries of the region;
- Pushing integration towards unity, and hence bringing about basic adjustments in Arab economies and enhancing economic interdependence.

- Setting up a New Arab Economic Order, capable of realizing the integration necessary for comprehensive development, and producing a pattern of division of labour which helps Arab countries to develop and to overcome external dependence. This would help in building up a New International Economic Order, aiming at reducing dependency, stopping the drain of the Third World wealth and creating just and equitable economic relationships.

These objectives look big, and may be taken as an endorsement of the views of the first school.

When we come to priorities for the next two decades, we fall in the realm of the second school. Consistency is achieved by stating that priorities are limited to areas of greater weight in joint action. Other activities may be introduced later, or even within the initial period if resources so permit. The list of priorities runs as follows:

1. Realization of military security for the Arab World, through strengthening its capabilities in all related fields.
2. Development of human resources and the labour force, and ensuring its mobility in response to the needs of member countries; maintaining the labour force within the region and expanding employment of Arabs to reduce dependence on foreign labour.
3. Acquiring technological capabilities, and adaptation of appropriate technology through encouraging all country and regional activities in this field, and adapting them to the needs and strategic objectives of the Arab world, including national security and basic industrialization.
4. Realization of food security through the highest level possible of independence in satisfying basic food needs. This includes increase in production and productivity, reduction of waste at all stages, and improvement of terms of exchange within the region and with the rest of the world.
5. Rationalization of energy through adapting oil policies to regional objectives, a better utilization of available resources of energy, and intensive co-operation in the search for substitutes.
6. Provision for basic industrial structures and development of pivotal industries (military industries; basic industries; engineering industries, especially production tools; oil industries, petrochemicals and chemicals; agrarian industries; building materials industries).
7. Directing joint action towards co-operation in planning for development of infrastructures, and implementation of its primary units: grids for electricity, communications, transport, scientific education and practical training. These have to cater to national development goals and the restructuring of the Arab economy.
8. Co-ordination of commercial, monetary and capital relationships with the rest of the world, and gearing them towards serving the fundamental Arab causes, and the realization of the highest yield.
9. Liberating the financial sector from its absorption in the world financial markets, channelling savings towards development and providing the monetary and commercial bases for joint action.
10. Creation of a regional planning activity which will be responsible for the

formulation of a joint plan and its follow-up. This planning would be imperative in areas of joint action, and indicative otherwise, hence country planners could co-ordinate their plans by referring to it. This activity should be in continuous five-year planning, starting from 1981. For this purpose there is need for unification of data bases, social accounting systems, planning techniques, raising the efficiency of planning agencies, techniques of evaluating projects at the regional level, and development of methodology for co-ordinating country plans to the regional plan. The need for a long-range plan based on a regional development strategy, as a framework for medium-term plans, was also emphasized.

To implement the strategy, a regional plan for joint action was to be formulated, where the Economic Council's Secretariat would assume the role of central planner, and the other Arab organizations would act as sectoral planners. The plan was to be eventually submitted to the summit meeting for approval. The plan would be implemented by Arab organizations, according to the preferences of each country. Follow-up would be undertaken by executing agencies, regional organizations and the Economic Council. The document called also for strengthening of joint action organisms, especially the AFESD and the AMF, implementation of Arab nation agreements and the co-ordination of activities of regional institutions. Member countries were asked to bring issues of joint economic action closer to the centre of decision-making, and to ensure consistency in views regarding various aspects of that action.

The strategy was referred to a group of official experts which met in Habaniya (Iraq) in early 1980, and was consequently approved by the Economic Council. Eventually it was endorsed by the eleventh summit meeting held in Amman (Jordan), in November, 1980. Before pursuing what happened in planning for its implementation, we should mention two incidents which are indicative of the confused state of mind concerning the scope and effectiveness of the strategy. The first relates to the views of the Iraqi government, expressed during the Habaniya meeting and further elaborated in the 1980 summit meeting. In the latter meeting, Iraq submitted a proposal for what it called the *Joint Arab Development Decade*. The main idea of the proposal was to allocate a sufficient amount of money, to be channeled through Arab funds and joint holding companies, for the purposes of accelerating development during the eighties, especially of the least-developed countries. In fact, if that was the purpose, then the proposal should have been considered as an integral part of the programme of implementation of the strategy. On the other hand, if that programme was not considered capable of catering for the suggested objectives, then there is something wrong with the strategy, and an amendment was in order. But the two documents were presented to and endorsed by the same summit meeting. Heads of State reduced allocations from $10-15 billion to $5 billion. They had in mind that the implementation of the strategy would add further financial burdens, and they started to fear their resources would run out by being poured into an endless pot. The net outcome was that neither was implemented.

The other source of confusion was the attempt of the Secretariat of the LAS to

meet the directives of the 1979 summit meeting (held in Tunis) concerning improvement of economic relations among Arab countries and with other regions, and the NIEO. Among the papers prepared on these topics was a proposal for a "Charter of National Economic Action". This included:
- Neutralization of economic action, to avoid harmful reflections of political differences;
- Preferential treatment for Arab products and products of joint Arab projects;
- Arab economic citizenship, ensuring Arab capital and other production factors rights equivalent to those of citizens; and liberating the movements and rights of Arab labour;
- Rapid reduction of developmental and income gaps among and within Arab countries;
- Adoption of regional planning for joint Arab projects as a means of ameliorating and regulating joint action, with full recognition of the joint economic action strategy, and the joint Arab development decades, and plans based on them. Countries were asked to include in their development plans an allocation of a given proportion of resources for financing projects of the regional plan;
- Collaboration in financing common Arab needs especially with respect to security of the Arab nation and development of human resources and infrastructure;
- Reconsideration of collective agreements in order to increase their effectiveness;
- Hastening the implementation of the measures mentioned in the AMF agreement concerning settlement of current payments, and the expansion of use of the Arab accounting dinar, and paving the way for creating an Arab monetary zone;
- Liberation of trade flows to help build up an integrated productive base, while giving joint integrative projects a preferential treatment vs. foreign projects with respect to finance and marketing. Entering world markets in a collective manner, according to a collective bargaining strategy, and elaboration of a regional storage policy for goods of strategic importance;
- Improving the structures of joint action organizations, to raise their efficiency and ensure co-ordination among them, and the fulfilment of tasks assigned to them by the joint action strategy; and
- In all their actions, member countries should bear in mind the ultimate goal of Arab economic unity.

Other parts of the Charter refer to relationships with other regions and the creation of a new economic order, bearing in mind closer co-operation with the Third World.

In a sense, the Charter emphasized aspects of the strategy, and it may be claimed that the contents could have been taken care of through rephrasing the latter. However, the confusion we referred to arises from the treatment of the concept of planning. The Charter, while recognizing plans emerging out of the strategy, introduced a new concept that was not proposed by the experts preparing it. Instead of mentioning planning with respect to joint action, the Charter now calls for

planning of joint projects. Thus we are faced with three concepts of regional planning:
1. Regional development planning, which is an element of the strategy;
2. Planning of joint action according to the strategy;
3. Planning of joint projects according to the Charter, and reduction of the imperative component to finance earmarked for the projects of that plan.

This created a topological problem which can be illustrated as follows:

Actions related to	Areas of joint action			Areas of a domestic (country) nature
	A regional plan		not included in plan	
	joint projects	others		
Development	a	b	d	f
Others	–	c	e	g

The region action plan covers the cells (a), (b), (c). Out of these, (a) represents joint projects in areas of priority of the strategy. The part (b) may include other types of projects (e.g. country projects) which are relevant to the plan. On the other hand, part (d) includes other joint and country projects in areas not covered by the plan (e.g. construction which was not included in priorities). Both (b) and (d) include types of joint action other than projects. The strategy covers cells (a), (b) and (c). Development shares (a) and (b) but includes (d) and (f) as well. This means that joint action is not a proper element of development. Being one of the areas of priority of joint action, development planning is, in principle, an element of it, which introduces a logical inconsistency. A true overall strategy, on the other hand, would cover all the above cells, from (a) to (g), and hence the development strategy itself.

This was the difficult situation which this writer faced as head of a group formed to formulate the first joint action plan. The point may be illustrated with respect to one single detail – the size of the plan and the finance available. In the absence of information on the size of a joint development plan, and of the volume of resources available for its finance, the size proposed for the joint action plan may look out of order. The point was resolved arbitrarily by assuming reasonable rates of growth and investment for the whole region and relating joint action to them. Actions in the form of projects were assumed to be around 10 per cent of total investments. Those which essentially take the form of current expenditure on research were assumed to be half of allocations to research. These latter were assumed to gradually grow to become 1 per cent of regional GDP. This gave a total of $62 billion. It should be borne in mind that not all this amount had to be provided as extra funds. The plan covers a wide range of activities, including projects of a country nature but with joint impact. The trend of assistance within the region gives an estimate of

$17.6 billion for the five year period 1981-85. Further, some $3.5 billion may be directly financed by the countries concerned, being donor countries. This brings the total to $21.1 billion, including the $2.5 billion coming from the development decade allocations. This provided a minimum of one-third of the former estimate.

Another problem emerged as a result of the lack of response of member countries to appeals to provide the secretariat of LAS with information on joint actions in which they would participate. A similar attitude was followed by Arab specialized agencies which did not allocate any of their resources to the identification of activities for the first plan. Ultimately, the expert group had to rely on previous programmes proposed by those organizations. It turned out that even in cases where such programmes were approved by respective Ministers or boards, they were not brought to the attention of Ministers of Finance or Planning. The result was that when the plan frame was presented to the Economic Council, it hardly gave any directives, but it asked for project proposals, with some indication in favour of the lower limit of the plan size. When those proposals were presented in the shape of project data sheets, two objections were raised. The first was that not all projects represented were joint projects. Second, it was not accepted that proposals should be presented to the Council from a group of experts without the direct involvement of country planners. Issues of sovereignty seemed to be involved.

It may be claimed that the preceding paragraphs represent a digression from the subject matter of this paper. However, they help to reflect the attitude regarding co-ordination of plans. Surplus countries had been leading the way out of a regional co-ordination. Their thinking seems to be along the following lines:

1. In spite of their endorsement of regional documents relating to joint action, including acceptance of regional planning as a means for mobilizing efforts and precipitating development, they have overtly expressed their rejection of the concept "regional planning for the Arab nation". They seem to resent opening a gate inviting undesirable economic systems. They equally reject any proposals which may be suspected to push public enterprises ahead of private ones.
2. They consider their peculiar situation to be their own concern, and should not be left for regional institutions. In line with this thinking, some of them formed the Gulf Co-operation Council (GCC) in which the weight of Saudi Arabia is quite marked.
3. Relations with the rest of the region may be defined through general agreements (ensuring free trade and free capital movements) and through joint projects. Beyond that, any co-operation or integration is to be the subject matter of deliberations of regional institutions, which are not to obtain any prerogatory rights.
4. The selection and implementation of those joint projects is not to be left to regional institutions. Final say should be with the donor countries through their Funds.
5. In general, joint actions should not supercede bilateral relationships. As mentioned before, the bulk of assistance was through bilateral channels. In spite of decisions included in documents such as the Strategy and the Charter to

strengthen the multilateral funds, the AFESD and the AMF, it needed some extra efforts to gain some increase in their capitals.
6. Even projects to be financed through allocations to the "Development Decade" were subject to selection according to criteria agreed by donor countries with no interference from regional agencies, including the Economic Council and the Summit conferences.

This brought the ambitions and efforts of past years to an end. In spite of missions sent by the LAS Secretariat to countries to discuss the contents of the joint action plan, and the adjustments introduced in that plan, the whole project entered "deep freeze". As a cover for retreat, the Economic Council decided to go ahead with one of the priorities to avoid delay. It decided to urge the relevant organizations to propose food security projects. Later, it requested financing institutions to give those projects appropriate consideration, within their normal practices of operation.

It is interesting to note that Arab thinkers were disillusioned about this outcome. During our meeting in Amman in 1980, as a group of experts preparing the studies to be presented to the next summit meeting, we did not hesitate to agree with H.R.H. Prince Hassan, Crown Prince of Jordan, that there was need for a think-tank which would help to convey to decision-makers the possible paths of action needed to achieve national objectives. Consequently, the ATF (Arab Thought Forum) came into existence under the chairmanship of Prince Hassan. The forum is at present considering ways and means of approaching decision-makers and affecting their attitudes.

CONCLUDING REMARKS

One may be interested in investigating the concept of joint projects more closely. The subject was dealt with in a conference held in 1974 in Cairo by the CAEU. Several studies appeared, and other conferences were held. The last of these was prepared by the AFESD and the Arab Planning Institute in Kuwait in March 1983. Its purpose was to supply heads of sectoral federations with methodological and practical issues relating to their role in the preparation of the joint action plan. Addressing that gathering on methodological issues, this writer observed that there were various meanings for the term "joint project":
1. The most popular one is the one relating to finance, where more than one country provides equity capital, and assumes some role in management. This seems to be the meaning which settled in the minds of those who limited joint action to such projects.
2. The Economic Council, at one point, adopted a meaning devised by its Secretariat. Projects to be included in the plan were those of a joint nature. Strictly speaking, this would limit the scope to projects along the borders of adjacent countries, mostly in infrastructure (e.g., common water resources, electricity grids, pipelines, etc.).

3. A third meaning would be projects that help achieve a joint or common objective. For example, all projects contributing to food security may be considered "joint" in this sense.
4. In fact, the Strategy introduced a different concept, namely those projects which help create mutual intetdependence among Arab economies.

It seems that the Secretariat of the CAEU, which played an important role in fostering joint projects, adopted an enlarged version of the joint finance concept. A joint project is a project in which two or more Arab countries participate. Participation may be in the form of financial or physical assets, land, a given technology, management, etc. The whole idea was motivated by the early successes of the RCD (between Iran, Pakistan and Turkey, which started in 1964). At any rate, the purely financial concept is a red herring. A certain project may succeed in attracting multilateral finance; and thereby, *a posteriori*, it may be considered joint. What are relevant to the discussion are the other features of the project which justify *a priori* considering it joint, hence capable of attracting joint financing.

The above is not intended to add another chapter to this essay. The question is the possibility of a more effective plan co-ordination if the joint-project school takes the lead. Going back over the history of the subject, we note that the main "joint companies" (created mostly under the auspices of the CAEU) are nothing more nor less than *joint holding companies*. They took the shape of a specialized fund, to which certain financial assets were allocated. As time goes on, those companies are assumed to create enterprises in their fields of specialization, fields which had been selected because of their importance to the Arab nation. The actual legal status of each of these enterprises may depend on conditions acceptable to the authorities of countries hosting them. But the fact remains that as the number of joint (holding) companies increases, more dispersion of the decision-making process takes place. Suppose that such enterprises were jointly managed. Decisions from the mother company, profit-oriented by nature, may conflict with those of country planners, in areas of investment, production, employment, wages, prices and trade. Such conflicts are not theoretical. In a country like Egypt, for example, some of the above aspects have brought about waves of adverse effects. A single aspect like wage rates in joint investment companies has shaken the whole economy, carrying with it inadequate income-distribution effects.

Thus we soon have another facet of the problem of *sovereignty*. Capital-abundant countries managed to frustrate regional planning efforts on the basis of preserving their own sovereignty. Their insistence on confining co-operation to joint-finance projects eventually forces capital-short countries to adjust their legislation and tailor their economies to the conditions acceptable to joint investors. This brings in the worst aspects of multinationals without necessarily bringing in the benefits sometimes ascribed to them. In fact, this was one of the main arguments presented by Iraq in their paper on the Development Decade. Unless some central agency like the CAEU or the LAS is building up an approved regional plan, defining clear roles for the so-called joint companies, both country and regional interests are liable to be lost in the jungle.

It seems, therefore, that there is a great need for constructive work in planning at the regional level, whether liked or not. This may be implemented by some non-official body, such as the Long Term Planning Group for Arab Countries. Experience has shown that over-emphasis of formulation and measurement of common objectives may frustrate the efforts of such a group. What they do need is a breakthrough in techniques of projection and planning at a regional level. Other types of research such as those of the UNU or the Centre of Arab Unity Studies would provide valuable inputs. But eventually there would be a need to put pressure on decision-makers. The ATF may be of help. But a legal "father" should be there. The Secretariat of the Economic Council, having believed in the issue for quite a long time, is eligible to patronize the new project. This is not meant to ignore the role of the Secretariat of the CAEU. But it is a fact that this institution has been more and more thrown in the shadows. Its long-standing will to build up a regional plan (and to see that it is imperative) has been hindered by lack of resources. The time may come in the very near future when this institution is dissolved in the Economic Council to save money!

While the major oil producing countries around the Gulf have recently devised a formula for their own co-operation, they will soon have to seek "external" contacts. Expected developments in oil during the 1980s may soon see surpluses dry up, except in one or two countries. They are now in a better situation to appreciate the need to diversify their economies and multiply their sources of income. The main way out if industrialization, with all its technological and social implications. But this means securing markets. It will soon be proved that general agreements such as those relating to trade and capital movements are necessary but not sufficient. If this is the case, then it will be hoped that these countries will eventually join neighbouring countries in appreciating the need for proper planning and plan co-ordination.

CHAPTER 8

Patterns of Regional Co-operation Among Arab Countries

Mohammed Imady

Arab Fund for Economic and Social Development

THERE IS HARDLY any need for an analytical or theoretical underpinning of the case for economic co-operation among countries, or, for that matter, among regions. There is sufficient evidence of the value and effectiveness of co-operation and the pooling of efforts, as against individual action, to make it unnecessary to articulate the argument for co-operation. But the case becomes stronger if the countries and/or regions concerned partake of similar or not widely different features and characteristics, and if, simultaneously, they suffer from insufficient development of their resources and development capabilities. In this instance, the potency of the argument becomes more evident.

The Arab countries, which occupy the region stretching from Morocco and Mauritania to the West, to Iraq and Kuwait to the East, have a yet stronger compulsion for co-operation, given the fact that, in addition to the general argument for co-operation, they have particular reasons and incentives for it. Thus, they share the same historical and cultural heritage, have one circuit of economic life which had remained unbroken for centuries until the establishment of the state of Israel in their midst, and hold great hopes for economic development, cultural rejuvenation, and security for themselves as individual countries, and for the region as a whole looked at as one entity. In addition, they aspire to achieve a large measure of unity among themselves and share a largely similar political outlook for the future. With regard to development and security specifically, they argue cogently in two directions: first, that their individual and collective interests interact and are mutually supportive, if correctly conceived and designed, and secondly, that development and security are also mutually supportive and can be better achieved through deep and far-reaching co-operation, not only in economic but also in other areas of life and action.

One aspect of the great merit and urgency of economic co-operation among the Arab countries, as among other regions of the Third World, is the desire shared by all Third World regions to witness the emergence of a New International Economic Order (NIEO). They realize that without co-operation which is intelligently defined and earnestly sought, it would be impossible to achieve the acceptance of the NIEO by the industrial countries and regions of the North, or, if the NIEO is accepted as a concept or objective, to have it acquire the content without which it would remain meaningless and rather empty.

Without going into a detailed characterization of this content, we can reiterate six expectations which would warrant being attached to the NIEO. These are:

1. Better international division of labour which would conform more closely to the new international economic realities, and embody the conviction of the Third World that the old economic order discriminates against Third World regions. The division of labour sought in the context of the NIEO must allow greater opportunities for the advancement of Third World countries, particularly in the areas of industry, agricultural and rural rejuvenation, education, the acquisition of technological skills and advanced productive capabilities, supportive sectors and activities, and generally in the generation of national product.

2. Fairer returns to Third World regions for their productive efforts and the exhaustion or utilization of their resources, which often constitute their major source of income, and which they are most eager to process in order to generate larger value added at home.

3. More efficient and less wasteful use of Third World resources, in circumstances which correct the practices of the past that have been extremely permissive in the use and depletion of these resources, and overly concerned with the narrow interests of the industrial regions.

4. Choice of more appropriate technology to suit the endowments and needs of the regions of the Third World. This would involve true co-operation between the industrial world and the developing regions, and among Third World regions, in the search for appropriate technology and the evolution of the capabilities of the workforce in these regions to acquire the skills called for by the new advanced technology.

5. The pursuit of alternative courses or patterns of development suitable to Third World regions, which take into account the cultural values, priorities, basic needs, and natural and human endowments of these regions, and do not push them towards the trap of attitudes and behaviour patterns conforming to the interests of the industrial world and its Transnational Corporations, or towards attitudes and behaviour patterns alien to their culture.

6. Respect for the national (and regional) will of Third World countries and groupings of countries, and provision of scope for independent decision-making. This is not to be understood as disregard for the intricate web of relations that connects the various countries and regions of the world, North and South alike, or for the interdependence that exists and the need to recognize both its reality and necessity. However, in the present context, interdependence is not to be understood as licence for the continuation of serious imbalance in North-South

relations, or to be used as a euphemism that permits the project of the *status quo* in power relationships between North and South into the future.

BACKGROUND TO ARAB ECONOMIC CO-OPERATION

The strong European drive for colonization in the nineteenth and twentieth centuries brought about a restructuring of economic relations among the Arab countries. It disrupted the close intra-regional relations that had been in existence since the meteoric emergence of the Arab/Islamic empire in the seventh and eighth centuries, and diverted the emphasis in the relations that were to follow the set-up of the colonial regime towards a new intensive and extensive relationship with the European colonial powers, in the service primarily of their interests.

It was the onset of the era of Arab political independence after the Second World War that provided the opportunity for the abolition of colonial structure and its exploitative economic pattern and fueled the desire to re-establish political unity.

Regional co-operation is the first step on the road to achieving this unity. It is hoped that regional co-operation will lead, step by step, to greater cohesiveness, complementarity, integration and eventually organic unity. This aim is manifest in the many agreements entered into and the institutions set up within the broad framework of the League of Arab States. That co-operation represents the mainstream of Arab thinking and feeling is evident in the fact that, as early as 1944 and 1945 when the protocol forming the League of Arab States, and then its Charter, were drawn up and signed, it was stipulated that the League would undertake to bring about economic co-operation and organize it among the member states. The ambitions of the Arab countries went beyond co-operation and reached for unity, with the drawing up in 1957 of the Agreement for Arab Economic Unity, and the establishment in 1962 of the Council for Arab Economic Unity.

Although the institutional framework formulated has sought objectives more ambitious than mere co-operation, pragmatism and the lessons of experience have made the Arab countries place emphasis on an intermediate objective between mere co-operation which could not be considered an adequate reflection of the historical and cultural ties among the Arab countries and the aspirations shared by them, and full economic unity, which is the most demanding objective among all forms of economic cohesiveness. Thus, although the various levels of cohesiveness continue to feature in the agreements in force and to form part of the functions of the institutions established to further the cause of cohesiveness, it is complementarity that has come to be the objective most frequently articulated, in official statements and in the relevant literature alike.

However, in more recent years, particularly since the mid-1970s, yet another term has come to be mostly used as expressive of the objective sought. This is Joint Arab Economic Action (JAEA). The neutrality of this coinage is probably what gives it the wide circulation it has, and why it was selected in the first place. It avoids the criticism that the term "co-operation" arouses for being insufficiently worthy of the efforts of sister countries, and that which the term "unity" arouses for being rather unrealistic under present circumstances.

JAEA has been given the highest stamp of authority through the approval by the Arab Heads of State in the Eleventh Summit Meeting in Jordan in November 1980, of the Strategy for Joint Arab Economic Action (SJAEA). Among other things, the SJAEA stipulated for a plan to be drawn for the JAE sector, and announced within its framework the Decade of Development. The latter is to be associated with concentrated efforts for the development of the six least developed Arab countries; it is to receive US $5 billion in addition to any other resource flows for development. (The programme of the Decade of Development is to be operated by the Arab Fund for Economic and Social Development.)

MECHANISMS AND MODALITIES OF CO-OPERATION

Arab economic co-operation in its various facets is sought through both official and private channels. The latter are too diversified and relatively atomistic to be covered in this paper, although some reference will be made to certain private sector efforts. The official efforts fall within two very broad institutional frameworks: the League of Arab States (LAS) and the Council for Arab Economic Unity (CAEU). Between them, they account for many agreements, mechanisms and modalities. The present paper will not be overloaded with anything like a complete listing of these, but reference to several among them will be made in the course of the discussion. It is worth noting here that the Economic Council of the LAS, recently renamed the Economic and Social Council, has taken the initiative in designing and launching many of the instrumentalities of co-operation. Likewise, the CAEU rightly claims credit for a number of other instrumentalities, including the initiation of the Arab Common Market in 1964. Within the private sector, the most energetic institution in the present context has been the General Union of the Chambers of Commerce, Industry, and Agriculture in the Arab Countries, the most recent initiative of which (May 1982) has been the resolution to establish a company for agricultural development with a capital of US $5 billion. Other private sector activities have led to the formation of several joint banks (some with non-Arab participation) and several other joint projects.

The two wings of the Arab region, the Maghreb and the Arab Gulf subregions, have also established frameworks of co-operation restricted to the countries comprised by them, motivated by the conviction that each of them has certain particular features that justify closer internal association. Neither grouping dissociates itself from the overall grouping that comprises the whole Arab region by emphasizing its particular needs, endowments and problems. The Maghreb grouping is the Maghreb Permanent Consultative Committee (formed in 1964) headed by the Conference of Ministers of Economy, with a Permanent Committee and a Secretariat. The Gulf grouping is the Gulf Co-operation Council (GCC) which was set up only in 1981, but has already distinguished itself with brisk activity and has spread the coverage of its functions to include all aspects of economic life, as well as security (both internal and external) and foreign affairs. While it is too early to assess the substantive performance of the GCC, it can already be said that it seems to be determined not only to achieve co-operation but also close co-ordination of policies and activities in the areas concerned. In contrast, the Maghreb Permanent Consultative Committee, though a much older body, has less to show in the record of its performance.

The many purposes that fall within the generic term "economic co-operation" are served by the various institutions and mechanisms to which reference has been made. These come under a number of categories. Several are official organizations (specialized agencies) such as the Arab League Educational, Cultural and Scientific Organization for Industrial Development; the Organization for Agricultural Development; the Arab Labour Organization; the Organization of Arab Petroleum Exporting Countries; the Arab Fund for Economic and Social Development; the Arab Monetary Fund; and the Arab Authority for Agricultural Investment and Development. In addition, there are a number of professional (syndical) bodies, such as the Federations of Arab Economists, of bankers, of labourers, of engineers, and so on. On the other hand, some are production and service companies, (potash, tankers, re-insurance, marine transport, livestock, fishing); while some others are groupings or unions of industries in the fields of iron and steel, textiles, chemical products, and insurance. In all, these institutions have a combined capital in excess of $23 billion; obviously, several have no capital but operating budgets, and the significance of these therefore goes well beyond the financial resources at their disposal. In addition to the categories listed for illustration, there are joint projects or ventures between two or more countries in the fields of banking, real estate and industry.

One category of institutions is worth mentioning here, although these belong to individual countries. They are the national development funds, whose services cover the whole Arab region. For this matter, the funds constitute one prominent illustration of Arab economic co-operation. The aggregate capital of the five funds in existence (in Kuwait, Abu Dhabi, Saudi Arabia, Iraq and Libya) is about $17 billion.

Another area of co-operation is that of training, although it has not witnessed very energetic endeavours. Several regional training institutions are in existence. They provide training in maritime affairs, planning, statistics, agriculture, vocational training and training in skills related to the oil sector.

Finally, the many ministerial and other councils organized on a functional basis embody another aspect of the co-operative effort. They constitute an important institutional mechanism of control and advisory and co-ordinative service. The ministerial councils fall under two broad categories: groupings of specialized ministers (such as those of finance, labour, industry, agriculture, health, and the like) who hold *ad hoc* meetings independently; and specialized ministers meeting in their capacity as governing councils of certain regional organizations, for example the ministers of agriculture meeting as the governing council of the Organization for

Agricultural Development, or the ministers of finance as the governing council for the Arab Fund for Economic and Social Development, or for the Arab Monetary Fund.

Mention ought to be made here of certain special cases where economic co-operation was expected to reach a high level of cohesiveness approaching integration or even unity. These are cases where political unity was first decided upon by sovereign states, and where close economic relations were to be a function of the close political relations designed and/or entered into. They include the merger of Egypt and Syria of February 1958 which was severed in September 1961; the Egyptian-Syrian-Libyan Federation, which was established in 1971 but was never effectively consummated; and the Syrian-Jordanian phased overall integration which was initiated in 1975. The last-named instance is of particular interest, although its evolution has been stopped. The interest arises from the fact that Syrian-Jordanian integration was the best studied of the three cases mentioned, its phases were carefully designed and rationally interconnected, and its scope went well beyond economic life (agriculture, industry, banking, trade, transport) to include education and political institutions. (At the present moment, seemingly serious steps are being taken to establish close complementarity between Egypt and Sudan, with initial emphasis on economic complementarity. But the endeavour is still in process and cannot therefore be judged.) In all these instances, economic integration was not the objective primarily sought and emphasized, but one which was expected to be achieved as a major by-product of political unity.

Special reference ought finally to be made to three bodies whose functions explicitly include the promotion of economic co-operation – using the term here in its broadest connotation. The first is the Economic and Social Council, which sets out to further the cause of co-operation through the agreements it has drafted and ratified, the institutions it has established to undertake the varied co-operative functions stipulated for in the agreements, and the joint projects set up and launched by it or by the institutions or organizations formed by itself.

The second body is the Council for Arab Economic Unity, which by its designation and statutes is the specialized institution *par excellence* for the promotion of economic co-operation, complementarity and unity among the Arab countries. The CAEU has also fathered several agreements, institutions and joint ventures which together constitute an embodiment of economic co-operation of significant dimensions.

Finally, there is the Arab Fund for Economic and Social Development (AFESD). One of its three formal objectives is to promote joint programmes and projects, and thereby further economic co-operation. In addition, the technical assistance programme of AFESD, and its active participation in many regional activities, make it a significant institution for the generation of ideas related to co-operation and joint Arab economic action, as well as an effective instrument for the translation of ideas into concrete policies and action. Of particular significance here are the Fund's programme (undertaken jointly with the UNDP) for the identification and initial study of a large number of joint programmes and projects; the initiation of the ambitious programme in agricultural development in the region which has culminated in the establishment of the Arab Authority for Agricultural Investment and Development; and the launching of programmes in the areas of children's education through films, and in telecommunications. The latest illustration of the recognition of the role of the AFESD as a promoter of co-operation can be seen in the delegation to it by the the Arab governments of the administration of the funds assigned to the Decade of Development which the Eleventh Arab Summit approved in Amman in November, 1980.

APPROACHES TO ARAB ECONOMIC CO-OPERATION

The title of the present paper speaks of "patterns of co-operation", but it would seem more appropriate instead to use the term "approaches" or "areas of emphasis". This is because the course of co-operation, irrespective of the intensity of such co-operation and the extent to which it went, has not developed sufficiently to form a distinct pattern. Indeed, it can be said that the Arab region has evolved, or emphasized, certain strands that could only become patterns in the full sense of the term if they are multiplied and woven together into an identifiable fabric.

Be that as it may, we can still identify the various distinct approaches or avenues leading to co-operation (and sometimes going beyond it to co-ordination and complementarity and some limited integration). These approaches often overlap and are not necessarily parallel; nor do they constitute pre-set phases of a long process which conforms in its entirety to a coherent conceptualization and deliberate design and structuring. These rigorous features can only be found in the latest approach, which is that of the intensification of JAEA.

Several approaches to co-operation broadly defined have been adopted over the years in the Arab region. They are not of equal importance, nor have they all been adopted with an equal degree of deliberation, since some have come to be resorted to spontaneously under the pressure of circumstances.

Trade liberalization and payments facilitation featured first as the most appropriate expression of Arab economic-co-operation, and for that purpose the highest body of the LAS at the time, the Council of the Arab League drew up the Convention for Facilitating Trade and Regulating Transit in 1953, along with its sister document, the Agreement for the Settlement of Payments for Current Transactions and the Transfer of Capital. The rationale behind the Convention and the Agreement was that if liberalization and payments facilities could be implemented, commodity exchanges among the Arab countries would be vastly expanded. During the Second World War, and in the decade or two thereafter, intra-regional trade was not insignificant, particularly that within the Mashreg and the Maghreb subregions. It was, however, smaller in value than that between each of the subregions and the Western (mainly European) countries.

The Convention was followed by several amendments, involving changes in the tariff rates that were to be reduced gradually, and the overall effect of trade liberalization efforts was an expansion in intra-regional trade. However, it soon became evident that the range of expansion was narrow and did not promise considerable widening, and that trade liberalization itself was well below the hopes and ambitions of the Arab countries. As indicated earlier, this led to the very ambitious shift to the objective of Arab economic unity, which was to incorporate unification of the markets of the adherents to the unity agreement, as well as of their economic, commercial, and fiscal and monetary policies, and to allow identical treatment to the nationals of other countries signatory to the agreement.

Several factors worked against unity, and even effective liberalization left a great deal to be desired. Although the formal initiation of the Arab Common Market, and the signing of a much broader and more encompassing trade agreement in 1981 were to intervene between 1953 and the time of writing in the autumn of 1982, intra-regional trade has not only remained small, but has actually declined as a proportion of the region's overall foreign trade. It now hovers around 5-6 per cent of the latter, while about 75 per cent of trade is conducted with the OECD countries, and the balance with the Socialist and non-Arab developing countries. (This applies both to imports and exports.)

By the late 1960s and early 1970s it had become quite clear to LAS and CAEU circles, as well as to many ministers and independent academics and businessmen, that the real trouble insofar as the modesty of intra-regional trade was concerned, was not with the restrictions and handicaps to trade in existence – though considerable and mostly irrational – but with the basic fact that there were not available all that many goods and services to put into the stream of intra-regional trade to begin with. Hence the drastic shift involving the placing of emphasis on the expansion and improvement of the productive capabilities of the Arab countries – in brief, on development. What form this shift finally took in 1980 with the adoption by the Eleventh Arab Summit of the SJAEA will concern us at the end of the present section.

Not much movement towards *substantive co-operation* was in fact made until the late 1960s and the 1970s, when a large number of regional organizations, syndical groupings, joint projects, associations of companies in the same field of activity, and joint banks and other financial institutions concerned with development were established. Among all these, joint projects were the most prominent concrete embodiment of Arab economic co-operation. By far, the major impetus in this respect came in what might be called the "oil era", beginning with 1974, although the first joint project had been set up as far back as 1956. (Today there are over 120 such projects, of which 40 have non-Arab partners in them. They fall under several sectors.) The joint-project approach has been felt to be the corrective answer to the inadequacy of the liberalization-of-trade approach. No doubt it is attractive and has considerable promise, particularly if it does not continue to be pursued on an *ad hoc,* rather arbitrary basis, but is put within the framework of a plan for the JAE sector with clear-cut sector and programme priorities which, in turn, are determined in the light of the region's fundamental interests, needs and problems.

The third approach has been *joint financing.* In fact, it represents the other side of the coin of joint projects, since the association among the parties that establish and own a joint project is based on their sharing in the capital of the project established. Here it might be argued that true economic complementarity and integration goes well beyond joint financing. In the first instance, complementarity involves differentiation in products, processes, endownments, and generally patterns of demand and supply – a differentiation that makes the exchange between the two parties involved an expression and a confirmation of complementarity.

In the second instance, integration involves the inter-meshing of the production capabilities of two or more parties. This could go well beyond the more pooling of financial resources in a joint project, and could take the form either of horizontal integration, where the similar productive activities or the products of two or more countries would be pooled together to provide one aggregate availability of the product in question, to meet internal demand or export demand, or it could take the form of vertical integration. In the latter case, each of the countries concerned would specialize in one phase or process of the production operation involved.

It ought to be admitted that the instances of complementarity in existence are mostly the result of accident or good fortune, and only in a few cases are they the result of deliberate planning and decision. Likewise, the instances of horizontal integration are simply the result of the similarity of products in one or more countries, which expands the availability of the products concerned for the internal or external markets. As far as vertical integration is concerned, some efforts are being exerted toward this advanced form of co-operation.

The next avenue of co-operation to record also involves financial flows, though of a different nature. We refer here to *flows within the Arab region for aid and development purposes*. A certain volume of aid has flowed before 1973 across national frontiers from one or more to one or more Arab countries. But the flow took substantial dimensions only after the autumn of 1973 upon the correction of oil prices, and the accrual to the oil-producing countries of vastly expanded revenues. Since then aid from the oil countries to their less fortunate sisters (and to other non-Arab developing countries) has been substantial. Its aggregate over the years 1974 to 1981 has been in excess of $41 billion, with the largest part going to the Arab countries. We refer here to official aid on easy terms; in addition there are certain aid payments that do not appear in national statistics because of their delicate political or military nature. Finally, this record leaves out of account capital flows where donors and recipients fall within the private sector.

It is only fair to say that Arab economic aid, as a proportion of the Gross National Product of the donor countries, is distinctly creditable. The proportion is more than ten times its counterpart for OECD countries, which are richer in absolute terms on a per capita basis, more advanced, and enjoy a national product which is reproducible, unlike the export of oil which is no more than the sale of a depleting non-renewable asset. We might add here, without injecting a plaintive note, that the Arabs hardly ever hear a word of appreciation from the OECD countries for their generous support of Third World development. Instead, the Arabs are increasingly asked to make expanded contributions to international bodies and programmes, when neither their resources nor their level of development justify the shift to them of the responsibilities of the advanced countries.

There is one type of financial flow which is not undertaken by the oil-exporting countries themselves, or by business firms for investment in other countries, but by the nationals of certain countries (particularly Egypt, Jordan – including Palestinians holding Jordanian citizenship – Syria, Lebanon, North and South Yemen, and Sudan), to their relatives back home. The *remittances* made run into some $4 billion a year currently, and they arise from the work and earnings of about 4 million expatriates from the countries listed resident in the oil countries (namely, Iraq, Kuwait, the United Arab Emirates, Qatar, Saudi Arabia, Lybia and, to a lesser extent, Bahrain, Oman and Algeria). In fact, the exchange between manpower and financial flows is a good illustration of complementarity, inasmuch as the countries which constitute the parties to the exchange "export" the resource in which they enjoy a comparative advantage: money in one instance, and manpower skills in the other. This is not to say that the endownments of each party to the exchange are restricted to that which goes into the exchange, but merely to underline the nature of the resources that it is desired to export in each instance.

The manpower movement involved is of great significance, well beyond its financial aspect and implications. It makes for rich human interaction among the citizens of different countries who feel bound together by very strong historical, cultural, political and economic ties. It also strengthens the appeal and the feasibility of greater Arab cohesiveness. At a time when the drive for Arab nationalism and Arab unity needs greater support, manpower movement keeps unbroken one important strand in the fabric of unity.

Finally, in the context of manpower, it ought to be stated that the movement constitutes a reallocation of human resources which is justified on purely economic grounds, and which is contributive to the acceleration of construction and development in the receiving countries. Without denying the hardship which the countries of origin of the expatriates are already experiencing because of the drain that is involved, particularly in the availability of certain critical skills, it could be safely said that on balance, the two parties to the exchange are distinctly better off with the exchange than they would be without it. The receiving countries have thereby telescoped the process of acquisition of the skills imported and shortened the period of waiting, had they had to train their own manpower, by at least one or two decades.

The next area of co-operation is *energy*. Arab co-operation in the formulation of oil policies relating to pricing, and volume of production determination, which is achieved through bilateral discussions but more often through multilateral discussions within the framework of the Organization of Petroleum Exporting Countries (OPEC) is real, substantive and effective. Furthermore, their co-operation within the framework of the Organization of Arab Petroleum Exporting Countries (OAPEC) is also real and significant, although it does not include price and volume determination. On the other hand, thanks to OAPEC, a substantial and highly instructive activity is undertaken for the benefit of the member countries and other oil-short Arab countries. This includes studies and seminars on the various aspects of the oil industry, the training of staff of oil ministers and national oil companies, information about the oil industry and a number of other areas of activity. In addition, OAPEC has succeeded in the formation of five joint companies that provide oil-related services (engineering, dry-docking, exploration, and so on), a training centre for training instructors in oil-related skills and a judicial board for the adjudication of disputes among member governments. Finally, OAPEC has considerably sensitized the Arabs to oil and energy issues through the conferences it has organized and the publications it has produced. This last function is vital in a world where energy plays a vastly important role and where the depletion of Arab oil resources is a critical issue.

The listing and brief discussion of the various approaches or avenues pursued for the intensification of economic co-operation and, hopefully, its promotion to the more satisfactory levels of complementarity and integration has left a serious gap unfilled. This is *education and the acquisition of advanced technological skills*. In neither case has a great deal been achieved, although the Arab League Educational, Cultural and Scientific Organization (ALECSO) has done creditable work and drafted a strategy for the harmonization of curricula, the obliteration of illiteracy, and generally the raising of educational levels. It would be fair to assert that the large steps taken in the expansion of educational opportunities and the improvement of educational quality have largely been the result of efforts undertaken by individual countries, not through collective or co-operative actions.

Likewise, although serious thought and many meetings have been gone into the elaboration of programmes for the acceleration, on a regional basis, of technological capability and the evolving of appropriate technology, precious little has actually been performed to show for the efforts. This is all the more regrettable considering the centrality of educational, research and technical capabilities as ends in themselves, and as instruments in the acceleration and deepening of comprehensive and meaningful development. Some important work has been undertaken by the AFESD by way of the generation of ideas, problem-analysis and the suggestion of instrumentalities and programmes for the development of human resources in general and manpower in particular; likewise, the Arab Labour Organization (ALO) has directed its attention to the latter subject. But it must be admitted that the harvest has been disappointingly meagre. A new effort is being deployed at this very moment, spearheaded by ALO and ALECSO, and we can only wish them greater success in bringing about concrete co-operative action in the most important fields of education and technology.

The strands of co-operation in the economic field, or in closely related fields, that we have attempted to describe and discuss in the preceding paragraphs, have only been arranged into one pattern and woven together into the fabric of joint Arab economic action recently, in the Strategy for Joint Arab Economic Action, and the main and supportive papers prepared around the SJAEA submitted to the Heads of State in the Arab Summit of 1980. With the approval of the SJAEA, the go-ahead signal has been given for Arab economic co-operation (under the more embracing though somewhat ambivalent title of "joint Arab economic action"). The unfolding of JAEA is to proceed according to a plan for the JAEA sector, where sector and programme priorities are set, within an internally-consistent system, for the achievement of the broad dual objectives of development and security.

The new approach, which could be also called the new framework for Arab economic complementarity in view of its coherent internal structure and its conceptualization and logic, takes its starting point from the inadequacy of the approaches adopted and pursued earlier, namely trade liberalization, the setting up of joint projects, and joint financing. While these are all objectives worthy of pursuit, they have by themselves been incapable of bringing about a large measure of co-operation and complementarity. The new approach, it is argued, corrects the inadequacies of the earlier approach – inadequacies which were partly internal, and partly the result of insufficient energy in the pursuit of the approach. We have already alluded to the inadequacy of trade liberalization. We would like to add here the haphazardness of the establishment of joint projects and their failure therefore to serve as a forceful factor in Arab development and complementarity. Finally, complementarity was not seen and treated as involving, of necessity, the inter-meshing of large areas of Arab productive capability, along with the widening and deepening of this capability through a process of healthy and wide-ranging development.

The new approach, instead, specifies that the emphasis should be on development, and that this development should have a regional focus, in addition to the individual-country foci. Thus, individual-country development plans should be in harmony with each other; hence the need for co-ordination between country plans, and between these and the plan of the JAE sector. It is argued in the documents of the Eleventh Summit of 1980 that if development is conceptualized, designed and pursued along these lines it would serve complementarity, and would also benefit from complementarity. Furthermore, such development-in-complementarity would serve the purpose of security, which is a vital and critical objective of the Arab region, considering the Zionist occupation of important parts in it, and its submission to continuous Great Power pressures that often go beyond the political to reach the military menace of intervention.

Furthermore, another essential condition is specified. This is *planning*. The new approach stipulates that the development of the joint Arab economic sector, which is to proceed in harmony with individual-country development efforts, can only optimize the use of resources and serve the dual purposes of development and security if it is planned. This would necessitate the provision of an overall conceptualization of objectives, strategy, programmes, projects and policies relating to the joint sector. The overall conceptualization also includes a provision for the machinery, instrumentalities and the financial resources needed for the conduct of the newly-perceived, planned, complementarity-oriented development. With this, the circuit is complete and the new pattern of co-operation acquires its fullness in the fabric of Arab economic life.

It remains to be added, though in brief, that the conceptualization established the priority sectors and/or acitivites that JAEA and the plan of the joint sector should embody. These are: (1) human resources and the work force, (2) the acquisition of inherent technological capability, (3) food security, (4) the optimization of energy policies, (5) the development of basic and engineering industries,

(6) the development of physical infrastructure, (7) the evolving of financial resources which are presently sub-optimally deployed. Given a multi-avenue approach to the tasks that such a conceptualization incorporates, and given a rational and internally consistent blend of the efforts exerted in the pursuit of the tasks, Arab economic complementarity was thought to be within reach in a rather small number of years. The basic assumption underlying this expectation was that there would exist the national and collective will and determination to turn the conceptualization into concrete achievement in due course. Given such a will and determination, there would be no serious financial or institutional constraints to block the way to achievement. It was on a note of optimism that no such constraints existed, that the Eleventh Summit of 1980 ended.

PAST PERFORMANCE AND THE OUTLOOK FOR THE FUTURE

It is not possible within the confines of this brief paper to undertake an evaluation of the achievements with respect to co-operation and complementarity among the Arab economies in the context of each of the approaches or avenues pursued, or by each of the insitutions that have been designed as instruments or modalities for co-operation and complementarity. Instead, we will present a global evaluation. This is warranted because five generalizations can be made which will apply in all instances. Furthermore, the explanations that will be presented for the shortfall of performance below the expectations will also apply to the approaches and instruments in general.

The first generalization is that most of the creditable performance registered has been in the realm of the establishment of joint projects in a number of economic sectors. This conclusion is tenable in spite of the disparity in the quality of performance among the projects, and of the fact that the establishment has not on the whole been guided by a system of priorities inspired by the desire to achieve as comprehensive a development as possible under the circumstances given.

The second generalization is that the oil era has witnessed the emergence of concrete complementarity insofar as the movement of a substantial Arab labour force to the oil-exporting countries, and of a substantial financial flow in the form of remittances from this expatriate labour force to its countries of origin, is concerned. Again, this can be stated although the flows have been spontaneous and have had some deleterious social and economic effects both on the host and the original societies and economies.

In the third place, a notable instance of co-operation is exemplified in the substantial financial flows from the oil-exporting countries to the capital-scarce countries for investment and development purposes. However, substantial as these flows have been compared with the decades before the 1970s, they are considered below the expectations and needs of the recipient countries.

Further, the most creditable institutional contribution to the cause and requirements of co-operation has been made by the development funds operating in the Arab world. Here we include not only the Arab Fund for Economic and Social Development, which is a regional institution, but also the other national funds whose area of service is the Arab region as a whole. The Kuwait Fund for Arab Economic Development rightly occupies the place of honour in the present context, being the oldest fund in the region, and the one with the largest volume of resources to draw on for the promotion of development.

Finally, it can fairly be said that co-operation and complementarity have made little progress apart from the exceptions made in the four preceding paragraphs. At the risk of oversimplification, we can identify five basic causes for the shortfall in achievements, in spite of the fact that over 35 years have passed since the espousal by the LAS of economic co-operation and complementarity as a central policy objective.

1. First, the historical explanation of the shortfall. This is due to the fact that the Arab countries had been under foreign domination for several centuries, including the long and disruptive period under European colonial rule. This in itself twisted the pattern of economic relationships and directed them outwards, rather than inwards within the region. The abnormality of colonialism has made it extremely difficult since independence to re-orient the Arab economies towards intra-regional co-operation and complementarity. As a result, the region is left with serious dependency on the Western industrial world and an unhealthy complementarity with its economies.
2. The pressure of narrow vested group interests within each country also works against genuine co-operation and complementarity. Often this pressure arises from insufficient realization of the benefits that can accrue through regional co-operation. But in other instances group interests have a legitimate fear that they would suffer from co-operation. In the latter case, compensatory mechanisms could forestall the hostility to co-operation, but the architects of co-operation and complementarity have so far failed to design such mechanisms.
3. The exaggerated attachment to, and interpretation of "national sovereignty" has often served as an alibi to the genuine striving for co-operation and complementarity. This is a case of economic logic being overpowered by political mythology.
4. The fourth explanation for the meagre achievements so far is the disparity in socio-economic systems and ideological outlooks. There is no doubt that this disparity creates objective obstructions to co-operation and complementarity. But there is also no doubt that human ingenuity can overcome many of the obstructions, by providing formulas and modalities of action which can minimize the impact of the disparity, particularly that the socio-economic systems have grown to be much less differentiated from each other than they were in the late 1950s and the 1960s.
5. Finally, Arab economic relations have been at the mercy of the quality of political relations prevailing, and as the latter have been subject to rather wide fluctuation in many instances, it has not been possible to place economic co-operative relations on a solid and stable foundation.

What, then, is the outlook for co-operation and complementarity, given the analyses and evaluation that have been presented? Is optimism warranted that the course of co-operation will be any smoother in the future?

Though it may seem paradoxical, the answer is Yes. This answer is not an act of obscurantist faith, but one based on two solid grounds. The first is that, in the final analysis, economic logic will prevail. It is a matter both of good economics and common sense that it is in the interest of the Arab countries to co-operate and to establish close complementarity among their economies. Before we move on to the second grounds for the affirmation, it would be useful to provide some substance, even if briefly, to the claim that economic logic works in favour of co-operation.

There is strong expectation that with the rapid pace of economic diversification, industrialization, and development in general, a larger volume and a wider variety of goods and services will be produced by most Arab countries in the coming years. And the process is continuous, in spite of some fluctuation and some shortcomings in the quality of development. Development will make it possible for the Arab countries to put into the stream of intra-regional trade many more goods and services, especially as production becomes more differentiated and sophisticated.

As far as the petrochemical industry in particular is concerned, the productive capacity already installed as well as that which is being installed is not expected by the mid-1980s to constitute more than 5 or 6 per cent of world capacity in the aggregate. This in effect means that there is a promising marketing scope for the products within the region, and also in Third World markets in general. It ought to be remembered in this connection that the petrochemical industry in its present state is, and for several years to come will remain, heavily biased in favour of primary products, much less secondary and tertiary (final) products. This means that the industry can be further projected into new directions and still find a market within the Arab region for much of its production. This is as true of fertilizers, insecticides and pesticides, as of synthetic fibres, dyes and paints, plastic goods, and the dozens of other products which are now a substantial component of the region's imports from the industrial countries.

Another opening for the region's products within itself will be created by the need for the recipients of Arab economic aid to pay their debts to the Arab creditors. They will have increasingly to depend on their exports to these creditors. This will have a dynamic effect on the diversification and sophistication of the Arab economies, and will widen the possibilities for exchange within the region. And the development in question will apply both to goods and to services.

With regard to the movement of Arab labour across national frontiers within the region, it may well be that the vast expansion of the volume which was witnessed between 1973 and 1980 may not be repeated. But it can also be argued that the present plateau of employment of Arab expatriate labour will be preserved. The fact that the youth of the oil-exporting countries are being educated and technically trained in ever larger numbers should not obscure the fact that the oil economies are expanding continuously, and that they have a large component of non-Arab expatriate labour. This should suggest that job opportunities for expatriate Arab skills will continue to be extensive for many years to come.

Large-scale industrialization depends on a solid and broad foundation of engineering industries. Most of the region's countries will be unable to establish and maintain these individually. Their compelling desire for industrialization will be an added impetus for co-operation. The same applies to extensive research and the attempt to create substantial cadres of leaders in technology.

The hardship experienced by the oil-exporting countries in 1981 and 1982 in selling as large a volume of oil as in 1979 and 1980, and the decline in oil export revenues, together suggest that capital flows within the region are bound to decline for a few years to come. It would be true that the answer to this unfavourable development cannot be a light-hearted faith in the reversal of the present depression in oil prices. The more convincing answer should be that the oil exporters have probably become fully aware of the inadvisability of placing a large part of their real and monetary investments in the Western money markets, and can legitimately be expected to divert a more substantial volume for investment in the Arab region. If this were to happen, and it is likely in our view, then the flows to the capital-scarce countries could at least be maintained.

Last but not least, the concern for food security can only be met satisfactorily though joint Arab efforts. This is increasingly becoming a matter of wide acceptance at the levels of opinion.

This analysis would be incomplete if we did not point to the impact of the large body of believers in Arab co-operation, particularly the intellectuals and opinion-makers, who are becoming increasingly sensitized to the power of the arguments for co-operation as being economically beneficial, in addition to being politically, culturally and emotionally necessary and desirable. The economic literature supporting co-operation, both official and by public institutions and analysts, is making itself felt at the decision-making level, as well as within the general public. Likewise, the dozens of regional organizations, with their leaderships and cadres, are an immense source of pressure for regional co-operation.

So far, we have been enlarging on the first grounds for the expectation that the course of co-operation will be smoother within the medium-term. The second grounds for optimism is that the very dangers that fragmentation in the Arab region present (politically as well as economically and culturally) will before long make it clear to decision-makers, opinion-makers and the public at large, that the only long-term safeguard and guarantee of national security, and the only road to comprehensive and meaningful development, lies in genuine and far-reaching regional co-operation.

Yet neither economic logic nor the realization of danger will operate by themselves to bring about that change in convictions, attitudes and behaviour patterns capable of smoothing the ground for co-operation and complementarity. In the final analysis, there will be a critical need for a re-education process at all levels of awareness and responsibility in order to show most clearly what substantial rewards co-operation could bring and what the substantial penalty of fragmentation would be. In closing, I wish to declare my faith that the Arabs will not fail to make a wise choice between the rewards and the penalty.

CHAPTER 9

Towards a Strategy for Arab Food Security

Khalid Tahsin Ali

Arab Fund for Economic and Social Development

FOOD PRODUCTION in the Arab world, viewed against the high growth rate of demand, has reached alarming proportions. The situation is clearly reflected in the developments of the recent past. During the previous 8 years (1974-1982)* agricultural production in the 12 Arab countries grew at the rate of 2.5 per cent annually, while demand, fueled by the combined effect of high population growth (2.9 per cent per annum during the 1970s), and per capita income (particularly in the oil exporting countries) grew at the rate of 6 per cent per annum. This wide disparity caused net agricultural imports to grow at the very high rate of 20 per cent per annum. Agricultural exports declined in volume for all major commodities. Thus a state of near equilibrium between imports and exports which prevailed at the outset of the last decade has been severely disrupted to the extent that earnings from agricultural exports declined to only 15 per cent (1981) of the cost of agricultural imports. The cost of these imports increased nearly twelve-fold in the past 12 years, from less than $2.0 billion (1970) to over $23.0 billion (1981).

Self sufficiency ratios (SSRs) declined sharply during the past 8 years, ranging from 20 to 40 per cent for different commodities. As a group, the Arab countries have maintained full self-sufficiency in the production of only two groups of commodities, none of them of basic or strategic significance, namely fruits and vegetables (108 per cent SSR) and cotton (140 per cent SSR). On the other hand, the region now imports 75 per cent of its requirements of sugar, 66 per cent of wheat and edible oil, 50 per cent of all grains and dairy products, and 33 per cent of meat (red and white).

In the process, 20 of the 21 Arab countries acquired a negative agricultural trade balance, while at the beginning of the last decade six of them enjoyed a positive one. The most disturbing feature in these developments is the fact that all the Arab countries with known and well documented agricultural production potential,

---

*The Arab Economic Report — 1983. The Agricultural Sector. Joint Publication by the League of Arab States, the Arab Fund for Economic and Social Development and the Arab Monetary Fund (in press).

sufficient to meet local requirements and provide export surpluses, are now net importers of food.

THE MAJOR ISSUES

Clearly the most important single issue facing agricultural development is the very uneven distribution of natural and financial resources among the countries of the region. With very few exceptions, this rather specific particularity of the agriculture sector of the region approaches a state of near dichotomy. Simply stated, the countries with abundant financial resources have very limited agricultural resource base in relation to their requirements and *vice versa*. This can be seen from a few relevant indicators.

More than three quarters of the cultivated area and irrigation water, and the same proportion of the rural population, are found in the 14 low and middle-income countries, a total of 33 m/ha of cultivated land (of which 8 m/ha is under irrigation) and 64 million rural people. Significantly, a much higher proportion of future potential is found in these countries. However, their combined GDP represents 34 per cent of the total Arab GDP, with an average per capita income of $710 (1980). The six least developed among these countries have a largely agricultural economy, and the majority of the population is rural. They possess one-quarter of the presently utilized land and water, 28 per cent of the rural population, but only 4 per cent of the combined Arab GDP, with an average per capita income of less than $400.

On the other hand, the seven high income countries possess the remaining one-quarter of the agricultural resources and rural population, as well as the remaining three-quarters of the GDP with an average per capita income of over $6,300. If the two countries with a good agricultural base are excluded from this group, we find that the remaining five possess only 6 per cent of the agricultural resources and rural population, but also 57 per cent of the total Arab GDP.

Detailed supply and demand analyses, as well as the present picture of agricultural imports, clearly indicate that, due to limitation of the resource base, the high income countries cannot achieve an acceptable level of food security (again with the exception of one or two) in the foreseeable future. With regard to low and middle-income countries, these analyses show that although many countries in this group have the potential for self-sufficiency and even surplus for export, their agricultural rate of growth achieved in the past 10-12 years has been rather disappointing due to a number of factors, most of them related to scarcity of development funds.

In the first half of this decade official appropriations for agricultural development averaged $3,300 per capita of agricultural population in the seven high income countries, $320 in the eight middle income, and only $135 in the seven low income countries, which is only 4 per cent of the high-income countries. The full spectrum ranges from an almost unbelievable $17,000, down to an equally unbelievable $70.

And this last figure concerns one of the countries with the largest unexploited agricultural potential in the Arab world. The high income countries appropriated an estimated $65 billion for their agricultural development in the first half of this decade, while the corresponding figure for the seven least developed countries is only $3.0 billion, much of it based on deficit financing and foreign aid which may or may not materalize. While these figures show the seriousness of the efforts of the high-income countries to develop their agriculture and transform their rural societies, they also reveal the inward-looking rather than regionally-oriented policies of the countries involved towards agricultural development.

This should not be taken to mean that there has been no serious co-operative effort. In fact there is growing interest and involvement of relevant joint organizations in agricultural rural development. Seven national and regional development funds and banks provide assistance for agricultural development to the needy Arab countries, mostly in the form of soft loans.

However, although the interest of these funds in agriculture is definitely on the rise, their combined loans to agriculture during the past decade did not exceed 6 per cent of the recipient countries' allocations, albeit very limited, to the development of this sector. Projections for the first half of the 1980s indicate that this picture is not expected to change substantially. In fact, the relative contribution of these funds may even decline due to increasing allocations of national resources.

In addition, there are a number of technical assistance joint Arab organizations, specialized or otherwise, which are involved in different aspects of agriculture. Although these are performing useful roles, they are all constrained by limited resources which renders their services hardly perceptible in relation to the magnitude of the problems. Lastly, there exists a number of joint agricultural investment companies and other types of bodies in the public, joint and private sectors, with capital participation ranging from two to fifteen countries. The results of their efforts are mixed, and in some cases too premature to assess. The overall picture, however, is that the financial resources available to these joint ventures are much too limited to make a real impact. Additionally, these ventures have tended to seek remunerative financial return in the short-term, and have necessarily concentrated their activities in "safe" projects. Therefore, the scope of their involvement has been severely limited, which has left untouched the wide horizon of opportunities which can only yield safe financial returns after a fairly long period of time.

However, it should be clearly recognized that the lofty objective of food security requires much more than what has so far been achieved and stipulated by Arab joint efforts. It, in fact, requires concerted and systematic efforts to bring together in a fully co-ordinated manner the various interventions required to achieve the specific economic and social objectives of agricultural and rural development. This entails not only the capability to co-ordinate and harmonize existing joint efforts, but also to intensify and multiply these efforts and to bring them in line with national priorities and plans. Obviously, to achieve this rather complex and multi-faceted task, a proper institutional set-up is required, which should draw its mandate from a legal instrument – an international treaty among co-operating countries. Such a legal and institutional framework should, *a priori,* formulate long-term and intervening medium-term perspectives for the food and agricultural situation in the region under different alternatives. And, accordingly, it should determine priorities, and modalities of interventions, within an overall strategy within which the roles of different regional and national efforts are clearly specified and fully co-ordinated.

The Arab world at present lacks such an approach and its legal and institutional requisites. Present joint efforts are fragmented among numerous institutions, there is a complete lack of an overall perspective, of collective objectives, and of a mechanism to co-ordinate, let alone integrate the efforts.

In brief, the central message of this paper is that, if the Arab world is to take the problem of its food security seriously, it has to develop a strategy of action which relies on the integrated approach to agricultural and rural development.

TOWARDS A STRATEGY FOR ARAB FOOD SECURITY

The proposed Lines of Action can be grouped into four categories:

1. Legal and Institutional Requirements

It is now deeply felt that an appropriate legal base and an institutional set-up is required to formulate a "Joint Arab Agricultural Development Strategy" within which the various issues are dealt with systematically and on a permanent and sustained basis. This should also afford an appropriate forum for the exchange of experiences and interaction of resources, for the formulation of suitable modalities of co-operation among the Arab countries, and for the co-ordination and strengthening of the activities of relevant, joint and national organizations.

Work on this aspect is already in progress as a joint effort between the Arab Fund for Economic and Social Development (AFESD), the Arab Economic Unity Council (AEUC), the Arab Organization for Agricultural Development (AOAD) and the Food and Agriculture Organization of the United Nations (FAO). It is expected that this work will propose a treaty and a number of subject matter protocols for Arab agricultural co-ordination and integration, and an appropriate institutional set-up which the AOAD will be strengthened to carry out the additional responsibilities required by the proposed treaty.

2. Long and Short-Term Perspectives

A number of "Lines of Action" are proposed. Their overall objective is to establish a clear and reliable picture with regard to demand, production and foreign trade in agricultural commodities and inputs, and their probable evolution in the short, medium, and long terms. This is basically a monitoring function and an early warning system, on the basis of which appropriate measures could be identified and implemented. Specifically, three Lines of Action are proposed within this category:

(a) Long-term (year 2000) Country Perspective Studies. These studies will develop projections up to the year 2000 at five-year intervals. In demand projections it will apply low and high variants; in production estimates it will employ three scenarios: a low or trend scenario assuming continuation of present conditions; a normative scenario assuming substantial support and policy changes, and a third high scenario assuming a high level of co-operation where financial obstacles are, by and large, eliminated. This work should form the basis, on country as well as joint Arab levels, for the determination of possible food security levels and their input requirements – land, water, machinery, pesticides etc., including financial inputs and time requirements.

(b) Short Term Perspective Studies (1985). These studies are to be designed to carry out in-depth analyses of the on-going agricultural and rural development plans, determine the reliability of their production targets from analyses of the different actions and policies included in these plans, and also to determine the effectiveness of implementation and major constraints. This work should lead to the identification of specific measures to relieve these constraints and achieve objectives.

(c) Standardization of Agricultural Planning Methodology. So far no attempt has been made in this direction, and therefore each country employs its own methodology in agricultural planning. Due to technical constraints the methodologies employed range considerably in reliability and sophistication. In the absence of a fairly uniform and sufficiently reliable planning system much of the future joint Arab effort would be hampered. This Line of Action, therefore, will attempt to establish an appropriate uniform methodology which would be adopted by individual countries in ways that would not interfere with the basic premises of the system. This work should also lead to the identification of specific measures to strengthen national capabilities in agricultural planning, follow-up and evaluation.

3. Co-ordination and Strengthening of Ongoing and Planned Joint Efforts

The third category is an effort to review and evaluate ongoing and planned joint Arab agricultural and rural development activities. The review should co-ordinate and intensify these activities, search for ways and means to increase their effectiveness, identify major gaps and, most important, search for ways of eliminating the obstacles facing some of the major initiatives in this area. The review would include:

(a) The regional and national Arab funds, the technical assistance organizations (AOAD, ACSAD,* specialized federations), and investment companies and organizations.†

---

*The Arab Centre for Studies of Arid Lands and Dry Areas.
†Arab Authority for Agricultural Investment & Development.

(b) Solutions to the stalled efforts of the AOAD concerning the Food Security Programmes, whose first stage of preparation was carried out two years ago but which have now been nearly halted due to lack of funds. The proposed efforts should not only seek funding for the pre-investment stages, but should also ascertain availability of funds for implementation.

(c) The development of an appropriate institutional set-up for the promotion and servicing of commercially viable investments in agricultural and food production and related areas, such as the production of inputs, marketing and processing. The potential for such investments is tremendous but the obstacles facing it, as was mentioned earlier, are also considerable. This could be an extremely rewarding undertaking which could yield rapid results. The proposed service should look at the investment climate in each country thoroughly and try to work out specific solutions to existing problems. It should identify suitable projects for investment and carry out the necessary technical and economic studies to promote these projects. The proposed institutional set-up could indeed become the focal point that would bring together the investment opportunities in the host countries with the financial resources seeking such opportunities.

One of the most important initiatives in this area is the recent decision (1982) of the conference of private Arab businessmen in Taif, Saudi Arabia, to form the Arab Agricultural Investment Company, with a capital of $5 billion. This is a clear indication of the potential and the willingness of the private sector to enter the agricultural and food area. The need is to guide, assist and promote this great potential. This development was further enhanced by the recent (February, 1983) resolution of the Arab Economic and Social Council. The resolution calls for the adoption of the integrated programming approach to joint Arab projects, particularly in the area of food security. A joint team, representing all relevant joint Arab organizations was created by the Council to see to the implementation of the above mentioned resolution.

4. Development Programmes in Selected Technical Fields

The fourth and last category includes a number of technical studies designed to come out with specific practical measures to be carried out in a co-ordinated manner at the country and regional levels. Each of the proposed studies is a complex of measures and activities requiring long and expensive efforts; however, each would deal with a fundamental problem of agricultural and rural development in the Arab world.

These studies and programming efforts include:

(a) A Programme for the Conservation and Development of Natural Agricultural Resources. The most important of these are surface and groundwater, soils, natural rangeland, forestry and marine fishing resources. The intended effort is designed to determine gaps in knowledge and the country's development effort, and accordingly to formulate plans of action at the country and joint levels as appropriate.

(b) A Programme for Agricultural Research and Development of Technology. The need for concerted serious effort in this most important field is all too obvious. The individual country's capabilities, although different in extent, are invariably inadequate. Furthermore, and due to considerable environmental similarities, this field of activities lends itself well to joint efforts based on ecological zoning rather than on artificial geographic boundaries. Several basic studies on the subject, which should form the basis of a suitable plan of action, have been carried out.

(c) Integrated Rural Development. It is now clearly realized that effective agricultural development should be humanized; technologies and infrastructures are useless in the absence of a contented, healthy, informed and motivated farmer. This social approach is now gaining rapid recognition at national and international levels. Some work has already been carried out. Completion, updating and reorientation of this work toward specific practical measures should receive high priority.

(d) Physical Infrastructures for Agricultural Development. The lack of sufficient physical infrastructure, particularly in the low income major agricultural countries, is seriously hampering the exploitation of the vast production potential of these countries. These include a vast number of components such as control and distribution of surface water, drilling for groundwater, hydroelectric power, transport and communications, storage facilities, fishing vessels and gear, agro-industries, etc. Information on the nature, location, priorities, time requirement and cost is a fundamental prerequisite of the medium and long-term development plan. Furthermore, infrastructural development receives high priority with the development finance institutions. Such comprehensive information may well lead to greater interest and investment at the national and joint Arab levels.

(e) A Programme for a Strategic Arab Food Reserve. Although a number of studies have been carried out at both the country and regional levels, no specific joint programme has yet emerged. The available information on this subject indicates that there are serious gaps in individual country efforts in this area, and that a considerable scope exists for joint action, mostly at a sub-regional level, thereby affording a greater degree of security at lower cost.

CONCLUSIONS AND RECOMMENDATIONS

Collective food security in the Arab world can only be achieved through a much higher level of co-operation than now exists among individual countries. A legal and institutional base, lacking at present, is essential for the development of a joint strategy.

Within the proposed legal and institutional base, Lines of Action, each providing a major thrust in a given sector, need to be developed and implemented. A numebr of these have been proposed. Initiation of action can start immediately. A co-ordinated programme of work may be developed and its financing and implementation distributed among existing regional organizations.

The U.N. system can play a catalytic and technical role. It can effectively contribute to the preparation and implementation of each of the proposed Lines of Action in co-operation with the relevant regional organization.*

---

*The Economic Department of the Arab League, The Arab Fund for Economic and Social Development, The Arab Economic Unity Council, and the Arab Organization for Agricultural Development.

CHAPTER 10

Regional Co-operation in Human Resource Development in the Arab Countries

Abdulla M. Ali and Mohammed Galaleldin

Arab Planning Institute

THE ARAB COUNTRIES probably represent the group of Third World countries most suited to regional co-operation and integration. In addition to a common culture and language, there is a geographic continuity and complementarity of resources. While European integration is possible without uniformity of language among the countries involved, the Arab countries do not face even a language handicap in attempting to integrate sets of neighbouring countries into larger units, or even in creating one Arab nation. But language is not the only issue. Complementarity of resources exist between the oil-rich and the oil-poor Arab countries. Significant flows of capital from the former group with their sparse population and relatively poor natural resources, and flows to them of labour from the latter group would improve the allocation of resources in all countries and maximize the welfare of the Arab region as a whole.

It is generally accepted that the development process is the development and utilization of human resources. The Arab region with a total population of over 160 million (in 1980) does not suffer a dearth of human resources. However, deficiencies in the quality and distribution of human resources throughout the region can be perceived as one of the most important factors in developing the area as a whole. As the size and density of population vary from one country to another, a redistribution of population in the Arab region would lead to better allocation of resources, optimal investment of natural and material resources, better mobilization and utilization of the labour force, equitable distribution of wealth, and increased satisfaction of basic social needs. This would be the beginning of a process of a genuine and comprehensive development at the level of the entire region if accompanied by a co-operative effort in the development of human resources.

A central element of human resource development in the Arab region is the system of education, including formal and informal components, and the social organization through which the energies of the people are mobilized. At both the national and regional levels, there are still serious deficiencies in the amount, quality and content of education. There are also extreme inequalities in the distribution of educational investments and opportunities between the different countries, indeed different zones of the same country, and between males and females. The target of eradicating illiteracy or of achieving compulsory basic education is very difficult for some Arab countries with large populations and/or scarcities of resources, such as the two Yemens, Sudan, Somalia and Egypt. A Pan-Arab educational plan seems the only way to hasten the achievement of educational targets.

The educational system in the Arab countries has been unable to meet the requirements for certain skills and highly qualified manpower, particularly in the oil-rich states. This has not only led to sizeable movrements of skills and professionals among the Arab countries, but also to significant inflows of labour from outside the Arab region. The modality of labour transfers is not necessarily in the best interest of both sending and receiving countries – or of the region as a whole – as far as comprehensive sustained development is concerned. Therefore, nationalization of these movements to maximize development potential in the region is urgently needed. This requires a systematic and scientific study in order to identify current and future availabilities and requirements of different types and levels of manpower in the whole region. Policy-makers must not only be aware about the shortages and surpluses, but also about how they have arisen, why they have been perpetuated and how they can be corrected. Drawing-up policies in this region requires regional co-operation and integration – not only in migration and education policies, but in economic policies as well.

Related to manpower and educational policies is the so-called "brain drain", or the emigration of highly qualified manpower to the advanced capitalist countries. The magnitude of this problem represents considerable losses in human resources and in the technological potential of the Arab region, and inhibits the integration of policies in the field of education, basic and advanced training, and technology transfer. The determinants and consequences of this phenomenon should be investigated thoroughly in all their social, economic and political implications in order to integrate plans for manpower and education and to find ways and means to attract Arab emigrants to work in the region and contribute to its development.

A related issue which must be pointed out is the magnitude, characteristics and causes of labour migration from the Meghreb countries to Western Europe. Research into the possible re-allocation of these immigrants to the Arab labour importing countries is needed. Improving labour market information in the Arab region is very important in this regard. The recent establishment of a regional Arab Employment Bureau in Tangier, Morocco, merits encouragement and support. It is hoped that this Bureau will lead to the growth of a common Arab labour market that would abolish or at least relax the legislative and administrative restrictions on the right of Arab workers and professionals to move freely within the Arab region, as had always been the case before the colonial period. Any progress in this direction would be extremely meaningful to Arab solidarity and unity, as this affects ordinary people. In this regard, it is very important to identify the legal and institutional issues facilitating or hindering labour exchanges in the Arab region. Studying the prevailing laws and decrees and their influence on migration in the region would help in drafting a Regional Charter that could be adopted as a common policy in the Arab region.

Health planning is essential to a strategy of human resource development in the Arab region. Although the provision of public health services, combined with public awareness as a result of education and communication, has resulted in better health standards during the past two or three decades, much more progress must still be achieved in personal and community health. Nutrition has to be considered as basic in this regard. The most recent statistics show not only high levels of mortality, but considerable differentials in morbidity and mortality levels among the different Arab countries, and within individual countries. A baseline assessment of current health conditions along with a better understanding of the social and biological determinants of morbidity and mortality must be provided so that effective measures can be taken to improve health conditions of the Arab society.

Without discussing other basic social and individual needs that are essential to the development and utilization of human resources such as security, freedom and participation and equal opportunities, we would like to stress that these needs as well as the ones mentioned before can only be fulfilled for the region as a whole through a genuine regional economic integration. This requires a higher degree of political maturity and greater co-operation. It seems that the oil-rich countries can afford to give substantial help and aid to the oil-poor countries without being greatly affected in their pursuit of development and prosperity. Persistent determination to follow the path of Pan-Arab solidarity and unity and to fulfil the dreams of economic self-sufficiency requires that the increasing gaps in wealth between the rich and the poor be arrested and the differences be reduced significantly.

An issue that needs special attention in our effort to develop and utilize human resources in the region is the position and role of women. Raising the participation of women in the labour force should be one of the main objectives. The economic participation rate of women can be raised through encouraging them to engage in activities that do not conflict with the disciplines of the prevailing value system. This would not however change women's roles significantly. It is therefore important to change the attitudes towards women's work. Although this cannot be done overnight, it would be effective if accompanied by some important technical actions such as provisions for transportation, child-care facilities, training, promotion and knowledge of available job opportunities.

Any regional approach to human resources development and manpower planning should aim to correct extreme inequalities in the distribution of wealth. Admittedly, the oil-rich Arab countries gave about five billion dollars per year to Third World countries as concessional Official Development Assistance between 1973 and 1980. A large share of this aid went to Arab countries – more than 70 per cent of it to the three "middle-income" countries Jordan, Syria and Lebanon. These countries have less than 10 per cent of the total Arab population and are known as the "confrontation states".

There are also striking variations in population distribution. The five least developed countries in the region have more than 20 per cent of the total population.

Two oil-rich countries, namely Algeria and Iraq, together possess another 20 per cent of the total population, while the richest Gulf countries have less than 10 per cent of the population. Half the population is concentrated in what we have classified as middle-income countries. (See Table 10.1.)

As the economic participation rate of the indigenous population is generally higher in the oil-poor countries, the percentage of the Arab labour force in these countries is much higher than that reflected by the population figures which include non-Arab population.

REGIONAL VARIATION IN LITERACY

As Table 10.2 shows, the rate of literacy ranges from 70 per cent for Jordan to only 17 per cent for Mauritania. Between these two extremes, there is a mixture of both oil-rich and oil-poor states. Some of the rich states such as Saudi Arabia have a low literacy rate (as a result of previously lacking infrastructures) and increasing expenditures on education have been provided. However, in all rich Arab states enrolment ratios are very high, as will be shown later. More resources and efforts are to be directed in these states for literacy campaigns for older age groups.

In the oil-poor Arab countries, with their relatively large and rapidly increasing

Table 10.1. Population in Selected Arab Countries (1981)

Country	Population (millions)	% of total
Egypt	43.3	25.7
Morocco	20.9	12.4
Algeria	19.6	11.6
Sudan	19.2	11.4
Iraq	13.5	8.0
Syrian Arab Republic	9.3	5.5
Saudi Arabia	9.3	5.5
Yemen Arab Republic	7.3	4.3
Tunisia	6.5	3.9
Somalia	4.4	2.6
Jordan	3.4	2.0
Libyan Arab Jamahiriya	3.1	1.8
Lebanon	2.7	1.6
People's Democratic Republic of Yemen	2.0	1.2
Mauritania	1.6	1.0
Kuwait	1.5	.9
United Arab Emirates	1.1	.7
Total	168.7	100.1

Source: Compiled from the World Bank, *World Development Report 1983*, Table (1) pp. 148 and 149.

Table 10.2. Literacy Rate in Selected Arab Countries (1980)

Country	Literacy rate % (15 years and over) 1980
Jordan	70
Tunisia	62
Kuwait	60
Syrian Arab Republic	58
United Arab Emirates	56
Egypt	44
Yemen, People's Democratic Republic	40
Algeria	35
Sudan	32
Morocco	28
Saudi Arabia	28
Yemen, Arab Republic	21
Mauritania	17

Source: World Bank, *World Development Report 1983*. Table (1), pp. 148 and 149.

population, it will be difficult to improve educational attainment substantially unless far more financial resources are made available from both local and regional sources.

MORTALITY DIFFERENTIALS AND THE RELATIONSHIP BETWEEN MORTALITY AND SOCIO-ECONOMIC VARIABLES IN ARAB COUNTRIES

In all the Arab countries, decline in mortality during the past few decades has been the dominant factor towards accelerated population growth. Gains in longevity have been experienced by all the national populations of these countries, rich and poor. However, the gains in mortality decline have not been uniform, either between the countries or within the countries. Differences in mortality levels exist not only between Arab countries but also within the countries such as rural/urban differences, male/female differences and differences by socio-economic status.

Table 10.3, prepared by ECWA, shows clearly that there are large differences in life expectancy among Arab countries. Life expectancy at birth falls within a range of 40.6 to 67.0 for males and 42.5 to 72.0 for females.

The *World Development Reports* of the World Bank are the other major source of data. The discrepcies between these two sets of estimates require considerable caution in interpreting results.

Generally speaking, the data presented in Table 10.4 suggest that traditional links between mortality and quality of living standards have been greatly loosened. Egypt, Jordan, Syria, Morocco and Tunisia have low income populations, but are

Table 10.3. Values of Measures of Mortality for Selected Arab Countries – Estimated by ECWA, 1980

Country	Nationality	Life Expectancy at Birth			Crude Death Rate			Infant Mortality Rate		
		M	F	T	M.	F	T	M	F	T
1. Bahrain	National	61.2	65.0	—	7.3	7.1	—	59.0	48.0	—
	Non-Nat.	63.7	67.5	—	5.0	5.0	—	49.0	38.0	—
	Total Pop.	62.9	66.8	—	6.3	7.1	—	57.0	45.0	—
2. Yemen, P.D.R.	Total Pop.	44.1	46.3	—	21.6	18.6	—	157.1	142.0	—
3. Egypt	Total Pop.	54.1	57.5	—	13.2	11.7	—	110.0	99.0	—
4. Iraq	Total Pop.	56.3	57.5	—	12.5	12.7	—	85.2	73.2	—
5. Jordan	Total Pop.	63.6	67.8	—	7.8	6.9	—	73.1	65.3	—
6. Kuwait	National	67.0	72.0	—	6.2	4.5	—	46.2	41.0	—
	Non-Nat.	67.0	72.0	—	5.1	4.3	—	26.2	21.0	—
	Total Pop.	67.0	72.0	—	5.5	4.4	—	37.0	32.0	—
7. Lebanon	Total Pop.	66.5	69.0	—	7.5	7.2	—	44.5	37.7	—
8. Oman	National	50.7	51.1	—	14.4	15.5	—	130.5	125.9	—
	Non-Nat.	67.5	72.5	—	4.6	3.5	—	53.0	47.0	—
	Total Pop.	54.6	53.7	—	12.1	14.0	—	112.4	116.3	—
9. Qatar	National	61.2	65.0	—	10.3	8.8	—	59.0	48.0	—
	Non-Nat.	66.2	70.0	—	3.6	4.6	—	39.0	28.0	—
	Total Pop.	65.2	67.9	—	4.9	6.3	—	48.4	37.3	—
10. Saudi Arabia	National	51.9	55.0	—	15.4	13.4	—	124.8	112.1	—
	Non-Nat.	67.5	72.5	—	3.7	4.4	—	53.0	47.0	—
	Total Pop.	56.3	58.0	—	12.1	11.9	—	114.3	102.8	—
11. U.A.E.	National	63.7	67.5	—	9.6	7.8	—	75.0	66.0	—
	Non-Nat.	67.5	72.5	—	3.2	3.9	—	53.0	47.0	—
	Total Pop.	66.8	71.0	—	4.4	5.4	—	62.0	54.0	—
12. Syrian, A.R.	Total Pop.	63.6	66.3	—	8.5	8.0	—	62.7	61.3	—
13. Yemen, A.R.	Total Pop.	40.6	42.5	—	23.4	21.1	—	177.5	160.7	

Source: ECWA – Demographic and Related Socio-Economic Data Sheets for Countries of ECWA (1982).

Table 10.4. Demographic, Socio-economic and Health Indicators for Arab Countries, 1980-1981

Country	Life Expectancy at Birth		Per Capita GNP		Adult Literacy Rate	Percentage of Urban Population		Physicians per 100,000 Pop.	Daily per Capita Calorie Supply as percentage of requirement	Infant Mortality Rate
	1980	1981	1980	1981	1980	1980	1981	1980	1980	1981
Bahrain	65	65	4,100	4,100	50	85	85	8.1	100	51
Yemen, P.D.R.	45	46	420	460	40	37	37	14	84	143
Egypt	57	57	580	650	44	45	44	103	117	110
Iraq	56	57	3,020	3,020	44	72	72	56	111	76
Jordan	61	62	1,420	1,620	70	56	57	53	96	67
Kuwait	70	70	19,830	20,900	60	88	89	169	110	33
Lebanon	66	66	1,200	1,200	70	76	77	189	100	40
Oman	54	54	2,570	2,570	38	22	22	5.2	99	114
Qatar	66	66	12,740	12,740	59	86	86	10.8	98	43
Saudi Arabia	54	55	11,260	12,600	25	67	68	61	120	111
Syrian, A.R.	65	65	1,340	1,570	58	50	49	43	117	60
U.A.E.	63	63	24,600	24,850	56	72	73	111	100	52
Yemen, A.R.	42	43	430	460	21	10	11	9	76	190
Algeria	56	56	1,870	2,140	35	44	44	38	101	114
Libya	56	57	8,640	8,450	45	52	54	137	147	97
Morocco	56	57	900	860	28	41	41	9	110	104
Sudan	46	47	410	380	32	25	26	11	101	122
Tunisia	60	61	1,310	1,420	62	52	53	27	116	88

Source: *World Development Report 1982 and 1983.*

found in the 57-65 interval of life expectancy. This confirms the strength of non-income influence on mortality.

Table 10.5 presents trends of mortality since 1960 for selected Arab countries. It may be seen that mortality has been steadily declining since 1960 in all these countries, as crude death rates and infant mortality rates have been declining and life expectancy at birth has been increasing. However, the gap between mortality levels in these countries remains large. The average annual increases in expectation of life at birth have been approximately one-half year since 1960. The largest gains over the past 20 years were achieved by Syria (15 years), United Arab Emirates (16 years) and Jordan (14 years). Among the Arab countries, Kuwait (Kuwaiti population) has the highest life expectancy at birth (70 years). This compares favourably with prevailing averages in the Western developed countries. On the other hand, in Yemen A.R. and Yemen P.D.R. life expectancy is below 50 years. It may also be noted that in 1960 as well, Kuwait had the highest expectation of life among the Arab countries and Yemen A.R. and Yemen P.D.R. were at the other low extreme.

URBAN-RURAL DIFFERENTIALS

Table 10.5 Trends in Life Expectancy at Birth, Crude Death Rate and Infant Mortality Rate for Arab Countries (1960-81)

Country	Life Expectancy at Birth			Crude Death Rate			Infant Mortality Rate		
	1960	1980	1981	1960	1980	1981	1960	1980	1981
Bahrain	n.a.	n.a.	65*	n.a.	n.a.	6*	n.a.	n.a.	51*
Yemen, P.D.R.	36	45	46	29	20	20	209	146	143
Egypt	46	57	57	19	12	12	128	103	110
Iraq	46	56	57	20	12	12	139	78	76
Jordan	47	61	62	20	10	9	136	69	67
Kuwait	60	70	70	10	5	4	89	34	33
Lebanon	58	n.a.	66	14	n.a.	8	68	n.a.	40
Oman	n.a.	n.a.	54*	n.a.	n.'a.	13*	n.a.	n.a.	114*
Qatar	n.a.	n.a.	66*	n.a.	n.a.	6*	n.a.	n.a.	43*
Saudi Arabia	43	54	55	23	14	13	185	114	111
Syrian, A.R.	50	65	65	18	8	8	132	62	60
U.A.E.	47	63	63	19	7	7	135	53	52
Yemen, A.R.	36	42	43	29	23	23	212	190	190
Algeria	47	56	56	23	13	13	165	118	114
Libya	47	56	57	19	12	12	158	100	97
Morocco	47	56	57	23	13	13	161	107	104
Sudan	40	46	47	25	19	18	168	124	122
Tunisia	48	60	61	21	9	9	159	90	88

Source: The World Bank, *World Development Reports 1982 and 1983*.
n.a. Not Available.
*Estimated by UN-ECWA.

The most obvious expectation regarding urban-rural differentials is that rural mortality is higher than urban mortality, given the differences in living standards between the two communities especially in the developing countries where social and health services tend to be concentrated in towns. Thus the urban-rural differentials could be due to class structure of the different populations, to environmental factors and to access to medical facilities. Available data do not permit the measurement of effects of these various factors. The findings of a study prepared by the population division of ECWA shows that rural mortality levels are higher than urban mortality in selected Arab countries.*

The data presented in Table 10.6 for selected Arab countries further confirm the existing urban/rural differentials. It can be seen that crude death rates and infant mortality rates are higher in the rural areas than in the urban areas. In rural areas where mortality levels are high, literacy programmes and public health and sanitation are the prime movers needed for achieving rapid change.

Little information is available on differentials in mortality in Morocco, Tunisia, Algeria, Libya, Egypt and Sudan. A study[1] in Algeria for the period 1969-71 revealed that infant mortality was highest for the sparsely settled rural areas and that it decreased with increases in population density. The study also showed that the rural differential was much higher for the second and third year of life than for infancy, indicating poor provision of medical care facilities in rural areas. Further infant mortality varied from 93 among families of professional and technical workers to 112 among those of artisans and labourers. Differences in neonatal and post-neonatal mortality rate by mother's education in Jordan were shown by the World Fertility Survey data (1970-74) for that country.[2] The figures for neonatal and post-neonatal mortality were 29.2 and 38.2 respectively for the period under study. The differential in early childhood mortality by education of mother was studied for Cairo city by analysing the 1976 Population and Housing census of Egypt.[3] The

Table 10.6. Crude Death Rates and Infant Mortality Rates in the Urban and Rural Areas of Selected Arab Countries at Selected Dates

Country	CDR (per 1,000 population)		IMR (Per 1,000 live births)	
	Urban	Rural	Urban	Rural
Egypt 1978[a]	9.7	11.0	—	—
Iraq[b]	9.7	12.8	76.3	104.5
Jordan 1978[a]	—	—	11.0	12.7
Syria 1977[b]	—	—	72.6	95.0

Source: (a) U.N. ECWA "Population and Development in the Middle East." 1982, ECWA, Beirut, p. 162.
(b) U.N. Demographic Yearbook 1981, pp. 298 and 327. The data for Iraq are the mean for the years 1973-74 and 1974-75.

*U.N. World Population Trends and Policies: 1981 Monitoring Report, Vol. I (New York, 1982) p.119.

results of this analysis showed that whereas 17 per cent of infants of illiterate mothers died before reaching the age of 5 years, only 5 per cent of infants of graduate mothers died.

Similar association between mothers' education and early childhood mortality was found in Jordan from its World Fertility Survey data (1976). To reduce sample errors and time fluctuations, averages of deaths of children up to ages 2, 3 and 5 years which corresponds approximately to mortality to age 4 were derived. The results showed that early childhood mortality of illiterate mothers was about 2.5 times higher than that of mothers with secondary level education.[4]

DIFFERENCES BY AGE AND BY SEX

At all levels of mortality and in all regions of the world summary indices of mortality such as life expectancy at birth nearly universally show lower levels of mortality for females than for males. Even in some rare instances when life expectancy at birth for females has been lower than that of males, analysis of death rates by age has often shown higher male mortality at nearly all ages, with exceptions occurring only during the early childhood years.[5]

The data in Table 10.9 present life expectancy at birth by sex for the period

Table 10.7 Probabilities of Surviving from Birth up to 5 years by Age and Education Level of Workers, Cairo, 1976

Educational Level	Probability of Survival Up to Age 5 Years			
	20-24	25-29	30-34	35-39
Illiterate	0.826	0.833	0.827	0.831
Read and Write	0.853	0.865	0.869	0.871
Primary	0.871	0.873	0.885	0.891
Preparatory	0.892	0.907	0.913	0.919
Secondary	0.915	0.925	0.928	0.929
High Diploma	0.892	0.930	0.936	0.914
University	0.933	0.942	0.947	0.947

Table 10.8. Childhood Mortality by Sex and Education of Mothers, Jordan 1976 (Average Proportions Dead by Ages 2, 3, & 5)

	Schooling of Mother				
	Illiterate	Literate	Primary	Preparatory	Secondary
Male	.1188	.0885	.0898	.0609	.0540
Female	.1239	.0999	.0885	.0764	.0405

1975-1980 for selected Arab countries. In all selected Arab countries, females show higher life expectancy at birth than males. The data also indicate smaller sex differentials.

Table 10.9 Expectation of Life at year of Birth for Selected Arab Countries, 1975-1980.

Country	Male	Female	Excess of Female
Egypt	53.6	56.1	2.5
Yemen, P.D.R.	42.9	45.1	2.2
Iraq	53.6	56.7	3.1
Jordan	62.4	66.0	3.6
Lebanon	63.2	67.1	3.9
Oman	46.2	48.4	2.2
Saudi Arabia	46.7	49.0	2.3
Yemen, A.R.	38.7	40.3	1.6

Source: U.N. Demographic Yearbook, 1981, Table 16.

Higher male than female mortality for all ages above 10 years is a general pattern experienced by all the selected Arab countries as shown in Table 10.10. However, the analysis of age-specific death rates indicates that with the exception of Egypt, there is no consistent evidence in any country of higher mortality among females during either infancy or childbearing years. It is possible that the relatively poor quality of the data raises doubts as to the validity of the observed differentials. Table 10.11 shows the age specific death rates for Egypt and Syria, based on a W.H.O. publication.

PHYSICAL QUALITY OF LIFE INDEX AMONG ARAB COUNTRIES

Among the Arab nations, the Arab oil-exporting countries held a special position because of huge surpluses in their balance of payments and accumulation of capital. The sudden and tremendous increase in the oil income of these countries during the past 30 years and particularly since 1974 has placed them among the richest countries of the world. But these countries exhibit huge gaps between the "social" and "economic" aspects of development which can be studied by comparing their per capita GNP (Gross National Product) and PQLI (Physical Quality of Life Index). The PQLI is composed of three indicators (life expectancy, infant mortality and basic literacy) which are known to be associated with other "social" indicators.[6] On the other hand, per capita GNP is the most convenient index of "economic" development. Table 10.12 shows the per capita GNP and PQLI for the Arab countries for the period 1980-81. The actual per capita GNP and PQLI figures for these countries are shown under columns one and two respectively. The expected PQLI values shown under column three are based upon results of regression analysis

Table 10.10. Age-Sex Specific Mortality Rates for Selected Arab Countries at Selected Dates

Age	Egypt 1976		Iraq 1977		Jordan 1979		Kuwait 1980	
	Males	Females	Males	Females	Males	Females	Males	Females
Under 1 year	172.5	173.2	19.9	15.3	14.5	12.6	40.8	35.8
1-4	15.6	19.1	2.2	1.9	2.4	2.0	1.9	2.0
5-9	2.1	1.7	0.8	0.6	0.9	0.6	1.1	0.7
10-14	1.9	1.3	0.7	0.6	0.8	0.3	0.8	0.4
15-19	2.0	1.5	1.0	0.8	0.7	0.5	1.6	0.6
20-24	2.7	1.5	0.8	0.9	1.2	0.6	1.3	0.5
25-29	3.2	2.1	1.5	1.3	1.1	0.7	2.0	0.5
30-34	3.2	2.1	1.9	1.7	1.0	0.4	2.1	0.5
35-39	4.6	2.8	2.6	2.3	2.0	1.5	1.9	1.3
40-44	5.8	2.8	3.6	2.8	3.1	1.9	3.0	1.7
45-49	9.8	5.1	4.7	3.1	4.6	2.9	5.1	3.9
50-54	14.9	7.3	9.0	5.7	7.7	3.1	10.3	7.7
55-59	23.1	11.7	11.3	6.0	12.5	5.2	16.7	7.4
60-64	29.7	15.7	19.7	12.5	16.0	8.1	28.0	17.2
65-69	58.3	38.8	25.2	15.7	24.6	14.6	40.1	33.3
70-74	73.7	49.5			33.2	14.1	69.5	42.5
75-79	165.0	227.0	55.8	45.1	51.2	24.3	91.6	74.6
80 and over					83.6	46.8	192.4	186.0

Source: U.N. Demographic Yearbook, 1981, Table 14. For Kuwaiti Population 1980, the source is "Annual Statistical Abstract", 1982 — Central Statistics Office, Kuwait.

Table 10.11. Age Specific Mortality Rates for Selected Arab Countries

Age	Egypt (1978)		Syria (1980)	
	Males	Females	Males	Females
0*	73.2	73.8	9.1	8.2
1-4	12.6	14.2	3.2	3.2
5-14	1.8	1.3	1.4	1.4
15-24	2.2	1.5	0.9	0.9
25-34	3.2	2.0	1.3	1.0
35-44	4.7	2.6	2.5	1.9
45-54	11.6	6.1	5.4	3.1
55-64	25.0	13.6	13.1	6.9
65-74	61.1	41.7	28.4	17.8
75+	150.4	186.5	86.1	59.0

*Per 1,000 Live Births.
Source: WHO, World Health Statistics, 1982.

of data of 154 countries.[7] The deviations between the actual and expected values of PQLI in absolute and in terms of standard error are shown under columns four and five.

All Arab countries other than Lebanon and Egypt have their actual social levels (PQLI) lower than that expected for countries with comparable levels of per capita

GNP. But for the OAPEC countries, the difference is more than twice the standard error, indicating the significance of their differences.

When comparison is made between the current values of PQLI and their values in 1977 in respect to a few selected Arab countries for which the requisite data was available to calculate the PQLI, it is observed that Saudi Arabia, Qatar and the U.A.E. have achieved appreciable increases in their PQLI during this short period, whereas there has not been much improvement in the values of PQLI for Iraq, Libya, Bahrain and Kuwait. It clearly deomonstrates that the latter countries had achieved the comparative level of social development measured in terms of higher expectation of life, literacy rate and lower infant mortality rate much earlier. It may however be noted that all the Arab countries have still to go a long way in achieving the level of "social" development attained by developed countries such as Sweden,

Table 10.12. Actual and Expected PQLI for Arab Countries, 1980-81

Country	Per Capita GNP (1980-81)	†Actual PQLI (1980-81)	Expected PQLI	Deviation from Expected PQLI	Difference in PQLI in Terms of Standard Error
1. Bahrain	4,100*	69 (61)	90	−21	−5.3
2. Yemen P.D.R.	440	38	44	−6	−0.4
3. Egypt	615	54	49	+5	+0.3
4. Iraq	3,020	51 (45)	89	−38	−9.6
5. Jordan	1,520	71	75	−4	−0.2
6. Kuwait	20,365	78 (75)	111	−33	−8.3
7. Lebanon	1,200	76	66	+10	+0.6
8. Oman	2,570*	48	88	−40	−10.1
9. Qatar	12,740*	73 (33)	102	−29	−7.3
10. Saudi Arabia	11,930	45 (29)	101	−56	−14.1
11. Syrian A.R.	1,455	70	73	−3	−0.2
12. U.A.E.	25,755	68 (35)	118	−50	−12.6
13. Yemen A.R.	445	25	44	−19	−1.1
14. Algeria	2,005	49 (43)	89	−40	−2.4
15. Libya	8,545	55 (43)	96	−41	−10.4
16. Morocco	880	49	57	−8	−0.5
17. Sudan	395	39	43	−4	−0.2
18. Tunisia	1,365	65	71	−6	−0.4

†Calculated values based on date in Table 5.
*Figures relate to around 1977.
(Figures in parantheses relate to the earlier period, 1977.)

the U.S.A., Japan, Switzerland and the U.K., which have PQLI in the range of 96 to 99.

EDUCATION AND TRAINING

No single question is more important to human resources development in general and manpower planning in particular than education and training. For this reason all Arab countries have given great consideration during the past decades to the expansion of formal education. For the Arab States as a whole, educational expenditure constituted 4.8 per cent of the GNP during the mid-1970s.[8] The oil-rich countries spent about 16 per cent and 13 per cent of their development plan and current government budgets respectively on education between 1977 and 1978. The share of development expenditure in the oil-poor countries was only 10 per cent during the same period.[9]

During the period 1960-1980, primary school enrolment has increased from about seven to about 20 million boys and girls. This means that for the whole region the enrolment ratio for children in the age bracket 6-11 has increased from about 46 to 70 per cent during the two decade period.[10]

However, the net enrolment ratio for primary education for the region as a whole was lower than the gross by about 10 per cent in the mid-1970s.[11] More than 10 million children were out of school in 1975 and 3 million more were estimated as drop-outs from the primary stage.[12]

It is clear that primary education has still a long way to go before ensuring basic reading and writing skills to all the population in the Arab nation. In 1970 it has been anticipated that universal primary education would have been fully realized by 1980. But as can be seen in Table 10.13, this target has been very difficult to realize in most Arab countries, particularly those classified as the least developed in the region. There are considerable variations in primary school enrolments between Arab countries. In 1980, the gross enrolment ratio was only 21 per cent in Somalia, 47 per cent in North Yemen and 51 per cent in the Sudan as compared with over 100 per cent in the more rich Arab countries.

These severe inequalities in basic educational opportunities call for urgent Arab co-operation to help oil-poor states in expanding primary education, particularly in the rural areas where the majority of the population lives. So far it seems that very little has been done to provide basic education to a relatively large number of children in the Arab countries with large populations and scarcities of resources.[13]

Although expansion of both academic and technical education is necessary, it will not suffice to achieve sustained development, or to meet the need for skilled manpower. The capabilities of the new generations have been frozen into obsolete and irrelevant theoretical academic programmes which have very little to do with the realities and problems of Arab societies.

Table 10.13. Enrolment Ratios for the First Level of Education in Selected Arab Countries (1970, 1975 & 1980)

Country		Enrolment Ratio (%)*		
		1970	1975	1980
Algeria	M	93	109	108
(6-11)**	F	58	75	81
	T	76	93	95
Egypt	M	88	89	89
(6-11)**	F	56	57	63
	T	72	73	76
Mauritania	M	20	24	43
(6-12)**	F	8	13	23
	T	14	19	33
Morocco	M	67	78	95
(7-11)**	F	36	45	58
	T	52	62	76
Sudan	M	46	59	60
(7-12)**	F	29	34	43
	T	38	47	51
Tunisia	M	121	116	118
(6-11)**	F	80	78	88
	T	101	97	103
Bahrain	M	115	107	110†
(6-11)**	F	88	85	93
	T	102	96	102
People's Dem. Yemen	M	91	110	93‡
(7-12)**	F	23	51	51
	T	57	81	72
Iraq	M	96	122	122
(6-11)**	F	41	64	110
	T	69	94	116
Kuwait	M	100	100	98
(6-9)**	F	76	86	93
	T	89	93	96
Oman	M	6	63	81
(6-11)**	F	1	24	43
	T	3	44	62
Saudi Arabia	M	61	72	77
(6-11)**	F	29	43	51
	T	45	58	64
Syrian Arab Republic	M	95	112	112
(6-11)**	F	59	78	87
	T	78	96	100
United Arab Emirates	M	121	107	117
(6-11)**	F	73	97	115
	T	98	102	116
Yemen, Arab Republic	M	23	59	82
(7-12)**	F	2	7	12
	T	12	29	47

*Gross Investment Ratio: Total enrolment of all ages divided by the population of the specific age group which correspond to the age group of primary schooling.
**Age group of primary schooling.
†1979.
‡1977.
Source: UNESCO, Statistical Yearbook 1982, Table 3.2, pp. 111-25-11-81.

Further, instead of stressing manual activity as a value, if not the sole basis for development and advance, the educational system consciously or unconsciously concentrates on the aristocratic concept of work. All forms of education in the different stages stress theories more than practice. They rely heavily on the transmission of information, and have in fact no proven theoretical or effective applied basis. This may be one of the main reasons why the productivity of graduates from such a system is very low. In fact, it has been estimated that the productivity average for the Arab scientist is less than 10 per cent of that of his counterpart in other countries.[14]

Arab education has failed to stress applied and technical skills in agriculture, industry and management. Most Arab countries suffer in varying degrees from shortages of skilled and technical labour. This has been the result of serious imbalances between vocational and academic education. The ratio of students enrolled in vocational training to the total number of students enrolled in the secondary level of all types of education has been extremely low in many of these countries. With the exception of Egypt, the ratio varies from only 2 per cent to 8 per cent in 1960 and declined to a lower range in 1970. It should be noted here that this ratio reaches more than 200 per cent in some socialist countries (such as Yugoslavia) and more than 100 per cent in some capitalist countries (such as West Germany).

If we take the number of students enrolled in all types of education at both the second and third levels of education, the ratio of those enrolled in applied programmes around the year 1980 would be only about 5 per cent for the Arab region, as compared with 40 per cent in Western Europe.

On the other hand, the number of students enrolled in faculties of Science or Engineering in all Arab universities is usually less than 30 per cent of the total, and in some cases, this proportion is much lower. For example, over 90 per cent of Sana' University students and more than 80 per cent of Qatar University students in the academic year 1982-1983 were enrolled in humanities faculties.

However, the most important imbalance from which Arab countries suffer may be that between the upper and middle cadres. Engineers, doctors, agronomists, and other university graduates outnumber the technical institute graduates. The result is the formation of a reversed employment pyramid, the top of which consists of university graduates and is larger than the body consisting of technicians and semi-technicians. In Iraq, the ratio of middle to upper cadres is 1:1.5.[15] In U.A.E., this ratio is 1:5 for the regular students in institutes and universities for the academic year 1978-1979.[16] In Kuwait, the ratio of technical institute students to those of science, engineering, petroleum, and medicine was 1:9 during the same year.[17] Such imbalances in ratios is even sharper for some fields of specialization, such as the case of medical doctors, nurses and health institute graduates.

Concerning the Arab world as an entity, the number of university engineering students was estimated at 85,000. Thirty-five thousand students were enrolled in technical institutes (technology and industrial) and students enrolled in the secondary industrial schools numbered 78,000.[18] Some studies assume that the ideal utilization of manpower requires the availability of 3-4 technicians and 20-40 skilled workers for each university graduate.[19] A UNESCO study reveals that the number of students registered in technical education all over the Arab world was only about 28 students for each 100,000 of the population in 1977, while the equivalent rate in a developing country such as Signapore was 515 students per 100,000 during the same year.[20]

All the above-mentioned rates and ratios are inadequate for the achievement of real development. The gaps may extend further, and labour demands will thus remain unsatisfied, especially in the Gulf countries. This state of affairs has induced many Arab countries, including oil-poor ones, to depend increasingly on skills imported from Asian or European countries. Many of the development projects which use capital-intensive techniques require increasing rates of skilled labour, which can hardly be supplied by the Arab countries in the short run.

As a matter of fact, the number of persons working in scientific and technical jobs in the Gulf countries is much higher than its equivalent in the rest of the Arab countries. In 1975, this rate was about 4.1 per cent and 4.4 per cent in Jordan and Syria respectively, while the equivalent rates were about 14 per cent and 10 per cent in Kuwait and Bahrain respectively.[21] This rate is expected to increase rapidly in the Gulf countries, especially in Saudi Arabia and the U.A.E. This forces them to import labour from India, Pakistan and from other Asian and European countries. They will continue to do so even in the medium and long-term if the education trends in the labour exporting countries remain as they are.

It seems difficult to encourage individuals to enter professions for which there are imbalances. However, there is increasing interest in those professions for which the demand is systematically declining. Table 10.14 gives us a clearer picture of the present incompatibility prevailing in countries such as Sudan, Jordan and Iraq.[22]

Yet, we have to point out the acute scarcity for some skilled and semi-skilled categories, such as mechanics, carpenters and construction workers. This has led to a dramatic increase in wages paid to these categories during the last few years, even in Egypt. Still it seems that public responsiveness to these professions is not encouraging, despite the high wages paid. This may indicate that factors other than financial remuneration may play a decisive role.

To adjust the above-mentioned disequilibrium, reverse the actual training and

Table 10.14. Imbalance in Demand and Responsiveness by Profession.

Profession	Expected Demand	Responsiveness	Financial Incentives	Moral and Social Incentives
Artisans	great	very poor	very poor	poor
Technical Assistants	great	very poor	very poor	poor
Science and Maths Instructors	great	poor	poor	average
Lawyers	little	good	good	very good
Agents & Brokers	little	very good	very good	good
Clerks	little	good	average	average

educational orientations, and plan labour and wages policies – while adjusting the sectoral disequilibrium in employment – a plan should be elaborated for the development and planning of human resources at the Pan-Arab level. Such a plan should be taken into consideration on the actual and expected needs of the different Arab countries. It should set up the educational and training policies necessary for the achievement of real development, and the required balance in demand for and supply of labour. Co-ordination, in this respect, is not enough, even if it were real and effective. Agreements and binding commitments should also exist to face the deficit, or to export the surplus labour within the same region, with no major reliance on the Asian countries to cover the deficiency, or European technical capabilities. In this way, every Arab country could avoid any surplus provision of certain professional categories which the economy is not able to absorb. Moreover, there would be no economic capacity to absorb them in the other Arab countries.

LABOUR MIGRATION IN THE ARAB REGION

Internalization of the movement of labour is vital for the socio-economic development of the whole region and for realizing Arab dreams for political integration. Serious steps towards economic integration would provide an appropriate framework for socio-economic development in all Arab countries, rich and poor. This would also facilitate planning manpower and migration on a regional basis in such a way as to overcome problems of underemployment and unemployment and avoid shortages in skills at the regional level. In order to propose policies in these directions, it is important to investigate labour migration in the region in some detail.

The direction, volume and geographic pattern of labour migration in the region is basically determined by the uneven distribution of resources between the oil-rich and oil-poor countries. The latter possess sizeable human resources and the former large oil revenues. The exploitation of oil resources and ambitious development plans for the oil-rich nations and the financial difficulties and modest development achievements of the oil-poor countries has led to wide disparities in econonic development and per capita income in the region. Besides the presence of the motivation for individuals to migrate, national policies in both groups of countries were also in favour of encouraging and facilitating the movement. The oil-rich countries, because of their desire to make up for their labour shortages, arising from the accelerated development that their local labour supply cannot satisfy. The oil-poor countries considered the movement of their labour to the other group as a temporary relief for their problems of unemployment and underemployment and at the same time as a possible source of foreign exchange earnings, through migrant remittances, that their economies badly need.

In 1975 there were 3.3 million temporary, non-national residents in the oil-producing and exporting countries in the Arab region, or almost one-third of the total population of these countries. Although the volume of this flow was not as large as the movement to Western and Northern Europe in the same period (6.3 million migrant workers), the proportion of migrants in total population and total employment in the labour importing countries in the Arab region is considerably high. Migrant workers provide nearly half of the total workforce and in certain countries like Qatar and the United Arab Emirates they assume an absolute majority (82 per cent and 85 per cent of the total workforce respectively).

Labour movement in the Arab region retains some characteristics that might not be shared by similar mass movements of labour in other parts of the world. Unlike the demand for labour in Europe which has been primarily for semi-skilled and unskilled workers, the demand of the Arab oil-producing countries for labour is for both highly skilled and unskilled labour. The movement is temporary in nature, where most of the migrants come with the idea that they will return to their home countries after a specific period of time. Finally, it is a transfer among developing countries, labour remaining largely with the Arab region.

The evaluation and scale of labour movement in the Arab region can be generally attributed to the labour market forces, supply in excess in the markets of non-oil producers and a high pressure of demand in the market of the oil-producing and exporting countries and the presence of wage differentials. Proximity of these markets which are in disequilibrium and the nature of the region and its people and the employment policies adopted in both groups of countries also contributed to this massive migration.

In considering the distribution of migrant workers between countries of employment, it can be seen that Saudi Arabia alone employs hearly half of the total (45 per cent). This is quite reasonable of course as Saudi Arabia is by far the largest in physical size. Its enormous oil revenues and reserves and ambitious development objectives make its requirements for labour more substantial. Libya ranks second (19.3 per cent), followed by the United Arab Emirates (15 per cent) and Kuwait (12 per cent). The share of Oman, Qatar and Bahrain in total are small (4.1, 3.1 and 1.7 per cent respectively).

Arab workers constitute nearly 73 per cent of migrant workers. Nearly a million and a quarter Arab workers were employed in countries other than their own. Asian workers constitute the second largest group (20 per cent). These were mainly from the Indian subcontinent and other South-East Asian countries. The rest came from Europe, Africa and others. The distribution pattern of migrant workers according to their ethnic background also varies between the different countries of employment. While Saudi Arabia, the Libyan Arab Jamahiriya and Kuwait have a higher proportion of Arab migrants in their workforce, the small-sized Gulf States of the United Arab Emirates, Oman, Qatar and Bahrain tend to employ higher proportions of Asians in their workforce. Over half of all Arab workers were employed in Saudi Arabia, constituting 90 per cent of its non-national workforce. Nearly a quarter of them were employed in the Libyan Arab Jamahiriya (almost 93 per cent of its total migrant workforce). Another 11.5 per cent of Arab workers were employed in Kuwait, making 70 per cent of its migrant workers.

The distance factor and the historical trade links between the Gulf States, especially those near the Gulf entrance and the large size of Asian populations, particularly from the Indian subcontinent, might give some explanation to the higher proportion of Asian workers in the workforce of this group. It might also be argued that increases of oil revenues and largescale economic development in these countries is relatively recent and that their demand for workers from outside has accelerated at a time when the surplus in the countries of origin had already been attracted by earlier importers. The distance factor equally applies in considering the larger share of Arabs in the labour markets of Saudi Arabia, Kuwait and the Libyan Arab Jamahiriya. The latter, for example borders Egypt, Sudan and Tunisia – all three labour exporters. Given the position of the three countries, their relative weight and inclination in the politics of the region, it is not surprising to see that these countries give preference to Arab employment. For Kuwait, the relatively earlier demand for foreign workers can be a further explanation. Table 10.15 shows the distribution of migrant workers by ethnic origin in the major countries of employment.

Among the major Arab labour suppliers, Egypt is the most important. Egyptians accounted for over 30 per cent of Arab migrant workers in 1975. The two other major exporters of labour are Yemen (22 per cent) and Jordan (including Palestinians) which accounted for 20 per cent of Arab migrant workers in the same year. These three countries combined exported over 950,000 workers, accounting for 73.5 per cent of total Arab migrant workers employed in the major countries of employment. Democratic Yemen, the Syrian Arab Republic, Lebanon and the

Table 10.15. Percentage Distribution of Arab Migrant Workers in the Arab Region, 1975

Country of Employment	Country of Origin & Percentage Distribution between Countries of Employment							
	Egypt (%)	Yemen (%)	Jordan & Palestine (%)	Democ. Yemen (%)	Syria (%)	Lebanon (%)	Sudan (%)	Others (%)
Saudi Arabia	23.9	96.6	66.1	77.9	21.3	40.3	76.3	22.8
Libyan Arab Jamahiriya	57.8	—	5.3	—	18.5	11.5	15.3	38.1
U.A.E.	3.1	1.0	5.5	6.4	6.4	9.0	3.2	14.6
Kuwait	9.4	1.6	18.0	12.2	23.4	14.6	1.9	20.7
Oman	1.2	—	0.6	0.1	0.6	2.2	1.1	0.4
Qatar	0.7	0.4	2.3	1.8	1.1	1.0	0.9	1.9
Bahrain	0.3	0.4	0.2	2.6	0.1	0.3	0.9	1.5
Others	3.6	—	2.0	—	28.6	21.1	0.4	—
Total (%)	100	100	100	100	100	100	100	100
No.	397.5	296.1	264.7	70.6	70.4	49.7	45.9	107.6
Percentage distribution of migrants by country of origin	30.7	22.4	20.4	5.5	5.4	3.8	3.5	8.3

Source: J. S. Birks and C. A. Sinclair, "Migration and Development in the Arab Region", ILO, Geneva, 1980. Table 10.

Sudan provided 5.5, 5.4, 3.8 and 3.5 per cent respectively. Other Arab countries were also responsible for smaller amounts. It is interesting to note that although Oman is considered a major country of employment, yet before the recent growth of its oil revenues, it was a source of labour supply to Saudi Arabia and other Gulf States, especially unskilled workers. In 1975 there were 38,000 Omanis employed in other countries.

The majority of Egyptians (58 per cent) go to the neighbouring Libyan Arab Jamahiriya, one quarter of them are employed in Saudi Arabia and nearly 10 per cent in Kuwait. Saudi Arabia is the largest employer of workers from Yemen (96 per cent of Yemeni workers were employed there in 1975) and from Jordan and Palestine (66 per cent). Another example of concentration of workers of certain nationalities in specific countries of employment is given by the distribution of Sudanese workers of whom three-quarters were employed in Saudi Arabia while another 15 per cent work in the Libyan Arab Jamahiriya. This apparent preference of migrants for particular countries of employment can be explained by geographical proximity, the particular nature of employment and the characteristics of the migrants, together with quickly developing traditions of migration. Once a flow of migrants has started to particular countries of employment, it creates its own momentum.[23] The presence of a number of certain nationalities in a particular country of employment will serve as a transmitting element of information on the labour market conditions in that country to their fellow citizens, which is an important factor in migration decision. Moreover, "Relatives and friends of similar background would help make the social transition easier for the recent migrant . . . ."[24]

The number of migrant workers has risen from 1.7 million in 1975 to 2.8 million in 1980. As can be seen from Table 10.16, the largest four labour importers – Saudi Arabia, the Libyan Arab Jamahiriya, the United Arab Emirates and Kuwait – still maintained the highest proportion. Yet this proportion had declined from 91 per cent of all migrant workers in 1975, to 84 per cent in 1980. This decline can be attributed to the emergence of Jordan, Oman, Yemen and Iraq as labour importers.

Another significant change that took place during this period is the rising trend of the share of Asian migrant workers at the expense of the Arabs. The share of Arab migrant workers has declined from 73 per cent in 1975 to 63 per cent in 1980 at a time when the share of Asian migrant workers has increased from 20 to 34 per cent.

Statistical data on age structure, distribution by sex and skills of migrant workers is very scanty. Available data on the age structure of the migrant population in Kuwait and the United Arab Emirates shows that the majority of migrants are between 15 and 59 years of age, as illustrated in Table 10.17.

Migration to the region is mainly for employment, it is reasonable then to expect that those within working age will migrate. The temporary nature of migration and the restrictions imposed by countries of employment toward accompanying of dependents give a further explanation.

The nature of the demand for labour and the social attitudes in the region towards employment for women indicate that migrant workers are predominantly male. The

Table 10.16. Distribution of Migrant Workers in the Arab Region by Sending Country and Country of Employment, 1980

Native Country		Saudi Arabia	Libyan Arab Jama.	United Arab Emirates	Kuwait	Qatar	Bahrain	Jordan (East Bank)	Oman	Yemen	Iraq	Total
Egypt		15.1	45.8	4.4	22.4	7.2	4.1	90.1	6.5	23.5	79.7	24.6
Yemen, A.R.		31.8	—	1.3	0.8	1.9	1.7	—	0.1	—	—	11.9
Jordan and Palestine		13.7	2.8	4.7	14.5	9.7	2.1	—	2.3	11.8	6.0	8.9
Yemen, P.D.R.		6.3	—	1.6	2.5	1.9	1.7	—	0.1	—	—	3.0
Syrian A. Rep.		2.4	2.8	1.4	9.2	1.2	0.2	—	0.6	5.9	—	2.9
Lebanon		3.2	1.0	1.6	2.1	0.9	0.4	—	1.5	2.9	3.6	2.2
Sudan		5.4	3.8	0.5	1.5	0.9	1.3	—	0.6	13.2	0.4	3.2
Maghreb		0.05	12.0	—	0.08	—	—	—	0.1	—	—	2.3
Oman		1.0	—	4.7	0.5	1.4	1.3	—	—	—	—	1.2
Iraq		0.3	—	0.3	10.6	—	0.5	—	—	—	—	1.6
Somalia		0.8	0.9	1.2	0.1	—	—	—	0.4	2.9	—	0.7
All Arab	%	80.2	69.2	21.8	64.4	25.2	13.3	90.1	12.4	60.3	89.6	62.5
	No.	820,550	277,300	897,000	243,800	20,200	9,010	68,500	12,030	10,250	112,500	1,763,840
India & Pakistan		5.8	17.8	59.9	20.9	40.7	56.8	5.9	82.8	29.4	7.6	23.1
Other Asian		9.1	4.9	5.0	2.6	5.6	14.8	1.3	—	1.8	1.2	6.0
All Asian	%	16.2	27.6	75.0	33.6	72.9	76.5	7.2	83.3	31.2	8.8	34.3
	No.	166,700	151,000	308,400	129,600	57,970	51,610	5,500	80,670	5,300	11,000	968,430
Others	%	3.6	3.2	3.2	1.4	2.0	10.2	2.6	4.2	8.5	1.6	3.2
	No.	36,000	17,200	12,900	5,300	1,600	6,900	2,000	4,100	1,450	2,000	89,450
Total	%	36.3	19.3	14.6	13.4	2.8	2.4	2.4	3.4	0.6	4.4	100
	No.	1,023,250	545,500	411,000	378,700	80,250	67,720	67,000	96,800	17,000	125,500	2,821,720

Source: Compiled and calculated from "*International Migration in the Arab World*". Proceedings of an ECWA Population Conference, Nicosia, Cyprus, 11-16 May 1981. Vol. II, pp. 750-51.

Table 10.17. Percentage Distribution of Population by Age Structure in Kuwait and United Arab Emirates, 1975

Country and Nationality	Age Group			
	15	15-59	60 or above	Total
Kuwait				
Nationals	49.5	46.8	3.8	100
Non-Nationals	39.7	58.7	1.5	100
United Arab Emirates				
Nationals	45.4	47.1	7.5	100
Non-Nationals	18.8	79.9	1.3	100

Source: N. Fergany, "Volume and Composition of Population and Workforce in the Arabian Gulf Countries". Seminar on Foreign Labour Migration in the Arab Gulf Countries. Centre for Arab Unity Studies and the Arab Planning Institute, Kuwait, 15-18 January, 1983.

proportion of female migrant labour is lowest in the Saudi Arabia and United Arab Emirates (less than 2 per cent) while it is relatively high in Kuwait (13 per cent).[25] Kuwait, a country which proceeded earlier in the development process, has been able to set its infrastructural base ahead of others. In 1975 it employed less than the average on construction and more in manufacturing. The order is reversed in Libya and Saudi Arabia. The role of the agricultural sector in Kuwait, and other Gulf States is almost negligible while it retains some importance in Libya and Saudi Arabia as revealed by the percentage of migrant workers employed in the sector.

Participation rates of nationals in countries of employment are very low while participation rates in countries of origin are relatively higher. The crude participation rate of non-nationals as compared to that of nationals in countries of employment is higher considering the characteristics of migrants – the fact that the majority are in the working age and they are predominantly male. The number of dependants is small due to the temporary nature of migration and the restrictions imposed by host countries. Participation rates, however, vary between countries according to the ethnic composition of the migrants and the degree of restrictions imposed. Differences in skill levels also have an effect. The more skilled is usually better paid and hence the more skilled migrants tend to travel with their families and settle for relatively long periods in countries of employment, while manual workers have a shorter duration of stay and less favourable employment conditions, consequently they are less likely to be accompanied by their families.

In general, the participation rate of migrants is much higher than that of nationals. In Saudi Arabia, for example, these rates are 49 and 22 per cent respectively and in the United Arab Emirates the difference is even greater — only 18 per cent for nationals compared to 55 per cent for non-nationals.

Among the migrant population themselves the participation rate of Asians is higher than that of Arabs. These differences are shown in Table 10.18 for Kuwait, Qatar and Bahrain.

Table 10.18. Participation Rates Differentials Among Different Nationalities

Nationality	Country of Employment		
	Kuwait	Bahrain	Qatar
Nationals	19.1	27.1	19.9
Non-Nationals:	47.9	71.9	63.9
Arabs	39.6	46.0	58.3
Asians	71.3	79.4	65.8
Others	45.9	47.0	

Sources: State of Bahrain, Cabinet Affairs, Directorate of Statistics, Bahrain Census of Population and Housing — 1981, Nov. 1982.
Kuwait, Ministry of Planning, Central Administration of Statistics, Census of the 1980 Census of Population, Vol. 1, Part 1, Sept. 1982.
Unpublished Results of the Demographic Survey of Qatar, 1983.

For Arab countries with high levels of employment the recourse to migrant workers is inevitable. Their initial stages of development require large investments in basic social and economic infrastructure which, even when all potential domestic workforces were mobilized, could not be realized without a large number of workers from outside. The increased revenues from oil encouraged increased spending by governments on ambitious development programmes, and thus additional flows of migrant workers were required. The increased number of migrants in itself necessitated additional numbers of workers to provide goods and services for the large numbers already existing. Generally, Arab countries have benefited from these labour flows: the basic infrastructures that they were able to build and the rate of growth they were able to sustain could not have been secured without migrant workers.

The magnitude of these flows, however, is considered substantially higher than it should be, given the size of the countries and of their indigenous population. The fact that, in some of these countries, nationals have increasingly become minorities, raises threats to sovereignty and to the survival of local culture and traditions. There is a majority of migrants, especially of Asian origin, whose language, culture and traditions are totally different from those of the host countries. The social expenditure to meet the increasing requirements of migrants is another point of concern. An important implication of recourse to the employment of migrant workers concerns the development of skills of nationals that will enable these countries to lessen their dependence on migrant workers when the real need for their services declines. It has been argued that the fact that migrants are readily available would discourage the incentive to skill formation. The present of alternative employment opportunities for nationals in the government and in business sectors discourages nationals from accepting hard or low-status jobs. The result is that some sectors of the economy, or at least some occupations, are totally left for migrant workers. "This is a limiting factor which narrows the range of skills and reduces the types of jobs that nationals are induced to acquire".[26] The long-run effect of this is that the need of migrant labour would be a permanent rather than a temporary requirement. This will establish a type of dependence on others which will limit the degree of control that national governments can have over their domestic markets, a situation in which no government would like to find itself.

BENEFITS TO LABOUR EXPORTING COUNTRIES

For the labour exporting countries of the region, the most outstanding direct benefit is the generation of foreign exchange through labour remittances. In fact, workers' remittances to their home countries have been continuously increasing through official and unofficial channels as well as in kind. Official flow of workers' remittances to the three larger labour exporters, Egypt, Yemen and Jordan increased more than four times between 1975 and 1980, from $1,050 million to $4,608 million. (See Table 10.19).

Caution has to be taken in interpreting the benefits derived from the increased volume of remittances. More important is the use to which they have been put. Their benefits can only be realized if they are invested in production, thereby strengthening local development. If this does not take place, the result is increased consumption expenditure by migrants' dependants or by migrants themselves on their return home. When productive capacity is not expanding, the increased demand for consumer goods will tend to push prices upwards or to increase imports to satisfy that demand. Obviously, the drain on foreign exchange might offset amounts secured through remittances. The experiences of other labour exporting countries reveal that although remittances were continually sent home by migrant workers, they did not necessarily generate a basis for local development.[27]

Reluctance of workers to put their money in productive investment can be expected as they lack information on profitable investment avenues or because of the limited investment opportunities in their country of origin. Besides, individual savings are relatively small and there is need for joint ventures. Able financial intermediaries and suitable government policies to mobilize these resources are generally lacking or relatively inefficient. Little has been achieved in directing these resources towards productive investment. The relative failure of many of these policies might partly be attributed to the fact that those who design these policies are not in a position to know the actual number of their migrant workers abroad, their income, occupations, duration of stay, etc.

The effect of migration on employment is another important issue. The rationale usually put forward for labour export policies is that it can alleviate problems of unemployment and underemployment. In the Arab world, this concept must be treated cautiously. Earlier in this paper we have shown that for labour-exporting countries, the proportion of skilled and semi-skilled workers that they can supply is limited by their stock of skills and the requirements. The need of countries of employment is for workers of all levels of skills besides the unskilled. Migration of unskilled workers, who are generally drawn from the traditional sector, can help to

Table 10.19. Countries of Employment: Workers Remittances, 1975-1980 (Million Dollars)

Country	1975	1976	1977	1978	1979	1980
Egypt	366	754.9	896.6	1,761.3	1,951.1*	2,641.4*
Jordan	166.9	410.8	470.2	520.0	600.2*	776.5*
Sudan**	150.7	183.3	244.7	257.2	290.0*	327.0†
Syria	195.0	205.0	363.0	371.0	379.2	388.0†
Yeman Arab Rep.	517.6	999.7	1,391.9	1,403.6	1,200.4	1,190.1
Dem. Rep. of Yeman	109.7	250.3	252.8	307.7	332.7	358.6
Total	1,505.9	2,804.0	3,619.2	4,620.8	4,753.1	5,681.6

*Estimated.
†Estimated using last year's growth rate.
**Includes some grants.
Source: Arab Fund for Economic & Social Development, Kuwait. A forthcoming report.

solve the problem of disguised unemployment thereby raising productivity. This is particularly true for the agricultural sector. But the drain on skills is the most serious consequence of labour migration. Due to the high demand for skilled and semi-skilled workers, migration began to draw upon the stock of productively employed workers whose place cannot readily be filled by equally qualified workers. Different attempts by national governments to limit the migration of certain skills often generate illegal channels of migration, as long as the pull factors are effective. The problem is worsening over time as the requirements of countries of employment call more and more for skilled and semi-skilled workers at the expense of unskilled workers. Nearly all countries of origin are now concerned by internal skilled labour shortages. This is seen by many as an obstacle to their own development programmes. Some of these exporters have had to import labour to satisfy their domestic demand.

Administrative and fiscal measures can be designed to discourage the drain of skilled labour. But since the control of the outflow of skills is not often feasible in practical terms and the need for foreign exchange is pressing, an alternative is to expand educational and training programmes to compensate for the loss in skills. Necessary funds for such programmes are not readily available, and skill formation is a long process. Besides, even if success if achieved, it can only be expected that most of those trained will then leave for countries of employment. Such expenditures will be a future loss added to earlier losses of amounts invested on human resources which countries of employment receive, already trained to start work.

The long-run implications of labour migration on the workers' countries of origin are even more serious. After the initial stages of development in countries of employment are completed, fewer migrant workers will be called for, especially the unskilled. The impact on countries of origin will be twofold: a decrease in foreign exchange earnings, and a problem of providing jobs for the returning worker. Recent developments in oil markets are expected to have their impact on the planned developments of countries of employment, and this in turn may act as an accelerator to the "return-home" process.

The majority of migrant workers live under harsh conditions in their countries of employment. There is always the fact of discrimination arising from the inequality of treatment and opportunity between nationals and migrants in matters of economic and social rights, including pay. The fact that workers are not organized, that there is a threat of immediate deportation, and that the home countries are unable to exert any genuine influence on the countries of employment, are major concerns.

THE LEGAL AND INSTITUTIONAL FRAMEWORK OF LABOUR EXCHANGE

Although there have been some assumed broad political and ideological division in the Arab region, representatives of the Arab countries have never been prevented from meeting regularly during the past three decades. In all of these meetings, the Arab states have stressed their determination to follow the path of Pan-Arab cooperation, integration and unity. Concerning labour migration and employment, the Arab Economic Council included in its Economic Unity Agreement of 1957 (which was ratified by 13 Arab States), "the freedom of labour exchange, of residence and of work". The general conference of the Arab Labour Ministers discussed the same issue in their first and second sessions. The conference at its third session (which was held in November 1967 and attended by 14 Arab States) adopted the Arab Agreement for Manpower Exchange (No. 2 for 1967).[28] The preamble of this agreement[29] was drafted to advance the Arab efforts and determination to achieve comprehensive unity and socio-economic integration. Thus, the Arab States decided to secure the freedom of labour exchange in the Arab Region making it the case of economic activities and realizing optimum employment. According to the agreement, the contracting parties "pledge to indulge the labour force exchange among them and to facilitate the pertaining office regulations", but to each of the contracting parties is conferred "an executive authority of its own in implementing the provision of this agreement".

Such an authority is to organize and supervise manpower exchange. The contracting parties also pledge to exchange all necessary data and information, giving employment priority to the Arab workers. According to the stipulations of this agreement, Arab migrant workers are to enjoy the rights and privileges of their native counterparts. They have the right to partly transfer their wages. The agreement also allowed bilateral agreements among the contracting parties. It presented a draft prototype bilateral agreement to guide those parties concerned. It includes some special details concerning labour and contractual terms. There is no doubt that bilateral agreements "allow room for political preferences and feelings of solidarity surpassing regionally or internationally agreeable minimum levels of transfer payments".[30]

It is worthwhile noting that the multi-lateral agreement did not include any stipulation concerning the expatriate worker's family, although the draft bilateral agreement allowed him to submit a request to be accompanied by his family. It does not stipulate any answer to such a request, or to the expatriate worker's right to training, to civil and union rights. Undoubtedly, Agreement No. 2 was clearly based on evident Arab unity prospects, though its stipulations were not at the level of such aspirations. However, only 6 out of the 14 Arab states which had previously agreed to it in 1967 have ratified it. These states were Jordan, Sudan, Syria, Iraq, Libya and Egypt.

After a lapse of eight years, the Arab Labour Conference, in its fourth planary session held in Tripoli (Libya) in March 1975, suggested that the socio-economic events occurred in the Arab region during the last decade have created such situations as to merit re-examination of the existing agreement for manpower exchange.[31]

Unfortunately, the re-examination of this agreement proved to be a setback. It deviated from the goal of achieving comprehensive unity, and of considering the Arab world as an integral socio-economic entity to secure the freedom of labour force exchange. As it was stipulated in Agreement No. 2, it regressed as to "regulate the labour force exchange, to face the development programme's requirements in every individual country, as to achieve the Arab economic integration targets".

Compared to the text of the 1967 Agreement, the amended agreement may be considered as a regional regression since it stipulates that "all job opportunities be kept to the native workers", restricting matters such as the special measures of "granting work licences and residence permits to the expatriate workers, including the renewal, non-renewal or withdrawal of such permits, not to mention the expatriate workers deportation terms from the host country." However, Arab migrant workers are to enjoy the same rights and privileges as their native counterparts enjoy and they have the right to complain to the competent authorities, and obtain all dues or privileges upon departure from the host country. They are granted a reasonable delay after the expiry of their residence permit; thus allowing them to properly adapt themselves and their families to the new situation.

One of the advantages of the amended agreement is its stipulation on the expatriate workers' right to request "the company of their family members (wife, children and parents) by granting them residence permits on equal terms with the migrant workers themselves". However, it left the door open to the host country authorities to procrastinate, and even to refuse, by stipulating that "the authorities will examine such a request, and will rapidly answer it within a period of no more than six months, starting from the day the request was submitted". The agreement also stipulated that "the migrant workers and their accompanying families are to enjoy the same rights and privileges enjoyed by their native counterparts in the host country", including job opportunities and training, letting "the migrant workers enjoy union rights, however, within the framework of the national legislations of the host country". Moreover, among the advantages of this agreement is its stipulation on each contracting party's pledge "to set up and implement both a short and long-run emigration policy suitable to its economic requirements", aiming especially at "encouraging labour force exchange among the Arab countries; encouraging the investment of Arab capital in investment projects capable of creating job opportunities to absorb surplus labour; giving priority to the other Arab countries' needs for manpower; and, working gradually to replace the foreign labour force by Arab workers". The agreement called the contracting parties to establish tripartite representation (governments, workers and employers) to carry out all activities and services accruing from joining the agreement. It called, as well, for the co-ordination among the concerned regional institutions. Thus, the agreement established an institutional framework consisting of regional elements, and a national co-ordination centre to work in the field of facilitating labour force exchange the spirit of the agreement. The amended agreement admitted, as well, the principle of bilateral agreements, and submitted a model agreement.

Strangely enough, most of the Arab labour exporting countries did not ratify the amended agreement. Some of these countries who had previously ratified the first agreement have not done the same with the amended agreement, such as Syria and Sudan. Only three countries ratified both agreements: Jordan, Egypt and Iraq.

In addition to both labour force exchange agreements, there is another agreement (No. 9 of 1977), and a recommendation (No. 2 for 1977) concerning professional guidance and training. They are both of specific importance in the field of labour force. As we have previously mentioned, most of the Arab countries experience a scarcity in technical and skilled labour force. Moreover, the Arab petroleum countries' labour market requires specific types of skilled labour adequate to the advanced technology they utilize, and who are not actually available in the Arab non-petroleum countries. It is difficult to face such a scarcity in the Arab labour market, without extensive Arab efforts in the field of training. Agreement No. 9 stresses Arab co-operation. It seeks to achieve Arab integration in the field of professional guidance and training, and aims at realizing marginal profits to each individual country from the available training capabilities in the Arab countries. It aims, as well, at inducing joint training cycles, in addition to collecting the necessary data to improve training efficiency and exchange it at the Pan-Arab level. As for the annexed recommendation to the agreement, it discussed Arab co-operation in the field of training with thorough details.[32]

BILATERAL AGREEMENTS

As was previously mentioned, the multilateral agreements concerning Arab labour force exchange have permitted the Arab countries to sign bilateral agreements organizing the labour force exchange procedures and terms among them. Some of these bilaterial agreements have been signed between labour exporting countries and the host countries, such as between Qatar and Egypt, Qatar and Tunisia, Libya and Sudan, etc. Although most of these bilateral agreements seem to have been implemented effectively, endeavours for co-operation and integration should be envisaged as multi-lateral treaties rather than bilateral agreements.

ARAB INSTITUTIONS

The Arab labour market has greatly expanded during the last five years. This has deeply affected socio-economic development in both exporting and host countries. This situation has necessitated the establishment of Arab institutional structures aiming at reinforcing Arab co-operation in the field of labour force exchange. Thus, the idea of an "Arab Employment Bureau" working within the framework of the Arab Labour Organization came into being. The project was submitted to the 8th session of the Arab Labour Conference in March 1980, in Baghdad. The conference agreed in principle on its establishment, with an interim period of two years "during which the establishment status will be drafted, its cadres be trained and its internal regulations be set up".[33]

The proposed bureau is an executive instrument, working within the framework of the Arab Labour Office, to achieve the following targets:

1. Collecting, organizing and publishing information on the labour market, including the labour force and employment supply and demand; and, the labour force exchange, its mobilizing factors and organizations. This will facilitate the labour force at the national level, through "supplying data, analysis and indicators on labour force and employment to the regional and national decision-makers and planners, and to anyone working in the formulation of industrial and other development projects, to help make sound policies and plans. Moreover, this will help the entire Arab world organize the labour market's own capabilities and resources, thus evading the exhaustion of these resources, and limiting the reliance on foreign emigration with its entailing risks".
2. Assisting in the absorption of the Arab labour force. This process starts with "the collection and provision of information, data and statistics on Arab manpower abroad (its resources, size and structure), and on the European host countries; their employment terms and social situation; and the host countries' future trends towards its continuation or liquidation."
3. Equilibrating the labour force supply and demand, through the contribution to joint Arab training projects, and through providing the necessary studies and surveys.
4. Implementing assignments within the framework of the Arab Labour Organization technical co-operation programme in the field of employment and labour market data amelioration.

THE POLITICAL FRAMEWORK FOR HUMAN RESOURCES DEVELOPMENT AND LABOUR-EXCHANGES

The Eleventh Arab Summit Conference adopted in November 1980 both the National Economic Activities Charter and the Joint Arab Economic Strategy. This action is considered a fundamental turning point requiring the revision of the legal and institutional situations controlling manpower exchange in the Arab countries. It is useful, in this context, to review the Charter stipulations and strategic elements concerning labour exchange.[34]

In the preamble to the National Economic Activities Charter, the Arab Kings and Presidents expressed their faith that the "Arab man is the development maker. Therefore, he should be its target". They aspired to facilitate labour force exchange within the Arab world boundaries, control migration abroad, and, stop "brain drain", or increase their contribution of these resources to the Arab region from where they are. The Arab Kings and Presidents expressed their full commitment to the Charter, and decided to mobilize their efforts, capabilities and resources to implement it. Concerning Arab relations, the Charter included the following elements concerning labour exchanges. Commitment to the principle of Arab economic citizenship includes:

1. Mutual preferential dealings: The Arab countries undertake the preferential dealings principle for the Arab factors of production including, naturally, the labour factor.
2. Commitment to the principle of Arab economic citizenship, including:
   – Treating the Arab worker as equal to his national counterpart in every Arab country in such a way as to get him the necessary guarantees and incentives.
   – Balancing the rights, privileges and facilities granted to the factors of Arab production contributing to Arab development, i.e., granting labour the same privileges given to capital.
   – Liberation of the Arab labour exchange, ensuring its rights and granting it the necessary facilities and assistance for its development.
3. Commitment to the principle of national economic joint solidarity. The Arab countries work for joint solidarity, each according to the decisions taken by the Arab Economic and Social Council, to finance joint Arab needs. This will especially include national security requirements, the development of human resources, and infrastructure projects.
4. The Arab countries will endeavour to orient Arab economic integration and co-operation toward the final goal of achieving Arab economic unity.

As for the Joint Arab Economic Activities Strategy, its target included "economic integration on the path of Arab economic unity". Its second priority was "the development and improvement of human resources and of the labour force in the Arab world, and securing its freedom of movement according to the requirements of economic development in the Arab countries". Its aims at "preserving this labour force within the boundaries of the Arab world, and increasing the reliance on Arab manpower, to decrease it on the foreign labour force". One of its programmes stresses the "setting up of policies, finding decisions which may facilitate the Arab citizens and Arab labour force exchange within the boundaries of the Arab world".

The decisions taken by the Amman Summit Conference also included the ratification of the "Joint Arab Funds investment agreement in the Arab world", which stipulates that employment priority be given to the host country's nationals, followed by Arab citizens, then to other nationalities with the required professional qualifications.[35]

THE "BRAIN DRAIN"

The so-called "brain drain" (the emigration of skilled manpower from the Arab region) has long aggravated all the imbalances mentioned above and critically inhibited the development of human resources. The magnitude of this problem is not exactly known. On the basis of the limited data available, Zahlan estimated that by 1976 the outflow of Arab scientists, engineers and medical doctors to Western Europe and the USA represented respectively 15, 23 and 50 per cent of the total Arab pool. This means that there were 7,500 scientists, 17,000 engineers and 24,000 physicians and surgeons working in the advanced industrial countries in 1976.[36] Between 1962 and 1977, the United States received some 18,200 professional, technical and highly qualified personnel (1,100 scientists, 2,500 engineers and 3,700 medical doctors).[37] The average number of professional and technical emigrants had been increasing year by year. For example, between 1973 and 1978, when the demand for labour increased substantially as a result of the boom in the oil-rich countries, the number of emigrants per year exceeded that of the previous period. In 1978 alone, the total number of Arab emigrants admitted to the U.S.A. was 14,712, of whom 1,722 were professional, technical and highly specialized workers.[38]

There is no doubt that the emigration of well-educated persons, some of them with immense practical experience, is a big loss to their individual countries and to the region as a whole. The emigration of specialized and highly skilled manpower from the oil-poor Arab countries to the oil-rich Arab countries or industrialized countries has affected adversely the socio-economic development not only in the fields of agriculture, industry and construction, but also in the vital sectors of education and health. As a result, some existing projects collapsed and proposed ones were delayed.

The circulation of highly skilled labour within the Arab region, though a great disadvantage to the labour-exporting countries, might be beneficial to the region as a whole, as it contributes effectively to the social and economic development in the receiving countries. In addition, it leads to more and more human interaction among Arab citizens and thus accelerates the drive for solidarity, integration and unity.

However, the continuation of the "brain drain" to the advanced countries cannot be justified on economic or political grounds. It is, however, very important to explore the real reasons for this emigration if efforts to integrate plans for manpower and educational policies to meet the social needs of the society are to be effective.

Several studies have attempted to explain the emigration of medical doctors, engineers, scientists and other professionals. The most accepted reason seems to be the irrelevance of the educational system to the needs and socio-economic environment and conditions of the great majority of the population. Other reasons include political upheavals and instability, inadequacy of research facilities, low salaries, rigidity of the civil service, lack of initiative and academic freedom. In short, it can be said that working conditions are far from being satisfactory to the aspirations and ambitions of these outstanding and highly selective professionals.

In view of the fact that most highly skilled emigrants are outstanding persons who are well-educated and trained and who have acquired immense practical experience in teaching and handling complex projects already in existence or planned to be undertaken in the Arab region, it is very important to find effective ways and means not only to stop the "brain drain", but to reverse the present trends. How this can be done will be discussed next.

PROPOSED EDUCATION, MANPOWER AND OTHER RELATED POLICIES

To start correcting the reversed cadre pyramid, decision-makers should not respond to the increasing pressures resulting from the growing valuation of university education, especially in the humanities. This type of education should be controlled, either through the establishment of more universities and faculties, or through using the prevailing institutions to accept and absorb more students.

As was said by Dr. Badran: "We should not consider this procedure as an interference in the student's freedom or way of life, or as determining the direction of his future arbitrarily".[39] The actual situation is, by itself, arbitrarily fixed by the students and their parents, and by the society and its prevailing institutions through their different pressures.

Here we have to take into consideration, not only the needs for manpower among university graduates, but the effectiveness of their contribution to the shape of the social structure, and to the formation of values and of social incentives, as mentioned by Dr. Ammar.[40] This is true when we take into consideration the expenses incurred on higher education and foreign missions, which represent a high rate in the Arab countries, especially in the oil-poor countries;[41] while general education (in which ten million children are enrolled, and which is thus vital to the large basis of the population) does not find proper attention or resources.

The special interest for general education requires a thorough review of the structure and content of the educational process – being an ideological process of decisive role in the formation of orientations and desires of both students and public opinion. This requires the connection of the general education to the countries' economic development requirements. It needs the formation and implanting of objective concepts in the children's minds towards manual, physical and intellectual work as a basic pillar for progress and development. Such a trend will help develop professional, manual and intellectual activities of children to forge and direct them to the desired ends.

EXPANSION IN PROFESSIONAL AND TECHNICAL EDUCATION

If general primary education and private education are able to change the students orientations towards manual productive labour, it will be possible to direct the students, in later stages, to different balanced specializations which may increasingly respond to the regional and national requirements. Therefore, the expansion of secondary school education should stop. Millions of students graduate from these schools after being taught specific stereotype subjects which are removed from their social milieu and which do not orient them to want production activities. These students have outnumbered their countries' needs, even in the Gulf countries. Instead, action should be undertaken to develop vocational and technical education, and to overcome the actual problems hindering its effectiveness. Wages, financial and social incentives should be reviewed. The "available alternatives" in theoretical academic education should be limited. Therefore, the individual's freedom of choice must likewise be limited.

At the Pan-Arab level, the importance of the contribution of the petroleum countries in establishing training centres and technical institutes in the labour exporting countries should be stressed in order to alleviate the burden of expenses the poor countries cannot afford.

Although the needs of Gulf countries for skilled and technical labour have increased, they face great difficulties in enrolling sufficient numbers of their nationals in their own centres and technical training institutes. In this case, these countries can take positive action to enrol the Arab newcomers' children in these institutions. The action taken by Kuwait, in this respect, deserves note. Its government decided in 1977 to give the Arab newcomers' children – born in Kuwait and living permanently there for a period of 10 to 15 years – the opportunity to enrol in professional training. Other conditions for enrolment include the service of the trainees in ministries, and in governmental and semi-governmental institutions for a period of 3 years for each year of training. It also stipulated that a sum equivalent to half of the remuneration paid to the Kuwaiti trainees be paid to them, on condition that they do not exceed 20 per cent of the total number of trainees. In all cases, priority should be given to the Kuwaiti citizen.[42]

This is an important development. Yet we consider some of the acceptance conditions – especially that of 20 per cent enrolment of non-Kuwaitis – as a limitation to the validity of this policy, since we know that the Kuwaitis' response to such centres is weak. Furthermore, a major part of the Kuwaiti trained graduates seek other jobs which have no relation to the skill they acquired. The Kuwaitis may, naturally, be given priority. Yet, to get the utmost benefit out of such centres, greater opportunities should be granted to the newcomers' sons who are able and willing to enrol in them. Such a trend should prevail throughout the Gulf countries, especially in Saudi Arabia and the U.A.E., yet with easier terms regarding the birth-place and the residence time span. Applicants who can satisfy the conditions of acceptance are few indeed, in these two countries.

To enlarge the skilled and semi-skilled labour force in order to increase demand for these categories, rapid training methods should be applied to create a larger skilled labour-force. On-duty training should be given greater attention. Iraq has taken important steps in this respect.[43] Still the gap is getting larger between vocational training output and Iraq's needs for a skilled labour-force.

Although there are acute shortages in skilled manual workers, the wages of these 'blue collar' workers are nevertheless lower than the wages of 'white collar' workers. It is important, therefore, to adopt new wages and incentives to influence the availability of the required types of skills at both national and regional levels.

ADJUSTING IMBALANCES IN SECTORAL EMPLOYMENT AND REDUCING UNDEREMPLOYMENT

In all Arab countries, increasing numbers on the working population graviate towards the tertiary sector. In the oil-rich countries specifically, we find that the tertiary sector employs the majority of both national and migrant labour. The industrial sector – despite enjoying a great part of invested resources – is unable to provide statistically meaningful manpower employment. Industrialization relies basically on the capital-intensive type, such as the steel industry in Qatar, and the petrochemical industries in Saudi Arabia.

Disguised unemployment, in the administrative and service activities, comes as a result of increasing and unbalanced public expenditures with a large material basis for the economy. This has led to a high increase in revenues in the petroleum countries, incapable of producing a natural development. A growing part of financing government expenditures comes through interval debts, or through deficit financing and external debts, rather than through self-generating inputs in the national economies themselves. This situation induces graduates and rural migrants to join the tertiary sector in growing numbers as it seems to offer better job opportunities than the other sectors.

There are several other reasons relating to disguised unemployment in the government apparatus. Among these reasons comes the absence of precise criteria fixing employment needs, thus leading mostly to exaggerations in estimates rather than real needs.[44] Moreover, the increase in some of the new jobs may be the result of the promotion of a certain employee. When higher positions are created, this will necessitate the provision of other new jobs such as secretarial work and others.[45]

All the abovementioned factors have led to rapid and disguised unemployment in the Saudi government apparatus: "Manpower in the government sector has become one of the highest in the world".[46] As a matter of fact, government employment was increasing at an annual rate of 21 per cent during the last decade,[47] despite the fact that most of the government public sector projects are implemented by the private sector.[48] The labour-force of the services sector has increased during the Saudi 5-Year Plan to more than 24,000 persons,[49] despite the fact that productivity has decreased in this sector at a rate of 6.4 during that plan.[50] If it was possible to measure productivity in the services, no explanation could be provided other than that great numbers have been absorbed without real need.

However, disguised unemployment is not confined to the government sector but is also found in other leading sectors. In the oil-rich countries, for example, in the transport, trade and construction sectors, labour-intensive methods are used similar to those in overpopulated countries suffering from scarce financial resources. As a result of large and increasing numbers of small shops, there is an unusually high percentage of the labour force in the trade sector. These numbers could be reduced significantly if these countries resorted to modern marketing where supermarkets and co-operatives can replace the huge number of small shops. Similarly, a plan for a well-organized public transport network will remove the need for thousands of taxi-drivers and mechanics. Also, a large number of construction workers can be spared by resorting to the mechanization of this sector.

Disguised unemployment can also be seen in many other forms: excessive errant traders, car cleaners, porters, doormen, servants, etc. It is quite clear that with better efficiency and better adjustment of the employment structure, one could maintain the same output with a substantial decrease in labour-force. This would also decrease the drain of skilled and semi-skilled manpower from the labour exporting countries which have begun to feel acute shortages in certain categories of labour.

Several studies have shown that there is a very strong positive association between participation rates of women and their educational level. In Bahrain, for example, the participation rates of national women in the labour force are over 75 per cent for university and other higher education institute graduates, 54 per cent for secondary school graduates, 12 per cent for primary education leavers and only 6.5 per cent for illerate women.[51] The situation in other Gulf countries is very similar to the case of Bahrain. Therefore it is very important to encourage education of women by all means. But this is not sufficient, as women in some countries are prohibited from public employment and in most other countries are concentrated in strictly limited occupations such as teaching and nursing. In fact, in certain countries, women are completely excluded from certain economic sectors. It is therefore essential to provide increasing employment opportunities in all sectors and professions.

MIGRATION POLICY

Benefits cannot be drawn from migration of labour, by any exporting country, unless a well-planned migration policy is formulated and executed. Only then can that country control and regulate the outflow of its workers and direct migrants' repatriated incomes to productive investment. Success in carrying out such a policy requires co-operation with countries of employment to block illegal channels of migration. Co-operation can go further to include some sort of compensation. Countries of employment are obliged, from an equity point of view, or from a feeling of solidarity, to compensate countries of origin for the loss in their human capital investment, even if that loss is temporary.

Furthermore, as many countries of the region are involved either as labour importers or labour exporters, co-operation and co-ordination between the two groups, or countries of each group, is necessary. This amounts to arguing that a regional employment policy is needed. An establishment of a Common Arab Labour Market can lead to a better utilization of human resources in the region. This can serve, in turn, as a base for a wider Arab economic integration which has been widely advocated in the region for so long. Under such co-operation migrant workers' conditions can also improve.

As an alternative to importing labour, labour-short countries can invest in countries where there is excess labour. This is exactly what Arab economic integration can facilitate for countries of employment. In examining the causes of labour migration in the Arab region, we have seen that it arises out of the uneven distribution of wealth and human resources. Economic integration can lead to a wider development in which all countries can gain, contrary to the present situation which tends to widen the gap and create, in the long run, a state of confrontation instead of co-operation.

POLICIES CONCERNING DOMESTIC SERVANTS

Related to disguised unemployment in the services sector is the large provision of servants and nurse-maids. Refrigerators, gas cookers and washing machines are increasingly widespread in the Gulf countries. Instead of liberating women from exhausting housework and allowing them to contribute to the production process, such technology has turned them into idle consumers. Moreover, they are importing domestic servants instead of playing a completely different role: that of replacing the newcomers in sectors of employment.

One suggestion is the elaboration of a strict policy banning the import of domestic servants, no matter what the reasons may be. Alternatively the government could provide effective and diversified services in all districts for working women and for housewives alike. Such services would include kindergartens, nursery schools, training centres of a professional nature for the non-working women, such as knitting, sewing, maintenance and repair of home appliances, etc. Part-time labour opportunities may be provided to suit non-working women's qualifications, abilities and home commitments.

As for the new generations, an end should be put to all types of discrimination between males and females[52] especially in the field of training and education throughout all stages and types of education and employment in the different economic sectors.

MORTALITY AND PHYSICAL QUALITY OF LIFE POLICIES IN OAPEC COUNTRIES

Assessing the social aspects of development measured through the Physical Quality of Life Index (PQLI) vis-à-vis the economic aspects in these Arab countries, it has been found that the nine OAPEC countries are entirely different from the rest of the world and the gap between their social and economic aspects of development is very large. The study highlights the paucity of reliable mortality data for most of these countries. Until vital registration systems in these countries are developed to provide reliable mortality statistics with complete coverage of population, it may be essential to encourage sample surveys on mortality and related subjects in these countries. Further, mortality differentials among these countries appear to be related to differences in social and economic levels. It is time, as recommended by the Population Division of the ECWA, to analyse mortality rates and formulate objectives that would lower the mortality level within a comprehensive social and economic framework for each population. Arab co-operation in this field, as in others, is quite essential.

RECOMMENDATIONS

1. For genuine integration to take place, there is an urgent need for a balanced and optimum use of both financial and human resources to achieve a higher level of socio-economic development for the Arab region as a whole.
2. Mutual assistance and co-operation in human resources development necessitates strong support of existing or proposed regional mechanisms.
3. The Arab Employment Bureau in Tangier, Morocco, should be supported and strengthened in order to enable it to play an effective role in labour market information and manpower planning at the regional level.
4. The Arab states should take more serious steps in establishing a Common Arab Labour Market which should abolish gradually the legal and institutional restrictions on the rights of Arab workers and citizens to move freely within the Arab region and to enjoy equality of opportunity and treatment in all matters of economic and social rights. The legislative and administrative framework

should be standardized for this purpose. Multilateral arrangements are a more favourable form of implementation than bilateral ones.
5. Regional vocational and technical education centres, such as those in Libya and Qatar, should be maintained and developed to satisfy some of the requirements of all Arab countries for teachers and skilled labour.
6. The oil-rich countries, particularly those importing large numbers of graduates and skilled labour should give increasing financial support to the existing regional and local training centres as well as participating in the establishment of new centres or compensating labour-exporting countries for the loss of highly skilled manpower.
7. To secure the needed skills in the quantity and quality required, Arab integration and common efforts should be directed to effective changes, improvements and expansion of education and training together with basic revision in the system of wages and incentives.
8. The current enrolment proportions should be considerably shifted in favour of vocational and technical education. This can partly be achieved through devising a system of incentives which includes better facilities and premises, scholarships for the students and higher wages, better working conditions and social status for graduates.
9. For regional co-operation in human resources development, particularly in the areas of education and training and labour migration, adequate data on current and expected supply of and demand for skilled labour and other employment indicators should be provided. The assessment of the situation should be reported regularly to help in educational planning and rationalization of labour movements.
10. Research institutes in the region should be more concerned about determinants and consequences of the "brain-drain" to help in integrating plans for manpower and education and in finding ways and means to attract Arab skills abroad to work in the region and to contribute to its development, particularly in reforming and strengthening higher education and research institutions.

References

(1) United Nations: *Levels and Trends of Mortality Since 1950.*
(2) Eduardo E. Arriaga: *Direct Estimates of Infant Mortality Differentials from Birth Histories"*, Paper presented at WFS Conference, London, 1980.
(3) Hamed Abou-Gamrah: *"Fertility and Childhood Mortality by Mother's and Father's education in Cairo, 1976"*, ECWA, Population Bulletin No. 19, Beirut.
(4) Brass William: *"Policies for the Reduction of Mortality Differentials"*. ECWA, Population Bulletin No. 19.
(5) U.N. World Population Trends and Policies: 1981 Monitoring Report, Vol. I (New York, 1982), p. 119.
(6) Morris, Morris D. 1979: *Measuring the Conditions of the World's Poor: The Physical Quality of Life Index.* New York: Pergamon Press.
(7) Riad Tabbarah: *Population, Human resources and Development in the Arab World*, in: Population and Development in the Middle East, ECWA, pp. 19-51.

(8) M. A. El-Ghannam, *The Arab World Year 2000,* Arab Planning Institute, 1981, p. 14.
(9) Paul Shaw. *Mobilizing Human Resources in the Arab World,* Kegan Paul International, London, 1983, p. 12.
(10) Ibid., p. 15.
(11) UNESCO, *Recent Quantitative Trends and Projections in the Arab Countries,* ED-77/MINEDARAB/Ref 3.
(12) Al-Ghannam, Op. cit.
(13) Zahlan, A. "The Problematique of Arab Brain Drain", In ECWA, *Population and Development in ECWA Region,* Beirut, 1982.
(14) Ibid.
(15) Republic of Iraq, Ministry of Planning, *Development of the Education Institutions in Iraq* (Baghdad, the Ministry, 1977); and, Republic of Iraq, Central Board of Statistics, Department of Social Statistics for University and Higher Education in Iraq for the academic year 1976-1977.
(16) United Arab Emirates, Ministry of Planning, Central Authority for Statistics, *the Annual Statistics Group,* Vol. 4, 1979.
(17) State of Kuwait, Ministry of Planning, Central Statistics Board, *The Annual Statistics Group,* Vol. 8, 1981.
(18) Dr. Said, Hashim M. and Dr. Al-Amy, Tareq A., *General Outlook at Facts On Technical Education in the Arab World* (Arabic): Paper submitted to the symposium on Planning Technical Education in the Arab World, Arab Union of Technical Education, Rabat, September 14-16, 1982, p. 7.
(19) Ibid.
(20) Ibid.
(21) ILO, *Yearbook of Labour Statistics.*
(22) Based on the writer's knowledge and experience.
(23) Birks, J. S. & Sinclair, C. A., "International Migration and Development in the Arab Region." ILO, Geneva, 1980.
(24) Azzam, Henry, "Labour Migration in the Arab Region: A Structural Analysis." *Seminar on Population, Employment and Mirgration in the Arab Gulf States.* The Arab Planning Institute-Kuwait and I.L.O. Geneva, Kuwait, 16-18 Dec. 1978.
(25) Z. Ecevit and K. C. Zachariah. Op. cit.
(26) Robert Mabro, "Immigrant Workers and Patterns of Economic Development." Paper presented to the Seminar on Foreign Labour Migration in Arab Gulf Countries. The Arab Planning Institute — Kuwait and Centre for Arab Unity Studies — Beirut, Kuwait, 15-18 January 1983. (Mimeo).
(27) S. Paine, *Exporting Workers: The Turkish Case.* Cambridge University Press, 1974.
F. Halliday, "Migration and the Labour Force in the Oil Producing States of the Middle East", *Development and Change,* Vol. 8, 1977.
Z. Ecevit and K. C. Zachariah, Op. cit.
(28) Arab Labour Organization, Arab Labour Office, Arab Agreement for Labour Exchange No. 2 for 1967, Cairo 1977.
(29) Some parts of this section are based on a study undertaken by Nader Fergany, previous Chairman of the Human Resources Department, the Arab Planning Institute. The study is published in El-Mustaqbal El Araby, (1982) (in Arabic).
(30) W. R. Bohning, "Perspectives of Arab Policies on International Migration" in *Population, Employment and Migration in the Arab Gulf States,* Arab Planning Institute, Kuwait, 1978, p. 499.
(31) Arab Labour Organization, Arab Labour Office, "Arab Agreement for Manpower Exchange, Amended, No. 4, for 1975, Cairo 1977.
(32) Arab Labour Organization, Arab Employment Establishment, Interim Documents (Baghdad, Arab Labour Organization, Arab Employment Establishment, 1981), pp. 71-72.
(33) *Ibid.,* pp. 4-15.

(34) League of Arab States, Secretariat General, General Administration for Economic Affairs, *National Economic Charter,* and, *Joint Arab Economic Activities Strategies:* Two papers submitted to the Eleventh Arab Summit Conference, (Amman, November 1981); *Economic Studies Backing the Major Papers,* 1980: Studies submitted to the Eleventh Arab Summit Conference, (Amman, Jordan, November 1980) 2G (Tunisia, League of Arab States, Secretariat General, General Administration for Economic Affairs, 1980) (therefore referred to as "the Studies").
(35) League of Arab States, Secretariat General, General Administration for Economic Affairs, "Joint Agreement for Arab Funds Investment in the Arab Countries", Paper submitted to the Eleventh Arab Summit Conference (Amman, November 1981), *The Studies.*
(36) A. Zahlan, "The Arab Brain Drain: Policy Reviews and Proposals" in ECWA, *International Migration in the Arab World,* Vol. 2, Beirut, 1982, p. 829.
(37) Paul Shaw, *"Mobilizing Human Resources in the Arab World",* Kegan Paul International, London, 1983, p. 172.
(38) A. Zahlan, op. cit., p. 831.
(39) Badran, Ibrahim: On Science and Technology Problems in the Arab World: The Cadres, Amman, 1978, p. 169.
(40) Ammar, Hamed: "On Arab Higher Education and Development", Al-Mustaqbal Al-Arabi, 5th year, No. 40, June 1982, pp. 125-238.
(41) Ibid, Table No. 2, p. 124 shows the ratio of higher education expenses to the total expenses incurred by education in the Arab World.
(42) The Council of Ministers Session No. 40/77, dated 21/8/77 – as mentioned in Hussein, Amal Mulla, Professional Training in the Kuwaiti Government Sector: A Study on Central Training Board, Arab Planning Institute, Kuwait, p. 57.
(43) See: The Arab Labour Office: Arab Symposium on Manpower Planning, Baghdad, December 1979, pp. 71-74.
(44) See Dr. Mansour, Hussein O., "Means and Ways of Realizing Labour Self-sufficiency in Government Apparatus". (Arabic), in a Seminar of Non-Saudi Labour Force in the Government Apparatus, Public Administration Institute, Riyadh, Rabi-Awal 1403 H., p. 232.
(45) Ibid., pp. 236-237.
(46) Ibid., p. 233.
(47) Al Adily, Nasser M., "Non-Saudi Manpower Behavioural Impact in the Public Sector, in Ibid, p. 155.
(48) Mansour, Hussein O., Ibid, p. 233.
(49) Ibid, p. 225.
(50) Ibid, Table 3, p. 224.
(51) The Population Census of Bahrain, 1981, op. cit.
(52) For more details, see: Galaleldin Mohamed A., "Discrimination Between Males and Females and Its Impact on the Women Situation and Role (Arabic), University of Jordan, Amman, 1982.

CHAPTER 11

Arab Development Aid Institutions: The Role of the Kuwait Fund

The Kuwait Fund for Arab Economic Development

ARAB AID to developing countries accelerated rapidly over the last decade reaching significant levels in absolute terms as well as in relation to the performance of other donor groups. Several bilateral and multilateral Arab aid agencies were established in the aftermath of the adjustment of oil prices in 1973* for the allocation and administration of aid. But long before that date an initiative was already taken by the developing State of Kuwait to establish in December 1961 the Kuwait Fund for Arab Economic Development.

In the present paper we shall consider the role of Arab aid agencies in development co-operation, with particular consideration given to the efforts of the oldest of these institutions, the Kuwait Fund. By highlighting the efforts of the latter, we focus on the nature of such efforts and the manner in which they were made. As aid provided by Arab development finance institutions is part of Arab aid in general, an overview of it is given first.

ARAB AID IN GENERAL

Three main groups of donors are usually referred to whenever Official Development Assistance (ODA) flows to Third World countries are considered. They are the DAC member countries, the Organization of Petroleum Exporting Countries (OPEC) members, and the Council for Mutual Economic Assistance (CMEA) countries. According to OECD sources net ODA flows from these main groups of donor countries reached a level of around $36 billion in 1980. It is estimated that 75

---

*In addition to the Kuwait Fund three other institutions were established before this date: the Arab Fund for Economic and Social Development (1968); the Abu Dhabi Fund for Arab Economic Development (1971); and the Libyan Arab Foreign Bank (1972).

per cent of this amount was provided by the DAC group, 20 per cent by the OPEC group, and 5 per cent by the CMEA group.

The OPEC group includes seven Arab countries* which provide the major part of OPEC aid. In fact, four of the Arab donors – Kuwait, Qatar, Saudi Arabia and the United Arab Emirates have so far been providing the bulk of what is considered "OPEC aid". For the period 1970-1980, these countries' net ODA constituted 80 per cent of OPEC's total for the entire period, and over 80 per cent of OPEC's aid in 1980 (Table 11.1).

Arab net ODA flows accelerated rapidly during the 1970s to reach $6.8 billion in 1980, equivalent to about 19 times their level in 1970, and constituting 2.34 per cent of the group's combined GNP for that year. This ratio is more than 6 times the corresponding figure for the DAC group, which is .37 per cent.

Again, considered individually, certain Arab donors performed extremely well in terms of GNP and in comparison to other major DAC donors. For example, Saudi Arabia's net ODA ranged between 2.6 and 5.62 per cent of its GNP during the period 1970-1980. Similar figures for Kuwait were between 3.88 and 10 per cent, for United Arab Emirates between 3.85 and 12.69 per cent, and for Qatar between 3.57 and 15.67 per cent. In contrast to this, none of the other DAC donors even reached a level of 1 per cent throughout the entire 1970-1980 period; and with the exception of Sweden, Norway, the Netherlands and Denmark, none of the other DAC donors succeeded in transferring net concessional assistance equivalent to the minimum target of 0.7 per cent of GNP,* as set by the United Nations over a decade ago.

The above comparisons which indicate conspicuously the high performance of the Arab group, do not take into account a host of other facts about Arab aid. First, all those Arab countries providing aid are themselves developing nations, and their economies are far from reaching the desired level of social and economic development. Second, dependence on one main export commodity (oil) renders their economies vulnerable to external factors beyond their control. Third, the "financial surpluses", so far realized by only a few of the Arab oil-exporting countries are neither a true sign of their wealth nor a measure of their income-generating capacities. These accumulated "cash balances", arising from the liquidation of depletable assets were not, due to limitation of absorptive capacity, readily transformed into productive investments. Consequently, they have been exposed to the ravages of inflation, foreign exchange fluctuations and other risks. Fourth, unlike much of the aid provided by traditional donors, Arab aid is free from any strings attached to procurement sources of goods and services; and does not seek to promote the donors' national economic interests, by way of seeking export markets for their products, or otherwise.

Indeed, the Arab aid initiative – promoted by moral and religious principles, humanitarian considerations, and a sense of belonging to the developing countries – is a new phenomenon of co-operation, committed to the cause of development and solidarity of the Third World.

*Algeria, Iraq, Kuwait, Libya, Qatar, Saudi Arabia and the United Arab Emirates.
*See OECD, Development Cooperation, 1981 Review (Table A.3).

Table 11.1. Net Concessional Assistance by OPEC Members 1970-1980 ($ Million)

	1970	1971	1972	1973	1974	1975	1976	1977	1978	1979	1980
Algeria	—	—	—	25	47	41	54	47	44	272	83
Iraq	—	—	—	11	423	218	232	61	172	847	829
Kuwait	148	108	—	345	632	976	621	1,517	1,270	1,055	1,188
Libya	63	53	64	214	147	261	94	115	160	105	281
Qatar	—	—	—	94	185	339	195	197	106	277	319
Saudi Arabia	155	160	204	305	1,029	1,997	2,415	2,410	1,719	2,298	3,040
UAE	—	50	74	289	511	1,046	1,059	1,238	717	1,115	1,062
Arab Donors	365	371	494	1,283	2,974	4,878	4,670	5,585	4,187	5,968	6,802
Iran	—	—	—	2	408	593	753	221	278	25	3
Nigeria	—	—	—	5	15	14	83	65	38	30	42
Venezuela	—	—	—	18	59	31	103	52	109	83	130
Non-Arab Donors	—	—	—	25	482	638	939	338	425	138	175
Total	365	371	494	1,308	3,456	5,516	5,609	5,923	4,611	6,106	6,978

Source: OECD, Development Co-operation, 1981 Review.

ARAB DEVELOPMENT AID INSTITUTIONS

Arab aid agencies comprise several bilateral and multilateral institutions which were established for the purpose of allocating and administering development assistance. With the exception of two institutions – the Islamic Development Bank and the OPEC Fund for International Development – all other development assistance institutions included in Table 11.2 are entirely Arab Organizations. The Islamic Development Bank and the OPEC Fund are considered under Arab aid institutions because of the major contributions made to their resources by Arab countries and, in particular, the Arab petroleum exporting countries. Both of these institutions are also members of the "Arab Co-ordination Group".* All Arab aid institutions provide concessional assistance, and have similar development objectives. The differences between them pertain to the scope of their operations and geographical coverage.

The rapid emergence of numerous Arab aid organizations with huge capital resources, and financial and administrative independence constitutes an important channel for external development assistance designed to serve the interests of aid recipients and to strengthen co-operation among the developing countries themselves.

The most evident part of Arab aid is that channelled by the development institutions. The latter as a group operate today in most of the developing countries – in the Arab world as well as in other countries in Asia, Africa and Latin America. They have so far been able to co-operate with more than 95 developing nations, by providing them with financial and technical assistance for a wide range of operations. Funds were provided to finance projects in various sectors such as infrastructure, agriculture, industry, and energy as well as a number of other operations including balance-of-payments support.

Annual commitments by the Arab aid institutions increased continuously during the 1973-1980 period, from a level of $59.5 million in 1973 to over $2.0 billion in 1977. Total commitments by these institutions reached about $4.9 billion in 1977, and rapidly increased to a total of over $14.0 billion in 1980 as is shown in Table 11.2 This acceleration of commitments was caused by the speed with which these institutions had to act in response to requests made by various developing countries, despite the fact that some of these institutions were only recently established.

The resources were committed for financing those projects which were considered of major importance and accorded high priority by the aid recipients. Although it is estimated that the largest portion (nearly one third) of these resources was directed to infrastructure, yet the combined share of both energy and agriculture exceeds that of infrastructure by some 7 per cent. These observations on the sectoral distribution of commitments reveal the recipients' needs to build up their infrastructure base, to develop energy sources, and to promote agricultural production

---

*All those shown in Table 11.2 are members of this group. The Libyan Arab Foreign Bank which is also a member is not reported.

Table 11.2. Evolution of Commitments by Major Arab/OPEC Aid Institutions (U.S. $ Million)

	1973	1974	1975	1976	1977	Total commitments end of 1977	Total commitments end of 1980
1. Abu Dhabi Fund for Arab Economic Development	—	55.1	46.2	169.4	138.1	408.8	901.0
2. Arab Fund for Economic and Social Development	—	127.3	200.8	336.3	362.6	1,027.0	1,250.0
3. Arab Bank for Economic Development in Africa*	—	—	—	79.5	76.0	155.5	598.0
4. Islamic Development Bank	—	—	—	—	120.3	120.3	1,465.0
5. Kuwait Fund for Arab Economic Development	59.5	143.4	343.1	324.5	411.8	1,282.3	2,526.0
6. OPEC Fund for International Development†	—	—	—	42.7	243.0	285.7	1,490.0
7. Saudi Fund for Development	—	—	282.7	458.3	841.1	1,582.1	4,159.0
8. The Iraqi Fund for Foreign Development	—	—	—	—	—	—	1,744.0
Total	59.5	325.8	872.8	1,410.7	2,192.9	4,861.7	14,133.0

*Not including commitments under the Special Arab Aid Fund for Africa, administered by BADEA, which amounted to $56 million in 1976 and $13 million in 1977.
†Not including commitments to IFAD, IMF Trust Fund and UNDP, totalling $477.6 million.
Sources: All figures for the period 1973-1977 from: OECD, Development Cooperation, 1978 Review, (*Table VII-13*).
Total Commitments at end of 1980 from: The OPEC Fund for International Development, OPEC Aid and OPEC Aid Institutions, Profile, January 1981.

essentially aiming at reducing the countries' dependence on imports for their energy requirements and basic food needs.

As new channels of aid, complementing ODA directly provided by Arab governments, the Arab aid agencies are now assuming a greater role in Arab ODA flows to Third World countries. For example, while net ODA provided by three Arab countries (Kuwait, Saudi Arabia and United Arab Emirates) amounted to $4.1 billion in 1976, only 241 million was channelled through the national development institutions of these countries. In other words, only 6 per cent of the countries' net ODA for 1976 was allocated by the related development institutions. The latter's role, however, increased rapidly between 1976 and 1980, as is evidenced by the growth of net ODA by three of the Arab aid institutions in relation to total net ODA by the countries concerned.

Table 11.3 shows the share of the three Arab aid agencies in total net ODA of the donor countries.

It is clear from Table 11.3 that the combined share of the three Funds in the total net ODA of the donors doubled, rising from 6 per cent in 1976 to 12.0 per cent in 1980.

The increasing role of these Funds in channelling aid becomes more evident by comparing the countries' ODA commitments with the aid commitments of the related national Funds. Based on total ODA commitments (about $14.5 billion) by Kuwait, Saudi Arabia and United Arab Emirates for the period 1975-1977, and total aid commitments (about $3.0 billion) by the three national Funds for the same period, it is estimated that the combined share of the three Funds in total commitments for the period is 21 per cent. This same ratio, however, rises to 28 per cent

Table 11.3. Share of National Development Institutions in Total net ODA (Per cent)

	1976	1977	1978	1979	1980
1. Abu Dhabi Fund	3.2	5.4	7.0	3.5	5.0
2. Kuwait Fund	23.5	10.7	14.2	18.1	23.5
3. Saudi Fund	2.5	7.8	11.5	13.2	10.4
Combined Share	6.0	8.0	11.5	12.0	12.0

Source: Based on tables IX-2 and G.1 in OECD, Development Co-operation, 1981 Review.

Table 11.4. Share of National Development Institutions in Total Commitments (Per cent)

	1975-1977	1978-1980
1. Abu Dhabi Fund	12.0	22.0
2. Kuwait Fund	33.0	46.0
3. Saudi Fund	19.0	25.0
Combined Share	21.0	28.0

Sources: Percentages are computed on the basis of: (1) Total ODA commitments by countries for the periods indicated, obtained from annual ODA commitments as in OECD, Development Co-operation, various Annual Reviews. (2) Total commitments by Funds obtained from Table 11.2.

for the period 1978-1980. The share of each Fund in the related country's commitments is as shown in Table 11.4.

The increasing role of Arab funds in channelling aid implies that a larger proportion of Arab aid is being administered with a view to realizing more effective use of resources. Administrative and technical organs are in existence within each Arab development institution to ascertain the technical soundness of investments and their impact on development. And in discharging their duties these institutions give considerable attention to the needs and problems of recipient countries. To this end, the "Arab Co-ordination Group" was established in recent years with the aim of co-ordinating the members' operations. The Co-ordination Group holds semi-annual meetings to review, discuss and exchange views on various aspects pertinent to its lending activities.

These meetings have so far led to a number of concrete results. Loan Agreements are now generally standardized and disbursement procedures determined. The institutions have also gone a long way in ironing out problems related to co-financing, follow-up of projects, etc. Despite these achievements further co-ordination is expected along these lines as well as in other areas, and a lot more is still to be done. The complex issues of development certainty require continuous and concerted efforts by all those involved in development activities in order to make more effective use of aid.

CONCLUDING REMARKS

The world economy is suffering from severe problems. The industrial countries have been faced with a prolonged recession and heavy unemployment accompanied by unprecedented high levels of interest rates. The developing countries' economic problems have been aggravated by the drastic drop in the prices of primary commodities, high interest rates, exchange rate fluctuations, unfavourable terms of trade, a decline in export volumes, as well as various kinds of protectionist measures and other barriers.

Against this background, one of the main issues currently discussed in a number of international fora concerns official development assistance. It is distressing to note that while the developing countries' needs call for more aid in order, at least, to avoid further deterioration of their prospects for growth and development, the volume of aid has recently levelled off. Not only that, but some traditional donors' attitudes towards the transfer of concessional flows has changed markedly, and unfortunately, their call for a more active role by commercial sources of funds comes at a time when the developing countries are struggling with an already heavy debt-servicing burden, and have only limited means of access to the international financial market.

The Arab oil-exporting countries are developing nations, and are still far from reaching the desired social and economic development. The temporary financial surplus of this group enabled it over the last decade to channel sizable concessional financial resources to other Third World countries, thereby enhancing development co-operation among the developing countries themselves.

National and regional Arab development finance institutions, established before and after the "oil revolution" in 1973 are gaining an increasing role in channelling and administering aid to the countries of the South, and they constitute today a significant framework for development co-operation among Third World countries.

The developed countries possess the means to do much more than what their ODA performance indicates. Yet, the volume of net concessional resource receipts of developing countries from non-OPEC donor groups throughout the last decade remained far below the "minimum" aid target in terms of the groups' combined GNP.

The economic interdependence of the world does not relieve the rich countries from the responsibility they have in keeping the "economic engines" working together. In order to avoid the worsening of the economic plight of the poor countries, the rich countries have, among other things, to increase their aid efforts and to relax the constraints which limit the effective use of the resources provided. The industrial countries' current problems should not loom above their intrinsic potential which enables them to bear a greater share of the resources required to meet the developing countries' urgent needs.

The developing countries need to make more concerted efforts to reinforce and strengthen the various schemes, institutions, organizations and other arrangements already established for promoting subregional, regional and interregional economic co-operation among themselves. They also need to explore further ways and means for utilizing their own resources through their concerted and co-ordinated efforts, making sure that the ground for economic co-operation among themselves, and related policies and measures are conducive to sustainable and lasting co-operation.

ANNEX

ACTIVITIES OF THE KUWAIT FUND

Soon after gaining full independence in 1961, the developing State of Kuwait established the Kuwait Fund for Arab Economic Development as an autonomous public body, with administrative and financial independence. The main purpose of the Fund was to assist Arab states in developing their economies, and to provide such states with loans for the implementation of their development projects and programmes. Important to note in this respect is the fact that the initiative to establish an aid agency was taken long before the adjustment of oil prices and despite Kuwait's relatively meagre financial resources at that time. Nevertheless, the initiative originally aiming at closer links of co-operation with Arab States in their developmental efforts remained an overriding consideration.

Soon after Arab oil-exporting states restored sovereignty over their resources in 1973, the mandate of the Kuwait Fund was extended, in July 1974, to include in its operations non-Arab developing countries as well. Today, the authorized capital of the Fund stands at KD 2 billion, its cumulative total commitments reached around KD 1,104 million by the end of December 1982, representing the value of 236 loans distributed over 58 developing countries, of which 16 are Arab, 25 African, 14 Asian, and 3 other countries.

As a development assistance institution, the primary function of the Kuwait Fund is the allocation and administration of financial aid to developing countries, and its main objective is "to assist Arab States and Developing States in developing their economies and, in particular, to provide such States with loans for the implementation of their development programmes." Although loans are the most apparent part of the Fund's all-inclusive aid efforts, they have always been considered only as a means of seeking the fulfilment of the desired objectives of development. Hence, realizing the fact that the requirements of development transcend the mere availability of financial resources, the Fund got involved in various developmental activities, which unlike loans, are not usually recorded in monetary terms, yet they are important in an overall measure of aid performance and as such they should not escape notice.

It is not the intention here to elaborate on the specifics of loans and grants provided to individual countries, but rather to highlight the main collaborative efforts of the Fund, the nature of the assistance provided in general, and the manner in which such assistance was made.

LOANS

The year ending 31 December 1982 marks the twenty-first anniversary of the Fund. During those years, the Fund has been able to cater to the needs of a wide spectrum of developing countries. In this respect, the Fund operations, which are essentially project-oriented, covered high-priority projects and programmes in such sectors as agriculture, power, transport and communications, water and sewerage as well as other industrial and infrastructure projects. As can be seen in Table 11.5, showing the geographical and sectoral distribution of Fund loans, two sectors (agriculture and power) together absorbed nearly half of the Fund's total loan commitments. This, of course, causes no surprise, but it reveals some interesting facts. While in selecting projects for financing, the policy of the Fund is to respect, in principle, the priorities set by the recipients themselves, and generally to turn down only those projects which fail to pass the rigorous appraisal made by the Fund's staff, the sectoral distribution of loan operations is in line with the recipients' needs to promote the production of basic food commodities and to develop indigenous sources of energy in order to cut down the foreign exchange requirements and reduce dependence on external markets.

Indeed, the Fund's operations in the power sector, constituting more than 27 per cent of total commitments, consist mainly of large hydro-power projects. The huge natural water resources of the developing countries, of which, according to present estimates, only a very small percentage (of the order of 4 per cent) has been tapped and developed, offer the developing countries an attractive opportunity in their search for alternative energy sources.

However, sometimes the viability of large multi-purpose projects, such as for land irrigation and generation of electricity, is hardly justified on the basis of national interests alone, but such projects can become viable investments through regional co-ordination and co-operation. Other similar examples of projects in various sectors may be cited, but the point to be noted remains the same, and that is that some projects which cannot be justified on the basis of limited geographical boundaries may stand a good chance of success by the concerted efforts and close co-operation of neighbouring countries which would be the ultimate beneficiaries of the joint action. To this effect, the Fund has always welcomed such regional projects and tried to assist the participating countries in working out feasible and sustainable arrangements leading to a more lasting co-operation among the countries themselves.

A quick look at the Fund's annual loan commitments given in Table 11.6 reveals a sharp rise in such commitments in 1975-76. This was due to the enlarged mandate of the Fund in July 1974 which enabled it to extend its operations to a large number of African and Asian countries. However, the preceding and succeeding years indicate noticeable fluctuations which were often misunderstood by observers, and therefore call for some clarifications. It has been the Fund's policy to commit itself to those projects whose implementation would otherwise have been hampered if financial resources were not made available at the right time. The size and pace of commitments, to be meaningful, should be considered jointly with the volume of disbursements. And for commitments to be of greater value to recipients, a more judicious policy in this regard should allow for greater flexibility in pipelining projects. In this sense, fluctuations may become inevitable, but not utterly undesirable.

TECHNICAL ASSISTANCE

Another activity in which the Fund has been involved concerns grants and technical assistance. The latter activity was introduced into the Fund's operations in 1971, as a result of the increasing evidence which showed that certain countries were unable

Table 11.5. Geographic and Sectoral Distribution of Fund Loans, 1962-82, incl. (Million K.D.)

Countries/Sector	Agriculture and Primary Sector	Transport, Communication and Storage	Power	Industry	Water and Sewage	Others	Total	Share of Total (%)
Arab	130.580	182.422	105.707	123.493	27.300	10.864	580.366	52.56
African	54.810	84.828	32.770	17.500	4.000	—	193.908	17.56
Asian	39.860	50.950	162.547	58.515	12.250	—	324.122	29.35
Other	3.700	2.130	—	—	—	—	5.830	0.53
Total	228.950	320.330	301.024	199.508	43.550	10.864	1,104.226	100.00
Share of Total (%)	20.74	29.01	27.26	18.07	3.94	0.98	100.0	—

to attract external financial assistance due to lack of well-conceived and prepared projects. Up to the end of 1982, the Fund's efforts in assisting to fill this gap in giving grants of a total value of around KD 14 million, spread over 28 countries, of which 10 are Arab, 14 African, and 4 Asian.

Table 11.6. Loan Commitments, 1962-1982, inclusive

Financial year (1 April-30 March)	Number of Loans	Amount (K.D Million)
1962/63	3	11.871
1963/64	3	6.216
1964/65	2	17.384
1965/66	1	1.674
1966/67	4	14.416
1967/68	3	10.181
1968/69	2	1.124
1969/70	1	6.996
1970/71	7	11.699
1971/72	5	11.141
1972/73	2	7.633
1973/74	8	31.435
1974/75	6	26.500
1975/76*	34	158.618
1976/77†	22	106.590
1977/78	14	57.326
1978/79	25	100.350
1979/80	20	72.297
1980/81	24	121.870
1981/82	34	214.945
July-Dec. 82	16	113.960
Total	236	1,104.226

*1.4.1975-30.6.1976.
†For this year and the subsequent years, the fiscal year begins July 1st and ends June 30th.

The major part of these technical assistance grants was directed to financing feasibility studies for projects in various economic sectors. The recipient countries and the Fund co-operate closely in the selection and appointment of consulting firms, the drawing up of terms of reference, and the supervision of the consultants' work. The active part played by the Fund within the framework of technical assistance is intended not only to ensure a high quality product, but also to give the recipients the opportunity to gain experience in tackling problems and issues related to their efforts in the development process.

CONTRIBUTIONS TO DEVELOPMENT FINANCE INSTITUTIONS

Apart from its main "business" of providing loans and technical assistance grants to Third World countries, the Fund is entrusted with the responsibility to act on behalf of the Government of Kuwait in various activities related to development co-operation. In this connection, the Fund makes direct financial contributions, out of its own resources, to a number of multilateral development finance institutions such as the Arab Fund for Economic and Social Development, the Arab Bank for Economic Development in Africa, the African Development Bank and Fund, and the Inter-Arab Investment Guarantee Corporation. Such contributions totalled around KD 106 million by the end of December 1982.

Although financial contributions to other multi-lateral development bodies such as, for example, the World Bank (IBRD), the International Development Association (IDA), the OPEC Fund for International Development, and the International Fund for Agricultural Development (IFAD), are made directly by the State of Kuwait, the management of the Fund is also assigned some role in representing the Government in those organizations, and therefore, through this role, the Fund is able to follow the activities of those institutions.

INITIATIVES

As a development institution with a relatively long history in development co-operation and a background of related experience, the Kuwait Fund has been aware of the fact that its mission cannot be fulfilled by the provision of financial assistance alone, no matter how much is being spent to establish factories, to construct roads, or to build other physical structures. It was therefore considered essential by the Fund to take, within the limitations of its means and capacity, certain initiatives aimed at promoting the building up of institutional and administrative structures as well as development-oriented institutions.

In this regard, some of the initiatives relate to: (1) assisting in the creation of certain multilateral development-oriented institutions, (2) providing financial assistance to a number of national development banks, and (3) providing technical assistance and financial support for strengthening national operational bodies and institutions.

In the first category, the Fund's initiatives include, for example, the Arab Fund for Economic and Social Development, the Inter-Arab Investment Guarantee Corporation, the Arab Bank for Economic Development in Africa, and the OPEC Fund for International Development. Such initiatives were of varying character and degree. For example, the proposal to establish the Arab Fund for Economic and Social Development and the preliminary documents for this institution were introduced first by the Kuwait Fund to the Arab authorities concerned. Subsequently, the Arab Fund was established. Again, the scheme for the Inter-Arab Investment Guarantee Corporation was proposed and sponsored by the Fund whose active participation in the scheme continued throughout the various stages of its elaboration and adoption.* The Fund's initiatives in the establishment of the other institutions were not as direct as they were in the case of the two examples thus far mentioned. Nevertheless, the Fund's experience and expertise helped constructively in making arrangements for and reaching agreements on the establishment of these institutions.

Another area to which the Fund gives attention is national development banks. The Fund has actively participated in the establishment of several such banks in various countries. For example, in Lebanon, Kuwait, North Yemen and Mauritania. Apart from this, some national development banks were granted loans to help them expand their operations and develop their capacities. Beneficiaries in this regard were development banks in Morocco, Sudan, North Yemen, Tunisia, Jordan and Mauritania.

Within the general framework of building up insitutions, it is considered that operational organizations, authorities, administrations and other structures are no less important than other bodies catering to the economic life and welfare of nations. The Fund's activity in this respect concerns the strengthening of managerial capabilities, promoting skills and advancing technical know-how for a more efficient utilization of human capital, and consequently, for a more effective use of resources. To this end, the Fund assisted in organizing and funding technical assistance missions to advise on economic planning and policies in such countries as North Yemen, South Yemen, Comoros Islands and the Maldives.

Although the Fund stresses the need to obtain the services of the most qualified and competent consulting firms, it also realizes the importance of promoting the technical capabilities and experience of consulting firms and expertise in the developing countries. In this respect, the Fund's policy is to encourage consultants from the developing world to participate in submitting proposals for the services required and, in particular, through their collaboration with other consulting firms from the developed countries.

With a view to promoting local capabilities and enterprise in developing countries and to fostering collaboration among the developing countries themselves, the Fund pays special attention to encouraging bidders (contractors) from the developing countries to bid for the whole project or a component thereof, as the case may be; and at the request of a recipient country a margin of preference is granted to local bidders when comparing bids received from local contractors with those of foreign contractors.

ADVISORY AND CONSULTING SERVICES

In its co-operation with Third World countries, the Fund tries always to ensure that the basic economic interests of the recipient countries, often among the least

---

* For more details on the initiatives leading to the establishment of the Arab Fund and the Inter-Arab Guarantee Corporation, see Abdlatif Y. Al-Hamad, *Building up Development Oriented Institutions in the Arab Countries*, Kuwait Fund Publications, October 1972.

developed, are protected. Various advisory and consulting services are rendered by the Fund and are geared towards fulfilling that objective.

A normal feature of the Fund's operations is that of trilateral co-operation – so to speak – in which there is almost always a third party from the industrial countries. Consequently, a major part of the Fund's daily activities relates to assisting recipients in their dealings with consultants, contractors, and suppliers, and also in tackling subsequent problems and issues.

In providing such services, the Fund identifies itself with the aspirations and interests of the recipients, and its leverage is used to ensure that contractual and other arrangements reached between recipients and third parties are based on more equitable and balanced terms and conditions. The strength of the Fund's leverage in taking specific attitudes with third parties stems from certain simple facts. First, the experience gained during twenty-one years of active involvement in development co-operation made the Fund familiar with the nature of the problems and issues usually encountered, and at the same time capable of providing appropriate advice on the course of action to be followed by recipients, as the case may be. Second, Kuwait, being primarily an oil-exporting country has no commercial interests to promote in external markets through aid-giving. Consequently, the Fund does not seek to solicit national economic advantages through its collaborative operations. Its primary goal for aid-giving is to accelerate development in the recipient countries; and to this end, it tries to utilize its power, experience and leverage in a way most advantageous to the aid-receiving countries.

Although it is difficult to measure the real impact of those advisory and consulting services in concrete terms, there is no doubt that their benefits are, more often than not, translated into more practical concepts of projects, more appropriate choice of technology and design, lower costs of investments, more equitable terms and conditions, and better performance.

CO-FINANCING

Another aspect of operations in which the Fund has been actively involved is that of co-financing. Large-scale projects such as for the development of agriculture, infrastructure or hydro-power, and other multi-purpose projects require resources that are beyond the means of any one donor to cope with. Financing such projects, therefore, requires close co-operation and co-ordination among co-lenders, especially those co-financiers whose policies and procedures are dissimilar. Co-financing by Arab aid agencies is greatly facilitated as a result of the similar procedures and largely harmonized policies realized by those institutions through their co-ordination efforts. Other non-Arab co-lenders, and in particular those providing tied aid, limit the scope for joint-financing, but very often this issue is resolved by resorting to parallel-financing whenever this is possible.

However, the Arab/OPEC donors have in recent years opened dialogue with their counterpart donors of the DAC and EEC groups with the aim of exchanging views on co-financing issues and other matters related to the development efforts of the two sides.

CHAPTER 12

Co-operation Between the Arab World and European CMEA Countries

Mihály Simai

Institute of World Economics, Budapest

MAIN TRENDS IN ECONOMIC RELATIONS BETWEEN EUROPEAN CMEA MEMBERS AND MIDDLE EASTERN COUNTRIES

ECONOMIC RELATIONS between European CMEA countries and the Middle Eastern countries are determined by several factors. The historical, political, geographical, economic and institutional/organizational factors of relations themselves are of a rather complex nature; each of them could be the subject of a separate analysis.

The process of economic and social transformation of the two groups of countries is in itself a source of important changes. The great differences among Arab countries in their population, market size, natural endowment, economic and social structure, development level, etc. are well-known sources of possibilities for, as well as limitations to co-operation with the CMEA countries. The CMEA countries themselves differ accordingly to their size, development level, and economic structure, and this influences their possibilities and practices of co-operation.

The extraordinary dynamics of CMEA-Middle Eastern trade in the 1970s are shown by the following factors (in no particular order of importance):

1. The geographical proximity of the two regions – in addition to obvious economies of transportation – has contributed to narrowing the "information gap" which is largely responsible for the inadequate evolution of some East-South flows.
2. The continuous accumulation of a scientific-technological potential in the CMEA countries and the high income elasticity of capital goods imports in the Middle East created a strong complementarity in supply and demand relations between the two groups of countries.
3. The strivings of most Middle Eastern countries for increasing national control over their natural resources during the early 1970s raised their "propensities" for establishing more extensive links with the socialist countries as a means of

enhancing their bargaining power vis-à-vis the transnational corporations of the industrially developed market economy countries.
4. States have emerged as the prime moving forces behind economic development in the whole of the Middle East, irrespective of political ideologies, during the 1970s. This phenomenon has been due partly to the relative lack and/or merchant attitudes of local entrepreneurs and partly to the fact that oil wealth accumulated in state budgets. This considerably and spontaneously favoured the involvement of socialist countries with their macro-centered foreign trade establishments and government-to-government attitudes.
5. The spectacular increase in the import needs of most Middle Eastern countries coincided with the growing constraints on expanding the socialist countries' exports to West European markets. A consequent shift stemmed from the quasi-residual nature of CMEA trade with developing countries.

The economic differentiation in the Arab World is growing. Even the oil producers are in an increasingly dissimilar position. Several countries established important industries in the 1970s; there are countries, however, where the oil incomes have not, as yet, led to substantial structural changes.

ACTUAL AND POTENTIAL CO-OPERATION BETWEEN CMEA COUNTRIES AND ARAB MIDDLE EAST STATES

The Middle East traditionally played a prominent role in East-South interactions. Its share of total CMEA exports to developing countries increased from 22 per cent after the first oil-price explosion in 1974 to 30 per cent in 1981, combined, however, with a sharply declining import share resulting in growing surpluses for the CMEA countries. The role played by the Middle East in East-South export flows (excluding the Soviet Union) is unique. The Middle East's share in LDC-directed exports of the smaller European CMEA countries grew from 33 per cent to 47 per cent between 1974 and 1981. The relevant export shares are in fact modest where total non-CMEA trade is concerned (6.7 per cent in 1974 and 11.1 per cent in 1981), nevertheless the overall figures do not reflect the importance of the Middle East in absorbing growing portions of the non-CMEA turnover of "socialist-made" manufacturers: 12 per cent in 1974 and 17 per cent in 1981. Similarly, the declining export shares of the Middle East to CMEA countries conceal the fact that the region supplied the lion's share of crude oil purchased by the socialist countries outside the CMEA region itself. The growing reliance of the smaller CMEA countries on Middle Eastern crude oil is a long-term phenomenon, since possibilities of increasing purchases from Soviet sources are limited.

The geographical pattern of CMEA exports to the Middle East shows increasing concentration in favour of one country, Iraq. The growing predominance of this market coincided with a fall in the relative shares of Iran and of the Gulf countries while the share of traditional partners such as Syria and Turkey remained constant.

The growing "Iraqi preference" of CMEA can be attributed to both positive and negative, i.e. pull and push effects:

Iraq had long received a good deal of assistance from several CMEA countries (Czechoslovakia, Hungary, Romania, the USSR) in developing its petroleum resources. Subsequently, co-operation could be more easily extended to non-energy fields, especially in view of the overall investment fever in Iraq. In 1975, a multilateral agreement between the CMEA and Iraq was signed. Without altering the basically bilateral character of co-operation, it secured an institutional framework for involving this market in the longer term planning practices of socialist countries. The socialist countries' role in developing the Iraqi defence sector has also contributed to reinforcing CMEA-Iraqi economic ties.

CMEA exports to the Middle East have been centered on Iraq due to some "push-effects" as well. The exports of the socialist countries had no direct access to the largest boom-market of the region, Saudi Arabia. On the other hand, they had a large share in the second biggest market, Iran, which produced extremely low import dynamics in the late seventies due to well-known political reasons. As far as the geographical pattern of exports from the CMEA is concerned, the most prominent feature is the decline of the Soviet export share. This appears to underline the marked cyclical sensitivity of Soviet exports to the Middle East.

Structurally, a deteriorating trend can be observed in socialist exports to the Middle East. The deterioration is especially marked if total CMEA exports are considered, although this can be misleading since a substantial part of Soviet exports cannot be fitted into the usual scheme of commodity breakdown. Nevertheless, the same trend – although less pronounced – surfaces also in the data of the smaller socialist countries. There was an indisputable decline in the 1970s in the share of manufacturers (including industrial semi-products) and a corresponding increase in the share of crude materials and mineral fuels with a quasi-constant share of agricultural exports. This trend is in contrast with the main structural shifts in the overall Middle Eastern imports where the share of capital goods tended to rise throughout the 1970s.

The collapse of the Iraqi and Iranian crude export capacities in 1980 resulted in a drastic fall in absolute terms of CMEA imports from the Middle East. In all, CMEA efforts to increase non-fuel imports from the Middle East are quite insufficient as compared to changes in the non-traditional export potential of the region. Surely, the decrease in volume of Middle Eastern, non-oil supplies is not a tendency to be maintained in the longer run, particularly with a view to the emergence of some second-tier newly industrializing countries such as Syria, Jordan, Cyprus and Turkey. During the past decades several important infrastructural industrial and agricultural projects have been implemented with CMEA assistance in the Middle Eastern Arab countries. While so far bilateral trade relations have predominated industrial co-operation is on the rise and some joint ventures have been established. Several CMEA countries are participating in the prospecting of oil and other natural resources. About 75 per cent of the total number of CMEA country exports in developing countries are concentrated in the Arab World.

Besides specialization, there is also some direct co-operation among the CMEA countries in their economic relations with Arab countries, usually within the framework of a general contracting system. This co-operation is promoted by the CMEA both directly and indirectly.

Taking into account the possibilities and the mutual interests of the CMEA countries and of the Arab world, it is clear that there is significant potential for expanding economic relations between them. Analysis of this potential must rest on long-term trends of structural changes in supply and demand, on geographic factors and the channels of communication so far established, as well as on the advantages of trade diversification for both parties:

- The import requirements of the European CMEA countries for oil will increase in coming years.
- It will be more advantageous for many CMEA countries to purchase some petrochemical products from abroad instead of increasing their own output.
- Certain countries in the Middle East may offer for export agricultural products (like citrus fruits) and industrial goods (especially light industry products) which may be of interest to some of the CMEA countries.
- Infrastructure development in the process of industrialization and agricultural development programmes offers good export possibilities for CMEA countries. These countries already supply about 5-7 per cent of the total machinery and equipment imports of Middle Eastern countries. (In certain cases these proportions are much higher.)
- The transformation of consumption, the improvement of the health services, housing, etc., also represent possible areas for co-operation, especially with the oil-exporting countries, in the field of industry, agriculture and services.
- The development of human skills in the Arab countries is an important field of co-operation with the CMEA countries, with great future potential.
- CMEA countries could be important partners in geological prospecting, the improvement of water supplies, designing large territorial development projects, and other service areas.
- There are important possibilities for increasing tripartite co-operation. These already represented a large part of trade relations at the beginning of the 1980s.

Intergovernmental trade agreements are instruments widely used in international trade. In trade between the European CMEA countries and most of the Arab countries such agreements determine the scope and the conditions of trade.

Practical experience proves, of course, that concluding a trade agreement does not automatically bring about trade-generating results. The role of intergovernmental agreements in comprehensive forms of co-operation – trade, industry, science and technology, and in the creation of mixed intergovernmental commissions – have been more important. Intergovernmental commissions themselves play a role of increasing importance in bringing about a more meaningful division of labour between the countries of the two groups.

Intergovernmental joint commissions usually play a key role also in the preparation of long-term (10 or 15 year) economic and scientific-technical intergovernmental agreements.

In a world economic situation of increasing complexity, beset with difficulties both for Arab and for European CMEA countries, there is understandably a growing demand for framework agreements on comprehensive, many-sided co-operation embracing as many sectors of the economy as possible. Various mixed intergovernmental commissions with their flexible and task-oriented organization are especially well suited for managing the implementation of such agreements.

NEW POLICIES, POSSIBILITIES AND ADJUSTMENTS FOR INTERREGIONAL CO-OPERATION

The strategic aims of interregional economic co-operation can be realized only if they conform to the changing possibilities and needs of the participating countries, or if the direction and structure of economic development in the countries change in harmony with regional interests. Of course, a readiness to develop and maintain interregional relations is also necessary. From this latter point of view the similarity of political, strategic and economic aims in the narrow sense, and a good knowledge of each other's efficiency are of great importance.

A comparison of the changes taking place in the Arab world with the interests and perspectives of CMEA countries suggests that there are possibilities for interregional co-operation.

Interregional co-operation, i.e. relations between the European CMEA countries as a group with Arab countries (or with any subregion within the area) requires the solution of many complex problems:

1. The scope and intensity of regional co-operation within the Arab world must increase. At present there are major political, economic, structural and institutional problems of inter-Arab co-operation. While there are important regional institutions, their role is limited by political difficulties and by legal and economic considerations. There are important financial institutions with great prestige and global reputation. There are very few Arab regional production projects, however. Initiatives for regional co-operation must, of course, come from the countries concerned. External actors (integration organizations, countries or transnational corporations) should participate in this process at the consent of Arab countries on the basis of mutual interest and benefits. If the Arab countries of the region are not ready for full scale co-operation and their economy is not developing along lines of complementarity, no harmonious relations will be possible with other regions on a multilateral scale. The participation of CMEA countries as a regional group would also be limited.
2. The character of regional and subregional co-operation among the Arab countries must be better defined. If efforts at regional co-operation are confined to customs-unions, or to the establishment of a few firms with joint funds especially in the private sector, concrete steps towards real integration in the region will be slow. Studies of the integration projects of developing countries (and more

specifically of Arab integration) reveal the reasons why regional projects fail or stagnate. It is evident that integration aiming at trade liberalization only does not lead to the desired results. This applies also to the Arab region, where the small achievements of the Arab Common Market and the large problems of subregional free trade areas proves the fact that integration confined to a customs union is not a feasible approach under present conditions in the respective countries. A joint development policy on the regional level, with production and development integration establishing a true division of labour and correcting and partially eliminating the market mechanism, would jointly develop the productive capacity of the region and serve as the basis of real integration. This qualititatively different approach to regional co-operation – based on large-scale inter-country projects within the public sector (or with the massive involvement of the public sector) with private firms supplying the market of several countries or promoting joint exports and common infrastructure development in transport and education – would also create a different level of opportunity for external participation. In this case regional co-operation would be closely connected with national planning. A regional mechanism similar to that which was developed within the framework of CMEA for the co-ordination of medium and longer term plans would be helpful. In this case, the participation of the CMEA countries could be more meaningful. The nature of the economies would facilitate broader co-operation both bilaterally and on the interregional level.
3. Regional and subregional economic institutions must be further developed. This is not an easy task; there are well-known political difficulties which go beyond the scope of analysis in this paper. There are also economic problems. Experts are probably available but the smooth running and management of the institutions is expensive. The costs are justified only by the achievements, which must be measurable, from the point of view of the member countries. Regional institutions must have the ability not only to co-ordinate regional interests but also to promote the co-ordination of interests with other regions.
4. Concerning interregional co-operation, non-discriminatory relations must be established between the members of the European CMEA region and all Arab countries. Interregional co-operation presupposes the absence of discrimination against the CMEA countries in the Arab world, and *vice-versa*. Mutually fair political and economic treatment must be accorded in the respective markets. Neither the necessary level of confidence nor the required degree of security can be achieved otherwise.

PROSPECTS FOR ECONOMIC RELATIONS BETWEEN THE MIDDLE EASTERN ARAB OIL-EXPORTING COUNTRIES AND EUROPEAN CMEA COUNTRIES

Because of their solvency, their dynamically expanding and many-sided import demand, their geographical proximity and the already established channels of co-operation, the oil-exporting countries of the Middle East could become ideal partners for the CMEA countries. Their importance is steadily growing not only because of the acute and probably lasting export-compulsion of the CMEA countries but also because of the slow-down of the fuels trade (or even its maintenance on a fixed level) within the CMEA. Thus in the course of the 1980s and '90s the Middle East will merit special attention from the socialist countries, not only as a source of foreign exchange earnings, but also as an increasingly important supplier of crude oil.

We have already indicated that in the near future the Middle East will remain one of the most dynamically growing, extremely import-sensitive regions of the world economy. It is also to be noted that as development policies become more balanced and rational, a slowdown in import dynamics compared with the second half of the 1970s must be anticipated. All this will produce a strengthening of quality and price requirements on the markets and increased competition among the suppliers.

What are the principal structural changes in imports to be expected? An undoubted and lasting rise can be foreseen in the share of complete *turnkey* and, even more, *production-ready* industrial equipment embodying modern technologies. A similar rise will occur over the next 10-15 years in the share of capital goods required for infrastructural development, at least in the "traditional" Iraqi and Iranian markets. No reduction can be expected as yet in any of these countries in the share of goods required to establish their welfare and educational infrastructure, and in the share of basic foodstuffs. On the contrary, below-average activity is to be expected (as a result of the gradual implementation of import substitution programmes) in imports of certain categories of vehicle, of durable and non-durable consumer goods satisfying "luxury" demands, of basic chemicals, building materials and, finally, in imports of mass consumer goods of the textile and canning industries.

Consequently, the Middle East will continue to offer wide-ranging possibilities for exports by the socialist countries but these can only be exploited if a comprehensive, co-ordinated and long-term structural policy is adopted. The critical element in this policy is the continuous adjustment in time and space to changes in Middle Eastern import structures because, as the above comments show, many presently important commodity groups exported by the socialist countries could diminish in importance and fall into the category of lagging import branches.

What structural policies should the socialist countries adopt if they are to stop the marginalization process that began in the last third of the 1970s for the European CMEA countries in the markets of oil exporters?

In the field of infrastructure development there are promising prospects for the socialist countries to participate as sub-contractors in the construction of complete electrical power systems, transport and communications systems, airports and port facilities. In this field the socialist countries may find themselves competing not only with Western companies but also with developing countries which have had spectacular successes in these fields in recent years (mainly India, South Korea and Brazil). The socialist countries will also have opportunities as prime contractors for the construction of health and educational facilities, water management (purification and irrigation) systems and local telecommunications network, provided that they will be capable of ensuring a higher degree of comprehensiveness, technical reliability guarantees, and continuous service and skill than in the past.

Industrial opportunities for the socialist countries are most extensive in the areas of extractive and light industries. In mining, extensive opportunities for participation exist in the geological surveys recently carried out in all these countries, the technical and know-how services (e.g. operation planning), and in mining infrastructure works (e.g. pipeline construction).

It is less likely that small countries such as Hungary, not in the vanguard of technical development, could contribute effectively to modern, high technology *heavy industrial* projects beyond occasional deliveries. This is a marginalization factor in itself, since it means exclusion from the programmes which determine Middle Eastern development policies over the long term and which consume a substantial share of imported capital goods. At the same time a favourable phenomenon for the socialist countries, partly offsetting these negative factors, in the increased attention devoted to *light industries,* in particular to small and medium-scale enterprises. In these fields (such as paper and canning industries, production of plastics, cables, pumps, textiles, building materials and simple electric consumer goods) a relatively wide range of possibilities will open for the CMEA, provided that the national industrial background proves more capable in the future of meeting more than usually complex demands created by the overall system of economic management.

We have already noted that, at least up to the end of the century, there will be no improvement in the rate of agrarian self-sufficiency in the Middle East. This will result in an increase in the volume (if not in the share) of food imports, while governments realize the economic as well as the social importance of agrarian development. Food imports will, to an increasing extent, consist of basic foodstuffs (grains, sugar, vegetable oils) which the socialist countries are not capable of exporting. The situation is different for imports of plant cultivation and stock breeding systems, water management and irrigation technologies and agricultural skills, where many socialist countries can compete. However, the degree of comprehensiveness may also be an important gauge of competitiveness in this field, in view of the integrated nature of Middle Eastern rural development. Successful participation in these projects assumes joint action or sub-contracting by two or more socialist countries.

Reliance on a single partner, inflexibility and lack of co-operation could have serious consequences for the policy of the socialist countries. In the Middle East the evolution of bilateral political relations seems to have a greater influence on economic and commercial relations than in other regions. The socialist countries must take into account that inter-governmental relations established with their base-market country could suddenly enter a serious (although generally only temporary) crisis which could also set back export turnover in the absence of suitable alternative markets. On the other hand, the same phenomenon, the sudden deterioration of relations with certain developed capitalist countries, could temporarily free new market segments for the socialist countries if they act with sufficient speed and flexibility. Therefore, the socialist countries must strive to reduce competition among themselves.

It is also evident that more meaningful co-operation between the European CMEA countries and the Arab world requires deliberate structural adjustments on a long-term basis. The European CMEA countries will have to take into account, in the elaboration of their medium-term (5 year) and long-term plans, much more than in the past those areas where structural changes are required in production and consumption in order to increase imports from the Arab countries.

The increase of CMEA exports also requires certain adjustments. It is not enough to create more export potential. Exports must be developed in a way which corresponds to the changing needs of the Arab world. The comprehensiveness of exports (exporting, for example, production systems, including machinery and equipment know-how and expertise) is an important requirement, which must be fulfilled on a regional and subregional basis.

From the point of view of CMEA countries with their systems of central planning it is also important to be able to rely on relatively stable partners, with whom long-term relations can be established. A deliberately organized long-term division of labour is not a one-way affair. It can be efficient and meaningful only when the nature of the economies and the interests of both partners are taken into consideration.

The interests of the Arab world require that regional and interregional co-operation with them should help in the solution of their basic problems: the elimination of backwardness, increase in the standard of living of their people, more social justice, and the strengthening of their position in a changing world economy. Interregional co-operation must also serve the long-term economic aims and interests of the European CMEA countries. These basic objectives should not be lost in the maze of technical details.

Table 12.1. Foreign Trade Relations between the European CMEA and the Middle East

Year	Exports (million $)	Annual growth rate (%)	Imports (million $)	Annual growth rate (%)	Balance (million $)	Share of Middle East surplus in the total LDC surplus
1974	1,943		1,458		485	24.4
1975	2,549	31	1,885	29	664	65.0
1976	2,849	12	2,313	23	536	36.0
1977	3,518	23	2,443	6	1,075	25.8
1978	4,578	30	2,569	5	2,009	30.8
1979	5,540	21	3,069	19	2,471	35.2
1980	5,815	5	3,336	9	2,479	40.8
1981	8,052	38	1,423	−57	6,629	80.3
1982	6,222	−23	1,955	37	4,267	—

Source: UN Monthly Bulletin of Statistics, 1983, No. 6.

Table 12.2. Trade Relations between the Soviet Union and the Middle East

Year	Exports (million $)	Annual growth rate (%)	Imports (million $)	Annual growth rate (%)	Balance (million $)
1974	873	—	699	—	174
1975	1,039	19	855	22	184
1976	1,111	7	1,004	17	107
1977	1,373	24	1,075	7	298
1978	2,158	57	1,100	2	1,058
1979	2,658	23	1,546	41	1,112
1980	2,210	−17	995	−36	1,215
1981	2,941	33	406	−60	2,535

Source: See Table 1.

Table 12.3. Commodity Structure of European CMEA Exports to the Middle East

	1974 (million $)	Market share (%)	1978 (million $)	Market share (%)	1981 (million $)	Market share (%)
Total exports	1,943	6.7	4,578	6.4	8,052	7.2
SITC						
0+1	8.3	4.0	7.6	5.2	8.3	5.1
2+4	7.2	11.2	3.2	8.2	8.6	21.0
3	1.1	0.7	2.4	2.7	10.7	7.3
5	5.1	5.2	3.9	4.6	5.5	7.0
7	45.3	9.3	41.3	6.3	30.4	5.8
6+8	25.2	5.9	12.7	2.8	18.1	4.4
9	5.8		28.9		18.4	

Note: Totals do not give 100 per cent as substantial parts of Soviet exports cannot be fitted into usual commodity breakdown.
Source: see Table 1.

Table 12.4. Commodity Structure of the East European Exports to the Middle East (%)

	1974 (million $)	Market share (%)	Middle East import structure	1978 (million $)	Market share (%)	Middle East import structure	1981 (million $)	Market share (%)	Middle East import structure (%)
Total exports	1,070	3.7		2,420	3.4		5,111	4.6	
SITC									
0+1	13.7	3.7	13.8	14.0	5.0	9.5	12.8	5.0	11.6
2+4	3.6	3.1	4.3	3.7	5.0	2.5	9.9	15.4	2.9
3	0.5	0.2	10.3	2.4	1.4	5.8	10.6	4.6	10.5
5	5.0	2.8	6.6	6.2	3.9	5.4	6.6	5.4	5.6
7	39.3	4.4	32.7	43.1	3.5	42.2	33.3	4.1	37.3
6+8	36.9	4.8	28.7	20.3	2.4	28.8	26.2	4.0	29.7

Source: see Table 1.

Table 12.5. Commodity Structure of the European CMEA Countries Imports from the Middle East

	1974 %	1974 (million $)	1978 %	1978 (million $)	1981 %	1981 (million $)
Total imports		1,458		2,569		1,423
SITC						
0+1	10.8	157	11.2	288	16.5	235
2+4	16.6	242	12.3	316	21.6	307
3	65.3	952	72.3	1,857	53.2	757
5	2.0	29	1.2	31	2.0	28
7	0.2	3	0.0	1	0.1	2
6+8	5.6	82	3.0	77	6.5	92

Source: see Table 1.

ANNEX I

Statements Made on the Occasion of the Meeting of the UNITAR Panel of Eminent Persons Kuwait, January 1983

ACKNOWLEDGEMENTS

Ervin Laszlo

THE PANEL of Eminent Persons of the UNITAR Programme on Regional and Interregional Co-operation met in the State of Kuwait in January 1983 to consider the prospects and possibilities of regional co-operation in the Arab world, as well as interregional co-operation between Arab countries and other parts of the world, especially developing countries.

The discussions of the Panel were wide-ranging, and covered the basic principles and goals of regional and interregional co-operation as well as the role of regional and international bodies, including the United Nations, in supporting and promoting such co-operation. The breadth and depth of the issues raised are reflected in the communiqué ("Summary of the Issues") which was drafted in the final hours of the two-day meeting and was formally presented at the closing session. Because of its intrinsic interest, the final communiqué has been translated into several languages and distributed to the government representatives of members of the Group of 77 as well as others in the developed and in the socialist countries.

The meeting was under the distinguished chairmanship of H. E. Abdelatif Al-Hamad, Minister of Finance and of Planning of Kuwait. It is to his initiative that the meeting owes its organizational structure, itself an example of regional co-operation. For indeed, the meeting was co-hosted by the Kuwait Fund for Arab Economic Development, the Arab Fund for Economic and Social Development, the Organization of Arab Petroleum Exporting Countries, and the Arab Planning Institute. Each of these bodies exercises a region-wide activity which, in the case of the Kuwait Fund and of OAPEC, involves extensive interregional elements as well.

As Director of the Programme I wish to acknowledge the outstanding preparations and meticulous attention to detail by the Arab Planning Institute and its director, Abdulla Mohammad Ali. I wish to thank the Kuwait Fund and its Director-General Faisal Al-Khaled for the use of its beautiful conference facilities and for support in all aspects of the meeting's implementation. Deep gratitude is owed as well to the Arab Fund and its President and Director-General Mohammed Al-Imady, especially for the detailed scientific preparations which the Fund has undertaken to enrich the meeting, and the UNITAR Programme itself, with fresh insights into Arab co-operation in its various dimensions. Last, but not least, special thanks and appreciation go to Ali Attiga, the distinguished Secretary-General of OAPEC who, as member of the Panel of Eminent Persons and long-time champion of regional co-operation in the Arab world and in developing countries in general, proposed holding the meeting in Kuwait and worked closely with the UNITAR Programme Secretariat in seeing the preparations through the various stages.

STATEMENTS

Abdelatif Y. Al-Hamad

Minister of Finance and Planning

MAY I EXTEND to you a hearty welcome in the name of the Government and the People of Kuwait and on behalf of the host Institutions, the Arab Planning Institute, the Arab Fund for Economic and Social Development, the Kuwait Fund for Arab Economic Development, and the Organization of Arab Petroleum Exporting Countries, as well as the United Nations Institute for Training and Research, and wish you a comfortable, enjoyable and at the same time productive stay in Kuwait.

We are indeed honoured and pleased to host this meeting in this country. It is symbolic that this meeting should be held in the buildings of the Kuwait Fund, and that it should be the first of its kind to be held in the new premises. It is symbolic of the importance Kuwait has always given to co-operation among the countries of the South, and the emphasis it has laid on such co-operation.

South-South co-operation has been a key factor in Kuwait's international policies and relations. The fact that the Kuwait Fund, which is hosting this meeting, is the oldest institution in the developing world for development co-operation among the developing countries themselves is an important example of the value and the potential of co-operation among countries in the South. The Kuwait Fund, which is the senior sister of the other institutions in the region, is an institution of which we are proud, not because of what it does for the benefit of people in the South but because of the symbolic value of the co-operation among ourselves in the South. It is a symbol of self-reliance without which we in the South are not going to be able to confront the challenges that will face us in the future. For that reason I am particularly pleased to welcome you here – not only to Kuwait, but to the premises of the Kuwait Fund – and to underline the importance we in this region give to the efforts of this distinguished Panel and to say that we will always support the pragmatic and realistic approach to the immense problems that face us in the South without which we have little chance to confront the realities of the future in our relationship with the North.

I am sure there are many more qualified and distinguished people around the table here who can speak with more authority than I could do, and therefore it is with great pleasure that I welcome you once more to this meeting and wish you all success in your deliberations and assure you of the support and the importance we in this country and in this region attach to this effort.

Ali A. Attiga

Secretary-General of the Organization of Arab Petroleum Exporting Countries (OAPEC)

On behalf of the Organizations hosting this meeting and in my capacity as a member of the Panel, I have the honour and pleasure to welcome you all. I want to express special thanks to His Excellency Abdelatif Al-Hamad for taking some of his precious time to open our session with his eloquent and inspiring address. Indeed his presence with us and the fact that we are meeting in the premises of the Kuwait Fund demonstrates once more the pioneering spirit and the standing commitment of the State of Kuwait to the cause of development through co-operation among the developing countries. It is not only appropriate that we meet in Kuwait, but it is also fortunate that we convene in the Kuwait Fund and that our meeting should be opened by Minister Al-Hamad, because the Kuwait Fund pioneered an effective policy of regional and interregional co-operation among developing countries more than two decades ago. It was under the leadership of Mr. Al-Hammad that the Kuwait Fund progressed from its limited regional role to its present worldwide activities and commitments. May I also express my thanks and deep appreciation to His Excellency Agha Shahi, Chairman of the Board of Governors of UNITAR, and His Excellency Mr. Farooq Sobhan, President of the Group of 77 for honouring us with their presence.

It is a source of encouragement for those of us who have been engaged in promoting regional co-operation through organizations outside the United Nations system to see that at long last the United Nations, through the good work of UNITAR, is beginning to realize the value and importance of the regional approach to development based on regional institutions and joint projects originating from and belonging to the countries concerned. Indeed, it is only through regional and interregional co-operation that trade and development can become two inseparable ingredients of a highly complex process of economic and social development.

What we now call developed countries have long realized the overriding importance of this fact and made use of it on national and regional bases as far back as two centuries ago. Thus, in the United States it was generally agreed, almost from the beginning, that irrespective of the number of states that may be established within the Union, they should not have any power to obstruct the normal growth and expansion of interstate commerce. Similarly, in the great subcontinent of the Soviet Union, one of the most significant developments brought about by the Socialist Revolution of 1917 was the establishment of a large economic unit within which no regional authority would have power to obstruct the overall development and growth of the Union as a whole. In each of these cases we can safely conclude that rapid development required the expansion of trade and that greater and more varied trade gave rise to greater and more diversified development.

Except for China and Brazil, other large economic units which had existed, politically at least, prior to World War II were, of course, made up of the colonial systems that had governed much of Asia and Africa for a long time. Unlike the examples of the United States and the Soviet Union, these "economic units" were each composed of one ruling power (which was usually technologically and militarily advanced) with many other colonial territories linked to it in a superior/inferior relationship. In such a relationship a certain degree of specialization developed, but not economic integration. This specialization consisted largely of having the colonial territories produce raw materials, using cheap labour and consuming processed and manufactured products, exported by the ruling powers. This kind of relationship accentuated the problem of unbalanced growth within these units and ultimately contributed to their disintegration as political entities. In their place new patterns of economic relationship have emerged.

Parallel with the fragmentation of the former colonial territories into many independent sovereign states, some of the former colonial powers initiated a process of economic co-operation and integration among themselves, which had far-reaching consequences on the trade and development patterns of the newly independent countries in Africa and Asia. Thus, while the implementation of such highly successful measures as the Marshall Plan and the scheme for the European Economic Community had the effect of promoting economic integration in Western Europe, the opposite was the case in the developing countries. As economic blocs among developed countries began to be established and expanded, the initial impact of this development was economic fragmentation and excessive competition for export markets among developing countries. Such fragmentation was contrary to the normal prospects of regional integration and trade expansion among developing countries. Moreover, excessive competition for highly organized export markets reduced the individual bargaining power of these countries to a dangerously low level. Here again, we see that whereas trade and development were given the most favourable conditions with which to interact in Western Europe, the opposite was the case in the newly independent countries of the Third World.

Perhaps one of the most serious and devastating aftermaths of post World War economic development, as far as the developing countries are concerned, has been the introduction of a highly powerful element of dissension among the developing countries. This came about largely as a direct result of the way in which the newly formed economic blocs among developed countries have sought to link their former colonies, which are now formally independent, into a special relationship that differentiates between them and their neighbours on the basis of their former colonial associations. This development has, in many cases, hindered the evolution of regional economic co-operation among the developing countries, since in many geographic regions there were two or more different and often antagonistic colonial regimes. These differences were reflected in the economic relations among developing countries, which belong to the same regions, but had been under the domination of different colonial powers.

With all of these historical considerations in the background, developing countries find themselves, although numerous, terribly weak in economic power and bargaining position in world trade. Their large number and their historical economic role under the colonial system, as well as their ability to reach a reasonable degree of organization and co-ordination of their mutual interests, made it necessary for each of them to compete against the other in the sale of their limited and homogeneous exports. The markets for which they were competing belonged to a few highly developed countries, whose mutual interests were largely co-ordinated and whose external trade policies were designed to promote economic growth and integration within their regions. These developments gave rise to a situation where the supply of the exports of developing countries was highly competitive, while the demand for these exports was organized and administratively manipulated. When the oil exporting developing countries tried to break away from this rigid pattern, they were wrongly accused of holding the world to ransom. Unfortunately for the developing world, their success may prove to be only temporary. Perhaps developing countries will now realize that if OPEC member states lose their bargaining position in world trade, it may mean a loss for all developing countries.

Perhaps historians will designate the seventies as the decade of international disappointments and frustrations with excessive and prolonged conferences, seminars, summit meetings, workshops, commissions, panels, task forces and dialogues or monologues. With this background in mind, I hope that this panel will succeed in assisting UNITAR with its global Programme of Regional and Interregional Co-operation under the able and dedicated leadership of Dr. Ervin Laszlo. Let us hope that this Programme will make a significant contribution towards better understanding of the problems and opportunities of co-operation among developing countries, and between them and the developed nations. Indeed it is not only a matter of choice, but it is also our professional and moral duties to do our utmost in helping to make this hope become a reality.

Mohammed Said Al-Attar

*Executive Secretary of the United Nations
Economic Commission for Western Asia
(ECWA)*

The Arab countries, including those in Western Asia, have, with varying degrees of success, endeavoured to forge closer economic relations among themselves since the establishment of the League of Arab States in 1945. To this end, they have attempted various approaches giving, over a period of more than a quarter of a century, prominence to the issues of trade liberalization and the formation of a common market. The limited progress achieved on these fronts – and the new prospects arising from the substantial increase in the overall financial capabilities of the region – contributed to the recent shift of emphasis to the promotion of co-operation in the field of production, notably through the establishment of joint ventures and the supporting institutions and legislation. Concomitantly, expression of support for subregional forms of co-operation became more vocal, culminating in the formation of the Gulf Co-operation Council (GCC) in 1981 (comprising Bahrain, Kuwait, Oman, Qatar, Saudi Arabia and the United Arab Emirates); and a tendency in favour of enabling the private sector to play an active role in the co-operation process began to emerge. The governments' more comprehensive approaches to regional co-operation and integration found their main expressions in the adoption, by the Eleventh Arab Summit Meeting, in Amman in November 1980, of a Strategy for Joint Arab Economic Action until the year 2000, and in the approval of the Arab Economic and Social Council of a new Convention for Facilitating and Developing Trade between Arab States to replace the 1953 Convention.

Notwithstanding the efforts and intentions, progress in realizing declared objectives in this important field remains below expectations. This has been largely attributed to the insufficient means for executing the political will which aims at closer economic co-operation. In this respect, the slowness in obtaining visible results from the integration process and the difficulties encountered in reconciling various interests have been a determining factor. However, while the importance of the political factor cannot be played down, the level and quality of this co-operation have been adversely affected by the inadequate preparation and analysis of the factors helping achieve co-operation or those obstructing it; the deficient assessment of the feasibility of the prerequisites for various forms of co-operation; and the absence of plans and operational programmes to achieve progress.

The promotion of regional co-operation and integration is a central preoccupation for the Economic Commission for Western Asia. By virtue of its comprehensive terms of reference, accumulated experience and expertise, proximity and closer contacts with member countries, the Commission has taken the initiative and participated in measures and efforts aimed at strengthening economic relations among its member countries which constitute an important part of the Arab world. This crucial role has been demonstrated by the work programmes of the Commission during the last ten years through a composite of interrelated activities comprising research, advisory services, training programmes and meetings. In these endeavours, the Commission has sought to co-operate closely with the regional organizations concerned and to benefit from the experiences of the other developing nations.

The Expert Group Meeting on Feasible Forms of Economic Co-operation and Integration in Western Asia, held 14-18 December 1981, was but one of the most pertinent activities of the Commission in this area. The objective of the Meeting was to bring about a better understanding of the economic factors that promote economic co-operation and integration among the countries of the region and to help formulate alternative policy options for action at the national and regional levels. Special emphasis was given to attaining benefits from the experiences of other regional groupings of both developed and developing countries by examining the obstacles to, and benefits from, closer economic co-operation and identifying the most feasible forms of co-operation arrangements.

While the search for viable forms of economic co-operation in the region has continued to be sought through the traditional and comprehensive schemes – in terms of both content and geographical scope – instruments and approaches emanating from decisions taken at high political levels, the often rather "passive" nature of these instruments, and the tenuous commitment to achieve their declared objectives, have resulted in advocating more "active" approaches where the basic feature is that they originate in initiatives taken at the low echelons of the decision-making process. Chief among these are the inter-Arab multinational joint ventures and producers associations. These instruments offer numerous advantages in terms of flexibility, participation in decision-making and management, complementarity, dynamic linkages, organizational and resource allocation efficiency, and the like. The various organizations engaged in promoting co-operation and integrating in the region need to determine the best way of embedding such instruments into the broader framework of co-operation and integration schemes among the Arab countries as a whole and in subregions thereof.

It is heartening to note that UNITAR has joined other member institutions of the United Nations system in seeking ways and means of enhancing co-operation among developing countries. The Meetings of the Panel of Eminent Persons of the UNITAR Programme on Regional and Interregional Co-operation in the 1980s will no doubt give impetus to work which is underway at various levels on this subject. The Meeting of the Panel in Kuwait marked yet another milestone towards the realization of co-operation and integration objectives among the countries of the ECWA region.

I am confident that the publication of the research material prepared by UNITAR on various aspects of the subject and the ideas and findings that have emerged from the deliberations of the Panel in Kuwait will make a valuable contribution to the limited literature available in this field. More importantly, it will provide policy guidelines for action aimed at promoting economic co-operation and integration among the countries of the ECWA region and between them and countries in other regional groupings.

Farooq Sobhan

Chairman of the Group of 77 in New York

On the occasion of the meeting of the Panel of Eminent Persons of the UNITAR Programme on Regional and Interregional Co-operation in the State of Kuwait, I wish to call attention to the relevance of the Programme and of this Meeting to the objectives of the Group of 77 adopted in Caracas.

The Caracas Programme itself notes that "co-operative efforts among developing countries" are by no means new. Several programmes have already been agreed upon and implemented to varying degrees, as evidenced in the various subregional, regional and interregional groupings.

Resolute action is now required to ensure the implementation of the Programme of Action of Economic Co-operation among Developing Countries adopted at this meeting in a concrete, coherent, integrated and time-bound manner, a programme that will have mutually beneficial results for all developing country members of the Group of 77.

The Caracas Programme, even though it is structured around eight priority sectors, was clearly designed to build upon and strengthen the subregional, regional and interregional experience with ECDC. While the calendar of meetings drawn up at Caracas was intended to be global in nature and participation within the Group of 77, action in each sector is envisaged at the regional and interregional level. In the chapter on Trade, for example, the importance of regional and interregional action is reiterated in each sub-sector or area of activity covered by the Programme. The Programme calls for:

- *expansion of trade among the developing countries* through adopting commercial policy measures at the national as well as the regional and interregional levels . . .

- *the trade information system* . . . could be considerably strengthened by more effective use of existing trade information in the subregional, regional and interregional institutions . . .

- *co-operation among STOs* . . . and meetings aiming at fostering ECDC should be organised . . . at the subregional, regional and interregional levels on a regular basis . . .
- *multinational marketing enterprises.* . . . technical and financial assistance should be provided on an urgent basis to intensify ongoing preparations and to support the process of sectoral negotiations envisaged at the regional and interregional levels for the establishment of this type of enterprise . . .
- *national enterprises, joint ventures and improved utilization of existing capacities in the field of services* . . . action should be at two levels . . . subregional and regional . . . and interregional . . .
- *TCDC in the field of trade* . . . more active exchange of information among the secretariats of the various subregional and interregional groupings of developing countries.

The pattern is repeated in all other sectors of the Caracas Programme. It is one of the tasks of the Chairman of the Group of 77 in New York to ensure that this essential aspect of the implementation of the Programme gets the attention intended for it by the Conference. This is being done, as envisaged in the Programme, in several ways.

At the intergovernmental level, the Chairman in New York has been asked to maintain close liaison with the national focal points for ECDC set up by member states. As a corollary, he will also establish close links with the secretariats of regional and interregional groupings. These links will ensure continuous interaction between the centre, represented by the Chairman in New York, and the regions. The Chairman is expected to act as an information clearing-house, and as a catalyst of action by member-states on ECDC programmes in follow-up to Caracas.

A concrete example of the regional and interregional aspects of the Caracas Programme are the recurring mandates for the creation of information systems in each of the priority sectors. The Chairman in New York has now taken on the task of putting together a comprehensive information network for the developing countries that would draw upon regional and interregional experience and systems.

The Caracas Programme, among its operational modalities, suggested the creation of Action Committees. The formation of these Committees was codified at the first Intergovernmental Follow-up and Co-ordination Committee Meeting in Manila. It is expected that groups of three or more countries from regions would get together to share national experience and form subregional, regional or interregional Action Committees on the basis of common needs or interests.

At the non-governmental level, the Caracas Programme called for the establishment of links with research institutions in the various regions. This is being done, both to draw upon specialized and regional experience, and to disseminate ECDC information as widely as possible.

A meeting of research institutions from all regions is being organized in Mexico shortly to organize and increase their input into the implementation of the Caracas Programme.

Thirteen of the meetings envisaged in the Caracas Programme have now been held. Recommendations emerging from these meetings have reinforced the regional and interregional content of the programmes designed to implement the Caracas Programme. As an instance, the Meeting on Food Security held in Manila decided that a follow-up meeting should consider the experience garnered in the ASEAN.

The meeting on Capital Goods held in Algiers decided that one of the mechanisms for follow-up should be the organization of regional seminars and exhibitions, where countries could explore and discover complementary needs and capabilities. Similarly, in the finance sector, the Jamaica meeting recommended that co-ordination with the regional and interregional financial institutions of the developing countries should be strengthened. All these recommendations are being followed up.

Perhaps most important of all in the implementation of the Caracas Programme is the question of information. Without adequate and up-to-date information on what other countries, other regions are doing, it will be impossible to have ECDC implemented. This is why it is essential to have an information network for developing countries in place as soon as possible. A beginning has been made on this vital project, after the Tunis meeting on TCDC, which recommended the establishment of a multi-sectoral information network for the developing countries.

Once these steps have been taken, the practical implementation of the Caracas Programme will be well under way. There will be a continuous exchange of information among research institutions in the South; manufacturers, traders, scientists and technologists will benefit from continual contact at the regional and interregional seminars, and the information generated by these contacts will be stored and disseminated by the Group of 77's information network. ECDC will then have developed from a programme to a reality.

Ervin Laszlo

Director of the Programme

The UNITAR Programme and Interregional Co-operation was initiated in 1980. It owes its existence to a sudden turn in world economic conditions and relations around the beginning of the present decade. The turn was undoubtedly for the worse. The great objectives of a new international economic order, which were elaborated with such care in the latter part of the 1970s, seemed to recede into the background. Global negotiations, which were to bring at least some of the many weighty issues to the stage of active negotiations between all members of the international community, could not get started.

Many compromises had to be made in the elaboration of the Development Strategy for the Third Development Decade, and we are awaiting its mid-term review to see how far even its more modest objectives are on the way to realization. The 11th Special Session of the General Assembly reflected in its debates and conclusions this turn of events. It prompted those of us who are charged with trying to see ahead, and bring useful knowledge to the attention of the U.N. family, to cast around for ways in which another turn in events could be furthered, this time one that is for the better.

We at UNITAR realized, like so many others before us and especially since, that closer forms of co-operation are needed among developing countries to bolster their self-reliance and provide an effective platform for the negotiation of their demands for a more equitable economic order. South-South co-operation has been long on the agenda of international conferences, but never has there been a need for it comparable to that which we have today in the mid-1980s. Such co-operation can take many forms: economic and technical, social, cultural and political. In the context of the turn of events at the beginning of this Development Decade, economic and technical co-operation – ECDC and TCDC as they have come to be known – have assumed paramount importance. The question we face is how such co-operation can be implemented in practice. There are several necessary conditions of successful co-operation, regardless of who the co-operating partners are. There must be a complementarity of interest; there must be solidarity; and there must be political will to build on them. Relations need to be based on enduring factors, not those that may change overnight. For these reasons we are looking to countries that have something in common, such as natural resources (rivers, coastlines, forests and mineral deposits), human resources (skills, aptitudes and a labour pool) and common cultural resources (a history of shared struggles, a common language, religion and social systems). Such elements are prevalent among countries that are neighbours. Of course, neighbours also have their disagreements. But could inherited fears and conflicts not be outweighed by inherited ties – when mutual relations could bring benefits, while continued conflict, unco-ordination, and unbridled competition could only bring more troubles?

These are the questions we identify with the letters "RCDC", which stands for Regional Co-operation among Developing Countries, and they are not a substitute for, or anything other than, South-South co-operation in the economic and technical fields. RCDC is a promising operational modality of ECDC and TCDC. Such operational modalities are crucially important. They spell the difference between declarations of noble goals with little or no follow-up, and the evolution of a more equitable and mutually beneficial economic system.

To explore how the international community may respond to specific proposals for regional co-operation, we organized, in May 1980, a conference at the United Nations on the theme "Regionalism and the New International Economic Order". The response of some developing countries was cautious at first, but became strongly supportive when we made clear that by "regionalism" we mean neither political bloc formation, nor the fragmentation of Third World unity. To avoid any possible misunderstanding, we abandoned the term "regionalism" in favour of "regional co-operation", and added to such co-operation the interregional dimension. Interregionally, groups of developing countries can forge co-operation among themselves, as well as with the industrialized countries, both East and West.

The basic concept is simple and logical. At a time when hardly any nation in the world can be truly self-sufficient, interdependence with those with whom one can develop lasting and dependable relations is better than with others who are intent mainly on exploiting it for power or profit and are ready to relinquish the relations when they can no longer guarantee either. The developing countries, for the most part late entrants in the world economic system, are more and more interdependent: they experience great difficulty in becoming autonomous and self-reliant. Many are forced into the position of economic colonies, by relations of dependence on one or a few industrial countries, often including the former metropolitan power. They could, however, exchange such dependence for a more equitable and dependable form of interdependence with other developing nations, who share their region or subregion.

A new economic order can, perhaps, be built step by step. Developing countries co-operating and integrating their basic economic processes in various subregions can form region-wide relations of mutual benefit and support with one another. The emerging regional groups can interact with one another and create new outlets for their products and new inputs for their processes of production. The countries of the North, whether in groups or individually, can enter into interregional arrangements with the consolidating groups of developing countries. The world economy would become better balanced and more secure. A path of mutual growth would be initiated.

This, in its briefest outline, is the Regional and Interregional Strategy for Collective Self-reliance. It was discussed at our U.N. conference on the basis of two dozen technical studies that explored many of its manifold aspects. From these studies and the discussions we distilled a series of proposals. I shall mention them here one by one, because they merit serious attention.

In the field of *development finance,* we proposed the creation of regional financing facilities which would have the task and ability to establish a body of principles to underlie the facility's loan philosophy; which would emphasize domestic production rather than export dependence; and disseminate a body of economic precepts and accounting principles capable of analyzing Third World developments in its technological, financial, demographic, ecological, social and cultural dimensions.

In regard to *industrial production,* we suggested the creation of regional centres which would formulate an investment code that offers preferential treatment for regional businesses by way of long-term loans, investment guarantees, and assured markets for the end products; and promote joint ventures among developing countries involving the supply of inputs and raw materials, location of industrial plants, and pooling of technical and managerial skills.

In the field of *trade and marketing,* similar centres are needed. They would act as the central clearing-house for marketing intelligence on prices, surpluses, shortfalls, distribution outlets, and shipping conditions to promote intra-regional trade, and study the development plans of Third World countries and how they may be enmeshed with their exporting strategy and strengthening of their infrastructural facilities. The activities of the centre could later be expanded to include downstream marketing operations in stocking, transport, finance and related ancillary services.

In the area of *agriculture and rural development,* regional centres were proposed in order to develop a common agricultural policy, taking into account price support systems, stockpiles and sales; and devise programmes to improve agriculture *inter alia* through such measures as appropriate fertilizer production, irrigation, prevention of soil erosion, storage, marketing and creation of transport and distribution systems.

Science and technology centres would, in turn, promote regional and interregional co-operation in field testing, adaptation, joint industrial research, evaluation and extension of technologies; develop appropriate regional technological capabilities; and enhance regional capabilities to adequately transfer and control imported technologies.

The more appropriate and beneficial use of *endogenous energies, natural resources and environments* would be promoted by regional centres that would establish joint regional enterprises for the R & D, exploration, exploitation and preservation of endogenous land and ocean-based natural and energy resources; identify all existing and potential energy resources required to sustain regional development; and establish an energy clearing system at the regional level to promote and facilitate the interregional exchange of appropriate forms of energy.

Last, but not least, *social, cultural and educational policies* could be co-ordinated and harmonized through regional centres that would determine the development aspirations of indigenous populations and examine the impact of imported technologies and modes of economic and social organization on the cultures with a view to increasing socially equitable employment opportunities, reducing conflict and preserving the useful and appropriate elements of the cultural heritage of the nations and the region as a whole; review educational materials and curricula in regard to their appropriateness to impart required skills, provide useful knowledge, and sustain the basic values of human dignity, compassion and solidarity with a view to establishing a regional common market for knowledge; and co-ordinate the research, development and application of new educational materials and techniques with due regard for ethnic and national diversity, as well as for the commonality of problems and opportunities within the region.

The creation of such a broad regional infrastructure in different parts of the world calls for a detailed knowledge of the opportunities as well as obstacles, the costs as well as the benefits, of regional co-operation. Also the existing institutions must be analyzed, and the possibility of their reform or restructuring explored. Consequently we could not end our endeavours in the field of regional and interregional co-operation with the publication and dissemination of the results of the U.N. Conference. We were morally and intellectually obliged to create the scientific infrastructure for the detailed investigation of the conditions under which regional co-operation can be implemented. We recalled the words of the Secretary-General who, in his Opening Address, said that we should "consider the question how the United Nations family could become more effective in helping to implement the many already existing plans and programmes of action for regional co-operation . . . and give thought to how the appropriate new concepts and policies could be developed and brought to the attention of the Secretariat and the United Nations system". Shortly after the Conference, therefore, we convened a Working Group to study ways and means of setting up a sustained research effort in this domain within UNITAR. The Working Group, which met periodically during 1981, was composed of representatives of the Under-Secretary-General for International Economic and Social Affairs, the Secretary-General of UNCTAD, the Administrator of UNDP, and the Regional Economic Commissions. On the recommendation of the Group we focussed our efforts on the human and the institutional aspects of regional co-operation, and identified a number of major research tasks. These can be summarized in the following questions: what are the economic and social sectors and areas where regional co-operation is especially appropriate and beneficial? What is the size and nature of the regions and subregions where co-operation offers optimal chances of success? Which are the complementarities and the opportunities of reciprocal trade, investments, joint ventures and similar arrangements among two or more subregional or regional groupings, on the South-South as well as on the North-South level? What institutional structures and mechanisms are required to implement potentially advantageous schemes of subregional and regional co-operation? And, finally, what would be the appropriate attitudes and policies on the part of developed countries if they would wish to assist developing countries in evolving regional and interregional schemes of co-operation?

These questions are the cornerstones of the research currently being pursued by our international network of research institutes. The projects are grouped under three headings: *regional* co-operation among developing countries; *interregional* co-operation among developing countries, as well as between developing and developed countries; and *general functional* issues which apply to all efforts of co-operation regardless of region and of level of development.

The projects of research under these headings – some 40 in number – were harmonized and co-ordinated with each other in a workshop organized by the German Foundation for International Development in Berlin, in November 1981. They were presented to the Programme's Panel of Eminent Persons at its Inaugural Meeting held in Brussels, in May 1982, on the invitation of the European Community and the Belgian government.

The Panel, created to guide the work of the Programme and produce a report on the conclusions for transmission to the Secretary-General, used the occasion of the Brussels meeting to define its own role. It will guide the international research network in the selection of the topics of research and in assessing its plans and projects in view of implementation, and it may also wish to conduct hearings with practitioners of subregional and regional co-operation and consult with the economic and social organs of the United Nations, in particular with the Regional Commissions. The Panel made clear that the final report of the Programme is to be addressed both to political leaders and to the public at large. The report shall present a clear and concise development co-operation philosophy, and project a compelling vision of the objectives to be achieved.

Since May of 1982 the great majority of the research projects of the Programme have been actively launched. The preliminary reports on research in progress were submitted to the Panel at its First Regular Meeting, held in Kandy, Sri Lanka, on the invitation of that country's distinguished Foreign Minister, in September of 1982. The reports focused on patterns and possibilities of co-operation within and among the subregions of Asia, as well as between Asian developing countries and the countries of the other regions of the world. On the basis of a review of the reports, the members of the Panel assembled in Sri Lanka unanimously adopted a declaration. The document, known as the Kandy Declaration, acknowledges that the purely bilateral strategy of international relations does not adequately meet the needs of either the developing or the developed countries, and that the best promise for collective and human survival and progress, and even for the preservation of human values and civilization as a whole, is held by co-operation. It calls on UNITAR to bring to a full and successful conclusion its studies on regional and interregional co-operation, and to generate a purposeful dialogue between political leaders, policy-makers, research institutions and the intellectual community to yield concrete results. As Director of the Programme in UNITAR, I am dedicated to achieving these ends.

It is in this context that I particularly welcome the present occasion, here in Kuwait. Our Programme is fortunate in having for the second Regular Meeting of its Panel of Eminent Persons a venue in the Arab world, where regional co-operation has a rich and long history. I am conscious of the great efforts of the Arab world to establish fair and beneficial ties among its own peoples. I am convinced that such co-operation can and will have far-reaching consequences for all the countries of the world, developing as well as developed, since Arab regional co-operation is the basis for numerous interregional ties which can do much to bring the world economy into much needed balance and harmony. Some two dozen research reports and two position papers have been prepared for this meeting, on various aspects of regional and interregional co-operation of particular relevance to the Arab nation. The conclusions the Panel will draw from them will be a guide to the further evolution of the Programme and will, I believe, demonstrate with force and clarity that regional co-operation in the 1980s is both necessary and feasible.

I wish to thank the organizers for the auspices they are providing for this meeting of crucial importance, and for embodying, in the very organization of this event, the principles of regional co-operation. All four of our host organizations are regional bodies: the Kuwait Fund for Arab Economic Development; the Arab Fund for Economic and Social Development; the Organization of Arab Petroleum Exporting Countries; and the Arab Planning Institute. Their joining together in this endeavour is itself a shining example of the will to explore together paths of solidarity and collaboration. It is fitting that the two position papers of our meeting, on Arab regional and interregional co-operation respectively, should have been prepared by two of our hosts. It is fitting that one of the major Arab projects should be the work of another one of our hosts, and that the executive officer of the fourth should be a member of our Panel. It is also fitting that the Arab League itself should have assumed the role of co-ordinator of all the research projects dealing with co-operation among Arab countries.

Permit me to express my deep gratitude to all the participants of this meeting, members of the Panel, the Advisory Board, the International Research Network, and of other bodies and organs who collaborate with us. Without them the goals of this Programme cannot become more than a wistful dream. With their help, and with yours, Mr. Chairman, and the four co-hosts of this meeting, the goals of the Programme – goals of a new and more equitable world economic order achieved through co-operation and solidarity – may yet become reality.

ANNEX II

A Summary of the Issues Raised by the Panel of Eminent Persons at its Meeting in Kuwait

THE PANEL of Eminent Persons of the UNITAR Programme on Regional and Interregional Co-operation reviewed progress by the Programme's international research network in its studies of issues concerning the activities of the Programme in the context of the present international economic situation. In crystallizing the issues, the research studies and reports prepared by Arab scholars and institutions were noted as being of particular significance.

The Panel recognized the obstacles facing regional and interregional co-operation as an element in South-South co-operation but stressed that implementing such forms of co-operation may be the only feasible way to resolve the complex problems facing the international community in this decade.

The main points stressed by the Panel were the following:

1. Balancing Relations between the United Nations System and Existing Regional Intergovernmental Organizations

The United Nations system should plan and implement its activities in a manner that would complement and support the work of regional intergovernmental organizations in developing countries. Instead of creating new regional institutions, better use should be made of those that already exist. While global aspects of planning should remain with the United Nations system, regional project and programme planning and implementation should be the responsibility of the intergovernmental regional organizations with the help and support of the U.N. Regional Commissions and other U.N. bodies. Generally speaking, it would be necessary to further investigate the way a two-way and mutually beneficial co-operation could be developed between the United Nations system and regional intergovernmental bodies so as to establish systemic relationships between them to support efforts towards regional co-operation.

2. Meeting the Financial and Administrative Requirements of Effective Regional Co-operation Institutions

Important financial and programmatic implications result from any plan to deliver development services based on the concept of regional administration of regional needs. Close attention must be paid to the financial weakness of regional groupings, which has impeded any fair test of regional capabilities in the past. The practical impediment is the lack of an adequate framework for the allocation of responsibilities and financial resources. The premises of an effective scheme include:
- According regional bodies adequate responsibility for regional economic planning and execution;
- Interrelating the complementary development functions of global and regional agencies;
- Strengthening regional development capabilities by channelling increased financial and technical resources through global agencies to the appropriate regional organizations.

3. Choosing the Regional Group to which Developing Countries Wish to Belong

In the past, the determination of developing countries to be members of regional groupings was attributable to their northern partners, and this led to the definition of regions in the South which did not necessarily correspond to geopolitical or economic realities. At times this was associated with the desire of some industrialized countries to maintain certain developing countries within their political ambit. Efforts should be directed to promoting endogenous definitions of regions, whether on the basis of geographical contiguity, similarity of production, or the complementarity of their economies, in ways deemed by countries in the regions themselves to best serve their interests.

4. Achieving a Balanced Assessment of Past Failures of Regional Co-operation in Order to Point the Way Toward More Promising Future Directions

The high rate of failures of schemes of regional economic co-operation cannot be attributed to any one cause. Regional co-operation can neither be reduced to a simple question of trade on the one hand nor is it tantamount to an operation of transfer of resources on the other. The inequality of distribution of benefits is one of the causes of failure but not the only one. The reasons for past failures should therefore be further investigated, region by region, with a view to deriving policy recommendations concerning pitfalls to be avoided in the future. The investigation of past failures should be joined with the study of those aspects of co-operation which have been instrumental in contributing to successes in regional schemes. Yet

ANNEX II

it would not be sufficient to derive policy recommendations for regional co-operation in the future from the study of past successes and failures alone: there is also a beneficial multiplier effect in bringing together regional groupings and organizations to exchange experiences, as recognized by the Panel in regard to the consultations it wishes to undertake in the future (para. 10).

5. Some Preconditions of a Successful Implementation of Schemes of Regional Co-operation

In order to guarantee the success of regional and interregional co-operation, the following factors should be investigated in depth:
(a) *The political will of national governments.* The political leaders need to recognize that the only desirable future available to many countries is one of collective self-reliance founded upon joint economic interest. Schemes of co-operation can succeed only if political leaders constantly press for their realization.
(b) *Legal, technical and administrative obstacles.* The establishment of a regional scheme is a painstaking and often highly technical operation which needs to be carried out by expert civil servants and technicians. The expertise of the United Nations specialized agencies and organs, and existing regional institutions can be of great assistance in tackling legal, technical and administrative obstacles to implementing projects of regional co-operation.
(c) *Public support.* Favourable public opinion is fundamental in achieving success in regional co-operation. The opposition or support of citizens can play a significant role in frustrating or sustaining initiatives adopted by national governments. Therefore, original approaches for motivating public support have to be found. The final Report of the Panel of Eminent Persons can contribute to this cause by being in simple language, understandable to the average reader.

The modalities by which the above factors are approached in practice are equally important. For regional economic co-operation to become effective, operational programmes need to be implemented in order that:
(i) Policies and incentives conducive to regional economic co-operation be integrated within overall national development plans and policies;
(ii) Appropriate mechanisms be promoted for this purpose at both the national and the international level; and
(iii) Schemes of regional economic co-operation be based on clearly identified sectors and projects, where such co-operation would be particularly effective and where it would ensure the mutuality of benefits (as noted below).

6. Taking into Account the Mutuality of Concrete Interests as a Motivation for Achieving the Goals of Regional Co-operation

Since concrete interests have remained the main causes of action at national and international levels, the joint interests of states in a regional framework is a primary pre-requisite of feasible and realistic schemes of regional co-operation. One or two detailed case studies can demonstrate the existence of important joint interests, for example, in the area of food security, human resource development, energy, industrial development, trade, or development financing. Several studies already presented to the Panel demonstrate the existence of such interests in the Arab region itself, in areas such as joint projects in numerous economic sectors including rural as well as human resource development, complementarity between the movement of a substantial Arab labour force to the oil-exporting countries and a substantial financial flow in the form of remittances to the countries of origin; significant financial flows from the oil-exporting countries to the capital-short countries for purposes of investment and development; and the promotion of regional development by major development funds, such as the Kuwait Fund for Arab Economic Development, and the Arab Fund for Economic and Social Development.

7. Assuring that Aid and Technical Assistance do not Discourage Regional Co-operation Programmes

Aid and technical assistance should promote regional co-operation specifically by avoiding the duplication of small-scale projects among members of a regional group, as this would induce economic fragmentation and reduce opportunities for enhancing collective self-reliance and interdependence in the region.

8. Modalities for Interregional Co-operation

Co-operation between regional groups – interregional co-operation – should make the fullest possible use of the existing multilateral channels and mechanisms created by regional bodies in each of the co-operating regions, thereby avoiding conflicts among the members and within their respective administrative sectors.

9. The Relevance of the Programme to the Purposes of the United Nations

The Programme is important for the future of the United Nations in general and for increasing the efficiency and relevance of the Organization in particular. In the decades since the establishment of the United Nations a complex structure of intergovernmental regional and subregional institutions has been set up. Many of these institutions are working within the framework of the United Nations and the specialized agencies, and they accumulate valuable experiences and enhance regional co-operation in different areas. Other institutions and bodies are working outside the United Nations structure. The Programme is the first attempt to analyze these initiatives and organizations in an integrated global perspective. Thus, for the economic security of each country it could provide valuable insight into the results, the shortcomings and the immense reservoirs of experience in these areas. It could contribute to a better understanding of the problems which hinder progress in the field of co-operation among developing countries, and could reveal fresh possibilities in global institutional co-operation for the implementation of the Third International Development Strategy. Never before have the difficult problems of regional and interregional co-operation been investigated in a similarly comprehensive, interdisciplinary and international framework, through the participation of important political personalities, scholars, research institutions and representatives of regional bodies from every continent, including countries with market economies, developing countries and centrally planned economies. The findings of the Programme may prove to be especially helpful for the Regional Economic Commissions, for the Specialized Agencies, and for the entire United Nations system.

10. Future Consultations of the Panel

In order to enhance the effectiveness of its own role, the Panel of Eminent Persons expressed the wish to have three kinds of meetings and consultations:
1. Systematic consultations with the United Nations Regional Economic Commissions and their Executive Secretaries;
2. Similar consultations with the Executive Officers of regional intergovernmental organizations active in the region where the Panel meets;
3. Joint consultations with the Executive Officers of the major regional intergovernmental organizations at a central location for a sustained exchange of views and exploration of the possibility of a harmonization of their activities.

Index

Abdullah Cairo, Dr. I.S. 146
Abu Dhabi Fund for Arab Economic Development (ADFAED) 91, 95, 137, 163
Africa
  Anglophone states 10, 11, 19
  and Arab world ix-x, 75, 89-97
  and CMEA countries 102-19
  complementarities ix, 9, 19-24
  co-operative institutions 6-8
  cultural values 4
  economic dependence 2-3
  Francophone states 11, 21-3, 35, 43
  intergovernmental organizations 13-18, 72-4
  political differences 10-13, 35-6
  Portuguese states 13
  see also development aid
African Development Bank (ADB) 6, 23-4, 72, 74, 75
African Malagasy Community (OCAM) 35
agriculture
  Africa 19, 48, 50
  Arab world x, xi, 128, 136, 143
  aid to 108-9, 113-14, 138, 175-81, 227, 263
Air Afrique 23, 53, 72-3
  as model 72-3, 74, 78, 81
Algeria 19, 32, 126, 168, 186, 191
Al-Sagban, Dr. A. A. 145
Ammar, Dr. 215
Andean Pact 30
Angola 94, 112

Arab Agreement for Manpower Exchange 209
Arab Bank for Economic Development in Africa (BADEA) 89-97 *passim*, 97-100, 137
Arab Common Market x, 124, 131, 133, 142, 143, 166, 245, 256
Arab Co-ordination Group 227, 230
Arab Economic and Social Council 164, 256

Arab Funds for Economic and Social Development xi, xii, 95-6, 98, 124, 140, 142, 145-6, 152, 156, 164-5, 172, 178, 236
Arab Labour Organization 212
Arab Monetary Fund 124, 152, 153, 156, 164
Arab Organization for Agricultural Development 143, 163-4, 178
Arab Organization for Investment Guarantee 139, 145
Arab Thought Forum 156
Arab Unity Studies Centre 146, 158
Arab world
  Amman summit x, 93, 124, 152, 162, 165, 212, 256
  and Africa 89-97
  Baghdad summit x, 149
  complementarity 161, 167-71 *passim*, 183, 244
  co-operative institutions 95-6, 162-5, 177-8, 212, 245
  and CMEA countries 166, 224-5, 240-50
  countries of 124-30
  ministerial councils 163-4
  political structures 164, 172, 212-14, 247
  socio-economic indicators 125-6
  see also development aid
Arusha conference 54-5
Asian migrants 133, 136, 137, 199, 201-2
Association of African Political Scientists 44
Association of African Women for Research and Development 44
Ayari, Dr. Chedly 89, 92

BADEA *see* Arab Bank
Badran, Dr. 215
Bahrain 168, 195, 201, 256
  education in 199, 218
balance-of-payments deficits 63, 65, 95
Balassa doctrine 133
Barilochi group 146
Belgium 12, 13, 18

Benin 12, 21, 24, 30, 94, 98
  railway 18-19
Birks and Sinclair 136
Botswana 44, 94
'brain drain' xii, 50, 184, 214-15, 221
Brazil 53, 59, 69, 254
Britain 10-13 *passim*

Cameroon 19, 24, 44
Canada 59, 73, 124, 126
Cape Verde 14, 24
Caracas Programme 258-60
CEAO *see* West African Economic Community
Central African Customs and Economic Union (UDEAC) 12, 20, 22, 25, 27, 31
Central African Republic 19
Centre Africain d'Études Monetaires 27
Cesaire, Aimé 4
Chad, 19, 21, 27
Chiekh Anta Diop 4
Chile 53, 69
CIMAO *see* West African Cement Co.
Club of Rome 146
CMEA *see* Council for Mutual Economic Assistance
CODESRIA 44, 114
colonialism viii, 11, 12-13, 36
COMECON 11, 32
Common Afro-Mauritian Organisation (OCAM) 23
Common Arab Labour Market xii, 184
common markets *see* economic communities
Commonwealth African Region 39
Community Development Fund (FCD) 27
Congo 12, 13
co-operative institutions 6-8, 162-5, 212, 245
Council of Arab Economic Unity (CAEU) 123, 131, 133, 142-8 *passim*, 152, 157-66 *passim*, 178, 209
Council for Mutual Economic Assistance (CMEA) xii, 59
  and Africa 102-19
  and Arab world 166, 224-5, 240-50
currencies ix, 24-7, 153
customs zones 13, 27, 29-30, 31

DAC *see* Development Assistance Committee
developed countries
  and developing countries viii, 2, 4-5, 42-3, 59, 63-4, 90-1, 160-1, 241

development aid
  Arab aid 89-97, 137-40, 163, 167, 171, 173, 185, 224ff *see also* Kuwait fund
  CMEA aid xiii, 111-12
Development Assistance Committee (DAC) 224, 239
development co-ordination 140-56
development institutions 227
development planning ix, 1-3, 49, 140-58
Diouf, Makhtar ix
Djibuti 126
domestic servants 219-20

East African Development Bank 72
East African Economic Community (EAEC) 12, 19, 23, 27, 30, 31, 35
Eastern Europe *see* CMEA
Economic Commission for Africa (ECA) 54-5
economic communities 13-24
Economic Community of Great Lakes Countries 12
Economic Community of West African States (ECOWAS) 12-16 *passim*, 20-9 *passim*, 35, 72
economic co-operation 258-60, 261-5
  Africa viii, ix, 9ff, 34-51
  Arab world 140-56, 246-50, 256-8
  CMEA countries 102-19, 246-50
  see also JRMEs; trade
economic crisis 46-7, 90, 260
Economic Integration and Trade Expansion (EIATE) 145, 146-7
ECOWAS *see* Economic Community of West African States
education
  Africa ix, 17, 22-3, 34, 36-8, 40-8
  Arab world xii, 138, 163, 169, 183-4, 196-200, 211, 215-217, 263
Egypt 4, 92, 93, 111, 124, 131, 133, 137-8
  economic co-operation 142-4, 164
  education 184, 198, 199
  migrants 135-6, 168, 202-8 *passim*, 210, 211
  mortality rate 187, 191, 193
  PQLI 194
El-Imadi xi
El-Imam xi
energy 24, 151, 168-9, 227, 263
Ethiopia 11, 37, 44, 112
European Development Fund 16, 79
European Economic Community (EEC) 11, 19, 20, 22, 31, 75, 239, 254
exports *see* trade

INDEX

financial co-operation
  Africa 6, 7
  Arab world xi, 153, 166-7, 170, 238-9
  CMEA countries 110-12
Food and Agriculture Organization (FAO) 114, 178
food security viii, xi, 5, 150-1, 156-7, 174, 175-81
foreign exchange 59, 63, 64-5, 74-5, 200, 207
France 11, 13, 21, 24-6
free trade *see* customs zones

Gabon 20, 41, 64
Gambia 24, 73
Ghana 12, 14, 18, 24, 26, 98, 112
  education 37, 41, 42, 44
  trade 21, 29, 32
Gross National Product (GNP) 126-8, 193-6
Group of 77 258-60
Guinea 12-15 *passim*, 18-20 *passim*, 24-5, 30, 94, 98, 112
Guinea-Bissau 24, 25, 94
Gulf Co-operation Council xi, 133, 155, 162-3, 256

Hassan, Prince 156
health 17, 38-9, 185, 191
Hogbe-Nlend H. viii-ix
Houphouet-Boigny, President 22
human resource development
  Africa ix, xii, 2, 34-51
  Arab world x, xii, 151, 168, 183-221
  see also labour force
hydro-power 17, 24, 233

illiteracy 36, 37-8, 184, 186-7, 191
imports *see* trade
incentive structures 49-50
Industrial Development Organization 142
industry 19-24, 54, 98, 113, 151, 247
  cement 20-1, 98
  petrochemical 173
  sugar 21-2
  see also JRMEs
infrastructure
  Africa 64, 77, 95, 100, 107-8, 109
  Arab world 138, 206, 227
  joint programmes 156, 246-7
Institute of National Planning, Cairo (INPC) 145
intergovernmental organizations 13-18, 267

International Bank for Economic Co-operation 32
International Monetary Fund (IMF) 26, 144
Iran 64, 157, 242, 246
Iraq 126, 130-1, 136-7, 168, 186
  and CMEA 241-2, 246
  economic co-operation 143, 144, 152, 157
  education 199, 217
  migrants 203, 210, 211
  PQLI 195
Iraqi Fund for External Development (IFED) 95, 163
Islamic Development Bank 94-6, 137, 227
Israel 91-3, 95, 159
Italy 15, 124
Ivory Coast 13, 14, 21-2, 24, 26, 28, 32

Japan 3, 63
joint ventures
  Africa xi, 20, 73-4, 110
  Arab world xi, 145, 153-8, 166, 170, 171
Jointly-owned Regional Minerals Enterprises (JRMEs) 52-83
  autonomy 70-1, 82
  finances 74-5, 77, 82
  personnel 75-6, 82
Jordan 131, 133, 143, 164, 186, 199, 242
  aid to 185, 237
  migrants 136, 137, 168, 203, 210, 211
  mortality rate 187, 190, 191

Kandy Declaration 265
Kenya 30, 37, 39, 47, 94, 98
Kiss, Judit xii, 102
Kuwait x, 94, 137, 142-3, 168, 190, 195
  aid 225, 229, 237
  education 198-9, 216
  migrants 201-8 *passim*
Kuwait Fund for Arab Economic Development (KFAED) xii, 91, 95-6, 124, 137, 139, 163, 172, 224-39
  activities of 231-9, 251-2, 253

labour force
  Africa ix, 7, 34, 40, 151, 199
  Arab world 151, 199
  skilled workers 49, 76, 214-15
  see also migration; manpower development
Lagos Summit viii, 37, 44, 46
Lagos Plan of Action 1-3, 7-8, 32-3, 54, 93
Latin America 9, 59
  Caracas Programme 258-60

League of Arab States (LAS) 91-2, 96, 98, 123-4, 131, 141-53 *passim,* 157, 161-6 *passim,* 172, 256
Lebanon 133, 137, 168, 185, 194, 237
Lesotho 37, 45, 94, 100
Liberia 3, 13-15, 20, 24, 26, 29, 92, 211
Libya 19, 32, 126, 135, 164, 168, 191, 195
   and aid 137, 163
   migrants 201-8 *passim,* 210
Libyan Arab Foreign Bank (LAFB) 95
literacy *see* illiteracy
Lome Convention 16, 22, 29

Madagascar 98
Maghreb region xi, 162-3, 184
Malawi 37, 40, 97
Mali 14, 19, 24, 38-9
   aid 94, 98, 112
   trade 28, 32
Mano River Union 13-15
manpower development 40-8, 54, 209-11
Mauritania 20, 21, 24-5, 32, 124, 126, 186, 237
micronationalism viii-ix, 2, 32
migrant remittances 136, 168, 171, 200, 207
migration 47, 184-5, 205, 208-11, 218-19
   Arab world 133-7, 168, 171, 173, 184-5, 200ff
   Asian migrants 133, 136-7, 199, 201-2
mine rehabilitation 79
mineral resources ix, 19-20, 52-83, 247
military security 151
Monrovia Declaration 1, 3, 5, 44
Morocco 133, 184-5, 187, 191, 220, 237
mortality rates 187-93, 220
Mozambique 40, 94, 100, 112
multinational corporations ix, 52, 55, 59, 66-9, 74, 77, 241
multinational projects 17, 23-4, 53ff

nationalism 2, 35, 50
national development banks 72-3, 75, 137-40, 163, 236-7
National Economic Activities Charter 212-13
natural resources viii, x-xi, 2, 54, 105, 180-1, 263
Network of Education Innovation for Development in Africa (NEIDA) 38, 44
New International Economic Order 5, 35, 91, 151, 160-1, 260
Niger 14, 20, 21, 24, 28

Nigeria 18, 19, 20, 32, 37, 39, 42, 45, 97, 112
   economic co-operation 13, 14, 24, 29, 30, 47
Nkrumah, Kwame 10, 11, 12, 24, 35

OCAM 23, 35
OCLALAV 32
OICMA 32
oil industry 20, 126-7, 132, 151, 168, 174, 241, 242
oil-producing states x, xii, 64, 90, 132-3, 174, 245-50, 255
Oman 23
OMVS 23
ONIGBOLO 21, 24
Organization of African Unity (OAU) vii, viii, 6, 11, 19, 35, 39, 44, 46, 54, 91-2, 96, 98
Organization of Arab Petroleum Exporting Countries (OAPEC) 132, 145, 168-9, 220
Organization of Economic Co-operation and Development (OECD) 75, 166, 167
Organization of Petroleum Exporting Countries (OPEC) 75, 168, 224-5
   OPEC Fund for International Development (OFID) 95, 137, 227, 237

Palestine 92
pan-Africanism viii, 10-13
parastatal enterprises 53, 66, 73, 77
Physical Quality of Life Index (PQLI) 193-6, 220
population distribution 185-6
procurement, discriminatory 77-8

Qatar 94-5, 124, 134, 168, 217, 221, 256
   aid 137, 225
   migrants 201, 211
   PQLI 195

Rahman, Dr. I.H.A. 146
railways 18-19
raw materials, 20-1, 27-8, 104-5, 113, 129-30
regional co-operation vii, 261-5, 268-71
   Africa viii, 1ff, 34-51, 112-14
   Arab world 123-58, 159-74, 183-221, 244-5
Regional Co-operation Tax (RCT) 27-8
Ritter A.R.M. x, 52

Ruanda-Burundi 12
rural development 50, 181

SADCC *see* Southern Africa Development Co-ordinating Committee
Sahelian states 14, 19, 22, 32, 48, 94, 98
Saudi Arabia x, 133-4, 155, 168, 186, 195, 199, 242, 256
 aid 94, 95, 98, 137, 163, 225, 229
 migrants 201-8 *passim*, 217
scientific co-operation 109-10, 263
Senegal 13-14, 20-3, 28, 29, 32, 44, 73, 98
Senghor, Leopold Sedar 4-5, 14
Sierra Leone 13-15, 24, 30, 37
skill training
 Africa 48, 49, 50, 75-6
 Arab world 169, 198-200, 216-217, 221
socialist countries *see* CMEA
socio-economic indicators 125-6, 185, 187-90
Somalia x, 37, 112, 124, 126, 133, 184, 196
South Africa 59, 90, 94, 95
Southern African Development Co-ordinating Committee (SADCC) 35, 46, 72, 74, 76, 100
sovereignty, issue of 155, 157, 172
Special Arab Aid Fund for Africa (SAAFA) 91
STABEX 16
state ownership 53, 59-62, 74
Strategy for Joint Arab Economic Action (SJAEA) 162, 166, 169-70, 213
Sudan x, 19, 124, 126, 133, 143, 191
 aid 112, 237
 education 184, 196, 199
 migrants 136, 202, 210, 211
Swaziland 37
Syria 131, 133, 143-4, 164, 185, 199
 and CMEA 241, 242
 migrants 136, 168, 210, 211
 mortality rate 187, 190, 193

Tahsin Ali xi
Tanzania 12, 19, 30, 39, 44, 73, 98, 112
 education 36-7, 40-1, 44
 manpower planning 45, 49
taxation 16, 66-7, 80-1
technology, co-operation with 109-10, 115, 151, 233-5
 transfer of 3-4, 114, 151, 263
telecommunications 19, 23, 25
Togo 13, 20, 21, 24, 30, 38
tourism 23, 137

trade 27, 262-3
 Africa/Arab 96
 Africa/CMEA 102-19
 Arab/CMEA 240-3, 248-50
 Arab region 129-30, 131-3, 153, 165-6, 170, 175-6
 liberalization of 29-30, 165-6, 245, 256
 minerals 55-62
 see also customs zones
transnational projects *see* multinational projects
transportation 18-19, 23
Tunisia 19, 132-3, 137, 187, 191, 202, 211, 237
Turkey 157, 241, 242

UDEAC *see* Central African Customs and Economic Union
Uganda 30, 39
underemployment 35, 217-18
unemployment
 Africa 41, 47-50
 Arab world 207-8
United Arab Emirates (UAE) x, 94, 124, 126, 134, 168, 195-6, 256
 aid 227, 229
 education 198, 199
 migrants 201-8 *passim*, 217
United Arab Republic (UAR) 143-4
United Nations 4-5, 44, 98, 225, 267
 Economic Commission for Africa vii, 13, 15, 65-6, 79, 83
 UNCTAD vi, 91, 145, 148, 182
 UNDP 66, 75, 98, 146, 164
 UNESCO 38, 114, 199
 UNIDO 114, 145
 UNITAR 8, 54, 114, 251-66 *passim*
United States of America (USA) 59, 214, 254
Union of Soviet Socialist Republics (USSR) 32, 254
 aid 108, 111-12, 115, 241, 242
universities 22, 43, 198-9, 215
Upper Volta 12, 14-16, 21-2, 24, 26, 28, 32, 98
urban centres 47, 48, 190-2

West African Cement Co. (CIMAO) 21, 24
West African Central Banks, Association of 27
West African Clearing House 24-7, 32
West African Customs Union (UDAO) 12, 21

West African Economic Community (CEAO) 11-14, 16, 19, 21-2, 23, 27-9, 31
West African Monetary Union (UMOA) 24, 25, 27
West African Unit of Account 25
women, position of 35, 185, 203, 205, 218, 219-20
World Bank 36, 72-5 *passim* 95, 98, 148
  1981 Report 26, 65, 79
World Health Organization (WHO) 39

Yemen 126, 168, 184, 190
  AR 136, 143, 196, 203, 237
  PDR 132

Zahlan 214
Zaire 13, 25, 26, 94
Zambia 19, 45, 76
  aid 92, 94, 98, 112
  education 36-7, 40-1
  minerals 53, 64, 69, 73
Zimbabwe 41, 45, 53, 94, 100
Zionism 90, 150